SOCIAL POLICY
Theory and practice

Third edition

Paul Spicker

This edition published in Great Britain in 2014 by

Policy Press
University of Bristol
6th Floor
Howard House
Queen's Avenue
Clifton
Bristol BS8 1SD
UK
t: +44 (0)117 331 5020
f: +44 (0)117 331 5367
pp-info@bristol.ac.uk
www.policypress.co.uk

North America office:
Policy Press
c/o The University of Chicago Press
1427 East 60th Street
Chicago, IL 60637, USA
t: +1 773 702 7700
f: +1 773 702 9756
sales@press.uchicago.edu
www.press.uchicago.edu

© Paul Spicker 2014

British Library Cataloguing in Publication Data
A catalogue record for this book is available from the British Library

Library of Congress Cataloging-in-Publication Data
A catalog record for this book has been requested

ISBN 978 1 44731 610 7 paperback
ISBN 978 1 44731 609 1 hardcover

Cover design by Qube Design Associates, Bristol
Front cover image: istock
Printed and bound in Great Britain by TJ International, Padstow

FSC
www.fsc.org
MIX
Paper from
responsible sources
FSC® C013056

Contents

List of tables, figures and boxes

immunity

About the author

Paul Spicker holds the Grampian Chair of Public Policy at the Robert Gordon University, Aberdeen. His research includes studies of poverty, need, disadvantage and service delivery; he has worked as a consultant for a range of agencies in social welfare provision.

This book combines elements from *Social policy: themes and approaches* (Policy Press, 2008) and *Policy analysis for practice* (Policy Press, 2006). Paul Spicker's other books include:

- *Stigma and social welfare* (Croom Helm, 1984)
- *Principles of social welfare* (Routledge, 1988)
- *Social housing and the social services* (Longmans, 1989)
- *Poverty and social security: concepts and principles* (Routledge, 1993)
- *Planning for the needs of people with dementia* (with D S Gordon, Avebury, 1997)
- *Social protection: a bilingual glossary* (co-editor with J-P Révauger, Mission-Recherche, 1998)
- *Social policy in a changing society* (with Maurice Mullard, Routledge, 1998)
- *Poverty: an international glossary* (co-editor with Sonia Alvarez Leguizamon and David Gordon, Zed, 2007)
- *The welfare state: a general theory* (Sage, 2000)
- *Liberty, equality, fraternity* (Policy Press, 2006)
- *The idea of poverty* (Policy Press, 2007)
- *The origins of modern welfare* (Peter Lang, 2010)
- *How social security works* (Policy Press, 2011)
- *Reclaiming individualism* (Policy Press, 2013)

Preface

In the previous editions of *Social policy*, I identified three main aims. First, this book is a guide for students taking undergraduate and professional courses in Social Policy and Administration. Most books which aim to give an overview of social policy consider details, issues and developments relating to the social services in their country of origin. I've written a couple of books like that myself, most recently *How social security works,* which outlines the British system of income maintenance in some detail. This book is different. It offers an outline of the theoretical foundations of the subject and many of the issues which affect social policy in practice. It is written for an international readership. In the course of the last twenty five years, social policy has increasingly become an international field of study. My website, *An Introduction to Social Policy,* attracts visitors from more than fifty countries every day; it has had more than six million page views. I've discussed aspects of the work in this book with students and teachers from several countries, and I've tried to write it in a form that will be relevant and useful for people around the world. It does not consider the details of social policy in a single country, because that would limit its general application; and it explains the issues in much greater depth than would be possible if three-quarters of the book was discussing policy and politics in Britain, the US or any other country. It follows that this book needs to be read together with other texts and resources to be used to the best effect.

Second, the book shows what theoretical approaches to social policy can offer. The coverage of social policy is often descriptive, or based in commentaries about specific government policies; this book is quite different. Most of the structures and explanatory frameworks used here were developed for successive editions of this book, and you will not find them anywhere else. The purpose of theory in social policy is not just to help people understand, but to give readers structure, shape and different ways of looking at the information they are coming across. This may be a textbook, and textbooks are often dismissed by the academic establishment, but there is no reason why a book cannot be useful to students, accessible and original at the same time.

The book's third aim follows from that. This book was always intended to be a contribution to the development of social policy as a subject, and to the literature in its own right. This has been a long-term project, developing a systematic view of social policy as a multi-disciplinary, applied field of study. Richard Titmuss laid the foundations for the academic study of social policy, and his work is often referenced here; from this book, it should be possible to see the building.

This new edition brings together material from two texts: the second edition of *Social policy: themes and approaches* (Policy Press, 2008) and *Policy analysis for practice* (Policy Press, 2006). I wanted to put more material about practice into *Social policy*; I also wanted to put more about theory into *Policy analysis for practice*. In both cases, I had the problem that I had already written a different book covering the areas I wanted to consider, often using the best material in a different context. It made sense, then, to combine the books, and that is what I have done. The tone of *Policy analysis for practice* was less formal than this book is, but more importantly its material was firmly rooted in practice in Scotland and the UK; the aims of *Social policy*, and its readership, are international. What you are reading is much closer, then, to the previous editions of *Social policy* than to *Policy analysis*, but the change in the sub-title reflects an important shift of emphasis. This edition has also had a moderately large injection of new material, including some 30,000 words and about 200 new references that were not in the tributary works. This may not always be obvious; if I have been successful in dovetailing the material together, it should be difficult to see the joins.

A book like this covers many issues, and I have to accept that some readers will only look at parts of it. It has always been true that many people who study social policy are doing it as an add-on for specialised and professional courses, such as social work, nursing, housing management and public administration. Beyond that, rather too many courses in the UK have lost sight of what social policy is about, and some students will find it difficult to relate most of the book to the content of their degrees. That is not a problem with this book, but it is a fault of some contemporary courses that present themselves as being about social policy. If you are a student learning about social policy, and you are not being shown how it can be used in practice, you should protest. Seize a pitchfork, fire the flaming torches and storm the castle (I speak, of course, metaphorically). You are being short-changed.

Paul Spicker
The Robert Gordon University

CHAPTER 1

Introduction: the nature of social policy

The nature of social policy
Social policy and the academic disciplines
The uses of theory
Studying social policy

The nature of social policy

What is social policy?

Social policy begins with the study of the social services and the welfare state. It developed from 'social administration', a field devoted to preparing people for work in the social services in practice. One of the best known descriptions of the field comes from David Donnison:

> The teaching of Social Administration began in Britain before the First World War ... 'for those who wish to prepare themselves to engage in the many forms of social and charitable effort'. ... The social services are still the main things they (students) study. That means they are also interested in people's living conditions, the processes which lead to the recognition of human needs and problems, the development of organised means for meeting needs and resolving problems, and the impact which social services and social policies have on living conditions and on society in general.[1]

This is where the study of social policy started, and it is still central to understanding what the subject is about. The social services are mainly understood to include social security, housing, health, social work and education – the 'big five' – along with others which raise similar issues, such as employment, prisons, legal services, community safety ... even drains. Drains (not to be confused with sewers) are worth a moment of our attention. The draining of surface water is important to control

---

[1]   D Donnison et al, *Social policy and administration revisited*, London: Allen and Unwin 1965, p.1

flooding, to limit problems from insects, and to prevent the spread of disease.[2] If one is concerned not just with topics that are dramatic and emotionally exciting, but with the kind of things that are important to people, which are intended to make people's lives better, which might be taken for granted when they are there and make life intolerable when they are not, then drains are a fairly good example.

This book has a strong emphasis on practice, but it is not only about practice. Donnison continues:

> Narrowly defined, social administration is the study of the development, structure and practices of the social services. Broadly defined, it is an attempt to apply the social sciences ... to the analysis and solution of a changing range of social problems. It must be taught in both these senses if it is to be of any value.[3]

The watershed in the development of social policy was an essay by Richard Titmuss, written in 1955, on the 'Social Division of Welfare'.[4] Titmuss argued that it was impossible to understand the effects of welfare policies in isolation from the rest of society; there were many other channels through which 'welfare' was delivered. The theme was picked up, for example, by Hilary Rose in an essay on the 'Sexual Division of Welfare', in which she argued that it was not possible to understand the impact of policy on women without putting this into its social context.[5] The present-day focus on social policy rather than social administration reflects a general trend for people working in the field to be less interested in the details of how services are run, and more in the broader sweep of policy and politics.

Although the practical issues the subject used to be mainly focused on are not always treated as central to the field, they haven't gone away. On the contrary, they have developed very substantially. Issues like strategic planning, governance, partnership working and user participation have become part of the language of everyday practice in

---

2   See e.g. S Cairncross, E Ouano, 1990, Surface water drainage in urban areas, in J Hardoy, S Cairncross, D Satterthwaite (eds), *The poor die young*, London: Earthscan.

3   D Donnison, 1961, The teaching of social administration, *British Journal of Sociology* 13(3), cited W Birrell, P Hillyard, A Murie, D Roche (eds) 1971, *Social aministration*, Harmondsworth: Penguin, p.9.

4   R Titmuss, 1955, *The social division of welfare*, in Essays on 'the welfare state', London: Allen and Unwin 1963.

5   H Rose, 1981, Rereading Titmuss: the sexual division of welfare, *Journal of Social Policy* 10(4) pp 477–502.

central and local government. There is a new administrative language, covering topics like needs assessment, performance indicators, targets and audit. Beyond that, we've seen the growth of a range of relatively new concepts – issues like empowerment, voice and quasi-markets. There are a range of new techniques and skills, obviously including changes in computer technology, but including focus groups, interactive approaches to consultation, and participative research. At a time when many people working in social policy had lost interest in social administration, the field has been growing, developing and changing.

What does social policy study?

Social policy and administration is about problems as well as policy; about ends as well as means. Titmuss suggested that the major fields of research and teaching were:

1. The analysis and description of policy formulation and its consequences, intended and unintended.
2. The study of structure, function, organisation, planning and administrative processes of institutions and agencies, historical and comparative.
3. The study of social needs and of problems, of access to, utilisation and patterns of outcome of services, transactions and transfers.
4. The analysis of the nature, attributes and distribution of social costs and diswelfares.
5. The analysis of distributive and allocative patterns in command-over-resources-through-time and the particular impact of social services.
6. The study of the roles and functions of elected representatives, professional workers, administrators and interest groups in the operation and performance of social welfare institutions.
7. The study of the social rights of the citizen as contributor, participant and user of social services.
8. The study and role of government (local and central) as an allocator of values and of rights to social property as expressed through social and administrative law and other rule-making channels.[6]

Social policy has always been study for a purpose. It is aimed in the first place at administrators and professionals in the public services who

---

[6]   R Titmuss, 1968, *Commitment to welfare*, Allen and Unwin, pp 20–24.

need to know about the problems and processes they will be dealing with. It has expanded beyond this, but the central focus of the field is still practical and applied. Although Titmuss's description of the field invites consideration of the wider distributive implications of social welfare policy, it does so mainly as a counterpoint to his central interests in needs, problems and diswelfare. Many people would argue, as Tawney did, that the problem of poverty is also the problem of wealth: Orton and Rowlingson, for example, argue that 'it is high time social policy analysts put riches on the agenda'.7 The simple truth, however, is that the study of social policy hasn't been genuinely concerned with riches, and the kind of material which is studied in courses in social policy departments and published in social policy journals does not normally include studies of the position of the relatively advantaged, unless it is done by way of contrast. There is a good reason for this: studying the lifestyles of the rich tells us little or nothing that we need to know about practice. People who are preparing for public service are much more likely to be concerned with disadvantage, deprivation and social protection.

Social policy, at its core, is the study of social welfare and the social services. The main areas which it studies are

- policy and administrative practice in health administration, social security, education, employment services, community care and housing management;
- the circumstances in which people's welfare is likely to be impaired, including disability, unemployment, mental illness, intellectual disability, and old age;
- social problems, like crime, addiction and family breakdown;
- issues relating to social disadvantage, including 'race', gender and poverty; and
- the range of collective social responses to these circumstances. This is often interpreted in terms of responses by the 'welfare state', but in different countries it may equally be understood as extending to mutual aid, voluntary effort or industrial organisation.

Several generalisations might be made about this field of study.

---

7   M Orton, K Rowlingson, 2007, A problem of riches, *Journal of Social Policy* 36(1) pp p 75.

1. *Social policy is about welfare*   The idea of welfare is used in a number of different ways. In its widest sense, welfare can mean 'well-being', and in that sense it is taken to mean the benefit of individuals or groups, which is the way the term is used in economics; people increase their 'welfare' when their material goods increase and lead to increased satisfaction. However, the idea also refers, more narrowly, to certain sorts of collective provision which attempt to protect people's welfare. 'Social welfare' commonly refers to the range of services provided by the state. (It should be noted that 'welfare' is also sometimes used, particularly in the United States and more recently in the UK, to refer to certain types of benefit, especially means-tested social security, which are aimed at people who are poor.) There is no 'correct' usage, and there is considerable scope for confusion, because people writing about welfare may want to refer to any of the different uses.

Social policy is sometimes represented as being about 'well-being' in general. Fiona Williams, for example, describes the field as studying 'the relationship between welfare and society, and different views on the best means of maximising welfare in society'.[8] Hartley Dean writes:

> Think for a moment about the things you need to make life worth living: essential services, such as healthcare and education; a means of livelihood, such as a job and money; vital but intangible things, such as love and security. Now think about the ways in which these can be organized: by government and official bodies; through businesses, social groups, charities, local associations and churches; through neighbours, families and loved ones. Understanding these things is the stuff of social policy.[9]

Hartley and I have disagreed about this.[10] Social policy is concerned with well-being, but it isn't about well-being in all its forms. It does not have much to do with the good things of life; for example, despite what he says about 'vital but intangible

---

8   F Williams, 1989, *Social policy: a critical introduction*, Brighton: Polity, p.13.
9   H Dean, 2005, Social Policy, Brighton: Polity, pp 1–2.
10 P Spicker, 2004, Saving social policy, *Policy World* 1(1) 8–9; H Dean, 2004, What next for social policy?, www.jiscmail.ac.uk/cgi-bin/webadmin?A2=social–policy;3328cad7.0412

things', the subject has very little to say about love, partnership and emotional nurturing. Nor is it even about 'the study of the social relations necessary for human well-being';[11] that does include needs, but it seems to include studies of family, friendship, religion, leisure, commerce and entertainment, and the study of social relations in these general terms is the province of sociology rather than social policy. It is much more true to say that social policy is concerned with people who lack well-being – people with particular problems or needs – and the services which provide for them. The kinds of issue which social policy tends to be concerned with, then, include problems like poverty, poor housing, mental illness, and disability. The boundaries are indistinct, however, because often people's needs have to be understood in terms of the facilities available to others; our idea of good housing, an adequate income or good health affects our view of what people need or what is a problem.

2. *Social policy is about policy* Social policy is not centrally concerned with the study of social, economic or political relationships, problems, or institutions, though it overlaps with all of those and more; it is interested in issues like this because they are important for understanding policy and practice. Social policy does not study food in itself, but it does affect the regulation and distribution of food; it is not concerned directly with child development, but it is with education and services to help children; it is not concerned with physical health, but it is very much concerned with policies to promote health and the provision of medical care. The distinctions between the areas of interest are hazy, and there are many issues which lie in disputed territory. The core things to understand about a policy are its origins, its goals, the process of implementation and the results. If we are to accept that social policy should be studied in its own right, rather than through specific issues like food or health, we ought to show that there is some value in considering the elements in policy and administration which are common to different issues. This is something which this book has to do.

3. *Social policy is concerned with issues that are social* The 'social' element in social policy should not be confused with policies for society: social policy is not much concerned with broadcasting, shopping, religious worship, communications or etiquette, even if those things are critically important for social life. The reference

---

[11] Dean, 2004.

to 'social' issues is there to imply that there is some kind of collective response made to perceived social problems. There are issues which are important to welfare which are not social, in the sense either that they are personal (like child development, love, and friendship) or that they go beyond the social (like the national economy, or international relations). They may touch on areas of social policy at times, but they are not the main focus of the subject.

4. *Social policy is an applied subject* Saying that the subject is applied is not the same as saying that it studies issues that matter – other social sciences do that, too; it is applied because it is also saying what should be done about them. Social policy has three characteristic modes of operation. The first is that it is concerned with prescriptions as well as analysis, and outcomes as well as processes. If knowledge is not geared to practical effects, it is not much use. The second issue is that it generally starts with problems and issues, and finds methods and approaches which fit the problem, rather than the other way around. The third point, which follows from the other two, is that the study of social policy is multi-disciplinary. Dealing with a wide range of situations, and beginning with problems rather than methods, means that there can be many different ways to tackle the issues. Although some methods will be more appropriate than others, the selection of methods has to depend on context; there is no single route to truth.

The scope of the subject extends across a broad spectrum, because social policy usually seeks to understand social responses by trying to put material into some kind of context. This context may be of many kinds – historical, social, economic and psychological among them. But the study of the context is not social policy in itself, even if it is of interest to students of social policy. That is important, if only because it distinguishes social policy from the other subjects, and helps to explain what the limits of the subject are. Social policy is not a subject that studies topics in social science as items of interest in their own right. The study of broadly-based issues like culture, the body or globalisation are helpful for understanding policies and responses to issues; sometimes they are necessary; but they are not an adequate substitute for the study of social policy in themselves.

Box 1.1: Richard Titmuss

Richard Titmuss was Professor of Social Administration at the London School of Economics from 1950 until his death in 1973 (his last book, *Social Policy*,[12] was published after his death). Social administration was a university-level subject long before Titmuss, but he did more than anyone else both to define the character of the subject, and to establish some of its characteristic methods of argument. Titmuss's perspective was strongly influenced both by the moral collectivism of Christian socialism and the empirical practicality of Fabian social thought. He rejected both the formalism of economic theory, and the positive, supposedly value free approach that dominated sociology in the 1950s. He argued for a subject that brought together empirical evidence with a strong base of values and norms. It was not enough, though, to show that an option was morally superior; it had to be practical, and to yield beneficial results. His most ambitious work, *The Gift Relationship*, is dated in its empirical approach. but not in the arguments; he attempted to show that giving blood was not just morally better than selling it, but that it was better in practice too; more blood was given, and it was better quality, than it was in countries where blood was sold instead.[13]

Titmuss's preference for writing essays rather than longer arguments[14] makes it difficult to give an over-arching summary of his views. The critical issues were the failure of the market, the inadequacy of purely selective social services, and the superiority of collective and universal approaches. Markets failed because the economic benefits that they promise – information, quality, and choice – could not be reliably provided for in fields such as medical care. The advocates for selective services suffered from 'administrative naivety'[15] – they assumed better information than anyone could hope to have, the services failed to reach the people they were intended for, and they were often profoundly stigmatising and socially divisive. Collective approaches were needed both as an effective response to these problems, but beyond that because they promoted social integration and participation in society – the process we have since come to call 'social inclusion'.

Policy and provision change rapidly; theoretical arguments only develop very slowly. Titmuss continues to be read partly because of his role in defining social policy, but also because of the continuing importance of many of the themes he identified: the balance between society and government, the

---

[12] R Titmuss, 1974, *Social policy*, London: George Allen and Unwin.
[13] R Titmuss, 1971, *The gift relationship*, Harmondsworth: Penguin.
[14] e.g. R Titmuss, 1963, *Essays on the 'welfare state'*, London: Allen and Unwin.
[15] R Titmuss, 1967, Universal and selective social services, in *The Philosophy of Welfare*, Allen and Unwin, p 138.

clash between philosophy of the market and collective provision, the conflict between universal and selective approaches to social policy, and his focus on the importance of distributive issues in understanding policy.

Why does social policy matter?

Why does social policy continue to focus on social services in particular, and what is the justification for concentrating on its main area of study? The most obvious reason is probably the most practical one: people who have an interest in the social services, and who want to pursue careers in related fields, want to know more about them. But there are other reasons besides – not least that social policy offers a way of studying the kinds of issue which matter to people in real life. Social policies are important; they affect the way that people live. If social policy is exciting as a study, it is because it engages with serious social problems, looks at how those problems can be dealt with, and examines strategies for putting responses into practice. Social policy has often drawn in people who are concerned about social wrongs, and who want to put them right.

It is difficult to prove that any academic study 'matters'. The things it studies may be important, but that does not mean that studying it makes any direct contribution. Poverty, suicide, disability or child abuse are not (or should not be) subjects for entertainment or prurient interest. Understanding more about them is often important in the personal development of students, but it is not always clear whether the study does anything for people who are poor, emotionally distressed, disabled or victimised. There are three main arguments for studying the problems.

- Social policy is an important part of professional preparation. The people who are studying it are often going to work in fields – like social work, nursing, housing or education – where they will come into contact with people in these kinds of situation, and they will understand the situations a little better.
- People who have studied social policy have made a considerable contribution to policy making. It has always been true that careful, considered research tends to have less effect on policy than a sharp blow below the belt, a point I shall return to in due course, but there are many cases in which research into social problems has had a major effect on provision: examples in Britain are Booth

and Rowntree on poverty,[16] Bayley on social care,[17] or Rowe and Lambert on residential child care.[18]

- The study of social policy can help to change the way that people think about the issues. This is the main defence of any academic subject. The people who are most likely to be affected are its students; social policy stresses, not only a certain set of intellectual disciplines, but the importance of particular types of social experience. Through those people, it affects a wider society; this kind of study does help to change social behaviour and attitudes. Like many academics, I still have a naive faith in the value of study, and the effect it is likely to have on the way that people think. The better people understand a social issue, the more complicated it seems to become. As part of the process, simplistic solutions and ideological dogmas have to be rejected; so, people try to come to terms with different views about an issue before selecting whatever seems best. Part of the purpose of a book like this is to challenge some of the comfortable certainties we all have.

Social policy and the academic disciplines

The problem-oriented character of social policy means that methods and approaches have to be selected to fit the issues, rather than the other way round. To deal with problems in practice, social policy needs to draw on the insights of a wide range of academic subjects. Social policy, Donnison argues 'is not a discipline; it is a field in which many disciplines must be brought to bear'.[19] A reader in the subject in the 1970s described social policy as a form of 'applied social science', seeking to identify its relationship to a range of disciplines.[20] That still seems appropriate today, though some writers, including Fiona Williams and Pete Alcock, have chosen to describe social policy as a discipline in its own right.

---

[16] C Booth, 1889, *Life and labour of the people in London*, London: Macmillan 1903; B Rowntree, (1901), *Poverty: a study of town life*, Bristol: Policy Press, 2000.
[17] M Bayley, 1973, *Mental handicap and community care*, London: RKP.
[18] J Rowe, L Lambert, 1973, *Children who wait*, London: Association of British Adoption Agencies.
[19] D Donnison, 1975, *Social policy and administration revisited,* London: George Allen and Unwin, p.13.
[20] Birrel et al, 1971.

The view of economic theory given in economics textbooks does not do justice to the work that economists do in practice.[28] Much of what economists do professionally in relation to social policy is similar to the work of other policy analysts – using theory to understand, seeing what happens and finding ways to explain it, identifying and trying out different options. Conventional economic theory tends to give the impression that the answers are certain; more typical is an awareness that life rarely conforms exactly to the textbooks, that predictions don't work, and that no generalisation can ever be made without some reservation or qualification.

Public policy The boundaries and approaches of social and public policy can be defined in very similar terms. Minogue describes public policy as follows:

> The search for a general explanatory theory of public policy necessarily implies a synthesis of social, political and economic theories ... Public policies do things to economies and societies, so that ultimately any satisfactory explanatory theory of public policy must also explain the interrelations between the state, politics, economics and society. This is also why people from so many 'disciplines' – economics, politics, sociology, anthropology, geography, planning, management and even applied sciences – share an interest in and make contributions to the study of public policy.[29]

There are, however, important differences in the areas of interest, and the subject matter is not the same. Public policy is centrally concerned, by this account, with the study of the policy process. Social policy is not centrally concerned with the process, but with the content of policy. Public policy may be concerned with content in so far as it offers an insight into process; social policy is concerned with process in so far as it offers an insight into content. Public policy is of interest to people from different disciplines because they need to know about the policy process; social policy uses material from different disciplines because this is how the problems of social policy have to be addressed. This has implications for the agenda; public policy is interested in issues like

---

[28]   See e.g. J Sachs, 2006, *The end of poverty*, Harmondsworth: Penguin.
[29]   M Minogue, 1993, *Theory and practice in public policy and administration*, in M Hill (ed) *The policy process*, Hemel Hempstead: Harvester Wheatsheaf, p.10.

pensions, defence or energy policy, because they are examples of the kind of process the subject is concerned with, but it is not interested in substantive issues like poverty or need in their own right.

There are many other subjects which also make a contribution – among them economics, history, epidemiology, geography, management, psychology, philosophy and law. Social policy has a chameleon-like quality; whatever it is taught with, it tends to adopt something of the character of that subject. There are, however, areas which social policy does not really touch on, and it may be helpful to review some of the areas which social policy does relate to, contrasted with some others which it doesn't have much to do with. Some indications are given in Table 1.1. The material in this table is subject to the reservation made earlier – there are very few issues which social policy might not have something to do with – and there are always exceptions.

The effect of using different kinds of approach is that social policy sometimes comes up with ideas which are distinctive to the subject,

Table 1.1: Social policy and the social sciences				
	Relationships	**Processes**	**Problem areas**	**Institutions**
Sociology				
Shared interests	Gender	Socialisation	Deviance	Family
Distinct interests	Personal relationships	Social interaction	Military power	Religious worship
Economics				
Shared interests	Labour market	Recession	Economic inequality	Public spending
Distinct interests	Money market	Trade	The firm	Banks and finance houses
Politics				
Shared interests	Power	Legislation	Race relations	Government
Distinct interests	Political change	Voting	International relations	Party structures
Psychology				
Shared interests	Pro-social behaviour	Child development	Attitude change	Psychiatry
Distinct interests	Crowd behaviour	Mentation	Perception	–
Social work				
Shared interests	Worker-client relations	Community care	Child abuse	Social care
Distinct interests	Family functioning	Counselling	Group interaction	–

because they do not properly 'belong' anywhere else. Ideas like altruism, stigma, welfare rights, and poverty are used in other subjects besides social policy, but they are not always used in the same way. There is a characteristic literature in social policy, and a particular way of understanding the concepts.

Box 1.2: Social science and social policy

Social policy has been identified with 'applied social science', because it uses the methods of social science to describe, analyse and evaluate policy. However, social policy does not finish with social science. Social policy is also about developing policy – identifying what policies are doing, examining the effects, and offering prescriptions for practice.

One of the justifications given for many academic studies in social science is that understanding an issue might suggest a way to solve it. Many sociologists know better than to make such a claim,[30] but even eminent scholars overstate the case: Anthony Giddens, for example, has written 'The more we understand about why poverty remains widespread ... the more likely it is that successful policies can be implemented to counter it.'[31] Pawson and Tilley suggest that what analysts do is to look for a 'generative mechanism' (that is, a set of causal relationships) which can explain what is happening, and go from that to identify appropriate responses.[32]

This misrepresents what social science can do. Social phenomena are complex; there is not one problem to solve, but many. Poverty, crime, unemployment, addiction, mental illness, and so on are all made up of many issues, not one. Arguably that is precisely why they are difficult. It follows that if there is not a single issue to deal with, the idea that there is any generative mechanism at the core is uncertain. The first task of social science is to identify what the issues are; explanation comes only later, if it comes at all.

The next problem to face is that even where there is a clear, identifiable issue, there may be several generative mechanisms to consider, not one. Take, for example, the case where a local firm closes down, making people unemployed. Understanding the issue might typically require understanding of the productive sector the firm is in, the local labour market, the system of social protection, the national economy and international trade. A relatively simple problem starts to look very complex when all the generative mechanisms are considered. If it is possible to identify causes in social science,

---

[30] see H Lauder, P Brown, A Halsey, 2004, Sociology and political arithmetic, *British Journal of Sociology* 55(1) 3–22.

[31] A Giddens, 1989, *Sociology*, Cambridge: Polity, p.23.

[32] R Pawson, N Tilley, 1997, *Realistic evaluation*, London: Sage, esp. ch 3.

their identification usually takes the form of a range of contributory factors, rather than direct mechanisms.

The most critical flaw in the argument is that even once these issues are resolved, it does not follow that there will be a practical solution. The way into a problem is not the way out of it. If you fall down a well, what you know about the principles of gravity will be next to useless, and reviewing the process of falling in will probably not help much either. In the same way, understanding issues like poverty, unemployment or inequality does not necessarily mean that a solution presents itself. There are measures that do seem to have worked – economic growth as a response to poverty,[33] public works as a response to unemployment[34] or the impact of social insurance on resources[35] – but they have little to do with explanations about cause, and everything to do with outcomes.

Social science provides prescriptions for policy in a different way. The process of understanding, analysing and explaining issues is essential for marshalling and selecting evidence. Descriptive statements rarely mean much in their own right; if facts are important, it is because they relate to some kind of context. Social policy depends on social science to do that. The methods and approaches used in the social sciences can be invaluable; but even a good explanation is uncertain to provide a secure basis for policy. There comes a point, then, where social policy parts company with the other social sciences.

The uses of theory

The 'theory of social policy' is not generally taught as an academic subject, though many social policy degrees offer courses in applied political or social theory. The practical use of theory is that it helps to make sense of policy, and to understand the patterns of thought which lead people from general principles to practice. People who work in the field should be aware not only what the problems are, but what elected representatives, officers and fellow workers believe about them, and what they see as legitimate action in the field of policy. If writing about social policy often begins with theory, it is for a good

---

[33] D Dollar, A Kraay, 2000, Growth is good for the poor, at http://elibrary. worldbank.org/doi/pdf/10.1596/1813-9450-2587 P Spicker, 2007, *The idea of poverty*, Bristol: Policy Press.

[34] H Hopkins, 1936, *Spending to save*, New York: Norton; K Subbarao, C del Ninno C Andrews, C Rodríguez-Alas, 2012, *Public works as a safety net*, Washington: World Bank.

[35] W Korpi, J Palme, 1998, The paradox of redistribution, *American Sociological Review* 63(5) 661–687

---

reason: theory provides a framework for discussing issues, and some criteria for choosing what to extract from the noisy hotchpotch of information that practice throws up.

Theory works through description, analysis and normative examination. One of the primary purposes of theoretical description is to provide a basis on which to categorize, or classify, phenomena. The most used approaches for classifying common factors are:

- *comparing reality with an ideal*, such as the model of the 'welfare state' or the ideal of the 'free market';
- *identifying categories according to theoretical criteria*, such as the distinction between universal and selective social benefits, or rationing supply and demand (a distinction drawn straight from economic theory);
- *using 'heuristic' categories.* This is an academic term used to excuse rules of thumb, and categories that are convenient, useful, drawn from empirical information or related to practice. Examples might be distinctions between different kinds of organisations, budgets or management arrangements; many of the bullet-point lists in this book are of that type.
- *'family resemblance'*, grouping similar clusters of ideas together – an example in this book is the discussion of poverty in Box 5.1; and
- *relative approaches*, where distinctions are made by juxtaposing and contrasting different situations – high-spending and low-spending countries, women and men, the position of people with and without disabilities, and so on.

Analysis generally takes place in two stages. The first stage is to break down complex issues into their component elements; that makes them less complex, and easier to grasp. The second stage is to identify the relationships between those elements. The process of classification helps with both of these stages; equally, the process of analysis makes it possible to say which classifications matter, and why.

Social policy is concerned with changing the world, not just with understanding it. It relies, to a degree which is very unusual in the social sciences, on evaluation – making judgments about situations. Those evaluations depend on the application of norms – expectations, standards or rules against which policies and practice can be judged. This can mean different things, because the norms which are applied can be moral or technical, defined socially or by 'experts'. 'Poverty', 'homelessness' or 'mental illness' are not simply technical descriptions of a set of conditions; they are terms which are used to considerable emotive and political effect, and the way they are defined depends strongly on what kind of response is being called for. The kinds of norms which are used, then, contain much more than simple descriptions against which policies might be judged; they are moral concepts.

When theory is used well, it should help to clarify ideas and thinking about social policy, and to identify what the options are. Sometimes, unfortunately, theory can get in the way of understanding: there are some celebrated (and feted) writers – Foucault is one of the worst examples – who refer to complex ideas in ways that could mean many different things. This is not much use to students or practitioners who are trying to make sense of what is going on. There are two important tests. First, good theory avoids ambiguity – it says what it means, and does not leave it to readers to interpret for themselves. That is often difficult in social policy, because many of the ideas that are used – ideas like welfare, community, health, care or need – are part of everyday life, and most people will come to a discussion with their own ideas of what the words mean. It follows that writers always need to explain their terms if they want to avoid being taken at cross-purposes. Second, theory should help to make sense of the issues; it does not leave it to the reader to sort out the mess. Theoretical writing needs to be lucid and accessible. If it is not clear, and not comprehensible, it is not good theory.

Studying social policy

It is unusual for books in this area to discuss the methods and approaches of social policy systematically, partly because that is thought of as the province of the academic disciplines, and partly because it is not always consistent with a focus on current policy. This book is intended to establish a theoretical foundation for understanding social policy – and to make the case for treating social policy as a valuable field of study in its own right. But it is not comprehensive; this book needs to be read together with the kind of introduction which describes services, agencies and issues in the context of a particular country.

I return to the methods and techniques of social policy in the final part of the book. In the interim, students who are new to the subject should be looking at different kinds of research and commentary in social policy to give them a taste of what the subject is like. Studies on poverty have developed considerably in the last twenty-five years, shifting the field from a narrow focus on economics and household incomes to a broader, richer understanding. Drèze and Sen's *Hunger and public action* is a provocative, unsettling book, using arguments from economics, politics and history.[36] Drèze and Sen argue that people do not starve because there is not enough food where they live, but because they have no right to the food which is already there. Governments, political rights and democratic structures can change things. The *Millennium Survey* in the UK applies a particular kind of survey method for identifying and understanding the way people in a society understand poverty; it asks people what they think is essential, and then tries to identify who is not able to afford those things.[37] The World Bank's *Voices of the poor* brings together research from developing countries where poor people are asked about their experience, and what matters to them.[38] The result is one of the best books ever written about poverty.

These are all examples of conventional books and reports. In recent years, there has a significant shift away from the use of academic literature in the conventional sense. It has always been true of social policy that much of it lived in a 'grey' literature, contained in short pamphlets and reports rather than books and academic journals. The arrival of the Internet has opened up this kind of material to the world: the rules of public services, local authority reports, the records of organisations, are easily and directly available. Much of this work is ephemeral, because the issues which it deals with are likely to be concerned with the policy of the moment. It is worthwhile to browse through this kind of material at the outset, because it helps to explain what kind of enterprise people working in social policy are engaged in.

ISSUE FOR DISCUSSION

Is social policy different in kind from other areas of public policy, such as policy on energy, the environment or culture? Does it need to be studied distinctly?

---

[36] J Drèze, A Sen, 1989, *Hunger and public action,* Oxford: Clarendon Press.

[37] D Gordon, L Adelman, K Ashworth, J Bradshaw, R Levitas, S Middleton, C Pantazis, D Patisos, S Payne, Townsend, J Williams, 2000, *Poverty and social exclusion in Britain,* York: Joseph Rowntree Foundation.

[38] D Narayan, R Chambers, M Shah, P Petesch, 2000, *Voices of the poor,* World Bank/Oxford University Press.

PART I
SOCIAL POLICY AND SOCIETY

CHAPTER 2

Welfare in society

The social context of welfare
The person in society
Social networks
Inclusion and exclusion
Society and social policy

The social context of welfare

Welfare has to be understood in a social context. That statement is axiomatic for most writing on social policy, but it verges on the trivial – it says very little about what kinds of life people lead or what will make their lives better. Its importance rests not so much in what it says, as what it denies. Much writing about politics and economics relies on individualistic premises. Jeremy Bentham wrote that

> The community is a fictitious body, composed of the individual persons who are considered as constituting as it were its members. The interest of the community is, then, what? – the sum of the interests of the several members who compose it.[39]

If we were to accept this, we should be concentrating on the individual, not society. Economics begins as a discipline with a idealised model of the individual, not with a review of perspectives on society, and it could be argued that analysis for social policy does not need to either. Methodological individualism works from the assumption that people are individuals, and that social behaviour consists of the combined preferences of lots of people, all acting independently. But it can be misleading to focus on the actions of individuals to the exclusion of others. There are social actions, and relationships. Relationships are not only developed between people; there can be relationships between or within organisations, like government and industry, or administration

---

[39] J Bentham, 1789, An introduction to the principles of morals and legislation, in M Warnock (ed) *Utilitarianism* Glasgow: Collins (1962 edition), p 35.

and professions, which are not reducible to the interactions of the people who are involved.

Welfare is inherently a social concept. It is easier to see that some assumptions are being made if we try to put another word in this section's opening sentence in the place of 'welfare': 'X has to be understood in a social context'. The phrase makes sense if we use words like 'housing', 'health care' or 'education'. It makes very little sense, though, if we substitute related, but relatively specific, phrases like 'central heating', 'pharmaceuticals' or 'studies in biology' instead. The point is that the first three examples already assume a social content; the second three do not. Welfare is taken in a social sense; it is assumed to have a social content; and it is evaluated normatively on that basis. Understanding the social context is part, then, of the process of understanding social policy.

The social context, and the range of relationships people have in society, is complex. It is difficult to identify all of the relevant relationships in a book of this kind, but fortunately it is not absolutely necessary to do so – this is not an introduction to sociology. A book like this does need, though, to map out the general terrain, to introduce the concepts which are most directly relevant to social policy, and to show how they relate.

This is a difficult, and disputable, process. One of the central things to bear in mind is that virtually all the concepts in the study of society are *contested*: there is not one meaning of words like 'the individual', 'the family' or 'the community', but many. This makes it difficult to talk sensibly about a 'policy' for families or communities: the question it immediately prompts is, 'what does that mean'? As knowledge of the area of discourse develops, the issues become progressively more confused, not less; there is not much room for certainty.

The person in society

Human beings The first, and most obvious thing to say about people is that they are human beings – they have bodies, they have physical needs, for things like food, water and shelter, and they have human needs, for things like contact with other people. There have been attempts to interpret 'welfare' in a restricted, 'biological' sense apparently divorced from social circumstances: people need so many calories a day, so many vitamins, so much water and so on, and their welfare can be said to be protected when they have these things available. This is usually referred to in terms of 'subsistence' or 'basic needs'.[40] Peter Townsend was always very critical of this kind of argument, which is often used to justify a minimalist, mean approach to welfare: for the poor, Townsend wrote, the argument 'carries the dangerous implication that meagre benefits for the poor in industrial societies are more than enough to meet their needs.'[41] The idea of subsistence should not be dismissed out of hand, if only because issues like nutrition and water supplies are so important for human beings: Lipton has argued for a 'biological' approach to poverty not least because so many people in developing countries have their physical needs unmet.[42] But the biological approach can never really be sufficient, either; people's food intake is not simply a question of nutritional constituents, but what is socially acceptable as food (insects, dogs and rats have a nutritional value), available and edible (about a third of the world's population cannot digest the dairy products comfortably eaten by the rest).

The biological character of human beings is taken for granted most of the time – until the moment when issues about our physical humanity surfaces into political argument, when arguments about biology become very contentious indeed. The body is important for welfare, and there is a growing literature in social policy about it.[43] For people in extreme poverty, the body is the most important asset a person has; the ability to sell labour, to move about, or associate with other people, often depends on a person's physical attributes, like beauty or physical strength.[44] In developed economies, the issues which focus around the body may be less stark, but they are still crucial; they include disability, body image, health and sexuality. At the same time, these arguments are not genuinely, or even principally, biological; they have to be seen through the lens of a social context.

Individuals The idea that we are 'individuals' is widely held, though it is not always clear what it is supposed to mean. We do not live in

---

[40] P Spicker, S Alvarez Leguizamon, D Gordon (eds) 2007, *Poverty: an international glossary*, London: Zed.

[41] P Townsend, 1985, A sociological approach to the measurement of poverty – a rejoinder to Professor Amartya Sen, *Oxford Economic Papers* 37 p 664.

[42] M Lipton, 2001, Poverty concepts, policies, partnership and practice, in N Middleton, P O'Keefe, R Visser (eds) *Negotiating poverty*, London: Pluto Press.

[43] See e.g. K Ellis, H Dean (eds), 2000, *Social policy and the body*, Basingstoke: Macmillan.

[44] See D Narayan, R Chambers, M Shah, P Petesch, 2000, *Voices of the poor: crying our for change*, World Bank/Oxford University Press.

isolation from other people; we grow up in families, and the way we develop and the way we live is constantly conditioned by other people. Some views of individualism are descriptive: they emphasise that while people are born and raised in society, they think and act independently. Friedrich Hayek argued:

> there is no other way toward an understanding of social phenomena but through our understanding of individual actions directed toward other people and guided by their expected behaviour.[45]

But he also condemned

> the silliest of the common misunderstandings: the belief that individualism postulates (or bases its arguments on the assumption of) the existence of isolated or self-contained individuals, instead of starting from men whose whole nature and character is determined by their existence in society.[46]

Individualism is as much a moral concept as a descriptive term – a belief that, regardless of social relationships, every person should be treated as an individual. In the past, it was a radical doctrine, used to challenge the established order of society; putting the stress on each person separately makes it difficult to justify social structures which oppress people and deny them the opportunity for self-expression or personal development. In modern society, much of this radical purpose has been undermined. Individualists argue that since what we have is the product of individual action, we have to leave the results alone.[47] Individualism has become a conservative doctrine – a justification for the maintenance of existing social structures, rather than a means of criticising them.

Individualism is important as a way of thinking about society. There are still many established social structures which oppress particular groups; liberal thinking has played an important role in opposition to sexism and racism. Possibly the most fundamental objection to sexism is that gender is taken to obliterate women's individual characteristics, so that women are assumed to slot into certain social roles. 'Liberal

---

[45] F Hayek, 1948, *Individualism and economic order*, Chicago: University of Chicago Press, p 6

[46] Hayek, 1948, p 6.

[47] See e.g. F Hayek, 1976, *Law legislation and liberty*, London: RKP.

feminism' – the argument that women should have equal opportunities to men – is an important branch of feminist thought.[48]

Individualism also plays an important role as an analytical approach. Methodological individualism is central to much thinking about economics, and particularly of micro-economic theory – that is, theory about the way in which parts of society or industry behave. The assumption is made that if a number of people all make individual decisions, then the extremes are likely to be cancelled out; it is possible to think about the 'average' individual, and to make predictions about collective social behaviour by examining the behaviour of this person'.[49] This has been a very effective mode of argument, but there are dangers: the economic idea of the average man, *homo economicus*, should not be confused with real people, many of whom are neither 'men' nor 'average'. It is probably true, for example, that the demand for health care falls when the cost increases, or that landlords overall respond to financial incentives; but it does not follow that we know how all patients or landlords are going to behave, and in social policy the behaviour of minorities is very important. Methodological individualism becomes dangerous, politically, when economists assume that everyone is going to behave in the same 'rational' fashion. When some do not – it is questionable whether anyone does, let alone some people[50] – the assumption that a measure will increase welfare may well be wrong.

The person A 'person' is not quite the same thing as a human being or an 'individual'. Many organisations – voluntary groups, churches, or businesses – are treated as 'persons' in law; they are given rights, like the ability to make contracts or to take legal action. Some human beings are denied the same status. In sociology, persons are defined mainly in terms of their social relationships – the roles they have, and the connections they have with others.[51] People who are cut off from

---

[48] M Humm (ed), 1992, *Feminisms*, Hemel Hempstead: Harvester Wheatsheaf, ch 7; J A Kourany, J P Sterba, R Tong (eds), 1993, *Feminist philosophies*, Hemel Hempstead: Harvester Wheatsheaf.

[49] I M D Little, 1957, *A critique of welfare economics*, Oxford: Oxford University Press.

[50] S Keen, 2011, *Debunking economics*, London: Zed, pp 70–72.

[51] R Dahrendorf, 1973, *Homo sociologicus*, London: Routledge and Kegan Paul.

social relationships, like people institutionalised with dementia, can become non-persons.[52]

It is not good enough, then, to consider 'human beings' simply in biological terms. Human beings are social animals, and there are social aspects to our needs. Social contact (or 'affiliation'), affection, reproduction and living with others are also basic to the human condition. By asserting that people are social, we move towards an important insight: that their welfare is defined in terms of the society of which they are a part. The heading of this section – the person in society – is tautologous. If there is no society, there is no person. If we are trying to improve people's welfare, it is helpful to try to understand something about the way that people are, and how welfare policies will change their conditions.

Social networks

The family The family is probably the most important social unit in modern society, if only because it is the base for a great part of social interaction; most people live in families with other people. The idea of the family goes far beyond that, however; the term disguises a number of different functions which conventionally are packaged together. A central element is the experience of families with children – the family is basic to socialisation, or preparing people for society – but the family is equally important for the development of a whole set of relationships – including partnering, parenting, friendship and affiliation; and the connections between adult members of a family – like the relationship between adult children and their ageing parents[53] – can be crucial for policy. The provision of domiciliary support by the state is generally built around the pattern of care which a relative delivers – and governments have to recognise that that care is often greater than anything the public services can deliver.[54]

The idea of the family is used, however loosely, to refer to many kinds of household where people who are related by birth or marriage live together, and more broadly to networks of kinship – covering grandparents, aunts and uncles, and so on. The vagueness and generality of the idea makes it difficult to make much sense of the term in relation

---

[52] E Miller, G Gwynne, 1972, *A life apart*, London: Tavistock; P Spicker, 2000, Dementia and social death, *Self Agency and Society* 2(2) 88–10.

[53] H Qureshi, A Walker, 1989, *The caring relationship: elderly people and their families*, Basingstoke: Macmillan.

[54] M Bayley, 1973, *Mental handicap and community care*, London: RKP.

to policy; 'family policy' can be taken as narrowly or as widely as one wishes. Where there are formal 'family policies', they tend to be policies specifically geared to families with children. Family policy in France is a notable example; support for families and the promotion of the birth-rate has long been accepted, by both left and right, as a central part of state activity.[55] But writing about 'family policy' usually means something less specific, and in many ways more deep-rooted, than any formal policy. The role of the family in society is taken to define the limits of social policy – the point at which the social becomes the private. The UN Convention on the Rights of the Child declares a conviction that the family is 'the fundamental group of society and the natural environment for the growth and well-being of all its members and particularly children' and continues:

> States Parties shall respect the responsibilities, rights and duties of parents or, where applicable, the members of the extended family or community as provided for by local custom, legal guardians or other persons legally responsible for the child, to provide, in a manner consistent with the evolving capacities of the child, appropriate direction and guidance ...[56]

There is arguably a presumption here that the state and collective services will not normally intervene. The formal rules which govern intervention in cases of domestic violence, child abuse or sexual abuse are written in the shadow of a substantial unwritten code, which begins from the position that families should be shielded from intervention unless there are very strong reasons to the contrary. That leads in practice, Cornford and others argue, to some ambivalence in the construction of the family for the purposes of social policy: while governments on the one hand assert the positive value of 'the family', in practice there tends to be a focus on problematic relationships. Examining the information systems used in education, health and social work, they comment that in practice 'the model of family is dominated by intergenerational relations of parenting and caring' and that 'the state's concerns with families ... are heavily conditioned by a

---

[55] R Talmy, 1962, *Histoire du mouvement familial en France*, Paris: Union Nationale des Caisses d'Allocations Familiales.

[56] United Nations, 1989, *Convention on the Rights of the Child*, preamble and article 5.

model of the family as a source of risk to children or as a (potentially incompetent) ally'.[57]

The community There are significant ambiguities in the concept of community: Hillery, in a classic article, identified 94 different definitions. The only thing they had in common was that they all dealt with people,[58] though even that may not be true – I have certainly come across some approaches to 'community regeneration' which seem to be about buildings instead. For simplicity, communities might be defined in at least four different ways.

1. A community is sometimes seen in geographical terms – people who live together in a specific location. This was the prevailing view in the sociology of the 1950s and 60s, where family, work, leisure and social contact would all happen within a limited area;[59] the position now seems dated, but it continues to shape the construction of 'community' for the purposes of policy.

2. A community might be seen as a social network which comes about through a set of interactions between people. This does not have to be geographical – we also talk about the 'Jewish community' or the 'gay community', and part of the reason for doing so is that membership of such communities defines patterns of social contact as well as other kinds of experience. Welfare systems in Europe often depend heavily on this kind of community, or 'solidarity', which offers the opportunity to use existing social networks as a basis for developing mutually supportive arrangements.[60]

3. People might be thought of as a community if they have a culture in common. The term 'culture' is generally used to identify a set of behaviour patterns; it might refer to language and history, common experiences, norms and values, and life-style. This tends to be at its most important in discussions of nationality and race, but for practical purposes it may also be important to identify sub-culture within a dominant culture – structured variations from the norm. The idea that there might be a 'culture of poverty'

---

[57] J Cornford, S Baines, R Wilson, 2013, Representing the family, *Policy & Politics* 41(1) 1–18.

[58] G Hillery, 1955, Definitions of community: areas of agreement, *Rural Sociology* 20 111–123 .

[59] M Young, P Willmott, 1957, *Family and kinship in East London*, Harmondsworth: Penguin, 1962.

[60] P Spicker, 2006, *Liberty, equality, fraternity*, Bristol: Policy Press.

was very influential in the US in the 1960s, when policies against poverty were often directed towards educating people out of the supposed 'culture'.[61]

4. People might be considered to form a 'community' when there are interests in common: the 'business community' might be an example. It is possible, however, to have interests in common without any social contact; this overlaps with the other main approach to defining social groups, which views groups in relation to the social structure.

Although the idea of community has never truly played a very large part in the politics of welfare, it has been a recurrent theme. 'Community care' builds on the strength of community networks; 'community policing' uses neighbourhood networks to build up trust and effective working relationships. But the term does not always have a specific content; communities are generally accepted as legitimate, and placing policies in relation to communities has been an important way of justifying the policies. Among the services which have been justified in terms of community there are 'community industry', 'community transport' and 'community arts'. This seems mainly to mean that these issues are socially oriented – indeed, the term 'social' could have been used as well as the term 'community'.

The workplace The workplace is an important forum for social interaction, though it is more than that: work and work status are tied in with the economic structure of society, and so with class, status and power. In much of Europe, the workplace has been the central location from which organised social action has been developed. Mutual insurance to deal with social contingencies and 'solidaristic' arrangements tends to depend on an association with a particular place of work or professional group.[62] In several countries, including France and Australia, social policy is concerned as much with industrial relations as it is with the provision of welfare. In France, there are special insurance 'régimes' for people in different occupational groups – for example, for rail workers or power workers. In a number of other countries, the trades unions have been responsible for the administration of benefits and services, such as unemployment benefits in Denmark,

---

[61] O Lewis, 1966, *La Vida*, London: Panther; C Valentine, 1968, *Culture and Poverty*, Chicago: University of Chicago Press.

[62] J Clasen, E Vie_brock, 2008, Voluntary unemployment insurance and trade union membership, *Journal of Social Policy* 37(3) 433–452.

or the former arrangements for health services in Israel.[63] Equally, employers may take on the responsibility for 'occupational welfare', the provision of services to their workers: the best known model is Japan, where firms – acting as a larger 'family' – can take responsibility for education, health and pensions.[64]

If the importance of the workplace in social policy seems to have been diminished in recent years, it is chiefly for two reasons. One is that the state has been increasingly seen as the main route through which welfare can be provided; where the state fails to provide, responsibility has been undertaken primarily by women and the family. The second is that people can only participate in such a system if they have work; the attention of many writers in social policy has shifted away from people in work, which was the traditional concern of nineteenth-century collectivists, towards those who are excluded from the labour market, or marginal to it.

The nation Nationhood might be held to consist of a shared history, culture or language; it is sometimes associated, like community, with geographical location; it might be seen, like citizenship, as membership of a political community. These disparate meanings are often used simultaneously, which makes nationhood rather an odd concept;[65] it is difficult to know whether it can sensibly be included in a consideration of the social context of policy, or whether it should be treated instead as a political ideal. In Belgium, conflict between different groups with different national identities has led to pressure for decentralised policy, but Béland and Lecours argue that this is not simply a reflection of social structures; the social arrangements reflect more complex, diffuse and overlapping networks of solidarity, and the boundaries cannot be explained only in terms of the supposed 'national' identities.[66]

This influence of 'the nation' on social policy is in most cases a negative one; like the idea of the 'family', nationhood is used more as a restraint on policy than a means of developing or encouraging it. Nationhood seems to define, for some, the limits of moral responsibility; it is

---

[63] U Yanay, 1990, Service delivery by a trade union – does it pay?, *Journal of Social Policy* 19(2) 221–234.

[64] Ka Lin, 1999, *Confucian welfare cluster*, Tampere (Sweden): University of Tampere; I Peng, 2000, A fresh look at the Japanese welfare state, *Social Policy and Administration* 2000 34(1) pp 87–114; T K Uzuhashi, 2001, Japan, in P Alcock, G Craig (eds) *International social policy*, Basingstoke: Palgrave.

[65] E Kedourie, 1993, Nationalism, Oxford: Blackwell.

[66] D Béland, A Lecours, 2005, Nationalism, public policy and institutional development, *Journal of Public Policy* 25(2) pp 265–285.

---

common for different rules to apply to nationals and non-nationals, or for immigrants to be denied benefits and services which are available to others (see Box 2.1).[67] . There is a moral argument for this kind of discrimination, which is referred to as 'particularism'; because social responsibilities are developed within the framework of a particular society, they are only binding within the context of that society, and the same standards cannot legitimately be applied elsewhere.[68] The standard case against this argument is universalist, implying that moral standards should be applied to everyone.

Box 2.1: Support for migrants

The UN estimates that there are 214 million migrants worldwide – at 3.1% of the world's population, a surprisingly modest figure.[69] Some 30 to 40 million of these are 'unauthorised' or illegal migrants. Immigration is mainly into the richer countries of the northern hemisphere; three quarters of all migrants are in 12% of countries.[70]

One of the dilemmas that confronts many welfare states is the issue of support for migrants. If welfare is based in solidarity, or networks of social relationships, then people coming from beyond those networks do not have the same entitlements as those who are within them. If it is based in rights of citizenship, it is not clear that migrants are part of the political community who are entitled to those rights. The exclusion of migrants is, in the view of some, justifiable. Unsurprisingly, then, different kinds of welfare system offer different levels of support to migrants.[71] In some, they are able to establish earned rights through contribution and work-record; in others, this is much more difficult. It remains true, however, that migrants are likely to work in lower-paid employment, and to have lower benefit entitlements, than the host populations.

The argument for including migrants is threefold. The first is the universalist argument that migrants, like other people, have human rights – rights which people have as part of common humanity. The problem with this argument

---

67   M Bommes, A Geddes (eds) 2000, *Immigration and welfare*, London: Routledge.
68   P Spicker, 1996, Understanding particularism, in D Taylor (ed) *Critical social policy: a reader*, London: Sage.
69   United Nations Population Division, 2010, World migrant stock, at http://esa.un.org/migration
70   International Organisation for Migration 2013, Global estimates and trends, at www.iom.sk/en/about-migration/facts-figures
71   A Morissens, D Sainsbury, 2005, Migrants' social rights, ethnicity and welfare regimes, *Journal of Social Policy* 34(4) pp 637–660.

---

is that if it applies to people who have entered a country, it applies equally to people who have not entered the country. It is not clear that the obligation to a person from Africa to Europe looking for work is any less than the obligations to someone who continues to live in Africa – indeed, if human rights are related to needs, there may be an argument that the claim of the person still in Africa is greater.

The second is an argument about the society which the migrant joins. The effect of not extending the same protection to migrants as to others is to create a two-tier society – a society in which some are included and some are not. This is tolerated in some societies, but many others would find it unacceptable. (The argument is often described as one about racism or xenophobia, but it is more general than that: it applies equally to all forms of exclusion within a society.)

Third, there is a view that society incurs a special obligation to its migrants, in return for their contribution to the economy, culture and social life of a community. This view is not universally shared, because some people view the change associated with migration with horror; but many of the world's most successful, vigorous societies are migrant cultures.

The universalist values held by many writers on social policy have favoured an internationalist perspective. Titmuss expressed reservations about the idea of the 'welfare state' because it seemed to him to assume that welfare fell mainly within the area of one state, rather than being the responsibility of everyone.[72] Beveridge described his report as being a contribution to the 'common cause' of the allies.[73] These issues have been of great importance in the past, and with the resurgence of nationalism in Europe, and the challenges posed by the European Union, they seem set to grow in importance now. The European Union has been developing a policy based on the progressive extension of 'solidarity', networks based on mutual responsibility; the kinds of solidarity which are being developed are likely to cut across national boundaries. However, solidarity, like nationhood, has the potential to exclude people as well as to include them; both concepts can be taken to define the limits of social responsibility, and so to define not only who should be protected, but who will be left out.[74]

---

[72] R Titmuss, 1968, Welfare state and welfare society, in *Commitment to welfare*, London: Allen and Unwin.

[73] Beveridge Report, 1942, *Social Insurance and Allied Services*, Cmd 6404, London: HMSO, p 171.

[74] P Spicker, 2006, *Liberty, equality, fraternity*, Bristol: Policy Press.

Banting suggests that where there is ethnic diversity, there is a potential tension with solidaristic systems, and diverse societies tend also to set limits on welfare systems.[75]

Inclusion and exclusion

The growth of individualism in the post-war period has made some people working in the English-speaking tradition reluctant to accept that a 'society' means anything. The philosopher Michael Oakeshott criticised the idea as implying an association without saying anything about what the connection really is,[76] and Margaret Thatcher famously commented that 'there is no such thing as society'.[77] 'Society' is often taken in the English-speaking literature to be a single, monolithic structure. The approach to the subject in Europe, and particularly in France, has led to a different understanding of the basic idea. In Catholic social teaching, people are represented as part of a set of social networks. The networks are held together by mutual support and obligation – the principle of solidarity.[78] (Some of the literature mistakenly attributes this idea to the sociologist Emile Durkheim; Durkheim was using, and trying to refine the meaning, of a well-established concept of the day.) From birth onwards, everyone finds themselves part of social roles, and networks of obligation – the obligations of family, community and social contact. The representation of society as a series of concentric circles, represented in Figure 2.1, is a useful shorthand, but the connections between and across the circles are just as important; because of solidarity, the networks overlap and intertwine. A society is a network of such networks.[79]

There are people, however, who are not fully integrated into social networks. Some people are 'marginal', in the sense that they stand on the periphery of such a society. Some are excluded altogether.[80] The idea of 'social exclusion' was developed initially in France to refer to people who were not part of the networks of solidarity that others

[75] K Banting, 2005, The multicultural welfare state, *Social Policy and Administration* 39(2) pp 98–115.

[76] M Oakeshott, 1975, *On human conduct*, Oxford: Clarendon Press.

[77] M Thatcher, Interview for Women's Own, at www.margaretthatcher.org/document/106689

[78] N Coote, 1989, Catholic social teaching, *Social Policy and Administration* 23(2), pp 150–160.

[79] See P Spicker, 2000, *The welfare state*, London: Sage.

[80] S Paugam, 2004, *La disqualification sociale*, Paris: Presses Universitaires de France.

Figure 2.1: People in society

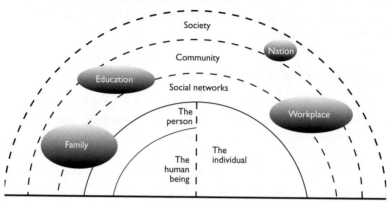

experienced – people who were left out of the systems of support developed in welfare states.[81] This idea was soon enough extended to refer to people who were not included in relationships of solidarity – people who were left out, shut out or pushed out. People are left out when the support that is available does not extend to them – for example, unemployed school leavers or long term unemployed people who have been able to contribute to social insurance schemes. They are shut out when they are barred from participating in society – like asylum seekers who are denied the ability to work or to contribute. They are pushed out when they are deliberately rejected. For much of the last century, people with intellectual disabilities were institutionalised, moved to 'colonies' and denied the chance to have children, so that their 'degeneracy' would not spread to the rest of the population.[82]

Social inclusion, conversely, is the process of combating exclusion – seeking to ensure that people become part of the networks of solidarity and support which apply to others. In France, benefits for *'insertion'* combined financial support with a set of agreements intended to bind people to social networks. That has been eroded by an increasing emphasis on participation in the labour market, and the *Revenu minimum d'insertion* – which had been a model for policies in several European countries[83] – was replaced in 2011 with a *Revenu de solidarité active,* which places a greater obligation on claimants to justify

[81]   R Lenoir, 1974, *Les exclus: un français sur dix*, Paris: Seuil.

[82]   See E Carlson, 2001, *The unfit*, New York: Cold Spring Harbor Laboratory Press.

[83]   P Spicker, 1997, Exclusion, *Journal of Common Market Studies* 35(1) pp 133–143.

solidaristic support. The European Union has agreed to emphasise 'active inclusion',[84] a principle intended to complement inclusion with the active participation of recipients and others.

Stigma

The problem of 'stigma' refers to the experience of social rejection and loss of status which people suffer when they receive services. There are physical stigmas: people can be socially rejected if they have some kind of attribute or characteristic which sets them apart, like a physical disability or a disease. Mental stigmas are associated with problems like mental illness and addiction. There are moral stigmas, when people are rejected because of something they have done or are thought to have done, like lone parents and offenders – and even, in the case of abused children, what people imagine they may be going to do in the future.[85] There are stigmas related to dependency and the receipt of social services. And there are, besides, people whose status is already low – like people on low incomes, or people living in poor areas. These different types of stigma overlap: people who are disabled, lone parents or mentally ill are also likely to be poor, while people who are poor or mentally ill are often morally condemned.[86]

> ## Box 2.2: The moral condemnation of welfare recipients
>
> People rely on other people, and there are moral obligations to help others. The main obligations are based in
>
> - humanitarianism – recognising the needs of others, through common humanity
> - solidarity – recognising mutual obligations to others in society
> - charity – moral duties to help others
> - reciprocity – the mechanisms of exchange which require people not just to make return for benefits, but to help those who have helped others, and

---

84 European Commission, 2008, Commission Recommendation 2008/867/EC of 3 October 2008 on the active inclusion of people excluded from the labour market [Official Journal L 307 of 18.11.2008].

85 H Ferguson, 2007, Abused and looked after children as 'moral dirt', *Journal of Social Policy* pp 123–139.

86 P Spicker, 1984, *Stigma and social welfare*, Beckenham: Croom Helm (online at www2.rgu.ac.uk/publicpolicy/introduction/books/Paul Spicker – Stigma and Social Welfare – ebook.pdf).

- rights – the recognition of moral obligations inherent in the status of each individual.

There are two common ways of resisting these obligations. One is to deny that people are genuinely in need, or deserving of help. The other main form of resistance is to say that there is something about the character or behaviour of the dependent person which removes any moral obligation people may feel toward them – that they are bad people, that they are lazy, feckless or degenerate, that they are morally accountable for their own choices, and so on. The recipients of welfare are 'othered'; they are said to be different from everyone else.[87] I referred earlier to the problem of stigma; the stigmatisation of poverty is one of the most consistent elements in the delivery of welfare over hundreds of years. The terms that have been used over the years – the lumpenproletariat, the residuum, the abyss, the submerged class, the underclass – are all ways of condemning the 'disreputable poor'.[88] Poverty is widely associated with dishonesty, sexual immorality and dirt.[89]

In the context of social welfare provision, this kind of stigmatisation is closely associated with the idea of dependency. Dependency is itself a stigmatised condition[90] – the receipt of resources and services involves, Pinker suggests, an exchange of status for help.[91] People who are physically or financially dependent are assumed to be psychologically dependent. The provision of welfare encourages a 'dependency culture';[92] people are trapped in dependency by the provision that is made for them;[93] the problem of dependency is growing.[94] The evidence for these propositions is very weak. If dependency is being encouraged to grow, the number of benefit recipients of working age should be expected to increase when the economy expands

---

[87] R Lister, 2004, *Poverty*, Brighton: Polity.

[88] D Matza, 1967, The disreputable poor, in R Bendix, S M Lipset, *Class status and power*, 2nd ed, Routledge and Kegan Paul.

[89] P Spicker, 1984, *Stigma and social welfare*, Beckenham: Croom Helm.

[90] See N Fraser, L Gordon, 1997, Dependency demystified, in R Goodin, P Pettit (eds) *Contemporary political philosophy*, Oxford: Blackwell, p 618.

[91] R Pinker, 1971, *Social theory and social policy*, London: Heinemann.

[92] See e.g. L Mead, 1992, *The new politics of poverty*, New York: Basic Books; H Dean, P Taylor Gooby, 1992, *Dependency culture: the explosion of a myth*, Hemel Hempstead: Harvester Wheatsheaf.

[93] C Murray, 1984, *Losing Ground*, New York: Basic Books; Centre for Social Justice, 2009, *Dynamic Benefits: towards welfare that works*, London: CSJ; Cabinet Office, 2010, The state of the nation report: poverty, worklessness and welfare dependency in the UK, www.cabinetoffice.gov.uk/media/410872/web-poverty-report.pdf

[94] Murray, 1984; Mead, 1992.

---

as well as when it contracts; it does not. If people were being trapped in dependency, they should be claiming long term; but unemployed people are very unlikely to claim benefits for the very long term.[95] The main groups of which this is true are pensioners and people with severe disabilities, and the reasons why they need to claim for long periods have much more to do with their circumstances than with any incentives developed in the benefits system.

The problems of stigma apply to many of the people who social services are intended to deal with, often long before they come into contact with the services. Jeremy Bentham argued, long ago, that there was nothing particularly humiliating about forcing poor people to wear a badge to show that they were dependent on the parish for relief; after all, aristocrats sported coats of arms, and war veterans wore medals. The problem that the paupers were experiencing was not the badge in itself, but the social rejection of their condition.[96] There are arguments to support the position: means-testing in the tax system may not be liked, but it is not usually described as stigmatising. It may be possible, on this argument, for social services to be organised so as to disguise the condition. For example, psychiatric wards situated in general hospitals are less likely than psychiatric hospitals to identify to the world that a patient is receiving psychiatric care; and attention to children in schools does not seem to attract the same concern as attention through social work.

At the same time, it is important to recognise that social services also carry a stigma in their own right. Part of this is the association with other people who are stigmatised. Receipt of care in a psychiatric hospital carries a stigma, and there is some reason to think that having been in a hospital is more likely to lead to social rejection than the symptoms of the illness itself.[97] A standard complaint about basic social assistance is that 'it lumps the unemployed, sick, widowed, aged and others into one undifferentiated and inevitably stigmatised category.'[98] One of the central arguments for universal services has been that the

---

[95] M Bane, D Ellwood, 1986, Slipping into and out of poverty: the dynamics of spells, *Journal of Human Resources* 21(1) pp 1–23; DWP Statistics, 2012, http://statistics.dwp.gov.uk/asd/asd1/adhoc_analysis/2011/oow_ben_duration.xls

[96] J Bentham, Papers: 1831–32, 154b, pp 602–604.

[97] D Phillips, 1963, Rejection: a possible consequence of seeking help for mental disorders, *American Sociological Review* 28(6) pp 963–972.

[98] P Townsend, 1976, *Sociology and social policy*, Harmondsworth: Penguin, p 126.

inclusion of everyone in the target group makes it possible to protect the vulnerable without stigmatisation.

Stigma has been an important element in the development of social policy; even as the deliberate imposition of stigma was part of the punitive policies of the Poor Law, its removal became one of the symbols of the 'welfare state'. It has been accused of being a 'myth'. Klein refers to the effects it is supposed to have on the take-up of benefits as 'the phlogiston of social theory: a label attached to an imperfectly understood phenomenon.'[99] But myths have an important role. What people believe in a society, Thomas and Znaniecki famously argued, is likely to be true in its consequences.[100] Whether or not 'stigma' refers to a real set of problems (as I believe it does), concerns about stigma have had a major effect on policy. Titmuss, for whom stigma was one of the central concepts in the study of social welfare, argued:

> there should be no sense of inferiority, pauperism, shame or stigma in the use of a publicly provided service: no attribution that one was being or becoming a 'public burden'. Hence the emphasis on the social rights of all citizens to use or not to use as responsible people the services made available by the community.[101]

Society and social policy

In order to understand the impact of social policies, we have to know something about the situation which policies are trying to affect. Welfare services have been criticised at times for problems, like the persistence of poverty, which have their origins in society rather than the services which respond to them. Problems of this sort have to be understood, in the first place, in social terms, because it is through the social structure that problems of poverty and inequality occur.

One view of 'social policy' has been that it consists of policy to change the nature of a society. Townsend, for example, suggests that social policy refers to 'the institutionalised control of agencies and organisations to maintain or change social structure and values'.[102]

---

[99] R Klein, 1975, *Inflation and priorities*, Bath: Centre for Studies in Social Policy, p. 5.

[100] W Thomas, F Znaniecki, 1918, *The Polish peasant in Europe and America,* Chicago: University of Chicago Press.

[101] R Titmuss, 1968, *Commitment to welfare*, London: Allen and Unwin, p.129

[102] P Townsend, 1976, *Sociology and social policy*, Harmondsworth: Penguin, p 6.

Ferge, by contrast, distinguishes social policy (as policy for welfare) from policies which are intended to change society, which she refers to as 'societal' or 'structural' policy.[103] There is an argument for seeing any social policy in structural terms, but in general social policy does not have to set out to alter social relationships. It can happen, then, that social policy does not affect or address inequalities – or that, even if social policy makes a difference to inequality, it does not make very much. In these cases, the explanation lies in the study of social relationships, and not in the policy.

Taking social relationships as given means that, on occasions, academic writing about welfare in society tends to give the impression that welfare is a sort of optional add-on to the existing economic or social structure. This is a convenient way of describing the impact of policy, but it is not really the way the world is; work, income, wealth and material goods have developed in a context in which some welfare services were already available, and this affects issues like security, the value of work and the importance of social status. When we consider individual policies it may be helpful to begin from the proposition that there is a status quo which the policy will somehow affect. We can then try to work out what the effect of a policy is, by comparing it with what we believe would happen if nothing was done, or with the effect of other alternative policies. There are reservations to make about that position – the social context is often too important to be left out – but we will come to those in due course.

ISSUE FOR DISCUSSION

Are we responsible for other people, and if so, which other people are we responsible for?

---

[103] Z Ferge, 1979, *A society in the making*, Harmondsworth: Penguin p.55.

CHAPTER 3

Inequalities

The structure of inequality
Inequality of resources
Redistribution

The structure of inequality

Inequality refers not to the fact that people are different, but that people are advantaged or disadvantaged in social terms.[104] The most important patterns of this advantage and disadvantage concern class, status, and power; they are manifested in inequalities in economic capacity, race or ethnicity, and gender.

Class

The idea of 'class' is commonly understood in three ways. In Marx's thought, class is defined by people's relationship to the system of production in society. Marx believed that there were two main classes in 'capitalist' societies: the bourgeoisie, or capitalists, who owned and controlled the means of production, and the proletariat, who sold their labour power. These were not the only classes, although Marx believed that the others would fade in importance; there was also the rump of the old feudal aristocracy who owned land, an intermediate group of entrepreneurs who owned their own production, and a 'lumpenproletariat' of poor non-workers who Marx dismissed as social parasites. The Marxist use of class is not very important for policy purposes, but it still shapes the way in which many people think about class relations.

The second use refers to economic position. Max Weber argued that a class consisted of a common set of economic circumstances.[105] By this criterion, there are a large number of classes in society: we might distinguish many groups, including owners, managers and workers; salaried and waged employees; professional, bureaucratic and manual workers; or workers and non-workers. Weberian analyses

---

[104] P Spicker, 2006, *Liberty, equality, fraternity*, Bristol: Policy Press, ch 3.
[105] H H Gerth, C W Mills, 1948, *From Max Weber*, London: RKP.

have been used, for example, to distinguish different 'housing classes' according to what kind of tenure a household occupies,[106] or to distinguish the characteristics of an 'underclass' who are marginal to the labour market and dependent on benefits.[107] This kind of argument has been important for welfare because it defines the groups to which a response is necessary. Peter Townsend's argument that disabled people should be seen as a class[108] is based on the hope that a general social response – a universal benefit for all disabled people – can be arranged in response. In the 'underclass' debate, the idea has been used to identify a group of people who are at the bottom of the heap – a point which can be interpreted to support or to criticise people in that position. There are strong objections to the term from some who see the argument as a way of lumping together people in very different circumstances and blaming them for their circumstances.[109]

Thirdly, class refers to a set of relationships between economic circumstances and social status. The identification of class with occupation is the basis of the conventional classification used in much social science research, which ranges from social class I to V or VI, or by advertisers who classify people as A, B, C and so forth. Economic factors alone are not enough to determine class; occupation, and to some extent the educational qualifications required for different kinds of education, is taken as a major indicator of status. This has probably been the most influential of the various concepts of class, because it lends itself to empirical analysis – indeed, one could argue that it is principally an operational definition of class rather than a theoretically based set of distinctions. If we wish to study the effect of inequality in relation to resources, health, education or housing, classification by socio-economic status has proved to be one of the most robust and most effective ways of doing it.

Status

The concept of status itself has a range of different uses. Status can be seen as a form of structured social identity, defining the way that

---

[106] J Rex, R Moore, 1967, *Race, community and conflict*, Oxford: Oxford University Press.

[107] W J Wilson, 1987, *The truly disadvantaged*, Chicago: Chicago University Press.

[108] P Townsend, 1979, *Poverty in the United Kingdom*, Harmondsworth: Penguin.

[109] R Lister, 1990, *The exclusive society*, London: Child Poverty Action Group; H Gans, cited in F Gaffikin, M Morrissey, 1992, *The new unemployed*, London: Zed Books, p.84.

---

people see themselves and that others see them. To say that people have a certain status means that they will have certain opportunities, or life chances, and will be able to live to certain material and social standards; Weber comments that status 'is in the main conditioned as well as expressed through a specific style of life'.[110] The pursuit of equality in education has often been concerned with access to the structure of opportunities determined by educational and occupational status; this is true both of the concern to offer opportunities to working-class children for higher education,[111] and in the US the use of 'affirmative action' to enhance the prospects of African-Americans to become doctors and lawyers.[112]

Status can also be seen in terms of social roles. People have various roles in society; a status consists of a set of roles, which conditions expectations about the way people are to behave and how others are to behave towards them.[113] This view has been particularly important in understanding the position of people on benefits, who have notably low status; the effect of failing to contribute to society is to be in breach of social norms, with the consequence that people are stigmatised and socially rejected when they are out of work for an extended period.[114]

Overlapping with this, status can be seen as a quality of social esteem; people have 'high status' when they are treated with honour, and 'low status' when they are stigmatised. Part of the aim of 'welfare states' has been to invest citizens equally with a status entitling them to draw on the resources of the society: Titmuss argued that universality – the establishment of rights for all citizens – was intended to remove degrading differences in their status.

> One fundamental historical reason for the adoption of this principle was the aim of making services available and accessible to the whole population in such ways as would not involve users in any humiliating loss of status, dignity or self-respect. ... If these services were not provided by everybody for everybody they would either not be available at all, or only for those who could

---

[110] M Weber, 1967, The development of caste, 28–36 of R Bendix, S M Lipset, *Class, status and power*, London: Routledge and Kegan Paul (2nd edition) pp 31–32.

[111] H Silver (ed) 1973, *Equal opportunity in education*, London: Methuen.

[112] R Dworkin, 1985, *A matter of principle*, Cambridge Mass: Harvard University Press.

[113] R Linton, 1936, *The study of man*, New York: Appleton-Century.

[114] P Spicker, 1984, *Stigma and social welfare*, Beckenham: Croom Helm.

afford them, and for others on such terms as would involve the infliction of a sense of inferiority and stigma.[115]

Power

Power is understood in different ways, and different sorts of power are exercised in various ways by different groups.[116] Power is defined by Russell as the 'production of intended effects'.[117] Against this, Lukes argues that power is not only to do with what is intended. If someone is powerful, or in a dominant position, other people will often act in the way they think appropriate; this implies that a number of effects might not be intended at all.[118] Saying that people have power can mean that they have the capacity to do things, that they change the way that other people behave, or that they are in relationships of dominance.

Michel Foucault interprets a range of issues in social policy in terms of the exercise of power – among them, sexuality, mental illness and punishment. For Foucault, power is based in relationships between people, and it comes as much from the people who are subject to it as it does from those who exercise it.[119] People are subject to norms and codes of conduct which affect how they live, how they understand themselves, and how they use their bodies: 'bio-power' controls the smallest aspects of people's behaviour in society. It is so complex and pervasive that it cannot be avoided. 'Power is everywhere, not because it embraces everything, but because it comes from everywhere.'[120] The problem with that position is that if power is everywhere, and exercised all the time, it does not tell us anything about the differences between people's positions, between social norms and the exercise of power. Foucault makes no useful distinction between the position of poor people, children, or women – or, for that matter, politicians, soldiers and investment bankers. That means the argument tells us nothing useful about policy.[121]

---

[115] R M Titmuss, 1968, *Commitment to welfare*, London: George Allen and Unwin, p. 129.

[116] P Spicker, 1988, *Principles of social welfare*, London: Routledge.

[117] B Russell, 1960, *Power*, London: Unwin.

[118] S Lukes, 1978, Power and authority, in T Bottomore, R Nisbet (eds) *A history of sociological analysis*, London: Heinemann.

[119] M Foucault, 1976, *Histoire de la sexualité: la volonté de savoir*, Paris: Gallimard, pp 123–7.

[120] Foucault, 1976, p.122.

[121] See M Mullard, P Spicker, 1999, *Social policy in a changing society*, London: Routledge, ch 10.

For the purposes of analysing social policy, there are three major questions to answer.

- *What kind of power is being considered?* Power is exercised in different ways. Lukes distinguishes coercion, influence, authority, force and manipulation.[122] The context in which power is exercised changes its character: economic strength, social influence and political power are connected, but they are distinct; they may well be held by different people and expressed in different ways.
- *How far is power concentrated?* Elite theorists argue that power is exercised or held by relatively few people; this might take the form of a ruling élite, a small number of people able to make all the important decisions, but it might also be based on a restricted number of elites who exercise power in particular contexts.[123] Pluralists believe it is diffused across many different groups, so that no one group has the power consistently to sway decisions. Pluralism is often misrepresented by non-pluralists to mean the belief that power is equally and fairly distributed in society,[124] but that is not needed for the idea; it means only that no-one has enough power to be consistently in control.
- *Who benefits?* This question represents an important challenge to many of the assumptions behind welfare policy: welfare policy is not necessarily intended to benefit the recipients. Some 'social control' is mainly directed for the benefit of others (like child protection, which involves substantial controls on parents, or slum clearance, which improves the material standards of the wider society), but there are other aspects, like penalties for refusing jobs which are offered, which can be argued to serve the interests of employers.

The structure of power in society is sometimes referred to as a way to explain why decisions, actions, accepted values and even failures to act work in the interests of some people rather than others. For example, a forceful argument about the nature of power has been made by

---

[122] S Lukes, 2005, *Power: a radical view*, Basingstoke: Palgrave Macmillan, pp 21–2.

[123] C Wright Mills, 1956, *The power élite*, New York: Oxford University Press; T Bottomore, 1966, *Elites and society*, Harmondsworth: Penguin; S Keller, 1963, *Beyond the ruling class*, New York: Random House; J Lee, 1963, *Social leaders and public persons*, Oxford: Oxford University Press.

[124] P Dunleavy, B O'Leary, 1987, *Theories of the state*, London: Macmillan.

feminists who have argued that society is fundamentally patriarchal.[125] Patriarchy has a range of uses – like any other concept in social science – but in its simplest form, it can be taken to mean men have power over women. This power is expressed both in the sense of direct control and in the sense that women have to alter their patterns of behaviour to accommodate the demands of a male society; Marxist feminists have argued that it is reflected in the sexual division of labour and the way in which men are able to control resources both inside and outside the home.[126] Redressing the balance implies not simply 'equality', in the sense of the removal of disadvantage, but empowerment; unless women gain power equivalent to men's, the disadvantages will subsequently recur.

The association of inequality with interests can however lead to a distorted perspective. Any coercive action can be seen as a defence of social order, and so of the status quo, but this is not just in the interests of those who are powerful – poorer people are disproportionately the victims of crime. It is easy to represent any inequality which arises after a policy has been put into practice seen as the result of deliberate intent; but in an unequal society, any policy which does not actually shift the balance is likely to have unequal effects, and no intention or relationship of dominance is required to explain the consequence. Power is important only if it has some identifiable effect.

Divisions of identity

Class, status and power are all associated with ideas of social stratification – the division of society into layers or hierarchies, where people are situated in relation to people who are above and below them in the social order. There are also some starker divisions, which cut across these concepts – circumstances where identification of a group places the members of that group consistently at a disadvantage. Society can be seen as divided – for example, between rich and poor, male and female, or 'black' and 'white'. Other examples where this happens might be in relation to ethnicity, tribal identities, and some religious groupings – for example, between Protestant and Catholic or Sunni and Shi'ite. These relationships can sometimes be translated into terms

---

[125] K Millett, 1977, *Sexual politics*, London: Virago, ch 2; M Humm, *Patriarchy*, 1989, *The dictionary of feminist theory*, Hemel Hempstead: Harvester Wheatsheaf.

[126] E Wilson, 1977, *Women and the welfare state*, London: Tavistock; H Hartman, 1992, Capitalism, patriarchy and job segregation by sex, in M Humm (ed) *Feminisms*, Hemel Hempstead: Harvester Wheatsheaf.

of class – traditional Marxism argued that non–economic divisions like patriarchy were a distraction from the real struggle – but the opposite is likely to be true: where people are oppressed because of race, gender or identity, they are likely to be disadvantaged in other ways, too, including economic disadvantage.

Gender is one of the principal dimensions used to understand relationships in social policy. Gender acts as a primary dividing characteristic because the position of women is conditioned in terms of a set of roles and expectations associated with their gender. These roles and expectations determine the range of opportunities available to women and men. The understanding of gender divisions is important, not simply because issues affecting women are part of the agenda which social policy must tackle, but also because a number of the traditional concerns of social welfare – like poverty, health and old age – have important gender-related dimensions.[127] There is a strong argument, for example, that poverty is being 'feminised', because women are considerably more vulnerable to the conditions of poverty. (This position seems to assume that something has changed; it is quite possible that poverty has always reflected gender divisions.[128])

'Race', like gender, is a socially constructed concept; unlike gender, the term covers a wide range of different types of characteristics, and it is used variously to indicate physical differences, cultural issues and historical antecedents. This very diversity makes it difficult to offer sensible generalisations about the circumstances of 'races', and the political abuse of the concept prompts some need for caution. Unlike gender, the issue is not mainly a question of roles and expectations; 'race' divides society because the combined effect of prejudice and racial differentiation is to limit the scope of people from different racial groups for social action. Racial discrimination refers to the deliberate use of adverse selection as a means of putting people from particular racial groups in an inferior position, but deliberate discrimination is not necessary to explain much racial disadvantage; the cumulative effect of denial of access to the resources, opportunities and conditions of life available to others is a deepening and extension of the experience of disadvantage.

---

[127] See M McIntosh, Feminism and social policy, and C Pateman, The patriarchal welfare state, both in C Pierson, F Castles, 2006 (eds) *The welfare state reader*, Brighton: Polity.

[128] J Millar, C Glendinning, 1989, Gender and poverty, *Journal of Social Policy*, 18(3) 363–381.

The common factor here is an issue of identity. People are not just seen as being different; they share a common social position in relation to others. Identity alone is not enough to bring people together in social groups – there is no guarantee that being a woman, a Filipino or a Shi'ite will bring with it solidarity or relationships with others who have the same identity. It can, however, be enough to generate disadvantage.

Inequality and social structure

There are four main ways of describing structural relationships of inequality.

- *Hierarchical inequality* The first is that society contains complex levels of inequality; wherever in the structure one is located, there is generally speaking someone above and someone below. This is sometimes described as a 'hierarchical' structure, though strictly speaking any set of rankings, including a stratified structure, might also be seen as hierarchically ordered; the important point to note is that the distribution of status and resources is continuous rather than discontinuous. Income and wealth are not simply split between the 'rich' and the 'poor', with the result that any categorisation of the level of 'poverty' might be arbitrary; the claim that there are divisions or stratified levels is often a convenience, imposed as a means of interpreting the data.
- *Stratification* A stratified society is split into a range of levels. The class system is not, by most accounts, divided into 'upper' and 'lower' classes; rather, there is a series of different classes who occupy different social positions. Information about inequalities in health uses information about class because it works as a way of following through differential opportunities and prospects over time.
- *Social divisions* Social divisions – are the 'fault lines' of a society. Distinctions which are important in one country might seem unimportant in another. The distinction in Northern Ireland or the Netherlands between Catholic and Protestant scarcely seems to matter in writing on social policy in Britain or the US. In Italy, regional differences are important; in Belgium, linguistic differences; in much of Africa, the key differences are tribal. These divisions are based in common identities. Groups of people can be distinguished from others by virtue of certain characteristics; people who share an identity can be grouped with

others, and the group as a whole is disadvantaged relative to other groups. Women are disadvantaged in relation to men; people born into certain castes are disadvantaged relative to others; some minority ethnic groups, such as gypsy travellers, are liable to be treated badly by others.

• *Postmodern views* An alternative set of views which has gained increasing currency in the course of the last twenty years is a 'postmodern' critique of society. Postmodernism is difficult to pin down, but the core of the argument is that society is no longer understandable in terms of the patterns of thinking which characterised most of the twentieth century. There is, instead, diversity – a rainbow effect of different identities, possibly individualised or atomised, often coupled with uncertainty about the nature of social relationships. According to Giddens, we have moved beyond tradition, and beyond scarcity.[129] The society Giddens is imagining here is one where poverty and need have ceased to be among the primary effects of disadvantage. This is not a situation many people working in social policy in practice would recognise. (Peter Taylor-Gooby has been critical of postmodern approaches; he argues that they undermine the radical and critical impact of social policy as a subject.[130])

These views are often held simultaneously, even if there are tensions between them. But different understandings about social structure do lead to differences in approaches to policy. Stratification and hierarchy can be modified by giving people the opportunity to be socially mobile, and to cross boundaries; postmodern diversity can be manipulated, even if it is difficult to pin down; but the divisions of gender and race do not really allow people to cross. In a hierarchical society, measures which help some people necessarily change their position relative to others; this can mean that poor people gain at the expense of slightly less poor people, or even that richer people from one group like women might gain at the expense of poorer people in another. In a postmodern society, the effects of policy become unpredictable and uncertain. Where society is divided, by contrast, the gains to some people in a group might help to advance the whole group – which is one of the justifications for trying to ensure that women are appointed to boardrooms, or that African-Americans can become lawyers.

---

[129] A Giddens, 1994, *Beyond left and right*, Cambridge: Polity Press.

[130] P Taylor Gooby, 1994, Postmodernism and social policy: a great leap backwards, *Journal of Social Policy* 23(3) pp 385–404.

Box 3.1 Policies for equality

Equality does not mean that people are the same – equality between men and women, for example, does not mean that there are no physical differences. It is about the removal of disadvantage. The methods by which equality is pursued[131] include

- *equality of treatment.* This is treatment without bias, prejudice or special conditions applying to people. (It is not treating everyone the same – equality of treatment in health services does not mean that everyone must have abdominal surgery!)
- *equal opportunity.* This can be the opportunity to compete (in which case it is the same as equal treatment), or the chance to compete on the same footing as others (which may require some redress before the competition starts).
- *equality of provision.* There are arguments for standardisation of delivery in a range of services, particularly health and education. 'Standardisation' implies working to common standards rather than uniformity, but the effect of applying common standards implies both a common foundation and generally applicable criteria or access to higher levels of provision.
- *basic security.* A lack of basic security is caused by 'the absence of one or more factors that enable individuals and families to assume basic responsibilities and to enjoy fundamental rights.'[132] The concept has been promoted in international organisations by ATD–Fourth World. Providing basic security implies that societies need to establish basic rights, provide or secure provision of a common foundation of resources and services, and to ensure a level of redistribution that will prevent people from becoming excluded by their disadvantages.
- *equality of outcome.* Policies which are concerned with inequalities of income or health status are generally concerned with removing disadvantage in outcomes, and tend in consequence to imply differential treatment according to circumstances.

There are many sorts of disadvantage, and removing one kind of disadvantage does not guarantee equality in others. The inequalities which people are concerned with, Rae suggests, can concern

---

[131] See P Spicker, 2006, *Liberty, equality, fraternity*, Bristol: Policy Press.

[132] J Wresinski, 1987, *Chronic poverty and lack of basic security*, Maryland: Fourth World Publications, 1994 edition, p.2

- individuals – the comparison is made, for example, between rich and poor people;
- blocs in society – categories and large social groups, like women, racial minorities, old people or regions. A typical comparison might be between women and men, or old people with people of working age.
- segments – for example, a distinction confined to children or to women.[133] So, a comparison might be made between middle-class women and working-class women, or poor children with all children.

A policy which corrects one inequality (e.g. between women and men) can aggravate another (e.g. between rich and poor, if the beneficiaries are richer women). In the same way, there is a current argument in India that attempts to avoid gender discrimination – making sure, for example, that richer women are more equal to richer men – will discriminate between castes.

Inequality of resources

The structure of advantage and disadvantage leads to differential access to opportunities and rewards in society; with that, it is closely associated with inequality in command over resources. Resources are commonly considered in terms of 'income' and 'wealth'. Wealth is about the stock of resources that people have – their assets, and things they can use. Income is a flow – it is about the changes in people's circumstances between two points of time. On the face of the matter, it may sound as if wealth is more important, but most studies begin from the opposite pole; food, fuel and essential services usually depend on people's ability to make regular payments, and for people who have little resources, income is critically important. Income is also an important indicator, or signpost, of other issues. When the World Bank refers to incomes of $1.25 or $2 a day – their figures are entirely arbitrary – it cannot tell us very much directly about how people live; but it does, in most countries, tell us that people are either not part of a formal economy, or that they have a very marginal position. The European Union uses a different indicator, an income which is 60% of the median income. The median is the mid-point of the income distribution. This is a mark of inequality, not just of low income; people whose income is below this may be able to buy some essential items, but their access to

---

[133] D Rae, 1981, *Equalities*, Cambridge Mass: Harvard University Press.

social goods like housing will be limited, and they will not be able to participate in society to the same extent as others.[134]

The pattern of income distribution in most formal economies tends to follow the pattern of a lognormal curve – a big hump at lower levels, and a long tail of people on higher incomes. Figure 3.1 shows the pattern for the UK; it is based on figures for 2011,[135] but the purpose of the graph is to show the shape of the distribution, rather than specific Liberty, equality and fraternity information. The numbers 1–10 show deciles, or tenths of the population; the graph is shortened, because there is a long tail of people on high incomes in the 10th decile who are not shown. The mode – the figure that recurs most often – is well below the median, and consequently closer to the conventional threshold of poverty at 60% of the median. The mean average is much higher than the median, because it reflects the position of people on very high incomes. Median earnings for full time work[136] are well above the median household income – that happens because so many

Figure 3.1: The distribution of household income in the UK

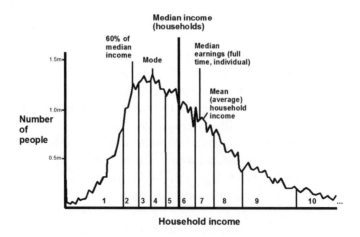

---

[134] P Spicker, 2012, Why refer to poverty as a proportion of median income?, *Journal of Poverty and Social Justice* 20(2) 165–177.

[135] From UK Department for Work and Pensions, 2012, *Households below average income*, London: TSO, p 27.

[136] Annual Survey of Households and Earnings (ASHE), 2012, 2011 Revised results, obtained at www.ons.gov.uk/ons/rel/ashe/annual-survey-of-hours-and-earnings/2011-revised-results--soc-2010-/2011-provisional-table-1.zip

households (including pensioners) have incomes that are lower than the incomes of people in work.

Inequality is commonly measured by the Gini Coefficient. It is easiest to explain in a diagram. The Lorenz Curve in Figure 3.2 maps the share of resources, from the lowest to the highest. The 'cumulative share' is how much is held by those at the bottom. In a simple economy where four people have £1, £2, £3 and £4, the bottom person has 10% (£1 out of £10), the bottom two have 30% and, the bottom three have 60%. The line at the centre of the graph shows where people would be if everything was shared equally. The curved line underneath shows the degree of inequality – the further it is from the centre, the greater is the inequality. The Gini Coefficient is a measure of the area under the line. It is described as a number between 0 and 1, where 0 is perfectly equal and 1 is completely unequal, though sometimes it will be presented as an index number between 0 and 100 (for example on the World Bank's website,[137] which for 2010 puts Colombia at 55.9, Nigeria at 48.8, Bangladesh at 32.1).

It is not surprising to discover that income and wealth are unevenly distributed; this is a pattern which obtains across many societies.

Figure 3.2: The Lorenz curve

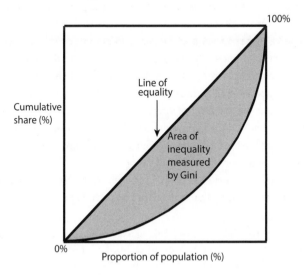

The possession of resources is often a key to access to the structure of social advantage; conversely, lack of resources implies cumulative disadvantages in material circumstances, life style, and opportunities. Extreme disadvantage in resources is generally referred to in terms of 'poverty', though it can be misleading to identify poverty too closely with inequality – in so far as poverty refers to the lack of resources, people can lack resources when others are in similar conditions, and measures which reduce inequality do not necessarily alleviate poverty.

Box 3.2: Explanations for poverty

Poverty is too complex to have a single cause, but discourses about poverty often tend to fall into predictable patterns – attributing poverty to a limited set of causes, and arguing for those causes to be responded to directly. The main classes of explanation for poverty are

- *Individual* Poverty is often represented either as the fault of the poor, or at least as something which can be attributed to their personal characteristics – laziness, lack of will power, lack of intelligence, poor decision making and so forth.
- *Familial* A recurrent element in discussions is the argument that poverty persists across generations, and poor families breed poor children. This may be because of inadequate parents, or because they suffer from a genetic defect or degeneracy. These assertions have repeatedly been shown to be false: in developed countries, poverty is much more generally experienced, there is considerable fluctuation in circumstances through the life cycle[138] and the impact of even limited social mobility through education, partnering and career greatly diminishes the prospect of intergenerational deprivation.[139] Evidence from social science is never allowed to stand in the way of a good myth, and the idea that people are trapped in a 'cycle of deprivation'[140] recurs whenever the economy falters.
- *Sub-cultural* Poverty has been attributed to the habits, behaviour and culture of the poor – another variant on pathological explanations. This

---

[138] L Leisering, R Walker (eds) *The dynamics of modern society*, Policy Press 1998; H Oxley, T Dang, P Antolin, 2000, *Poverty dynamics in six OECD countries*, OECD Economic Studies 30 7–52.

[139] A B Atkinson, A Maynard, C Trinder, 1983, *Parents and children*, London: Heinemann; I Kolvin, F Miller, D Scott, S Gatzanis, M Fleeting, 1990, *Continuities of deprivation?*, Aldershot: Avebury.

[140] *Benefits*, 2002, Special issue 35: The cycle of deprivation, thirty years on, 10(3).

is currently seen in discussions of the 'underclass'[141] which attribute their supposedly persistent and intractable poverty to such behaviour as 'violence, arson, hostility and welfare dependency.'[142]

- *Resource based* There is a view, represented for example in Green arguments, that there are simply not enough resources for some people to be rich while others are poor;[143] poverty happens because poor people do not have a large enough share of resources. Some of these arguments are based in the scarcity of resources, such as land or water supplies; others are based in structural inequality, because inequality denies people access to resources that would otherwise meet their needs.

- *Structural* Poverty can be attributed to the structure of society in two ways. The first is a reflection of the distribution of power in society – the production of disadvantage through the operation of class, capitalism and self-interest. The second sees poverty as the product of social organisation – for example, the effect of inequality, the structure of property rights, the position of women in society. There is no other explanation needed – if the structures work this way, then some people will unavoidably be poor while others are not.

- *External 'agency'* Lastly, there is a class of explanations which sees poverty as something which reflects deliberate action or inaction – the failure of governments, businesses, international organisations and so forth.

These explanations are not exclusive – it is possible to hold to some at the same time as others. Individual and structural explanations are not difficult to reconcile – the structure of society determines whether people are poor, while individual explanations claim to explain which individuals are affected. Similarly, aspects of poverty can be attributed to structure and culture, or culture and agency, at the same time.

Redistribution

Redistribution involves taking resources from some people and giving them to others. A measure is redistributive if the people who receive goods or services from a measure are not the same as the people

141 C Murray, 1994, *Underclass: the crisis deepens*, London: Institute of Economic Affairs.
142 K Auletta, 1983, *The underclass*, New York: Vintage Books, p.21.
143 R Johnston, 1989, *Environmental problems: nature, economy and state*, London: Belhaven Press, pp 5–6.

who pay for them. If we begin from the position that this payment comes from individuals or families, all social services are, by definition, redistributive in some way.

Redistribution is conventionally classified as vertical or horizontal. Vertical redistribution may be progressive (from rich to poor) or regressive (from poor to rich); for the most part, increasing welfare involves transferring money from richer people to poorer ones. Vertical redistribution can increase welfare in several ways.

- Vertical redistribution increases welfare if resources are worth less to richer people than to poorer ones. Many resources have a 'diminishing marginal utility'. Utility refers to their usefulness or desirability to the people who have them. 'Marginal utility' refers to the effect of small changes in the existing distribution. Taking a small amount of money from a very rich person will hardly be noticed; to a poor person, it can be the difference between eating or not eating. The marginal utility of a pound or a dollar is much greater, then, to the poor person than it is to the rich person. 'Diminishing marginal utility' means that as resources increase, each addition becomes less important. Several studies have found that while 'life satisfaction' is certainly associated with income, it also increases or decreases proportionately with income[144] – and if it takes 10% of income to see a step change in well-being, that is a lot more for a rich person than a poor one. That also means that if money is taken from rich people and given to poor people, it has a smaller effect in reducing the welfare of rich people than it does on increasing the welfare of poor people.
- Keynes also argued that a wider dispersion of income and wealth can be beneficial for the economy as a whole.[145] The reason is that the wider dispersion leads to greater levels of economic activity.
- Redistribution from richer to poorer people is essential to social cohesion. Sahlins suggests that the reason the principle is found throughout tribal societies is that it is necessary for the survival of a society; without redistribution, society becomes so fractured that it is not a society any more.[146]

---

[144] E Diener, R Lucas, U Schimmack, J Helliwell, 2009, *Well-being for public policy*, Oxford: Oxford University Press, p 171.

[145] J M Keynes, 1936, *The general theory of employment interest and money*, London: Macmillan.

[146] M Sahlins, 1974, *Stone age economics*, London: Tavistock.

- Inequality itself is damaging. *The Spirit Level* offers evidence linking inequality with a range of social problems, affecting whole societies, not just those who are disadvantaged. Societies which are more unequal tend to have more insecurity, worse health and more crime. The greater the degree of inequality, the more problems that are experienced by everyone, rich and poor alike.[147]

The main arguments which have been made to the effect that redistribution reduces welfare are:

- Rich people need incentives to produce, and by doing so increase the welfare of everyone. John Rawls claims, in *A theory of justice*, that this would lead most reasonable people to agree to some level of inequality in a society;[148] but there is no real evidence to support the contention that work effort is much affected by such incentives.[149]
- The concentration of wealth may have beneficial effects – de Jouvenel argues, for example, that much of our cultural heritage has been built on the previous patronage of rich people.[150]

There are also, of course, moral arguments concerning vertical redistribution. Redistribution from rich to poor is a moral imperative; the principle of charity is reinforced by most major religions. Box 2.2. referred to principles of humanitarianism, charity, reciprocity, solidarity and rights, while principles that work against redistribution will include property rights, reward according to desert rather than need, and the moral condemnation of the poor. There are further arguments based on issues of equality and social justice, considered further in Chapter 10.

Horizontal redistribution goes from one kind of group to another – for example, from men to women, households without children to families with children, or tenants to owner-occupiers. Barr makes a general analysis of pensions. Pensions redistribute resources

---

[147] R Wilkinson, K Pickett, 2009, *The spirit level*, London: Allen Lane.

[148] J Rawls, 1971, *A theory of justice*, Oxford: Oxford University Press; contrast N Daniels (ed), 1975, *Reading Rawls*, Oxford: Blackwell.

[149] see e.g. C Brown, 1983, *Taxation and the incentive to work*, Oxford: Oxford University Press; S Bonner, G Sprinkle, 2002, The effect of monetary incentives on effort and task performance, *Accounting, Organizations and Society*, 27(4–5) pp 303–345.

[150] B de Jouvenel, 1951, *Ethics of redistribution*, Cambridge: Cambridge University Press.

- from young to old
- from rich to poor, in so far as the ratio of benefits to contributions is greater for people on lower incomes;
- from poor to rich, in so far as richer people live longer
- from men to women, because women live longer and have earlier retirement.[151]

Horizontal redistribution is more complex than vertical, and the kind of arguments which are made for supporting families or women are not the same as those which relate to transfers from rich to poor. For the most part, horizontal redistribution is a way of changing patterns of behaviour in society, or encouraging behaviour (like raising children) which is seen as desirable for society overall.

Both horizontal and vertical redistribution might then have quite different effects from those implied by a principle of equality. Work on the welfare state in Britain suggests that much redistribution is not in fact from rich to poor or from one group to another, but rather from one part of an individual's life-cycle to another.[152] The effect is referred to by Barr as 'income smoothing'.[153] People, and societies, need to save for the bad times – the principle is in the Bible.[154] Sometimes this can be done privately, but in many cases the need goes beyond the capacity of individuals to provide for, and it has to be done collectively. A large part of redistribution for welfare provision is support for children, who repay when they are adults, for people who are sick, who pay when they are well, and for pensioners, who have paid while they were working.

Redistribution and equality

It cannot be assumed that redistribution will lead to greater equality. If redistribution goes to people who are poor, disadvantaged or in greater need, it may do; but it can go in other directions entirely. Rae reviews a series of different patterns in which redistribution might be thought to bring about a greater equality of resources.[155] He distinguishes four distinct tests:

---

[151] N Barr, 2004, *The economics of the welfare state*, Oxford: Oxford University Press, pp 199–201.

[152] J Falkingham, J Hills, C Lessof, 1993, *William Beveridge versus Robin Hood: social security and redistribution over the life cycle,* London: LSE Suntory-Toyota Centre.

[153] N Barr, 2004.

[154] Genesis, ch 41.

[155] D Rae, 1981, *Equalities*, Cambridge Mass: Harvard University Press.

- *maximin*, or 'maximising the minimum'. The word was coined by John Rawls.[156] The effect of raising the floor is both that the people with the least resources benefit, and their economic distance from the rest of the population is reduced.
- *minimax*, or minimising the maximum – that is, capping the incomes of those who are richest. This reduces inequality of resources overall; it may not noticeably benefit the poorest.
- *least difference*, or reducing the range of inequality – effectively a combination of the first two. It might be done, in principle, by taking money from the top and moving it straight to the bottom.
- *ratio*. If only the top and bottom of the distribution are changed, most people will not be touched. A progressive system of taxation and benefits works by charging more as people's incomes increase, and greater benefits as their incomes fall. The effects are felt throughout the income distribution – everyone's income becomes more like the incomes of the people above and below them.

If these approaches were taken to extremes, they might all end up in the same place, with incomes that are the same. In practice, they never will reach that point, and they look and feel very different.

The different meanings of 'equality' are much broader than the question of redistribution alone. Changing the distribution of income is not going, in itself, to guarantee equal rights relating to gender or sexuality, or protect the position of people in minorities. It is no less true that different approaches to equality may pull in contradictory directions – for example, in circumstances where group-based policies favour the position of better-off members of disadvantaged groups over poorer individuals.

There are limitations, then, to how far it is possible to achieve greater equality through a process of redistribution. That is not a fatal objection. The argument for equality has never been an argument for a fixed, absolute state. Tony Crosland, a writer much misrepresented in the literature, argued:

> How far towards equality do we wish to go? I do not regard this as either a sensible or a pertinent question ... We need, I believe, more equality than we now have ... The ultimate objective lies wrapped in complete uncertainty. This must be the case unless one subscribes to the vulgar fallacy that some ideal society can be said to exist, of which blueprints can be drawn. ... society at

---

[156] J Rawls, 1971.

any given moment either does or does not sufficiently embody these values; and if it does not, then further changes are required. ... But where, en route, before we reach some drab extreme, we shall wish to stop, I have no idea.[157]

If equality is about the removal of disadvantage, the pursuit of equality describes a direction of movement, not an ultimate objective.

ISSUE FOR DISCUSSION

If people's circumstances are improving, does it matter if they are disadvantaged?

---

[157] C A R Crosland, 1956, *The future of socialism*, London: Jonathan Cape, pp 215–17.

CHAPTER 4

Problems and responses

Social problems
Responding to social problems
Targeting: the focus of policy
Individuals
Individual and collective approaches

Social problems

Social policies are sometimes represented as responses to social problems. They are rather more than this, because there are policies which are not at all centred on 'problems'; any policy which is designed to change or maintain social structures or relationships could be described as a social policy, and it has been argued that the failure to make such policies can also be treated and analysed as a form of social policy.[158] But a focus on social problems is helpful in the first instance, because it helps to point our attention to some issues which affect all social policies.

Social issues become 'problems' because they need to be solved: some kind of response is called for. It is not always the case that people agree about what constitutes a problem. This might be because of lack of awareness. In Victorian times, for example, many people denied that there was a problem of poverty: Southwood Smith used to take selected dignitaries for a tour in London to persuade them.[159] More recently, doctors seemed unaware of the problem of physical child abuse, which was 'discovered' by radiographers;[160] child sexual abuse was hardly heard of until the 1980s, and there are still many who deny the existence of ritual abuse.[161] It might also, however, happen that

---

[158] P Townsend, 1976, *Sociology and social policy*, Harmondsworth: Penguin, p.6.

[159] S E Finer, 1952, *The life and times of Edwin Chadwick*, London: Methuen, ch 3.

[160] S Pfohl, 2003, The 'discovery' of child abuse, in P Conrad, V Leiter (eds) *Health and health care as social problems*, Lanham, Maryland: Rowman Littlefield.

[161] S Scott, 2001, *The politics and experience of ritual abuse*, Maidenhead: Open University Press.

---

people are aware of the conditions which others think of as a problem, and do not see a problem there. Many people do not think that hitting a child is problematic as long as it does not cause serious injury, and they hold that physical chastisement should be seen as a desirable part of a child's social and moral education. The view that children should not have less protection than adults has gradually been taking hold, and several countries have now legislated to prevent parents hitting children.

This example points to an important general issue: the definition of problems is different in different places. Definitions are not 'objective', if by this we mean that they are fixed on some standard which can be identified outside the context and society where they are applied. This does not mean that problems are 'subjective', however; they are not simply made up or arrived at by anyone. A better way to describe them is that they are 'inter-subjective', and the understanding of problems grows through a series of shared perceptions and beliefs.[162] Problems are 'socially constructed'; the pattern of relationships in society shapes the circumstances which lead to the problem, the way the problem is understood, and the extent to which it is perceived as a problem. Youth, old age, worklessness or educational attainment are not fixed, unchanging concepts; they mean different things in different places, and the way they are understood and responded to is different. This view of social relationships has led to an increasing emphasis in social research on 'abductive' studies, which try to understand the meaning of actions and reasons from the perspective of those involved in the research.[163]

The second major point the example raises about social problems is that they are social, which means that they occur in a social context and are recognised as such. Many problems are not social – for example, personal relationships, grief or pain. They become social at the point where they are constructed in social terms, or when a social response is called for. This requires some caution, because discussing whether or not issues are social can be taken in itself as an attempt to put them onto the social agenda. It could be argued, from what I stated earlier, that domestic violence is not a social problem. The trouble with this statement is that it is liable to be taken not as a description of how the problem is responded to (which would still be true for many of the countries where this book is read) but as a moral statement about

---

[162] P Berger, T Luckmann, 1967, *The social construction of reality*, New York: Anchor.

[163] N Blaikie, 2010, *Designing social research*, Brighton: Polity, p 105

what ought to be seen as a social problem (which would be highly disputable).

Understanding problems is important for social policy for a fairly obvious reason: it helps to understand what the problem is in order to respond to it. Part of the difficulty here is that people understand the issues differently. The problems of an abused child might be seen as a failure of family life; but they might also be seen as a reflection on the social acceptance of corporal punishment. Educational failure might be seen as the product of individual inadequacy, culture and upbringing or social deprivation. It often happens that the 'common-sense' assumptions made for policy rest on a series of complex, scarcely examined assumptions. It seems hard now to understand what policy-makers were doing when they bracketed mental illness with intellectual disability,[164] or child abuse and neglect with juvenile crime;[165] the associations are based in assumptions about the relationships between problems which now look wholly unconvincing. But equally questionable assumptions are made when, for example, racial issues are identified with poverty, or mental illness is linked to dangerousness. When social problems are recognised, they are interpreted or 'constructed' in a particular way; they might have to be reinterpreted, or 'deconstructed', to make an effective response possible.

Box 4.1: The misconstruction of problems

The history of social policy is festooned with examples of theoretical approaches which have gone sour – ideas which have misled practitioners, which have been misapplied, or which simply failed to deliver. Box 1.2 makes the case that trying to deal with the causes of problems is misconceived – not just because it is difficult to do, but because causal explanations do not lead to solutions. That is not the worst of it. People who think they know what the causes of a problem are often get it wrong. Sometimes they are positively dangerous.

A notorious example is the belief that social problems are inherited and biologically transmitted. This has been one of the most influential views in the history of social policy. In the late nineteenth century, the idea of 'degeneracy' was seen as the root of a range of inter-related problems – idiocy, insanity,

---

164 K Jones, 1972, *A history of the mental health services*, London: RKP.
165 Labour Party, 1964, *Crime: a challenge to us all*, London: Labour Party.

crime, poverty, worklessness and prostitution.[166] Boies, writing in the US, proclaimed: 'We believe it is established beyond controversy that criminals and paupers both, are degenerate; the imperfect, knotty, knurly, worm-eaten, half-rotten fruit of the race.'[167] According to Cooley, the sociologist better known for the idea of the 'looking glass self', 'such things as crime, pauperism, idiocy, insanity and drunkenness have, in great measure, a common causation, and so form, practically, parts of a whole.'[168]

The leading account of degeneracy at that time was a social study of a degenerate family, the Jukes. 'In the present investigation', Estabrook wrote,

> 2,820 people have been studied ... 2,094 were of Juke blood and 726 of 'X' blood who married into the Juke family; of these 366 were paupers, while 171 were criminals; and 10 lives have been sacrificed by murder. In school work 62 did well, 288 did fairly, while 458 were retarded two or more years. It is known that 166 never attended school; the school data for the rest of the family were unobtainable. There were 282 intemperate and 277 harlots. The total cost to the State has been estimated at $2,093,685.[169]

In fact, 'the Jukes' were not a single family at all – but it happened then, as it has happened in other cases, that the researchers were so certain they knew what the problems were that they didn't think that inconvenient details like that really mattered.[170]

The same confidence about identifying the cause was rapidly translated into policy. The initial response to degeneracy was to seek to isolate degenerates from the community; it was an important motor force in the development of colonies for people with intellectual disabilities, and for the building of large institutions, confining them along with people who were mentally ill.[171] Subsequently the emphasis shifted to eugenics, which sought to stop degenerates from breeding – preventing unfit people from having children. Indiana permitted involuntary sterilizations on eugenic principles

[166] See D Pick, 1989, *Faces of degeneration*, Cambridge: Cambridge University Press; E Carlson, 2001, *The unfit*, New York: Cold Spring Harbor Laboratory Press.

[167] H Boies, 1893, *Prisoners and paupers*, New York: Knickerbocker Press, p.266.

[168] C Cooley, 1902, *Human nature and the social order*, New York: Scribner, p.375.

[169] See A Estabrook, 1916, The Jukes in 1915, available at www.disabilitymuseum.org/lib/docs/759.htm.

[170] S Christianson, 1993, Bad seed or bad science?, *New York Times*, 8th February.

[171] Carlson, 2001.

in 1907, and Virginia passed a 'Eugenical Sterilization Act' in 1924, which was approved in the US Supreme Court. This was the model for the Nazis' eugenics law of 1933.[172] The Nazis began by preventing people from sexual relationships and isolating them from the community, proceeding only later to kill them.[173] Although Nazism gave eugenics a (deservedly) bad name, people with intellectual disabilities were routinely sterilised, in several western countries, until at least the 1970s.[174]

There are many reservations to make about the general proposition that social problems are inherited. There is little support in biology for the crude determinism of most of the arguments,[175] and the complexity of the different influences, coupled with some egregiously bad statistical methods,[176] makes many of the generalisations worthless; but this is about more than bad science. It shows what can happen when people are convinced that multi-faceted problems have a single origin. It shows what can happen when people try to address the cause, when that cause is attributed to a fault of the people who have the problems. And it shows what can happen when the decision-makers are absolutely convinced they are right.

Responding to social problems

The way that a problem is responded to is shaped by the way the problem is defined and understood, but it is not determined by it. Some responses to problems are *direct*, in the sense that the response is intended to deal with the immediate problem as presented. If people do not have money, they can get money. If they do not have a job, they can get work. This is sometimes criticised as a way of dealing with symptoms, rather than with the underlying problems. But relieving symptoms is not necessarily such a bad idea; at least it makes some things better, and there are circumstances in which one cannot deal

---

[172] P Lombardo, n.d., Eugenic sterilization laws, www.eugenicsarchive.org/html/eugenics/essay8text.html

[173] R Grunberger, 1974, *A social history of the Third Reich*, Harmondsworth: Penguin; G Rimlinger, 1987, Social policy under German fascism, in M Rein, G Esping-Andersen, L Rainwater (eds) *Stagnation and renewal in social policy*, NY: Armonk; P Weindling, 1989, *Health, race and German politics between national unification and Nazism, 1870–1945*, Cambridge: Cambridge University Press.

[174] J Trent, 1995, *Inventing the feeble mind: a history of mental retardation in the United States*, Berkeley: University of California Press.

[175] S Jones, 1993, *The language of the genes*, London: Flamingo.

[176] See e.g. J Ioannidis, 2005, Why most published research findings are false, *PLOS Medicine* 2(8) e124 doi:10.1371, obtained at www.plosmedicine.org/article/info:doi/10.1371/journal.pmed.0020124

with the root of a problem unless some obstacles are removed first. It is not impossible to respond to people's health problems while they are sleeping rough, but it is markedly more difficult.[177] The second kind of response is concerned with *causes* rather than effects. Addressing 'causes' is contentious, because it is difficult to find agreement about what the causes of social problems are (Box 1.2), and because sometimes the solutions are radically wrong (Box 4.1). However, strategies which address causes have been influential in policy, partly because they seem to offer solutions that are simpler than dealing with the problems, partly because of the fear that if the causes are not addressed then the problems will simply recur, and partly because of the dangerously misplaced confidence of their advocates.

A third approach is *key intervention*. The principle of key intervention depends on the argument that a focus on a small number of selected elements can have a critical effect on other elements. This is based on an analysis of the relationships between the elements. If the relationships between the parts are identified correctly, it may be possible within a complex set of issues to pick out the ones which will lead to change more generally. A simple example is giving support to child care in order to increase female participation in the labour market, or (more contentiously) offering support to landlords in an attempt to improve access to affordable housing. Other examples depend on a more elaborate set of assumptions about complex social relationships; for example, it has been argued that education is the key to equality,[178] or that democratic processes are key to the prevention of famines.[179]

Although it is possible to relate the response to problems to the patterns of social organisation considered in the previous chapter, there is no necessary link between them. Even if the problem is social, the response might be individual – or vice-versa. Table 4.1 gives some illustrative examples.

The way to reach lots of people individually might be to have a category-based policy (such as using nursery education to reach children in difficulties); conversely, there are many examples where socially determined problems like homelessness are responded to through individualised programmes for the homeless person. These responses are not 'right' or 'wrong', but both are subject to objections on the grounds of the misdirection of resources. The example of

---

[177] R Burrows, N Pleace, D Quilgars, 1997, *Homelessness and social policy,* Routledge.

[178] R Tawney, 1930, *Equality,* London: Allen and Unwin.

[179] A Sen, 2001, *Development as freedom,* Oxford: Oxford University Press.

	Table 4.1: Problems and responses		
	Responses		
Problems	*Individual and family*	*Community-based*	*Social*
Individual and family	Social casework	Child care	Health promotion
Community	Rehousing	Regeneration	Public order
Social	Unemployment	Local economic development	Public health

nursery education might seem to be wasteful, if the level of provision is extensive and the true target limited in numbers; in the worst cases it may fail to meet the needs of the target group, either by omission or because there is no way of directing resources to them within the system. The example of homelessness suffers from the problem that it involves a huge time and effort to deal with the effects of a major shortage of housing on an individualised basis; it may, beyond that, put an inappropriate responsibility on individuals for circumstances beyond their control.

Responses have to be translated into practical action. Policies are usually 'targeted', or aimed at somebody. The idea of targeting is much misunderstood; the word has acquired some very negative connotations, because it is often identified with a particular kind of policy that treats poverty as an individual fault and welfare as a public burden. The World Bank website suggests: 'The main objective of targeting is to deliver more resources to the poorest groups of the population.'[180] But there is no intrinsic reason why the target should be the needs only of the poorest; it may be possible, for example, to aim policies at broader categories of people (like lone parents or residents of particular neighbourhoods), and the World Bank once argued for 'indicator targeting', picking on regions, age groups, gender or other kinds of common characteristic.[181] Targeting means only that policies have to be directed at someone or something.[182] The next section considers some of the alternative focuses that might be adopted.

---

[180] World Bank, 2004, Social safety nets, at www.worldbank.org/sp/safetynets/Targeting.asp

[181] World Bank, 1990, *World Development Report*, Oxford: Oxford University Press.

[182] P Spicker, 2005, Targeting, residual welfare and related concepts: modes of operation in public policy, *Public Administration* 83(2) pp 345–365.

Targeting: the focus of policy

The 'focus' of policy refers to the people or social units who the policy directly affects. This is not quite the same as saying that they have to be intended to help particular people, because the people who are helped are not necessarily the people who the policy is focused on. The most effective response to unemployment, for example, is to expand the economy – the intention may be to help unemployed people return to work, but the focus of policy is the economy. Similarly, one way of reducing gender disadvantage might be to offer child care, but the focus of such a policy is on families with children, not on women.

Social policies have commonly focused on a range of different targets. They include policies aimed at individuals; families; households; communities; different kinds of social group; and the whole society. The question of which focus is most appropriate can be taken in two different ways: to what extent these groups can be seen as the source of the problems, and to what extent it is appropriate to focus on such groups as a means of responding to the problem. I plan to concentrate on the latter, but it is still important not to lose sight of the former, because ideas about causation play such a large part in the formation of policy.

Individuals

A focus on the 'individual' is usually read as a focus on the person who has needs or problems – though, as explained in Chapter 2, these ideas are not quite the same. Approaches to problems and policy which concentrate on dealing with people one at a time are usually described as 'individualised', although sometimes you will encounter the term 'pathological'. Pathological theories are those which see the cause of a problem in terms of the unit which has the problem; so, if individuals are poor, ill-educated or homeless, a pathological explanation is one which tries to find the reasons for their condition in terms of the characteristics or behaviour of those individuals. This is an important aspect of policies, but as ever it is necessary to make a distinction between what policies are intended to do and the methods which they use; individualistic policies do not have to be pathological.

The central argument for concentrating responses on individuals is that problems are always experienced at the individual level, even if they are also experienced at other levels. Any general policy which ignores their individual position runs the risk of not doing something for at least some individuals. Even in countries where there are general policies for the support of the population as a whole, there is usually some kind of 'safety net' to protect the position of people whose circumstances are different enough to mean they would not be protected otherwise. Closely related to this argument is an argument about effectiveness. If resources are going to be used to help people in need, it is important to ensure that people in need actually benefit, and the only way to be sure of this is to protect them at the individual level. Anything else risks people being left out. The point can be supplemented by an argument about the best use of resources; concentrating resources on the people who are most in need should give the maximum benefit with the minimum waste. This is also more directly redistributive; if money is taken from the best off and given to the worst off, society will be more equal.

Although these positions are often seen as following from an individualistic perspective, individualism is a much richer tradition than this suggests. For individualists, the individual is not only the basic unit in society, but also the unit which undertakes obligations, makes agreements, or tries to gain redress against injustice. Individual rights have proved in practice to be a very effective strategy for the delivery of welfare. If individuals gain entitlements, and are able to claim benefits and services themselves, and to have some kind of direct redress against the providers of services or the government, it introduces an important set of checks and balances, as well as making services much more responsive to the circumstances of the individual. The US constitution was designed around this principle; individual actions are protected by the constitution and the bill of rights, and constitutional action has been used to protect such issues as voting rights, racial equality and the rights of prisoners. A striking example is Wyatt v. Stickney, which established a 'constitutional' right for patients in mental institutions to have decent living conditions, including adequate meals, comfortable bedding and a TV set in the day room.[183]

The arguments for an individual focus are strong ones; but there are also compelling arguments against the concentration of responses on individuals. It may be desirable to identify individuals in need, but it is not easy to do; it requires some kind of test. Tests of need are likely to be intrusive and administratively complex; one of the arguments for 'indicator targeting', going for the broad range of problems rather than the individual level, is that it is often the only practical way to arrange services. The practical experience of individual testing is that

---

[183] *Harvard Law Review*, 1973, Wyatt v. Stickney and the right of civilly committed mental patients to adequate treatment, 86(7) 1282–1306.

it often leads to inefficiencies; many people who are entitled do not receive their benefits. Perhaps most important, individual tests of need are believed to be socially divisive; the effect of concentrating on the individual is often to attach blame to people for their circumstances.

Households and families

The basic units of contemporary societies are not 'individuals', but households and families. A household is defined in terms of a group of people who live together, sharing resources and responsibilities. Families are a special kind of social unit, defined in terms of a particular network of personal and social relationships and responsibilities. The two categories overlap considerably, though they are not the same – family relationships apply to many people who do not live together, and many people who live together do not have the kinds of responsibility which are encountered in a family. In the case of the family, it should be noted that there are other reasons why it might be thought of as the focus of policy – implicit in the idea of 'family policy' referred to in the previous chapter. There are certain social issues, particularly childbirth and socialisation, which are primarily addressed socially in the context of the family. That being the case, it is difficult to avoid consideration of how policies work at the level of families when these issues are discussed.

The central argument for concentrating responses on families and households is simple enough: it is how people actually live. People do have responsibilities to each other; they do share resources; they do share their liabilities. Measures which ignore the realities run the risk of becoming unfair, though the unfairness can work in different ways. Two people who share responsibilities with each other do not have the same resources and liabilities as two people who live separately. A lone parent is particularly vulnerable, because of the combination of reduced resources and much higher needs than each partner in a couple. These circumstances can only be distinguished by a rule which defines couples differently from lone parents, and from single people living with others. However, this kind of rule is the source of considerable potential conflict, and it often leads to intrusive and degrading enquiries. One of the problems associated with 'household means tests' (used in Britain in the 1930s) or the aggregation of resources in a family is that it calls for different responses according to the make-up of the household. This leads to differences and inequities in the treatment for example of same-sex couples, adults living with their elderly parents or people living with others who are not members of their family. This can lead to some perverse effects – for example, creating financial incentives for households to break up, requiring wives to give up work when their husband is unemployed, or encouraging children to leave home.[184]

There are other problems with this kind of focus:

- it is very easy to lose sight of individuals within a household or family. This has particularly worked against women; feminists have argued that women in a household or family which is well-resourced are not necessarily able to take advantage of the resources, and in some cases these women might be classified as 'poor' although the household cannot be.[185]

- there are problems and aspects of social disadvantage which derive from the structure of households and families, which have the effect of making many policies based on them inequitable. A woman is likely, because of conventional social structures, to interrupt employment in order to care for children or others. An arrangement which ignores this situation is inequitable. But taking the situation into account – offering, for example, support and extra resources – is likely to reinforce it, creating disincentives to alternative social arrangements.

- the objections which were raised against targeting individuals all remain; it is still difficult to identify needs, and inequities arise.

Box 4.2: Social casework

Social work calls for individualised responses to problems. The idea of 'casework', or direct social work practice, rests on the view that the social worker should be able to select methods that are appropriate to the needs of the person. 'Casework' typically includes

- problem solving (as advisor, broker or advocate)
- psycho-social therapy
- meeting the functional tasks of the agency

---

[184] M H Phillips, 1981, Favourable family impact as an objective of means support policy, in P G Brown, C Johnson, P Vernier (eds) *Income support*, Totowa, NJ: Rowman and Littlefield.

[185] J Millar, C Glendinning, 1989, Gender and poverty, *Journal of Social Policy* 18(3) pp 363–381; S Payne, 1991, *Women, health and poverty*, Harvester Wheatsheaf, London; but see S Cantillon, B Nolan, 1998, Are married women more deprived than their husbands?, *Journal of Social Policy* 27(2) 151–172.

- changing behaviour, and
- crisis intervention.

The fundamental principle of casework rests on the selection of appropriate responses after identification of needs. The role of the social worker, and the methods used, depend largely on the interpretation of the problems the worker is dealing with. Where the problems are personal, the responses might include

- psychodynamic approaches – trying to change the way that a person thinks and behaves;
- counselling, which is non-directive and encourages change from within;
- education;
- general support, often in combination with other professions (like medicine and occupational therapy); or
- contract work, where the social work negotiates an agreement with the client to bring about changes.

Where the problems are based in relationships with others, such as family members or peer groups, the methods might still be personal, but might also include

- family therapy – where all members are engaged jointly and individually
- groupwork – where people are dealt with together, either because they have common relationship issues (e.g. women's groups) or because the group as a whole needs relations within it to be addressed
- conciliation (as in marriage guidance) where people are brought together to resolve issues.

Problems with the social environment might call for very different approaches, including

- advice and advocacy
- community and neighbourhood work, and
- community education.

– though it is important to recognise that these still have a focus on the people who experience the problems, rather than the social issues themselves.

Some social workers would aim for a holistic approach, either by combining a range of methods aimed at different issues, or identifying key elements within a set of systems to bring about change strategically.[186]

Casework is intrinsically an individualistic activity. It depends heavily on the direct personal relationship between the social worker and the client, however the term 'client' is defined; it focuses on identifying the needs of the person; it generally tries, in principle, to offer a personalised response to those needs. This is sometimes problematic, because – as many social workers would argue – the source of the problems is not necessarily to be found at the level of the individual. It is not always reasonable to insist that people should adjust to the social environment; sometimes the social environment needs to adapt to them. But dealing with situations in practice, they have to do what they can – even when they know that the response is likely to be inadequate.

These approaches used to be central to social work, but their present-day role is less prominent than used to be the case; the social work profession has increasingly moved in the direction of 'care management' rather than casework. By contrast with casework, care management is characterised by planning and responsiveness to the needs of groups rather than individuals, and the specification of functional tasks.

Communities

It can be difficult to say just what focusing on a 'community' involves, because the term is so ambiguous. For this purpose, though, I shall concentrate on two kinds of approach: focusing on areas, and focusing on people with existing networks of responsibility, or 'solidarities'. The arguments for and against concentration on people with common identities, like racial or religious groups, are slightly different, and are considered in the next section.

Some of the arguments for focusing on communities as geographical areas are based in a view of what community life is like, or ought to be like. 'Community cohesion' has been interpreted in the UK in terms of living together well, implying social interaction and tolerance for diversity.[187] That assumes a link between geography and social networks which seems increasingly questionable in contemporary society – people increasingly live, work, maintain family relationships

---

[186] B Compton, B Galaway, B Cournoyer, 2005, *Social work processes*, Belmont: Brooks/ Cole.

[187] P Ratcliffe, 2012, 'Community cohesion': reflections on a flawed paradigm, *Critical Social Policy* 32(2) 262–281.

and socialise in different locations. However, the people for whom this is least true tend to be those who have been excluded from access to wider networks, and to some extent the focus on 'community' reflects a concern with a particular type of locale where deprivation has become concentrated.

The chief reason for concentrating on geographical areas, then, is that problems often present themselves on an area basis. There is a bad argument for this, and a good argument. The bad argument assumes that people with problems are best identified according to where they live. It is true that problems like poverty, crime and poor health tend to be found in higher proportions in the same places, but 'a higher proportion' is not the same as 'most'. Poverty and ill health are widespread, even in developed economies; most poor people do not live in poor areas. Equally, saying that an area has a high concentration of problems does not mean that most of the people who live there share those problems. The good argument is that some problems are area-based. The conditions found in geographical areas affect the people who live there – those who are not poor, as well as those who are. Issues of social organisation, economic development and the physical environment demand an area-based response. Issues like renovation, housing design, communications and social relationships need to be thought about spatially.[188]

Communities are not simply geographical units. Social networks are important as a basis for social provision. The cohesion of a community – another term imported from French social policy,[189] and misunderstood in Britain – depends on solidarity, the establishment of mutually supportive social networks. The term 'social capital' is also used to describe the value of such networks, because they clearly add to people's capacity to do things.[190] The work of voluntary organisations, the informal care given to children or elderly people, the connections between people in social clubs, are all examples of social capital. (The idea has been enormously helpful in persuading economists in international organisations to take account of the value of otherwise intangible social activities. Svendsen and Sørensen describe it as a 'methodological revolution ... where ... non economic resources are being included on the same footing with more visible, economic

[188] P Spicker, 2001, Poor areas and the 'ecological fallacy', *Radical Statistics* 76, pp 38–79.
[189] M Fragonard, 1993, *Cohésion sociale et prévention de l'exclusion*, Paris: La Documentation Française.
[190] R Putnam, 2000, *Bowling alone*, New York: Simon and Schuster, ch 19.

assets' – while at the same time they find that the networks they are investigating have little direct economic impact.[191])

Blocs

Groups of people who share common characteristics might be referred to (after Rae) as 'blocs' in society.[192] Women, minority ethnic groups, families with children, older people and disabled people are defined for this purpose not so much by what they have in common as by their difference from other blocs – the distinction between men and women, disabled and able-bodied, and so forth. Bloc-regarding policies may be aimed at identifiable social groups, but they are not necessarily based in a politics of identity – that would depend on participants sharing understandings about group membership. The policies are just as likely to be aimed at broad categories of people – women, adolescents and so on. The basic arguments for aiming at blocs are these:

- They are the source of the kinds of social disadvantage which social policy is so often trying to address. If there are problems of disadvantage, oppression or exclusion, there is a case for seeking to change the social relationships which bring them about.
- They set the context in which social policies have to operate. A policy which ignores social divisions can often have unintended effects, and might reinforce the divisions. For example, people in relatively advantaged groups are generally paid more than those who are disadvantaged; so, a pensions scheme which is based on past earnings will give greater resources to people who are already better off. Access to social services can be prejudiced by direct discrimination, but services which rely on waiting lists or residence – like housing or some forms of schooling – may also work indirectly against outsiders or people who are in less stable circumstances. One of the most trenchant and persistent criticisms of the welfare state has been that it tends to favour the middle classes, those who are already best provided for but who are in a position to use the services provided.[193]

---

[191] G Svendsen, J Sørensen, 2006, The socioeconomic power of social capital, *International Journal of Sociology and Social Policy* 26 9/10 pp 411–429.

[192] D Rae, 1981, *Equalities*, Cambridge, Mass: Harvard University Press.

[193] R Goodin, J Le Grand (eds), 1987, *Not only the poor*, London: Allen and Unwin.

- The approach is simple. The argument for 'indicator targeting' is at its most powerful in developing countries, where deprivation is widespread and fine distinctions are difficult to administer, but it still has its place in developed societies.

However, there are also considerable problems in addressing blocs adequately.

- There is a problem of equity. If policy is framed in terms of groups, the position of individuals might be ignored. The position of one large category of people is rarely uniformly worse than that of another. Giving preference to women may mean that a rich woman is given priority for service over a poor man. Creating opportunities for people in minority ethnic groups might create opportunities for middle class people in minority ethnic groups above other people in the ethnic majority. Support for families with children may divert resources from poorer younger and older households to others which have much better resources.
- The kinds of bloc considered here, like 'women' or 'minority ethnic groups', are very mixed, referring to large numbers of people in very diverse circumstances. The way in which the problem is constructed does not necessarily reflect all the divisions. The distribution of racial disadvantage in the UK, for example, needs to be understood in terms of cross-cutting influences of gender, ethnicity and religion,[194] but the main statistics are drawn from crude distinctions largely based on skin colour. There is a risk that blanket policies will favour some groups over others. This was one of the problems aired in the US courts about the policy of 'affirmative action'. In the Bakke case, a Jewish student sued a college (successfully) which excluded him from a medical course in favour of an African-American student with lower grades.[195]

It is important, too, to add a word of caution about bloc-related policies. The study of sociology points us towards a series of disadvantages and social divisions – among them, the position of women, 'race' and sexuality. That is not in general how social policy is constructed or designed. Where it is constructed differently for disadvantaged groups

---

[194] National Equality Panel, 2010, *An anatomy of inequality in the UK*, London: LSE.
[195] See R Dworkin, 1985, *A matter of principle*, Cambridge, Mass: Harvard University Press.

– with policies which treat disadvantaged people differently – most obviously in the apartheid régime of South Africa, or the institutional discrimination against women in Saudi Arabia – it is liable to provoke unease. Books on social policy often rely on sociological concepts to understand the distributive implications, but to understand the structure of policy we usually need to look at the issues in different terms.

The general public

Beyond issues like community and social cohesion, certain kinds of policy are intended to benefit people in general. In a sense, such policies are 'unfocused', because the benefits are not necessarily attributable to any particular individual or group. A public park, for example, is a facility available to anyone who wants to use it. It is very difficult to attribute specific gains or benefits to any particular users, and even any set of users. But there is little doubt in most people's minds that parks are a good idea, and the world is better for having them than not. Economists refer to such provisions as 'public goods'.[196] Other examples might be public services like police, transport and communications networks, though these are more disputable. They are used for the good of a society rather than identifiable groups or individuals in that society. Public goods are characterised by the absence of rivalry for their use, and their lack of exclusiveness. Some commentators add further conditions: a possible criterion is that people are unable to opt out of the good (like defence – once it is provided, everyone has it). Another potentially important factor is joint supply, so that there is no extra cost involved in providing for a further person – but there may still be a problem of congestibility, which is that public use of goods like parks and roads can change the character of the good, diminishing its value to other people.[197] There may well be rivalry for the use of public space.

The central argument for taking a generalised approach is that it increases the welfare of the public as a whole; people are better off. This is difficult to prove, because the costs are clearly attributable and the benefits are not, but it is still persuasive, because the communal benefits from parks and roads are fairly evident. Economists tend to judge this by the Pareto principle, the idea that a group of people is better off if

---

[196] S Bailey, 2002, *Public sector economics*, Palgrave.
[197] D Weimer, A Vining, 2010, *Policy analysis*, Harlow: Longman, p 72.

at least one person is better off, and no-one else is worse off.[198] The principle is highly disputable,[199] partly because people are reasonably sensitive to distributions that are unfair, partly because inequality does make people worse off – it disadvantages them. ('Economic distance' is, for good reason, one of the ways we define poverty: see Box 5.1.) In cases where it has been possible to attribute the benefits from such policies specifically, it often turns out that their effects are inegalitarian, favouring people who are already best provided for over those who are least well off. Parks are often located in places where they serve the middle classes; transport subsidies tend to favour people who can afford to travel most; sponsored cultural activities are favoured by the middle classes. This kind of policy has been objected to on the basis that the middle classes are liable to 'hijack' welfare services – though it can equally be argued that the services which are available to middle class people tend to be better for everyone else as well.[200]

Society

A policy for society – a 'societal' policy[201] – is focused on the relationships of society as a whole. Policies that are intended to change relationships in society – policies concerned, for example, with the family in general, culture, or national identity – can be seen as focused on society. In Chapter 2 I introduced a particular model of society, based on solidarity; it represents society, not as a single entity or common identity, but a network of networks. The idea of 'social capital', mentioned before in the context of community, has been another way of considering the issues. One view of societal policy is that it is concerned with approaches to strengthen those networks. The idea of 'social cohesion' has been represented in several ways. The Council of Europe reviews a long series of definitions: some based on social bonds, some on shared values and a sense of belonging, some on collective

---

[198] See e.g. L Kaplow, S Shavell, 2001, Any non-welfarist method of policy assessment violates the Pareto Principle, *Journal of Political Economy* 109(2) p 281–7; T Damjanovic, 2006, On the Possibility of Pareto-Improving Pension Reform, *The Manchester School*, 74(6) 741–754; A Hasman, L Osterdal, 2004, Equal value of life and the Pareto principle, *Economics and Philosophy* 20(2004) 13–23.

[199] See P Spicker, 2013, *Reclaiming individualism*, Bristol: Policy Press, s. 3.4.

[200] R Goodin, J Le Grand (eds), 1987, *Not only the poor*, London: Allen and Unwin.

[201] Z Ferge, 1979, *A society in the making*, Harmondsworth: Penguin p.55.

---

action, and some on harmonious co-existence.[202] There may, too, be policies intended to benefit society collectively. Policies for defence, culture and heritage or foreign policy fall into that category. One of the best examples of benefitting a whole society is macro-economic policy – that is, the management of the whole economy; the application of monetary policy or fiscal policy is not specific to particular individuals or groups, and the effects are experienced across society.

Individual and collective approaches

Welfare is understood differently when it is viewed from individualist or collective perspectives. One view of 'social welfare' is that it is nothing more than the sum of the welfare of the people who make it up; in the case of public goods like parks or roads, collective action can yield more benefit for each person than the cost to each individual user. But there is also a view that societies have interests and welfare which is distinct from that of any individual member; societies also need to survive, to reproduce themselves, and to flourish. If welfare is understood individualistically, it can be increased by making things better for more people, for example through growth, redistribution or insurance. If, on the other hand, it is interpreted collectively, there are different criteria by which the welfare of a society ought to be judged. Societies can be said to have 'needs', in the sense that there are things which are necessary for a society to survive. They have to maintain order, to deal with change, and to 'reproduce' themselves for the future.

The movement in the twentieth century to welfare states and the development of social services can be seen as a move towards collective approaches, including not only national schemes for social provision but a range of structural responses, like economic development and public health. It is not unequivocally collective, however. Many welfare systems are based on individualised responses – personal insurance, entitlement determined through an individual work record, or subsidised commercial markets, where people continue to act as consumers. Pensions are increasingly individualised, based on individual work record, rather than being available to all as of right; some countries like Sweden and Italy extend this principle to state pensions.[203] There has been a strong trend towards individualisation – choosing policies

---

[202] Council of Europe, 2005, *Concerted development of social cohesion indicators: methodology guide*, Council of Europe.
[203] Pensions Commission, 2005, *A new pension settlement for the 21st century,* London: The Stationery Office.

that relate to the circumstances of individuals, rather than people in groups or broader categories.[204] There are economists who argue that the best responses are always individualised,[205] because only individualised policies can adapt to individual cases, but that makes little sense. It is not self-evident that individual tuition is better than learning in schools, that providing drinking water to households in bottles is better than providing it through a water system, or that personal transport is better than public transport. They may be, and they may not; the issues have to be considered, and argued, in the circumstances where they apply. Unemployment was seen, in the post war period, as a structural phenomenon, and the main responses included economic development, regional policy, job creation through public works and social protection. In recent years the response to unemployment has been individualised, with a strong emphasis on 'activation' to re-engage the unemployed person in the labour market.[206] McKeen, writing in the context of Canada, comments that 'social policy has become social casework, writ large, and structural understandings of social problems have been all but eliminated from the calculation.'[207]

The general experience of social welfare provision has been that both individual and collective responses are necessary. Systems which respond to general needs can only cover populations comprehensively if they also have the capacity to respond to exceptions; and some of the needs which are being considered, like medical care and social care, often require highly individuated responses. On the other hand, systems which rely heavily on individualised responses cannot cope with the diversity and range of problems, even in highly developed economies like the United States. Once apparently individual problems, like interpersonal violence or alcoholism, become widespread, a generalised social response may be needed for services to be effective.

---

[204] See P Spicker, 2013, *Reclaiming individualism*, Bristol: Policy Press.

[205] L Kaplow, S Shavell, 2001, Any non-welfarist method of policy assessment. violates the Pareto Principle, *Journal of Political Economy* 109(2) p 281–7

[206] N Gilbert, R van Voorhuis (eds), 2001, *Activating the unemployed*, New Brunswick: Transaction, 2001; W van Oorschot, P Abrahamson, 2003, The Dutch and Danish miracles revisited, *Social Policy and Administration* 37(3) pp 288–304.

[207] W McKeen, 2006, Diminishing the concept of social policy, *Critical Social Policy* 26(4) pp 865–887.

ISSUE FOR DISCUSSION

If governments want to reduce obesity in the population, where should the focus of policy fall?

CHAPTER 5

Needs and welfare

Well-being
Needs
Need groups
Needs and responses

Well-being

Although the main focus of this book is on 'welfare' in a different sense, welfare is often taken to refer to 'well-being', whether or not people are living good, satisfied, contented lives – some examples of that use were given in Chapter 1. The idea of well-being is sometimes used to distance the discussion from practical issues of social welfare, and it needs perhaps to be taken with some caution on that account.[208] Well-being is understood by economists mainly in terms of what people choose. Choices are mainly determined according to the value that people attach to different options, and this is affected by norms, beliefs and emotions. The choices which people make can be understood in terms of their 'utility', or perceived value to the people making the choice. Figure 5.1 shows some conventional utility curves, also called 'indifference curves' because each curve describes a set of choices which are of equal worth to people. Well-being is increased when utility is maximised – in the graph, when choices are made from a higher curve – and reduced if utility is reduced. Utility is not necessarily increased by having more of something; once they have their basic quota, most people do not want more families, more spouses, or more parents. When people are considered as a group, welfare is held to be increased if the utility of the group is increased.[209]

---

[208] D Taylor, 2012, Well being and welfare, *Journal of Social Policy* 40(4) 777–794.
[209] D Winch, 1971, *Analytical welfare economics*, Harmondsworth: Penguin.

The economic analysis of welfare tends to emphasise what people choose – not what they need, what is in their interests or what they ought to have. There is a strong moral argument to say that people are the best judges of their own interests, but it is not the only view; it could equally be argued that there are 'objective' interests, things without which it is not possible for people to have welfare. They might include the necessities for physical survival, education, scope for autonomous action, and many other things.[210] In other words, welfare can be seen as depending on the satisfaction of 'needs', not just of choices.

Besides the view that choices are equivalent to well-being, there are some other contentious premises underpinning the economic approach. The second is that people's choices are rational – which may sometimes be true when differences are averaged out, but is often not true either for individuals or for a whole society. Third, people try to maximise their advantage; more is nearly always better. Figure 5.1 depends on a conventional economic representation of the choices people make – in this case, a choice between food and health care. The curves represent a range of choices where the choices have the same value to the person who makes them. One of the central assumptions made in this presentation is that people are generally willing to trade off one commodity in order to get more of another. A person will be willing to take a little less health care to get more food, or vice versa.

Figure 5.1: Utility curves: the economic representation of welfare

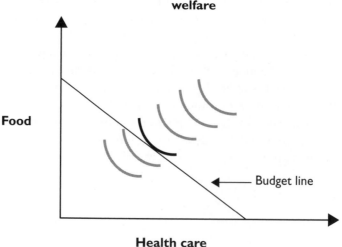

Health care

---

[210] L Doyal, I Gough, 1991, *A theory of human need*, Basingstoke: Macmillan.

Another is that higher indifference curves are always to be preferred to lower ones. Both assumptions are very questionable. The problem with the first is that some things are not practically tradable – there are admittedly circumstances where people go without food in order to have health care, or vice-versa, but in most cases the idea of balancing a budget between food and health care makes little sense. The problem with the second is the assumption that people will always prefer to have more. People can have too much food; and there are levels of health care that people do not want to receive – too much can stop a person living an independent life.

Fourth, it is assumed that choices are expressed effectively through the combination of individual choices within a market system. It might with equal justice be argued that the market system, along with the process of socialisation, shapes and constrains choices. Obesity is not rising in developed economies simply because individuals have made personal choices about food; it reflects the kind of food available, methods of preparation, methods of distribution and relative costs – not to mention all the other aspects of lifestyle which affect physical activity.[211] Fifth, analytical welfare economics generally takes it that a group is nothing more than the sum of the people who make it up: social groups, religious congregations, cities, cultural groups or nations have no specific interests that are not the interests of their individual members (though businesses, oddly enough, may have). Theoretical economists often trumpet the finding that social provision is inconsistent with the consequences of individual preferences as proof that it is incompatible with well-being.[212] All this shows is how limited the economic conception of well-being really is.[213]

Alternative views of 'well being' are related to other kinds of value position. Well being can be interpreted in terms of 'happiness', 'interests' or what is 'good' for people, and needs, understood as things without which they are liable to suffer.[214] One of the central problems in increasing 'well being' is that it may not be understood in the same way by different people, and the enhancement of welfare from one perspective may be seen as its reduction from another. Bernard Shaw

---

[211] T Lang, G Rayner, 2005, Obesity: a growing issue for European policy?, *Journal of European Social Policy* 15(4) 301–327.

[212] L Kaplow, S Shavell, 2001, Any non-welfarist method of policy assessment violates the Pareto Principle, *Journal of Political Economy* 109(2) p 281–7.

[213] A Sen, 1979, *Collective choice and social welfare*, Amsterdam: Elsevier, ch 6 and p 198.

[214] P Spicker, 1988, *Principles of social welfare*, London: Routledge, ch 1.

warns us not to do unto others as we would have them do unto us; their tastes may not be the same.

Needs

The idea of 'need' is used to refer to things that people must have – things which are, in some sense, 'essential'. Needs, Feinberg suggests, are 'welfare interests' – the things which people will be harmed if they do not have.[215] The sorts of interest that Feinberg thinks of as essential include

- physical health and vigour;
- physical integrity and functioning;
- the absence of pain or disfigurement;
- a minimum degree of intellectual activity;
- emotional stability;
- the absence of groundless anxieties and resentments;
- engagement in a normal social life;
- a minimum amount of wealth, income and financial security;
- a tolerable social and physical environment; and
- some freedom from interference by others.[216]

This is a popular sport for writers about need, who have often come up with lengthy lists of needs. The idea of 'basic needs' used at times in the UN refers to a list of essential items:

> Firstly, they include certain minimum requirements of a family for private consumption: adequate food, shelter and clothing, as well as certain household furniture and equipment. Second, they include essential services provided by and for the community at large, such as safe drinking water, sanitation, public transport and health, education and cultural facilities.[217]

Doyal and Gough have an even longer list, based on people's ability to participate in society.[218] Lists of this kind can never be final, because

---

[215] J Feinberg, 1973, *Social philosophy*, Prentice Hall, Englewood Cliffs N.J.: Prentice Hall, p 111.

[216] J Feinberg,1980, *Rights, justice and the bounds of liberty*, Princeton NJ: Princeton University Press, p.32).

[217] P Spicker, S Alvarez Leguizamon, D Gordon (eds), 2007, *Poverty: an international glossary*, London: Zed.

[218] L Doyal, I Gough, 1991, *A theory of human need*, Basingstoke: Macmillan.

needs are socially defined and constructed. They are constructed because they stem from a set of social relationships or they are the consequence of specific social arrangements. Children, for example, are dependent, not simply because they are weaker or less competent than adults, but because they are required to be dependent – they are not allowed to work and they have to attend school.

The 'social definition' of needs is a more complex idea. Social expectations and patterns of behaviour determine what is thought of as 'harm', as 'basic', or as 'necessary'; the meaning of 'need' is defined in such terms. The issue of 'disability' offers an example. One of the central concepts used in understanding disability is the distinction between the idea of disability as a physical limitation – sometimes referred to as the 'medical' model – and the idea of disability as a social concept. Understood in physical terms, a disability is the functional restriction which results from some kind of limitation – the inability to perform certain tasks. The social model re-interprets disability in a social context, arguing that limitations are as likely to arise from social assumptions, the design of the environment and the effect that such assumptions have on opportunities and capacity. Short-sightedness or colour-blindness are not generally treated as disabilities; the loss of an eye or a kidney are sometimes treated as disabling conditions, but not necessarily so. By contrast, amputation, disfigurement or previous experience of schizophrenia are often treated as disabilities. There may be a rationale behind this – the definition of 'disability' depends, at least in part, on the identification of conditions which are considered particularly problematic – but much of it is conventional.

The idea of need is particularly important for social policy in practice. Needs are what many social policies, and social services, respond to. Some of the needs are 'human needs', which everyone shares as a human being – for example, needs for food, water, warmth, shelter. But many, and possibly most, human needs are met through mechanisms which have little to do with social policy; people are typically fed and housed through the operation of economic relationships, not by the development of collective social action or social services. The focus of social policy tends to fall, instead, on areas where needs are not met through this sort of mechanism. By contrast with a general focus on human need, social policy is concerned with circumstances where needs remain unmet, and some kind of response is required; and with people in circumstances where they are likely to experience needs which are in some way distinguishable from the common needs that everyone has.

Box 5.1: Poverty: the absence of welfare

Poverty is a complex, multi-faceted, often disputed concept. For many writers, poverty is interpreted primarily in terms of economic resources, especially income. Several standard 'measures' of poverty, so-called, are based on people's income – for example, the $1.25 a day referred to by the World Bank, or the 60% of median income favoured in the European Union.[219] But the idea of poverty is also used in many other ways – among them, a description of how people live, a constellation of social problems, a set of economic relationships and a social experience. In those more general senses, it is one of the terms most often used to describe the state where people lack welfare.

There are scores of definitions of poverty, but within them it is possible to identify several clusters or 'families' of meaning – inter-related ways of understanding the idea. One set of approaches describes poverty in terms of material need.

1. Poverty as *need*. Poverty is sometimes understood as a lack of essential items, such as food, clothing, housing or fuel.
2. Poverty as a *pattern of deprivation*. This might refer to long-term need – malnutrition, living in slum housing, being trapped on a low income – but that is not the only pattern which is possible. Poverty is also characterised by insecurity. There may be a 'web of deprivation':[220] poor people's circumstances may change, but the lack of resources implies that they have to sacrifice some things to achieve others, and they are liable to move from one form of deprivation into another.
3. Poverty as a low *standard of living*. People who have low income or consumption over a period of time have to make do with less than others; poverty is identified with circumstances in which people are not able to use or get the goods, amenities or activities that other people can get. Charles Booth, who pioneered research on poverty in Victorian Britain, referred to poverty as 'living under a struggle to obtain the necessaries of life and make both ends meet.'[221]

---

[219] P Spicker, 2012, Why refer to poverty as a proportion of median income?, *Journal of Poverty and Social Justice* 20(2) 165–177.

[220] F Coffield, J Sarsby, 1980, *A cycle of deprivation?*, London: Heinemann; D Narayan, R Chambers, M Shah, P Petesch, 2000, *Voices of the poor: crying out for change*, World Bank/Oxford University Press, ch 11.

[221] C Booth, 1902, *Life and labour of the people in London*, London: Macmillan, vol 1 p.33.

Another group of definitions describes poverty in terms of people's economic circumstances.

4. Poverty as a *lack of resources* Someone who is in need but who has enough income would not be thought of as 'poor'. An international declaration, signed by many leading social scientists, claims that 'Poverty is primarily an income- or resource-driven concept'.[222]

5. Poverty as *economic distance* People whose income is significantly below that of the people around them are said to be at an 'economic distance' which cuts them off from full participation in society. O'Higgins and Jenkins explain: 'there is an inescapable connection between poverty and inequality: certain degrees or dimensions of inequality ... will lead to people being below the minimum standards acceptable in that society. It is this 'economic distance' aspect of inequality that is poverty.'[223]

6. Poverty as an *economic class* The relationship of many people to the economy – for example, marginal workers, elderly people and people with disabilities – means that they are not able to command resources in many societies, and that they are likely to be poor.

The third set of clusters treats poverty as a set of social relationships. Across the world, poor people describe their experiences and understanding of poverty in terms of their relationships to the society around them.[224]

7. *Social class* People's social position depends on a combination of economic position, educational attainment and social status. Poverty, for many, refers to the position of the lowest class, people who lack status, power and opportunities available to others.

6. *Dependency* Georg Simmel, the sociologist, identified poverty with dependence on assistance: 'The poor person, sociologically speaking, is the individual who receives assistance because of the lack of means.'[225]

8. *Social exclusion* The idea of exclusion covers a wide range of circumstances: it brings together people who are unable to participate in society because of poverty, vulnerable people who are not protected

222 P Townsend and others, 1997, An International Approach to the Measurement and Explanation of Poverty: Statement by European social scientists, in D Gordon, P Townsend, 2000, *Breadline Europe*, Bristol: Policy Press.

223 M O'Higgins, S Jenkins, 1990, 'Poverty in the EC: 1975, 1980, 1985', in R Teekens, B van Praag (eds) *Analysing poverty in the European Community*, Luxembourg: European Communities, p 207.

224 Narayan et al, 2000.

225 G Simmel, 1908, 'The poor', in *Social Problems* 1965 13 pp 118–139.

> adequately (like asylum seekers and people with disabilities), and people who are socially rejected (like AIDS sufferers and drug users.)
>
> 9. *Lack of entitlement* In international organisations, a 'lack of basic security'[226] has come to be understood in terms of people's rights. Amartya Sen argues that famines happen, not because of a shortage of food, but because poor people are not entitled to eat the food that is there.[227]

These views overlap, and there are ideas that cut across them: Peter Townsend's broadly based concept of relative deprivation, for example, takes into account a pattern of deprivation, resources, social exclusion and economic distance,[228] while Paugam's 'social disqualification'[229] encompasses class, exclusion and lack of security.

There is an eleventh cluster, or field of meaning. Nested in the core of the idea is a moral imperative – the sense, not just that poverty is serious, but that something must be done. That is one of the reasons why poverty is so difficult to define; any definition that fails to capture the moral compass is liable to be rejected as unsatisfactory. But it is also one of the reasons why governments may be reluctant to admit the existence of poverty: that admission carries with it a commitment to do something about it, and it can only be countered by either rejecting the definition or finding other moral reasons why it should not be done.

Need groups

Need groups refer to people in similar circumstances which require some kind of collective response. They include

- the times of the life cycle when needs are long-term and predictable, like old age and childhood;
- the position of people who are restricted in their abilities to undertake ordinary activity, like people with physical disability, chronic mental illness or intellectual disabilities;
- contingencies which people are vulnerable to at different points of their lives, like poverty, homelessness, sickness or unemployment.

---

[226] K Duffy, *Social exclusionand human dignity in Europe*, Council of Europe CDPS(95) 1 Rev.

[227] A Sen, 1981, *Poverty and famines: an essay on entitlement and deprivation*, Oxford: Clarendon Press, Oxford: Clarendon Press.

[228] P Townsend, 1979, *Poverty in the United Kingdom*, Harmondsworth: Penguin.

[229] S Paugam, 2004, *La disqualification sociale,* Paris: Presses Universitaires de France.

Although each of these categories is narrower than a general concern with human needs might be, it is important to recognise that these circumstances affect a very wide range of people. Everyone is at some stage a child; most people will eventually be elderly. It has been argued that up to a third of the population will receive psychiatric treatment at some point in their lives, which indicates high levels of risk, while over a third of all elderly people are likely to be physically disabled at some stage. And, on the World Bank's very conservative figure of $2 a day, over 40% of the world's population is poor.[230]

Needs in the life cycle

Childhood Children have, of course, the same needs as anyone else – needs for basic essentials, for emotional support. But they also have two further, distinguishable sets of needs. The first set of needs is developmental – the things a child needs to grow into an autonomous adult. Mia Kellmer Pringle identifies these as needs for love and security, new experiences, praise and recognition, and responsibility.[231] Most of these needs are not seen directly as the province of government, but one of the first provisions made for children in most countries is the provision of basic education; the Sachs report suggests that it is one of the most important initial measures to counter poverty.[232] The second set of needs is based on their dependency; it has to be recognised that children's capacity to meet their own needs is limited. The idea of childhood as a prolonged period of dependency and vulnerability is not new, but its length is; child labour laws generally date from the early nineteenth century, universal education in most countries is a relatively recent introduction – some developing countries are only in the process of introducing it – and the age of leaving school and entering the labour market has progressively been increased. The United Nations Convention on the Rights of the Child defines children's rights in terms which emphasise their dependency, and their place in the family: 'the child, for the full and harmonious development

---

[230] See World Bank, 2013, Poverty, at http://web.worldbank.org/WBSITE/ EXTERNAL/TOPICS/EXTPOVERTY/EXTPA/0,,contentMDK:20 040961~menuPK:435040~pagePK:148956~piPK:216618~theSitePK:43 0367~isCURL:Y,00.html

[231] M Kellmer Pringle, 1980, *The needs of children*, London: Hutchinson.

[232] UN Millennium Project 2005, *Investing in development: Overview*, New York: United Nations Development Programme.

of his or her personality, should grow up in a family environment, in an atmosphere of happiness, love and understanding.'[233]

It does happen, of course, that sometimes the needs of children reflect problems with the family: abuse and neglect are deficiencies in the family environment. In those cases, it may happen that children need to be separated from the family – usually going to substitute family care. In most cases, however, responses to the needs of children tend to be understood in the circumstances of the family. When a child is poor, it is because the family is poor – and the first step for getting support to a child, for example in engagement in education or obtaining health care, is to make arrangements to engage the family in the process. This has not always been true: compulsory education has been introduced despite the resistance of families, and schools have been used as the basis to provide children with nutrition and health care.

Parenthood The dependent position of children largely explains the demands that the family puts on the position of parents, but it does not explain everything about it. Many assumptions are made about the position of parents: for example, that biological parents have a special bond towards children and responsibility to them, that women will be the primary carer, that motherhood is not compatible with a role in the labour market. These assumptions are deeply entrenched, but they are very questionable. The arguments about the position of women are probably most familiar, and they have been increasingly challenged in the course of the last forty years or so, with the establishment of 'Second-Wave' feminism. The assumption of a biological link is no less capable of challenge. In France, parenthood is constructed legally as a social responsibility rather than a biological fact; parents are asked to accept children at birth, and if they do not do so, a child may be born with one parent, or no parents.

The effect of the assumptions is to condition a pattern of life where women are likely to interrupt their time in the labour market, and where family income falls at the point where a baby is born. There are different ways to respond to this. One has been to institute practices like maternity leave and maternity benefits; another has been to increase family allowances for very young children (because the point when a family is most vulnerable to a fall in income is when the child is too young to receive child care outside the family.) These are further examples, then, of needs which are 'socially constructed' – problems

---

[233] United Nations, 1989, *Convention on the Rights of the Child*, preamble.

which have developed, and which require a response, because of the social circumstances which produce them.

Old age   Old age is another social construct, and because the conventions differ in different social services, the discussion of old people's needs does not always take place on the same basis. For the purposes of social security, 'old age' is generally equivalent to pension age; and provision for old age has been stretched to cover support for 'older people', including people who are fit and active, but have effectively withdrawn from the labour market. In the case of children, it is possible to argue that children have needs which others do not. In the case of older people, the argument has little force. In so far as old people have common needs, it reflects retirement rather than old age – that is, the withdrawal or exclusion of people above a certain age from the labour market. The common needs of older people for income maintenance in retirement have been described as 'structural dependency'. Their dependency reflects their economic position and relationship to society, not just their capacity.[234]

When it comes to health and social care, the focus tends to shift to people who are much older – typically over 75. The condition of old people does reflect their capacities to some degree, but that degree is very limited; there is no intrinsic reason why a person who is 75 should be disabled or in ill health. Although elderly people are much more likely than others to be in poor health, this is not a necessary aspect of old age; poor health arises not simply because of old age, but also because diet, housing, occupation and lifestyle in previous times have not been conducive to good health. Having said that, hopes for improvement in the physical capacity of elderly people over time have not been generally realised.[235] A significant minority of elderly people are physically disabled, and in Europe dementia rises markedly with age, affecting 3.5% of people aged 70–74, 15.7% at 80–84 and 41% at 90–94.[236] The services which are provided for old people tend either

---

[234] A Walker, 1980, The social creation of poverty and dependency in old age, *Journal of Social Policy* 9(1) pp 49–75; M Fine, C Glendinning, 2005, Dependence, independence or inter-dependence?, *Ageing and society* 25 601–621.

[235] G Lafortune, G Balestat, 2007, Trends in severe disability among elderly people, OECD Health paper DELSA/HEA/WD/HWP(2007)2, Paris: OECD, www.oecd.org/dataoecd/13/8/38343783.pdf

[236] Alzheimer Europe 2009, Prevalence of dementia in Europe, www. alzheimer-europe.org/Research/European-Collaboration-on-Dementia/ Prevalence-of-dementia/Prevalence-of-dementia-in-Europe

to be dedicated to elderly people in poor health (such as residential nursing care) or based on the assumption that they are likely to be physically dependent (such as sheltered housing, which seeks to provide the reassurance to old people and their families by providing a backup or emergency service in the event of problems). In practice, large parts of general health services are necessarily used by older people, because they make up a large proportion of people in need of care.

Other common problems include poverty, reflecting an extended period on low incomes, and the low incomes of previous generations; isolation, as friends and families die or move away; bereavement, when spouses die; housing, because old people often live in older housing, which may be deteriorating or unsuitable for current needs; and the problems of carers. Many older people are looked after by their spouses, male or female, or by women in the next generation who are themselves ageing.

Limitations in ordinary activity

Physical disability Physical disability is not one issue, but a term referring to a wide range of issues of different kinds. It may refer, for example, to people who have lost limbs, who are blind or deaf, who have difficulty moving or walking, who are unable to sustain physical effort for any length of time, and so on. It sometimes refers to people who are physically different even if they are able to function physically in the same way as people without disabilities. Many people with disabilities do not think of themselves as 'disabled', and even among those who do, the effect of fluctuating conditions and the unpredictable experience of problems often means they do not think so all the time.[237]

The treatment of disability as if it was a single problem may mean that disabled people receive insufficient or inappropriate assistance. The problems that disabled people have in common are not so much their physical capacities, which are often very different, but limitations on their life style. Income tends to be low; at the same time, disabled people may have special needs to be met, which means that their costs are higher than others. Socially, people with disabilities may become isolated: as health declines, they struggle to manage on the resources they have, and they may be socially excluded.

---

[237] UK Department for Work and Pensions, 2013, Ad hoc statistics of disability, from the ONS Opinions and Lifestyle Survey, obtained at https://www.gov.uk/government/publications/disability-statistics-from-the-ons-opinions-and-lifestyle-survey-january-to-march-2013, 3rd July 2013.

The World Health Organisation identifies three elements in disability: problems in bodily function or structure, which they used to call 'impairment'; problems relating to activities, or 'disability'; and problems related to social participation, which they called 'handicap'.[238] The term 'handicap' is now considered unacceptable by many people with disabilities, and the idea of a 'social model of disability' has been adopted in its place – but, as Edwards argues, 'both are couched in terms of disadvantage due to social factors'.[239] The accusation in some texts that WHO had ignored the social dimensions of disability is not true.

The social model of disability understands disability in terms of the social norms and expectations which shape the experience of people with disabilities. The primary emphasis in services based on this model has been 'normalisation' (not 'independence', but the promotion of autonomy and 'social role valorisation') and 'empowerment'.

Mental illness 'Mental illness' is a broad term covering a range of conditions. The most important are

- *functional psychoses*, mainly schizophrenia and manic depression. Schizophrenia is itself a set of conditions rather than a single illness. It is characterised by a complex of symptoms including, e.g., a clouding of consciousness, disconnected speech and thought, variations of mood, feelings that one is being externally controlled, or hallucinations (which can be auditory, visual or tactile). Manic depression leads to severe and sometimes prolonged extremes of mood: in 'manic' phases, constantly active and extrovert; in depressed state, withdrawn and negative. Drug therapy can be used against the cycle
- *organic psychoses*, caused by infections, drugs, metabolic disturbances, or brain traumas
- *neuroses*, including anxiety states, phobias, obsessional states, hysteria, and some depressions, and
- *behavioural* disorders. These are not true 'illnesses'; they are identified as disorders because people behave differently to others, not because anything is malfunctioning. Probably the most important is psychopathy (also known as 'sociopathy'), which is characterised mainly by a lack of social awareness, consideration, or conscience towards others.

---

[238] World Health Organisation, 2000, ICIDH-2, WHO.
[239] S Edwards, 2005, *Disability: definitions, value and identity*, Abingdon: Radcliffe, p 20.

Mental illness is very common, but most of it is not treated by any specialist response, and in policy terms the forms of illness are less important than the experience of psychiatric care. For many years, mental illness led to prolonged hospitalisation, often in antiquated institutions intended to isolate 'mad' people from the community. The reasons for this movement have been the 'drug revolution' of the 1950s, which has made treatment possible outside hospitals, disillusion with the role played by large institutions, and substantial increases in the relative cost of institutional care.[240] The needs of psychiatric patients have to be understood in terms of this major shift in policy and practice. The trend to 'community care' should mean, in principle, that psychiatric patients are re-integrated into the community rather than isolated. The essential services include community psychiatric support, to enable continued health care and medication; social support, to counter the problems of social exclusion associated with mental illness; accommodation, including access to ordinary housing, and the provision of a range of supportive residential units, including half-way houses, staffed group homes; and access to income and employment opportunities. There has been a trend to favour shorter-term psychiatric care in general hospitals, and the use of the older hospitals has been changing, for example as a base for psychiatric services rather than a closed institution.

Intellectual disability Intellectual disability refers to a state of slow or impaired mental development. (This is not universal usage: in the UK, the term 'learning disability' is used, but in US literature, 'learning disability' refers to special educational needs. I have used the Australian term because it avoids the ambiguity.) Although it is sometimes associated with other conditions – a high proportion of people with the most severe intellectual disabilities are also severely physically disabled – most has no physical or organic origin. (Down's syndrome, probably the best known cause, accounts for only about a sixth of all cases.)

The effect of intellectual disability over time is not only a matter of 'learning', because development is important for a range of social activities, including physical competence and social functioning. The tasks which most children have to learn – like personal care, household tasks and basic education – become different for people who have to learn them at different stages of their life. The wide range of capacity consequently stretches from people with complex developmental and physical disabilities, who may not be mobile or able to manage basic

---

[240] A Scull, 1977, *Decarceration*, Englewood Cliffs: Prentice Hall.

self-care like washing or eating, through people who have difficulties with shopping, cooking, reading, or using money, to some who can do any of these things.

Because many intellectual disabilities develop from birth or early childhood, the problems have tended to be constructed in terms of aid to families. In practice, the main support for most people with intellectual disabilities comes, not from the state or voluntary organisations, but from families. The effect of services is to supplement the care given by these families.

Risk, vulnerability and insecurity

'Risk' is a clumsy term, which lumps together issues that ought to be understood distinctly. It can be interpreted in several ways:

- the probability that something will happen (like the risk of death or disability in smoking), identified in terms of incidence over time (in epidemiological terms, 'cumulative incidence');
- a 'lack of basic security', a term which is closely identified with poverty;
- insecure circumstances, which imply that policy has to deal with unpredictable contingencies; and
- vulnerability, which is the possibility that when things happen, the vulnerable person might suffer harm.[241] The opposite of risk is 'security'; the opposite of vulnerability is 'resilience'.

People can be vulnerable without being insecure (for example, low-paid public sector workers, who have secure employment but little capacity to deal with emergencies); they can be insecure, or 'at risk', without being particularly vulnerable (as many entrepreneurs are). It is vulnerability, rather than risk, which is the main focus of social protection policies.

Deprivation People are deprived when they have needs their resources are insufficient to meet. This is often identified with poverty. Poverty is a broader concept than need alone (see Box 5.1), but it is also strongly associated with deprivation, the situation where people have needs that they cannot meet because of lack of entitlement or resources. One of the ways in which poverty has been identified is

---

[241] P Spicker, 2001, Social insecurity and social protection, in R Edwards, J Glover (eds) *Risk and citizenship: key issues in welfare*, London: Routledge.

by a 'consensual' approach, describing what people ought to have but are unable to afford. There is a striking level of agreement about such norms. More than 90% of those surveyed in the UK consider these items to be essential: two meals a day, beds and bedding for everyone, fresh fruit and vegetables once a day, and a warm waterproof coat.[242] In this, the UK population is rather fractious – it is surprising that as many as 10% disagree. In Australia, more than 99% of those surveyed agreed that access to medical treatment, warm clothes and bedding and a substantial meal at least once a day are essential.[243]

Limited resources or low income are likely to lead to extended periods of deprivation, but people are liable to suffer whenever income is disrupted – and in a contemporary economy, disruption is commonplace. Low income children and parents commonly go without essential basic items.[244]

Homelessness Homelessness occurs when people have nowhere to live. This is, like the other categories in this chapter, a socially constructed concept. That statement may sound strange, because the question of whether people have somewhere to live seems like a simple matter of fact. The problem rests in the question of where people can live. In many developing countries, people who have nowhere to live have the option of squatting – finding an occupied bit of land and putting up a shelter on it. But this is not an option everywhere. There are some countries, like India, where the system of landholding is highly developed, and the opportunities to squat are limited. Housing and land tenure are generally distributed through markets, and in any market, the resources are most accessible to those with the capacity to command them – the money, the legal rights or the political power. (In parts of Africa, women are unable to hold rights in property, and poverty follows.[245])

If homelessness is about lack of access, and lack of entitlement, it follows that it is a broader issue than the question of whether someone

[242] S McKay, S Collard, 2003, *Developing deprivation questions for the Family Resources Survey*, University of Bristol.

[243] P Saunders, 2011, *Down and out: poverty and exclusion in Australia*, Bristol: Policy Press.

[244] H Aldridge, A Parekh, T Macinness, P Kenway, 2011, *Monitoring poverty and social exclusion 2011*, York: Joseph Rontree Foundation; New Policy Institute.

[245] UN Human Settlements Programme Global Urban Observatory, 2005, Global Urban Indicators Database, at www.unhabitat.org/publication/Analysis-Final.pdf, table

has a shelter. People with limited command over resources have to occupy unfit, unsanitary and inadequate housing, because they have to take the best alternative they can. 'Homelessness' is sometimes taken to mean not just that a person has no accommodation, but also to indicate people who live in unsatisfactory and insecure accommodation.

Unemployment 'Unemployment' means something only where there is employment, in a formal economy. Some poorer societies lack the structures for exchange and employment; integration into a formal economy is essential for economic development and the avoidance of poverty. The process of forming such an economy often creates hardship, and vulnerability.

Employment depends on a labour market, where people are effectively able to sell their labour. People are under-employed if the pattern of employment is insufficient to meet their needs or their skills; they are unemployed if they are without work, and unable to sell their work. The patterns of labour markets are diverse. There is nothing in the structure of a modern economy that guarantees that work will be available for everyone who ought to work, and at times labour markets create only limited opportunities for employment. Casual work, for example, is work which is available only intermittently – some industries have developed offering work on a daily or weekly basis, and in developing countries there are still patterns of work in some countries where people will sit at roadsides hoping to be picked up by an employer for a day's labour. Some work is seasonal, for example in construction, agriculture and tourism, and employment will only be available at certain times of the year. Some unemployment is 'cyclical': there are times in different industries when demand is strong, and others where it is deficient. Some is 'structural' – based in circumstances where the skills and capacities of the workforce are not related to the demand for labour from employers. Arguably the decline of manufacturing industry in Western Europe has left a serious structural problem for the labour force; the European Union's 'structural funds' exist to realign the supply of labour in regional markets with demand. 'Voluntary' unemployment occurs when work is available but people choose not to work at the wage available – for example, parents and carers who withdraw from the labour market, people who are discouraged, or people who take early retirement instead.

Responses to unemployment are usually made in one of two ways: an attempt to increase the demand for jobs, by stimulating the economy, creating work or subsidising jobs, or an attempt to deal with individuals who do not work, by education and training, incentive or punishment.

Employment is important for people, and it is especially important to avoid poverty, but it does not follow that everyone in a society needs to be employed; it may be possible to find ways to legitimate people's non-participation in the labour market, for example by reclassifying people who are unemployed as something else (lone parents, disabled, or incapacitated); removing people from the labour market through earlier retirement, military service or prolonging education.

Incapacity for work Like unemployment, 'incapacity for work' is a term of art; it depends on the structure of an economy and the alternatives available. It can refer both to a person's individual inability to continue to do work for which the person is otherwise qualified – for example, like the impact of vibration white finger on a machinery operator – or a presumed inability to do any work. Incapacity is often confused with disability, and in countries where no distinction is made between incapacity and disability, people with disabilities have to present themselves as 'incapacitated', while people who are unable to work because of a medical condition, such as depression, may have to present themselves as 'disabled'. But people who are disabled may well be able to work, and people who are not disabled (for example, people with a specific condition that prevents them pursuing their occupation) may not be.

The reasons for responding to incapacity are distinct from the reasons for responding to disability. Services for people with disabilities are usually concerned with meeting needs, compensating for disadvantage, meeting extra costs, improving personal capacity, and promoting employment, among several others. Services for people with incapacity are more likely to be concerned with social protection, income maintenance during interrupted employment and economic efficiency.

This catalogue of needs is far from exhaustive, and the defining lines are very blurred. In the first place, the categories all cover a range of diverse conditions. 'Older people' have little in common beyond age and the expectation of retirement. The range of physical disabilities is vast. Particular issues within the broad categories, like the problems of AIDS or child neglect, convey such a complex constellation of problems that they could reasonably be classified as categories in their own right.

Secondly, people in each category are vulnerable to a range of other problems. People who are poor are not simply short of basic necessities, such as food, clothing, fuel and shelter; they lack security, health, and the social position (like status and power) which might help them to improve their situation.[246] Homeless people tend to be poor – if they had command over resources, they could obtain housing; their conditions create problems with health;[247] often they are also marginalised in their community (because where there are social networks on which they can draw they do so).[248] Mental illness is commonly associated with problems in behaviour and communication, which have a profound effect on social relationships and the ability to function in a social context. People with mental illness are vulnerable to poverty, because they are unable to participate in the labour market, and to homelessness, because in addition to their poverty the networks of family and friends which others rely on are disrupted.[249]

Despite the limitations of such categorisations, there is a purpose in considering people in terms of such 'groups'. Even if the problems which people experience are complex and individuated, there are common patterns: the circumstances of people in the different groups reflect a common social experience. The exclusion of old people from the labour market has a profound effect on their circumstances, and common problems generally call for some kind of common patterns of response. In some cases it is the response itself, like the requirement that children should attend compulsory education, which defines people as constituting a group. Mentally ill people have varied circumstances, but the most common response – the experience of psychiatric care – has itself created common patterns of need, notably issues related to institutional care and subsequent discharge. Service responses are commonly planned in terms of the client groups to whom they are directed.

'Old' needs and 'new' needs In recent years, a number of writers have suggested that the focus on certain need groups has been superseded by the need to respond to new patterns of social need, arising out of a changing economic and social environment. These patterns include, for example, lone parenthood, long-term unemployment, the needs of young people, pressure to balance participation in the labour market

---

[246] P Spicker, 2007, *The idea of poverty*, Bristol: Policy Press.

[247] W Bines, 1997, The health of single homeless people, in R Burrows, N Pleace, D Quilgars, *Homelessness and social policy*, London: Routledge.

[248] N Pleace, 1998, Single homelessness as social exclusion, *Social Policy and Administration* 32(1) pp 46–59.

[249] N Crockett, P Spicker, 1994, *Discharged: homelessness among psychiatric patients in Scotland*, Shelter (Scotland).

with family care, and 'atypical employment biographies'.[250] These contingencies have contributed to a perception of 'new poverty', especially in Northern Europe.[251] However, there is nothing 'new' about most of these needs, or about policies to respond to them; the problems of lone parents, long term-unemployed people and the working poor were central to the Poor Law Report of 1834,[252] while issues related to gender became a progressively greater part of the social policy agenda throughout the twentieth century. What is relatively 'new' – though still not that new – is the recognition in various European régimes that welfare structures built around a regular employment record or stable domestic circumstances are unable to provide for many social contingencies. The Beveridge report, in the UK, developed provision to include a casualised labour force, but failed to account for issues like divorce; the gaps in the system became a concern with the 'rediscovery of poverty' in the 1960s. In France, the watershed came in the 1970s, with the recognition that the generalisation of social security would not extend to people without work records; in Germany, it arguably happened only later, with the reunification of East and West.

The idea of 'new' needs may have some value, nevertheless, as a political critique. One of the besetting problems of the welfare states has been complacency – the assumption that provision is basically satisfactory, and that people who fell through the net must have misbehaved in some way. The argument runs that because society has changed, so must welfare provision. This serves both as a salutary reminder that there are problems to be dealt with, and a convenient political excuse to engage with long-neglected issues.

---

[250] G Bonoli, 2005, The politics of the new social policies, *Policy & Politics* 33(3) pp 431–449; S Häusermann, 2007, Changing coalitions in social policy reforms, *Journal of European Social Policy* 16(1) pp 5–21.

[251] D Gallie, S Paugam, 2002, *Social precarity and social integration*, European Commission.

[252] S Checkland, O Checkland (eds) *The Poor Law Report of 1834*, Harmondsowrth: Penguin, 1974.

Box 5.2: Assessing the need for social care

'Needs assessments' have become an important aspect of the provision of social care. The shape of such policies is, roughly, that after an identification of needs, a range of appropriate responses is selected, and the test of whether policy is effective is whether the needs are met. There are various permutations of this procedure, but it is used in a wide range of services: examples are medical services, services for elderly people, special educational programmes, anti-poverty strategies social security provision, and housing provision.

Counting needs depends, in the first place, on counting problems. It is possible to respond to the same problems in many different ways: if someone finds it difficult to prepare meals, for example, a carer could be brought in to help with preparation, food can be delivered to the home, or the meals could be provided at another location like a lunch club which the person could attend. It makes little sense, then, simply to record that large numbers of people need meals. Isaacs and Neville suggest that the needs of old people can be classified in terms of the frequency and urgency of the response – 'long interval' needs are those which can be dealt with without someone attending every day, 'short interval' needs like help with dressing are those which call for a carer to help at least once a day, and 'critical interval' needs are those which are unpredictable and need someone generally on call.[253] That kind of classification has fallen out of favour, but it makes it possible to classify needs in terms of the time and attention that people need, and so to organise care and services so as to respond flexibly to the situation of the person who needs help.

The dominant model of needs assessment in health and social care has developed around the idea of a census of needs – a comprehensive count of every issue, and every demand. The stages are:

1. The needs of every individual are assessed.
2. The figures are aggregated to produce a global result.
3. Services are commissioned on the basis of the global figures.
4. Services are allocated to individuals on the basis of their assessment.

This puts things in quite the wrong order. If the aim is to respond to the needs of a population, assessing the individual needs of everyone in that population is not the best way to do it. From the point of view of the people planning and commissioning the services, assessing the needs of every individual is

---

[253] B Isaacs, Y Neville, 1975, *The measurement of need in old people.* Scottish Home & Health Department, Edinburgh.

slow, expensive and unreliable – censuses miss people out, they can have systemic biases (for example, because people are reluctant to seek help or report their problems), and by the time the count is done, needs will have changed. From the point of view of individuals in need, a global assessment does not help to deliver a sensitive, individuated response. Conversely, future provision is not necessarily improved by a precise assessment of individual needs at an earlier point. If services are allocated immediately consequent to assessment, then stages 2 and 3 are a distraction – they can only be helpful for planning services for future needs, which implies that they do not rely on individual assessment, and they hold up the allocation. If they are not allocated immediately, the implied delay breaks the link between individual assessment and provision. People's needs change over time, and by the time the services are commissioned and delivered, the individual who has been assessed is not likely to be the person who benefits.

Needs assessments have to serve two purposes. In the first place, they are used to deliver services to individuals. Second, they have to be capable of aggregation in order to yield global figures. The first function implies diversity, individual responsiveness and complexity; the second calls for uniformity, simplicity and mechanisms to share information. No system of needs assessment has ever squared the circle. For policy purposes, there is a good argument for uncoupling the two different approaches. Planners need only the global figures, and it is not crucial if they are accurate at the individual level. For service delivery, the converse is true; global figures are not very useful if the range of people identified are not actually being served.

Needs and responses

'Needs' refer, in part, to problems which people experience: people who suffer from mental or physical impairments, for example, are deemed to have 'needs' on that basis. Many of the needs described in this chapter are clearly socially constructed. Because 'problems' are often social, needs are too.

Needs are not just problems, however; they are also needs for something. We speak of needs for money, for domestic help, or for residential care. Needs have to be understood, not only in terms of problems, but also in terms of responses. People are thought of as being in need not simply because they have a problem, but because they are lacking something which will remedy that problem.[254] There are circumstances in which people with a degree of impairment have no identifiable 'needs' as a consequence: for example, many people with

---

[254] J Feinberg, 1973, *Social philosophy*, Englewood Cliffs NJ: Prentice-Hall.

mild dementia continue to function normally in their own home.[255] The response to a problem, like the problem itself, has to be seen in terms of the society in which it is happening. The definition of a need depends not just on the recognition of a problem – like disability, child abuse, old age and so forth – but an association of that problem with a particular kind of response. Items which might not have been thought of as 'needs' a hundred years ago – like inside toilets, washbasins or children's toys – have become recognised as needs because their absence presents problems and other more pressing problems no longer obscure their importance. Items which scarcely existed a hundred years ago – like telephones, computers, cars and fridges – are becoming needs as they become the main route to provide socially necessary facilities (communications, transport, or food storage). This also means that needs change over time.

There is no simple, fixed relationship between the kind of problems that people experience and the kinds of response which have to be made. Impairments are mainly responded to by trying to cure or repair the loss of ability; but impairments are only part of a general experience of disablement. Disability can be responded to by addressing an underlying medical condition, through treatment; it might be responded to by addressing the functional problems created by it – which implies either that a service is provided to help a person overcome functional limitations (for example, occupational therapy) or that services themselves seek to overcome those limitations (e.g. the provision of meals and home helps). But it might also be responded to by seeking to change social relationships. This can be done through the development or maintenance of relationships (in theory, one of the purposes of day care); reducing social disadvantage (which can be achieved by providing services, and by offering special facilities like holidays); or compensating for that disadvantage by the development of alternative patterns of social life (for example, through sheltered housing).

It is difficult, then, to establish precisely what services people 'need'. There is often not just one possible response, but a range of options. People who are socially isolated might have that isolation reduced in a number of ways: for example, by introducing a number of people into their home, like voluntary visitors or even 'companions'; by bringing them into contact outside their home, through lunch clubs or day centres; and by changing the home, which is commonly done through

---

[255] P Spicker, D S Gordon, 1997, *Planning for the needs of people with dementia*, Aldershot: Avebury.

sheltered housing or residential care. People who need housework done might have it done through domestic assistance, but they might also have it done through substitute family care or residential care. Strictly speaking, there can be no such thing as a 'need' for a lunch club or a home help; rather, there are needs which services of this kind may be able to satisfy to a greater or lesser degree.

The position is also complicated because people may be able to deal with their problems in different ways. Many of the 'needs' attributed to elderly or disabled people, including cooking, cleaning, and company, would not be experienced in the same way by a rich person; it is possible to buy the services of a cook, a housekeeper or a companion. Once the arrangement has been made the disabled person would not usually be thought of as still in need; and that implies that needs are, among other things, subject to the amount of money that a person has. This also means that it is difficult to separate the discussion of needs from the question of responses. Arguments about need are as likely to be arguments about resources as they are about the extent of problems.

'Needs' are not neutral concepts. Like most ideas in social policy, they have a normative purpose – they are used to make an argument for provision. It is implicit in the idea of need that some kind of response is possible – and it generally follows that something must be done. In most discussions of social policy, claims of need can be seen as a form of claim made against services.[256]

ISSUE FOR DISCUSSION

Are there needs which should not be met?

---

[256] P Spicker, 1993, Needs as claims, *Social Policy and Administration* 27(1) pp 7–17.

CHAPTER 6

Indicators – quantifying social issues

Measurement and indicators
Counting: enumerations and censuses
Presenting indicators
Anticipating change

Measurement and indicators

The first question that has to be asked about a problem is what kind of problem it is – that is why issues of definition and social construction are so important. The next step in policy discussions is usually to ask questions about its size and shape. The kinds of problems which are dealt with in public policy are often fairly ill-defined, and the implications are often uncertain. Numbers are used to give shape to issues, and to identify relationships.

Many people glaze over when numbers are mentioned, and if they are bored or puzzled, they tend to suspend their critical judgment. The moment something can be counted, it is likely to be treated as if it was a 'fact'. At times people may give the impression that well-known indicators, like the European poverty threshold (60% of median income) or the unemployment rate, are 'measures' of a problem, or that performance targets like 'reducing by two thirds the mortality rate among children under 5' (one of the UN's Millennium Development Goals,[257] discussed further in Box 6.1) are precise assessments of what is to be achieved. They are not. Numbers are used, in policy studies, as *indicators*. The word 'statistics' was originally coined to refer to the data compiled for the 'state', but most books about 'statistics' are now about something completely different, and the connection between 'official statistics' and the kind of 'statistic' which one learns about elsewhere in the social sciences is fairly weak, so it is helpful to have another word. The term 'indicators' is generally used to show that quantitative information about social issues represents not simple 'facts' but rather ways of putting together complex and uncertain information.

---

[257] United Nations, 2007, *Millennium Development Goals*, www.un.org/millenniumgoals/

An indicator is a signpost. It suggests the direction in which changes take place, rather than a specific measurement of social problems and responses.[258] Examples might be the crime rate, the unemployment rate, the level of public spending. Economic growth is measured using GDP (Gross Domestic Product), or GDP per capita; income inequality is tracked using the Gini coefficient. There are well known problems with most of these figures. They are built on a long series of judgments, and they are open to argument. Crime rates depend on reported crimes; unemployment rates fail to include many cases of marginal labour or exclusion from the labour market; governments manipulate public spending figures by taking certain transactions off the books. GDP goes up if a child leaves school to work in a sweatshop, and down if people are allowed to retire in old age; the Gini coefficient can fail to capture distributive changes in the middle of the distribution.

Indicators are not the same thing as measurements. A good measurement is accurate, precise, and reflects the characteristics of the issue it is measuring. A good indicator is associated with the issue, robust, consistent over time and available. For example, low birth weight can often be used as an indicator of poverty – that is, it often points in that direction. Where there are large numbers of children being born underweight, it is likely that their mothers are poorer; where there are small numbers, they are probably richer. But low birth weight is not the same thing as poverty, and the associations are not straightforward – at an individual level, we cannot tell how rich or poor someone is from the weight of their baby. Birth weight is a signpost, not a measure, and it needs to be taken with other signposts before it can be used meaningfully. Conversely, something can be a good measurement but a bad indicator. The measurement of criminal convictions is more accurate than recorded crime, because then the allegations have been put to the test, and recorded crime is more accurate than crime surveys (for the same reason), but crime surveys are generally a much better indicator of what is happening than recorded crime or conviction rates.

The extent of a problem: incidence, prevalence, distribution and intensity

Judging the extent of a problem – how big it is, how wide it goes – is done in four main dimensions. The first is the *prevalence*, or how frequently a problem is found. It is usually reported as a proportion

---

[258] See P Spicker, 2004, Developing indicators: issues in the use of quantitative data about poverty, *Policy & Politics*, Vol 32(4), 2004, pp. 431–40.

(e.g. 5% of a population) or a rate (3 people in 1,000), taken at a point in time – epidemiologists call this 'point prevalence' to distinguish it from prevalence over a period of time.

The second dimension is the *incidence,* how many new cases are happening. Increasing incidence usually implies increasing prevalence, but this is not necessarily the case – if more people exit from a problem group than come into it (for example by dying) the prevalence can fall when the incidence is rising.

The *distribution* of the problem is about the relative position of people with the problem compared with others. Distributional factors are used to identify causal relationships; they are also important for understanding issues like equality and disadvantage. In the consideration of social problems, however, prevalence and incidence usually matter much more. It is often true, for example, that people in minority ethnic groups are more likely than others to be poor[259] – that is important as an issue in equity, and a mark of racial disadvantage. That is not the same as saying that people in minority groups are likely to be poor – in the UK, at least, most are not.[260] It is not true that membership of a minority group is a passport to poverty, unemployment or overcrowding – saying that problems are 'more likely' is not the same thing. And it is not true that poor people are likely to be from minority ethnic groups. The assumption that people in racial minorities are poor is stereotypical – and, arguably, stigmatising of people in both categories.

A related fallacy is common in discussions of the influence of biological inheritance on social policy. Between 40% and 70% of the variation in obesity appears to be 'hereditable'. 'Hereditability' is often supposed to refer to the extent that relationships can be explained genetically, but what it actually shows is a variation in the distribution of issues, not in their prevalence. Obesity runs in families, but families are not only linked by genes; they commonly live together and share features of life-style, income and diet. Inheritance, then, is only one possible explanation out of many. If the causes of obesity were genetic – if obesity was inherited, so that some people were born to be overweight, and others were not – it should be possible to predict the prevalence (how many people are obese) as well as the distribution (which people are obese). In fact, the prevalence of obesity has changed

---

[259] L Platt, 2007, *Poverty and ethnicity in the UK,* York: Joseph Rowntree Foundation, at https://www.jrf.org.uk/bookshop/eBooks/2006-ethnicity-poverty-UK.pdf.

[260] P Spicker, 2002, *Poverty and the welfare state,* London: Catalyst.

rapidly, more than doubling worldwide in less than thirty years.[261] Genetic endowment changes very slowly – it takes generations. It follows that genetic inheritance cannot account for the change; any explanation has to lie elsewhere. The startling rise in obesity is the result of external factors, such as people's diets.[262] It is important, then, not to assume that higher proportions point to causal explanations, or that such distributions must have direct implications for the focus of policy. Neither proposition is necessarily true.

The fourth dimension to be considered is the *intensity* of a problem. Many of the indicators which are used are dichotomous: people are counted on the basis that they either have a problem or they do not. Many social issues, like poverty, disability or educational attainment, are not simple categories; they refer to complex, multi-faceted issues. The issue of intensity relates to the relative severity and depth of a problem. It may be important to consider not only the position of people with problems relative to those without, but also the relative position of people with problems, compared to others whose problems are more or less severe.

Counting: enumerations and censuses

Enumerations are attempts to count things; censuses (for the purposes of social policy, at least) are attempts to count people. Some censuses attempt to count everyone within a particular set of conditions – for example, a census of rough sleepers, or of people with dementia. The needs assessments for social care considered in Box 5.2 are another example. At local level, the most common form of enumeration comes from counts made of service statistics – the numbers of crimes reported or the numbers of people using particular services. These counts are subject to distortion, in two ways. The first is that, because they are based in service responses, any biases or omissions in the coverage of the services are carried forward to the statistics. For example, the system of assessment used for social care begins with individual assessments, which are aggregated to give information for purchasing services (Box 5.2). The count is conditioned by the range of services which is realistically available.

---

[261] WHO Global Health Observatory, n.d., Obesity, www.who.int/gho/ncd/risk_factors/obesity_text/en/

[262] T Lang, G Rayner, 2005, Obesity: a growing issue for European policy?, *Journal of European Social Policy* 15(4) 301–327.

The second distortion is one which applies to all forms of census; some people are hard to find, or do not want to cooperate. This does not happen randomly – for example, young males cooperate less with censuses, and in urban societies poorer people tend to be more mobile. This leads to systematic biases. For example, counts of rough sleepers are liable to underestimate the total numbers, because many rough sleepers have a pattern of varied, unstable arrangements made night by night.

The 'census of population' – that is, the count of the whole population – poses particular problems. This count is fundamental, because it provides the basis for most surveys and planning estimates. A census of population provides, in principle, a useful basis for the construction of indicators about a population, though fluctuating population means in practice that the results can never be absolutely precise. A census defines the denominators – the figures which are used to divide other figures and provide a proportion. Some countries have traditional, one-number counts: they include the UK, Ireland, Portugal, Spain, Italy and Greece. The most important enumeration of the population in the UK is undertaken in the ten-year Census. The problem with a ten-year census is that it rusts: the data become gradually less and less reliable over time, to the point where the figures can be seriously misleading. The data from the UK's 10-year census are between 2 and 12 years out of date at any point. The potential for social change within small areas is considerable, because of migration and redevelopment, and as a result the census is not very reliable as a basis on which to assess policy for small areas. Several countries use registers of information to count their population – most of the Nordic countries, and several countries in central Europe are moving in that direction.[263] Some statisticians have come to think, however, that sample surveys may be better than censuses in assessing situations overall. This is because a well constructed sample can avoid some of the systematic biases which are found in censuses. In France, the national census has been replaced with a rolling survey of the population, which offers a more secure basis for updating census material in the interim between counts.

---

[263] United Nations Population Fund, 2002, Population and housing censuses, New York: United Nations Population Fund, https://www.unfpa.org/upload/lib_pub_file/24_filename_pophousingcensus.pdf, p 62.

Presenting indicators

Indicators are mainly presented in one of three ways. The first is to use a 'headline' indicator: a simple, selective view. A good headline indicator is widely available, and easily understood. Commonly used examples are the use of income inequality as an indicator for poverty, or the growth rate as a proxy for economic development. These indicators are likely to be chosen because they are easily available and quantifiable, in preference to others which may be difficult or expensive to collect. In developing countries, infant mortality is widely used as an indicator of welfare: it is strongly linked with other issues, like poverty and adult health, and trying to improve it is a worthwhile exercise in its own right. The main problem with focusing on a headline indicator is that sometimes the indicator takes over the political debate – like the claimant count has for unemployment, or income levels for poverty. Complex issues need complex responses.

The second is to use a bank of multiple indicators – presenting lists of indicators, classified by theme. The Millennium Development Goals (Box 6.1) give one kind of example: they are summarised in 'progress charts' which show the overall direction of movement.[264] In the same way, the national performance indicators used by the Scottish Government lay out the indicators in a table, showing whether they have gone up or down or stayed the same.[265]

Hoernig and Seasons criticise this kind of approach, because the indicators are discrete and confined to particular issues.[266] They are right that single indicators should not be taken in isolation, but indicators can be interpreted in many ways. Interpretation is typically done by reading across a bank of indicators, looking for trends. Social, economic and environmental indicators have to be read together as well as separately. If indicators are concerned with complex problems, multiple indicators help to 'triangulate' or examine a problem from different perspectives. Indicators which move in different directions can confuse, but they also point to contradictory trends; indicators which move in the same direction confirm general trends.

---

[264] www.un.org/millenniumgoals/reports.shtml
[265] www.scotland.gov.uk/Publications/2007/11/13092240/9
[266] H Hoernig, M Seasons, 2004, Monitoring of indicators in local and regional planning practice, *Planning, Practice and Research* 19(1) pp 81–99.

Box 6.1: The Millennium Development Goals

The Millennium Development Goals (or MDGs) have been adopted by the 191 members of the United Nations (UN). They commit the UN, by 2015, to

1. eradicate extreme poverty and hunger
2. achieve universal primary education
3. promote gender equality and empower women
4. reduce child mortality
5. improve maternal health
6. combat HIV/AIDS, malaria and other diseases
7. ensure environmental sustainability, and
8. develop a global partnership for development.[267]

There are 21 targets, measured by 60 indicators – there used to be fewer indicators, but they have been gradually expanded. The indicators for the eradication of extreme poverty and hunger are as follows:[268]

Target 1.A:
Halve, between 1990 and 2015, the proportion of people whose income is less than $1 a day
(this was achieved ahead of schedule, and in some places the figure has been revised upward to $1.25)

1.1 Proportion of population below $1 (PPP) per day
1.2 Poverty gap ratio
1.3 Share of poorest quintile in national consumption

Target 1.B:
Achieve full and productive employment and decent work for all, including women and young people

1.4 Growth rate of GDP per person employed
1.5 Employment-to-population ratio
1.6 Proportion of employed people living below $1 (PPP) per day
1.7 Proportion of own-account and contributing family workers in total

Target 1.C:
Halve, between 1990 and 2015, the proportion of people who suffer from hunger

1.8 Prevalence of underweight children under-five years of age
1.9 Proportion of population below minimum level of dietary energy consumption

---

[267] www.un.org/millenniumgoals/
[268] http://mdgs.un.org/unsd/mdg/host.aspx?Content=indicators/officiallist. htm

The targets fall somewhat short of 'eradicating' poverty – halving it is not the same thing. The first of these indicators, an income below a dollar a day or $1.25, has been the subject of vehement criticism.[269] It is arbitrary; it is not a measure of poverty; it is dated; it is not clear what it means in different societies; it is not genuinely comparable. At that level, income can hardly be measured sensibly. All of that is true, but that does not mean it is not useful as an indicator. A daily rate makes it possible for researchers to check whether people have any formal income, and the main issue that is actually being identified is whether or not people can be said to be part of a cash economy. The second indicator, the 'poverty gap ratio', is nearly as arbitrary. It is a measure of how far below the poverty line people fall. It is supposed to be a test of how much money it would take to eliminate poverty. That sounds good in principle, until one remembers that poverty is being measured at a dollar a day; a little more than almost nothing is still almost nothing. The third indicator is a test of inequality. That is relevant, because people's ability to use resources in a society does not just depend on them; it depends on the people around them. The price of many important goods, such as land and housing, depend on the relative ability of people to pay.

The next group of indicators are mainly concerned with economic development. That has often been measured simply in terms of Gross National Product (GNP, or national income, which is the same thing. Some figures refer to GDP which excludes international trade). Economic growth is linked with some benefits,[270] but GNP has defects as an indicator, and it can increase while conditions are getting much worse; for example, if child labour spreads, GNP increases. A structure of employment assumes something about the growth of a formal economy, and two of the indicators are simply about whether or not people are in employment. However, an aspect of what has been happening in developing countries is that a small number are witnessing urbanisation at unsustainably low wages – more than half the employees in countries like Bangladesh, Guinea or Burundi are still on less than $1.25 a day – so indicator 6 is concerned with whether employees receive even this most minimal wage.

The last two indicators are concerned with diet. Calorific intake is not sufficient for a good diet – people can be malnourished and have excessive calories at the same time – but it is necessary. Underweight (being a low weight for one's age) is only one indicator of malnutrition – the others are

---

[269] P Townsend, D Gordon (eds), 2002, *World poverty: new policies to defeat an old enemy*, 2002, Bristol: Policy Press.

[270] D Dollar, A Kraay, 2000, Growth is good for the poor, at www.worldbank.org/research/growth/pdfiles/growthgoodforpoor.pdf .

wasting (losing weight, measured by being underweight for one's height) and stunting (being a low height for one's age, a sign of impaired development).

The third approach is to use a summary index. An example is the Index of Multiple Deprivation used in the UK to compare poverty by area,[271] or the Human Development Index used by the United Nations.[272] An index consists of a set of indicators which are compiled in order to produce a composite measure.

There are liable to be problems whenever numbers are used; just because something looks a number doesn't mean it should be treated like one. Social problems can't always be added together – they are not necessarily 'commensurate' or comparable on similar scales. Numbers are ordinal – two is greater than one – and aggregative – two plus two is four. The moment that numbers are used, people assume they behave like numbers should – they can be added together, divided, proportions can be established, and so on. Social problems are neither ordinal nor aggregative. For example, figures for mortality cannot meaningfully be added together with figures for income to construct indices of deprivation – but we do this kind of thing all the time. Housing is not self-evidently more or less important than education, and a person with three problems is not necessarily worse off than someone with one. In the studies of disability by the Office of Population Censuses and Surveys (OPCS), the points scheme used to measure disability was disregarded after the largest three problems were entered;[273] the experts who validated it felt, probably rightly, that after the three largest problems were taken into account, any others had only marginal weight.

The main issues in constructing an index are these:

- *Validity* Indices ought to mean what they are supposed to mean, but as they are summary figures at best, that is hard to check.
- *Reliability* Indices which are reliable within a particular social context, or at a certain period, are not necessarily transferable to other circumstances.
- *Inclusion and exclusion of relevant factors* Exclusions lead to important issues being ignored. Over-inclusion can lead to excessive weight being given to particular factors; the high level

271 Social Disadvantage Research Centre, *Scottish Indices of Deprivation 2003*, Oxford: Social Disadvantage Research Centre.
272 UNDP (United Nations Development Programme), 1999, *Human Development Report 1999*, New York: Oxford University Press.
273 OPCS (Office of Population Censuses and Surveys), 1988, *The prevalence of disability among adults in Britain*, London: HMSO.

of overlap in social phenomena related to deprivation makes the influences difficult to disentangle.

- *Quantification* Many indices ignore the problems of quantification and use sophisticated statistical techniques on the numbers, which depend on large assumptions about the character of the numbers and the relationships between them.
- *Weighting* Factors have to be given appropriate weights, which depends on appropriate quantification.[274]

It is possible to fix weights on issues normatively, in a 'points scheme': more points are given for the factors which people think are more important. Leaving things to expert judgment runs the risk of being arbitrary, so a growing number of indices have been put together using multivariate analysis, which assigns values according to mathematical formulae. Multivariate analysis is complicated. It works by identifying patterns in the data, finding the strongest possible relationships between variables, then putting related factors together to identify the strongest combinations of associations. In order to construct a composite measure, the numbers have to be standardised – they have to be the same kind of numbers, describing the same kinds of thing. Common methods are the use of percentages or proportions; indices of urban deprivation have been based on Z scores, which measure the relative position of a proportion within the overall distribution. The values assigned are then generally decided by running the material through the computer, and they are difficult to argue with without specialised knowledge.

Multivariate analysis demands a great deal from the sources of data, and decision-makers who know how to interpret the results. Where this kind of analysis is used, it tends to be developed by specialist researchers and then presented to agencies in the field as a complete package. It is questionable in those circumstances whether as a practitioner in social policy you would need to know how to construct a multivariate model yourself, but if you are faced with one in practice you should at least know what the issues are. The first set of problems rests in the nature of the task that is being performed. Wherever there are multiple variables, it can be difficult to decipher any pattern of relationships within the general noise. Statistics are usually framed in terms of associations, and associations can happen by chance, particularly where there are very large numbers of variables. The variables are supposed to be independent of each other (which sits uncomfortably with the idea that

---

[274]   P Spicker, 1993, *Poverty and social security*, Routledge, ch 3.

they are linked to some underlying factor). Unfortunately, in practice they are usually interdependent and it is difficult to distinguish effects. The computer will normally begin with the strongest relationship and weed out others which seem not to make a difference. When there is this sort of overlap – 'multicollinearity' – it matters crucially which factor goes into the process first. Even where there is a relationship, it may be unstable; the construction of an equation is built on a particular relationship, at a particular point in time. A multivariate analysis is generally only as good as the theory behind the explanations it is reporting.

The second set of problems is often hidden by the computer, but it lies in the nature of the statistical methods being used. For most of the conventional techniques to work, relationships are supposed to be linear, or describable by a line on a graph. Data should be normally distributed – that is, distributed in the bell-like shape of a 'normal curve'. After the processing has been done, the 'residuals' – the information that has been left out – are not supposed to show that there is more analysis left to do. In practice, most of these requirements are liable to be compromised. The data often have irregular distributions,[275] and they have to be shaped to fit the assumptions. Missing values are commonplace; they have to be worked round, averaged or ignored. Exceptional cases, or 'outliers', have to be thrown out of the analysis, or they will distort the results. Some data, like income distribution, can be made to fit the assumptions after transformation. But in other issues, like indicators of deprivation, the figures stubbornly refuse to look remotely normal even after all the standard transformations have been applied. To make up the Index of Multiple Deprivation in the UK, Noble and his colleagues followed up a range of transformations with 'shrinkage' of area data, adjusting data to reduce the effect of different sizes of area on apparent proportions. The results by the end of the process are still not quite normal, and not quite linear.[276]

Multivariate analysis is widely used – for example, the World Bank routinely recommends it for its programme evaluations – but it needs to be treated with some caution. The quality of the information going in is not always good enough to stand up to sophisticated mathematical manipulation. If basic mistakes in data entry or calculations are

[275] Social Disadvantage Research Centre, 2003, p 53.
[276] M Noble et al, 2001, *Meetings on Indices of Deprivation 2000*, at http://stats.lse.ac.uk/galbrait/indices/OxfordStatement.pdf

made, they are fiendishly difficult to spot.[277]   And hardly anybody understands what on earth is going on in these formulae – including many of the experts, because the level of information conventionally given in academic papers in social science is often not good enough to tell. Keeping things opaque is sometimes seen as an advantage – a 'technological fix' to silence political opposition – but it is not necessarily helpful.

Anticipating change

A goodly part of practical work in social policy is concerned with change: charting it, anticipating it, trying to bring it about. Indicators are commonly used to track changes, to give some evidence about what is happening. The simplest way to do this is to follow indicators over time, seeing whether they go up, go down or stay the same. As I have explained, indicators are not precise, faithful measures of issues, but if they work they should tell us, more or less, what direction things are moving in. If the basis of the indicator is changed – if there is a different figure, or a statistical 'refinement', or a different method of counting – that kind of comparison becomes difficult; so it may be more important to count things in the same way than it is to get the figure 'right'. The quality of the indicator is more likely to be improved by other indicators, getting more information from different sources; if all the signposts point in the same direction, that makes it less likely that the result is a quirk of a particular statistic.

Indicators are markers, rather than explanations. Some indicators are used because people think they stand for a wider issue. So, for example, the Scottish Government's Performance Framework tracks the abundance of terrestrial breeding birds as an indicator of biodiversity – itself an indicator of environmental enhancement – and delay in traffic journeys as an indicator of whether the country is an attractive place to do business.[278] If the connection has been identified rightly, these indicators should in principle co-vary with other indicators of the same issues. The theoretical justification for using the indicator does matter, but there is considerable scope for getting things wrong – in both the theory and the process of counting – and indicators should always be treated with caution.

---

[277]   European Spreadsheet Risks Interest Group, 2013, *Horror stories,* at www. eusprig.org/horror-stories.htm

[278]   Scottish Government, 2007, *National Indicators*, www.scotland.gov.uk/About/Performance/scotPerforms/indicators

---

Causal analysis

It is important to understand what such numbers cannot do, as well as what they can. The early sociologists, like Comte and Marx, were convinced that there were general laws of society, just as there were laws of nature, and that what we had to do was to identify the causes and the effects would follow. If one thing causes another, then in theory the effect should come about whenever the cause is present, unless there is something stopping it. That general assumption has proved to be fairly unreliable in social science, and that is not just because the numbers do not mean what they seem to mean. One reason is that social issues tend to be multi-faceted, with lots of processes going on all at once. That means that causal explanations tend to be partial at best. Second, a cause can only be effective when other things do not prevent it, and in a complex, chaotic environment, the pressures often lead in several directions at once. (That is a major reason why the predictions of economic theory are so often false.) Third, causation is very hard to detect. All we can say with certainty from looking at data is that one thing is likely to happen before another – and the lesson of history implies that social policy analysts have not been very good at identifying when that is true, and when it is not (Box 4.1). Causal explanations have to be handled with tongs – many serious social scientists are reluctant to use them at all. And that is true before we move to consider the practical application of causal predictions.

Causal connections, or 'generative mechanisms', are mainly identified through tracking patterns of association. In most social data, many things happen all at once. There may be patterns in the data, where one thing increases or reduces along with another, or where one factor (benefit receipt) goes up when another (employment) goes down. One of the primary methods used to disentangle causes is to 'control' for the influence of other factors. That means, simply enough, that a comparison is made between the circumstances where the other factor does apply, and where it does not. It can be difficult to mount formal experiments to do this in social policy – I will come back to the issue of 'control trials' when I discuss evaluation – but it may be possible to review the effect of different influences in a bank of data, for example dividing up the data to separate out the impact of important influences such as education or gender.

Some of the statistical techniques which are available to us make it possible to go fishing in a pool of data to see what the links might be. The literature on comparative social policy is stuffed with examples, where researchers take comparative datasets and look for associations and trends within the data. There are three serious weaknesses in the approach. First, the techniques that we use cannot tell us for certain that there is a causal link – that one thing makes another happen. What we look for instead is a statistical association, where one thing is unlikely to happen at the same time as another by chance. An association often suggests a relationship, but it is not proof of one. Some of the associations that have been identified in the past – for example, between unemployment and crime,[279] or between gender equality and rape[280] – are deeply contentious, and open to conflicting interpretations.

The second problem is that the approach can produce accidental results. An association is said to be 'statistically significant' if the chances of it happening are sufficiently remote to make it unlikely. Conventionally the test is set at a probability of 1 in 20, usually written in the form $p < .05$; that means to say that p (the probability that this will happen) is less than .05 (five chances in a hundred). However, one chance in twenty is not very long odds. Even if we look for a wider margin – say one in a hundred ($p < .01$) – one chance in a hundred is fairly sure to turn up if there are more than a hundred relationships examined. What this means, in a nutshell, is that during a fishing expedition connections can turn up by chance, and they will. Austin et al give an example from a large medical data set:

> The second International Study of Infarct Survival demonstrated that the use of aspirin during the acute phase of acute myocardial infarction reduced mortality in a group of more than 17,000 patients. A subgroup analysis demonstrated that aspirin increased mortality of patients born under the astrological sign of Gemini or Libra. ... we were able to identify multiple significant associations, all of them clinically implausible.[281]

They suggest that 'conclusions obtained from data mining should be viewed with a healthy degree of skepticism.' [282]

The third problem is about the way that variables are identified and defined. Most associations in social data look weak next to associations in biology or physical sciences. If the correlations are very high,

---

[279] S Box, 1987, *Recession, crime and punishment*, Basingstoke: Macmillan.

[280] R Whaley, 2001, The paradoxical relationship between gender inequality and rape, *Gender and Society* 15(3) 531–555.

[281] P Austin, M Mandani, D Juurlink, J Hux, 2006, Testing multiple statistical hypotheses resulted in spurious associations: a study of astrological signs and health, Journal of Clinical Epidemiology 59, 964–969

[282] Austin et al, 2006.

however, that is often a sign, not that the data show a strong relationship, but that the indicators are not sufficiently distinct. Sometimes the data come repeatedly from a particular source, which produces a 'common source bias'; sometimes the variables seem to be independent but they actually reflect the same underlying circumstances. For example, unemployment, lone parenthood and disability are all directly affected by benefit régimes, and consequently interconnected; they tend to increase when jobs are hard to find, because people make the claims which are most appropriate to their circumstances. It can be difficult to work out which factors are really important. This cannot be left to the computer to decide (though all too often it is); the importance of associations depends on the quality of the explanation which is given, not the mathematical process by which they are derived.

Forecasting, prediction and planning

Part of the purpose of looking at indicators and associations is to predict the future. This may sound flaky – if measurement has to be treated with scepticism, measuring an uncertain future is even more suspect. Predictions have a serious purpose, however. They are needed, in the first place, for a policy analyst to be able to say what the likely impact of a policy will be, and what difference the policy is expected to make; and, for the same reason, they are used to select appropriate policies and responses. Second, they are needed to plan services. A forecast is a statement about the future, based on the situation at present. Forecasting methods are widely used for basic service projects. Every housing plan has to have some basic statement of present and future needs. To build a primary school, an education department has to make some kind of statement of what the population of young schoolchildren will be in the years to come, when some of the prospective beneficiaries have not even been conceived. Third, and most contentiously, predictions are used to develop policies that anticipate long-term trends – for example, in pensions, health care expenditure or climate change.

Projections Projections are extrapolations of existing trends into the future. A projection is a conditional statement: it takes the form of saying that 'other things being equal, if we make certain assumptions, this will be true.' A sound projection should identify the conditions explicitly. The standard technique in projection is to draw a line on a graph, and to carry the line forward on the basis of the previous trend. The lines do not have to be straight. They may form patterns, like oscillations, cycles, growth curves (steeply rising), decline curves (flattening) or 'S' curves (starting slowly, leading to rapid growth, then slowing again). It is fairly common to see three lines being drawn, a 'high', 'medium' and 'low' estimate, to take account of uncertainty.

The lines are commonly drawn through one of three techniques:

- using historical data
- identifying 'moving averages' for previous time periods. Each result in the trend is based on the average of several time periods, rather than a single point. For example, indexes of house prices or price inflation are revised every month, to refer to the previous twelve months. This smoothes out differences in the data
- using weighted moving averages. The weights make it possible to give more recent time periods greater weight than more distant time periods.

This is only part of the story: not many projections in public policy are made quite so easily. Most complex problems – and practical problems tend to be complex – have several lines to consider, not a single one. Cohort analysis assumes that each section of an issue can be projected, and the results can be aggregated to give a total projection.

Population forecasting is a relatively straightforward illustration of the problems. Population is predicted by tracking cohorts in a range of age brackets, which makes it possible to predict patterns of fertility, ageing and mortality over time. At a global level, the pattern of population depends on the relationship of births to deaths. If more people die, the population falls; if more people are born, it grows. Deaths are linked to health, and births to fertility. For a biggish country like the UK, population is still largely determined by mortality and fertility, but migration plays a visible part. For a city, migration comes to play a larger role. The planning of schooling and old people's homes seems as a matter of common sense to depend on how many children or old people there are, but that will often not be determined by birth or death rates. By the time the focus moves to small areas, migration is central, and births and deaths matter relatively very little. For any small area, the number of children depends on how many families and people of child-bearing age move into the area. (Reports on London in 2012 suggest that there may be an under-supply of nearly half a million primary school places in the next three years.) The number of old people, similarly, tends to depend proportionately on what kind of accommodation there is in the area (which encourages old people to move or to remain in an area), and how many younger people move out. Simply put, the smaller the area, the more important migration becomes, and the less important mortality becomes.

Household formation is more complex, because the number of households depends not just on population, but on housing supply, household formation and fission (or breakup), when one household breaks up into two. In England and Wales, the national projections for the numbers of households are developed through the following procedures:

- the population is projected, both nationally and sub-nationally
- marital status is projected nationally (regional estimates are based on national estimates)
- the institutional population is calculated, and subtracted from the rest of the population
- household membership is projected from censuses and the Labour Force Survey
- the data are then broken down into sub-national areas, and discrepancies are smoothed out. [283]

This process is difficult, but it is still remarkably crude – there is nothing here to take into account the effects of economic change, social change or migration. That might help to explain why house-building has been subject to such radical under-investment and inconsistent development in the course of the last forty years.

Box 6.2: Malthus and world population

Thomas Malthus, writing at the end of the eighteenth century, argued that the growth of the human population must lead to disaster. Population, he wrote, grows in geometric proportion (2, 4, 8, 16) while food only grows in arithmetic proportion (2, 4, 6, 8).[284] We were going, then, to run out of food. But population could be limited only by war, famine, disease, or 'vice' (by which he may, or may not, have meant some kind of birth control). The famines of the nineteenth century were seen by Malthusians as the inevitable consequence of too many people trying to get too little food.

Malthusianism enjoys periodic resurgences in popularity, and certainly many of the critiques of developing countries begin from the supposition that

---

[283] Office of the Deputy Prime Minister, 1999, *Projections of households in England 2021*, www.odpm.gov.uk/stellent/groups/odpm_housing/documents/page/odpm_house_604206-01.hcsp#P5566_107468

[284] T Malthus, 1798, *Essay on the principle of population*.

overpopulation is the central problem.[285] There is a 'population explosion', which is going eventually to lead to some kind of disaster. The *Limits to Growth*, a phenomenally popular account of the 1970s, argued that population was growing to a potentially catastrophic level.[286]

There is a clear and obvious problem with this analysis. Malthus' *Essay on the Principle of Population* was published in 1798. More than 200 years later, the catastrophes he predicted have not happened, so we might reasonably have come to the conclusion that he was wrong. There were three important flaws in the argument.

The first, and most obvious, is that we can bear a much greater increase in population than Malthus reasoned. Some countries may be short of space, because their populations are confined by political boundaries, but the world is not short of space, and will not be in the foreseeable future.

Second, food production does not increase more slowly than population; it has generally increased at least in line with population. This is mainly, but not solely, the result of technological change; it is also true that an increasing population produces goods to meet its needs. Why, then, if resources are increasing, do famines occur? Incredible as it may seem, famine does not generally happen because there is not enough food. Drèze and Sen's authoritative study shows that famine comes about when people have no entitlement to the food which exists, which is a very different proposition.[287]

Third, population does not grow in geometrical progression – or, as Meadows et al suggest, 'exponentially'. (By 'exponential' they mean that growth is 'proportionate to what is already there'.[288]) Not everyone in a population has children at any time; fertility is proportionate not to the size of the population, but to the size of the female population within a particular age band. If people are living longer, the population will grow but the overall number of births will be about the same as before (and it will seem to fall as a proportion of the whole). Holding fertility at a constant rate would produce what Meadows et al call 'sigmoid' growth, which continues to increase but where the rate of growth diminishes. Even if we were to move instantaneously to replacement-level fertility, Cohen calculates that the population would not level off until 2150, with 8.4 billion people.[289] However, people do not simply carry on having children regardless of circumstances.

[285] See e.g. S McDaniel, 1990, People pressure, in C Mungall, D McLaren (eds) *Planet under stress*, Toronto: Oxford University Press; Meadows et al, 1992.

[286] D H Meadows et al, 1972, *Limits to growth*, London: Earth Island.

[287] J Drèze, A Sen, 1989, *Hunger and public action*, Oxford: Clarendon Press.

[288] D H Meadows, D L Meadows, J Randers, 1992, *Beyond the limits*, London: Earthscan, p.17.

[289] J Cohen, 1995, *How many people can the earth support?*, New York: Norton.

If we look at the growth of population in the developed countries, we see a remarkable phenomenon: that in those countries, natural population growth is static, or has even started to shrink, because people are not having enough babies to maintain the population. Whatever the reasons, the idea that people in general have babies at the same rate as previous generations is just plain false.

The reasons why fertility declines with development include

- the effect of urban society on the cost of having children
- the lengthening period of dependency of children, due to education and labour laws
- the changing role of women
- the economic effect of female employment, which leads to a loss of income if women leave the labour market to have children
- increasing education and later marriage, and
- the availability of contraception.[290]

One of the strongest associations, however, is the risk that a child will die. Where infant mortality is high, women have more children, because that is the best way to make sure that someone will survive. When infant mortality falls, so does fertility. The surest way to cut population has been to reduce the poverty that leads to infant deaths.

> The path to family planning in every country lies through the eradication of poverty, which in fact has historically been the main cause of over-population. ... It has truly been said that the best contraceptive is development.[291]

Parameters and modelling Projections depend on the assumption that 'other things are equal'. The assumptions behind that statement are referred to as 'parameters'. Parameters are often, wrongly, identified with limits; that is not what the term means. Once parameters have been identified, it should be possible to test what would happen if they were different. These are sometimes called 'what if?' calculations, because they address the question 'what if things were different?' In

---

[290] T Hewitt, I Smith, 1992, Is the world overpopulated?, in T Allen, A Thomas (eds) *Poverty and development in the 1990s*, Oxford University Press.

[291] K Gulhati, L Bates, 1994, Developing countries and the international population debate, in R Cassen (ed) *Population and development: old debates, new conclusions*, Washington DC: Overseas Development Council, p 53.

the US, they are referred to as 'sensitivity analyses', because they are identifying how sensitive the outcomes are to the assumptions.[292]

A 'model' is a statement about the relationships between different factors. Projections – conditional statements about current trends – tell us what happen if things continue in the same way. Models tell us what impact that variations in different factors are likely to have. Taking again the example of population, we might assume that, if other things being equal, levels of migration are likely to remain at current levels. Migration is clearly affected, however, by a range of factors, such as the state of the economy. So we can model migration in terms of different rates of economic growth, producing high, medium and low estimates of migration according to the variation of economic conditions. The more factors that are taken into account, the more complex the model becomes. Economic forecasting in the UK depends on a multi-factorial model maintained by the Treasury. Over the years, this model has become progressively more complex and sophisticated; every change in tax or interest rates is passed through the model to see what the likely effects might be.

Models are often expressed as equations. As a rule of thumb, plus and minus signs are used to imply that the effects are being produced by a mixture of different factors; multiplication and division suggest that the factors are working together in combination. Other models can be represented as 'decision trees', where at each stage there are different possible outcomes. A 'Markov model' is a sequence of possible events where the odds of going down each branch of the tree have been calculated. They can be used, for example, to examine possible outcomes from health care treatments.[293] If these approaches are not much used in public policy analysis, however, it is because they assume a level of knowledge and precision about likely outcomes which is rarely available in practice.

Prediction A prediction is, simply, a statement about what will happen in the future. Projections are conditional: their critical flaw that they begin by assuming that things will happen in the same way they have happened before – and so that, other things being equal, this is what will happen. Other things are rarely equal. It is unwise to project

[292] E Stokey, R Zeckhauser, 1978, *A primer for policy analysis*, New York: Norton, pp 233–236.
[293] K Kuntz, M Weinstein, 2001, Modelling in economic evaluation, in M Drummond, A McGuire (eds) *Economic evaluation in health care*, Oxford: Oxford University Press.

without some element of judgment, and reasoned predictions –
sometimes called 'judgment forecasts' – tend to be more convincing
than crude projections. Population forecasting is complex, but it lends
itself to projective techniques. For other, less tractable problems, such
as economic development or social change, there are more techniques
for collating judgments about the future. These do not have to be
done quantitatively. The 'Delphi technique' collates individual expert
judgments (a different process from inviting discussion between an
expert group). Experts are asked individually, and without prior
discussion, what they think; their positions are then compared and
contrasted.

'Cross–impact analysis' modifies the Delphi technique by putting
different influences into a matrix, examining how each factor interacts
with the others. This sounds complicated, but it isn't; a 'matrix' is
simply a cross-tabulation. If there are four factors to predict, like
'society', 'the economy', 'the population' and 'housing', a matrix is a
table with six cells, like this:

			Housing
		Population	
	Economy		
Society			

The respondents have to fill in each of the empty boxes.

A third approach is scenario building, 'that is, evaluation of alternative
possible futures, each corresponding to a different policy.[294] 'Scenario
building' gives an expert group the opportunity to examine their
assumptions qualitatively. There is an example of scenario building in
the Wanless report on the National Health Service (NHS). Wanless
was asked to look at 'technological, demographic and medical trends'
over the course of twenty years. As part of that exercise, it constructed
three scenarios:

- solid progress, with increasing life expectancy, service targets being
  met and a background of improving social conditions;

---

[294]   M Scriven, 1991, *Evaluation thesaurus*, 4th edition, p.267.

- slow uptake, with increasing long-term chronic illness, slow implementation of new technologies and limited change in service use;
- full engagement, with improving public health and improving service.[295]

As it happens, none of these scenarios raised major concerns about the viability of the NHS.

There is a tendency in some official reports to translate predictions into prescriptions for policy. Population is increasing, so people should have more contraception;[296] people are getting older, so pensions must be limited;[297] the climate is changing, so we must try to stop the change.[298] These statements are unwise. The problem is not necessarily that the policy does not relate to the problem – though that is sometimes true, too – but that prescriptions for future policy have to be based on more than prediction of a likely outcome. There are many possible policy prescriptions – often a much wider range than possible outcomes. The alternatives need to be examined; the outcomes of each option need to be predicted; and a prudent policy will consider not just what will happen if they succeed, but also if they fail. 'Robust' policies are policies which allow future changes in direction. Some policies don't. For example, the Stern Review's prescriptions for 'mitigating' or reducing climate change may – by the report's own account – have no effect at all, and the review does not consider policies for 'adaptation' or coping with climate change at all; 'mitigation' is not a robust option. Preparing policy for the future calls for acceptance of uncertainty, and a certain humility.

[295] D Wanless, 2002, Securing our future health, London: HM Treasury, ch 3; at www.hm-treasury.gov.uk/Consultations_and_Legislation/wanless/consult_wanless_final.cfm

[296] United Nations, Population Division, Department of Economic and Social Affairs, 2003, Fertility, contraception and population policies, New York: United Nations.

[297] Pensions Commission, 2005, *A new pension settlement for the 21st century*, London: The Stationery Office.

[298] HM Treasury, 2006, *Stern Review: The Economics of Climate Change*, London: TSO.

ISSUE FOR DISCUSSION

How can we deal with future problems – like population movement or environmental change – if we have no clear idea of the size of the issue?

PART 2
POLICY

CHAPTER 7

Public policy

The nature of policy
Formal processes: law and the state
Governance
Government and social policy
The social services
Comparing policies

The nature of policy

The idea of 'policy' is ambiguous, and often infuriatingly elusive. Politicians, when they use the word, generally seem to have in mind some sense of a deliberate set of approaches – the things they have chosen to do. When this is looked at in more detail, however, it fragments into a wide range of disparate issues. Hogwood and Gunn pick up a range of meanings of the term.[299] A policy might be, amongst other things,

- a label for a field of government activity and involvement – like 'family policy' or 'transport policy';
- an expression of a desired state of affairs or general purpose – 'our policy is to support the family';
- a set of specific proposals;
- the decisions made by government;
- a process of formal authorization (like the policy of a local authority, as opposed to 'practice' or 'agency discretion');
- a strategy, programme or agenda for action – a defined sphere of activity involving particular, inter-related measures;
- a theory or model where actions are assumed to produce certain results. Townsend argues that social policy 'can be defined as the underlying as well as the professed rationale by which social institutions and groups are used or brought into being to ensure social preservation or development. Social policy is, in other

---

[299] B Hogwood, L Gunn, 1984, *Policy analysis for the real world*, Oxford: Oxford University Press.

words, the institutionalised control of agencies and organisations to maintain or change social structure and values.'[300] Policy can be implicit, 'unspoken and even unrecognised'. On this view, it is possible to read back from the results to a set of intentions, and even to 'non-decisions' – points where policy fails to address issues because of its underlying assumptions;[301]

- the product of a process of decision making. This understanding is mainly used in academic discussions of the subject: when people ask what a 'policy' is they are actually looking at what has come out of the policy process. Stone, for example, describes policy formation as a process of negotiation or bargaining in the 'polis' or political community.[302] Policy is not rational; it is formed through bluff, bargaining, the use of influence, loyalty, horse trading and so on.

When welfare is considered in terms of 'policy', outcomes are often attributed, in some way, to design – that is, to the deliberate intentions of policy-makers. The description of methods and outcomes is often used as a way of identifying such intentions. There are dangers in trying to read intentions from effects; there can be a world of difference between what policy-makers intend and what actually happens. At the same time, understanding what policies are intended to do is an important part of understanding social policy in a more general sense.

Formal processes: law and the state

Many social policies are made and developed through the state. The limits of 'the state' are not always easy to define, because the term is used very loosely; depending on the context, it can be taken to mean several things – a system of government, a set of formal institutions, the public sector. Berki defines the state as 'an institutional structure whose primary and distinctive function is the maintenance of authority in a given territorial unit.'[303] There is a better-known definition by Weber, who defines the state in terms of its claim to the exclusive use

---

[300] P Townsend, 1976, *Sociology and social policy*, Harmondsworth: Penguin, p.6.

[301] P Bachrach, M Baratz, 1970, *Power and poverty*, Oxford: Oxford University Press p.44.

[302] D Stone, 2002, *Policy paradox*, New York: Norton.

[303] R Berki, 1979, State and society, in J Hayward, R Berki (eds) *State and society in contemporary Europe*, Oxford: Martin Robertson, p.1.

of force.[304] That is a mistake; it is authority, not force, that is central. The constitution of the USA reserves the use of residual force to its citizens, and in any constitutional state, the state can exercise only the powers which are granted to it.

The narrow interpretation of this structure is that the state is concerned with the formal political institutions of a society. A wider view of the state would describe it as the means through which governmental power is exercised (which could include, for example, schools or hospitals) or the full range of government activity (which might include sponsorship of the arts). The formal political institutions of a society are conventionally classified in three categories: legislative (or law-making), judicial, and executive (concerned with government and the civil service). The United States has a strong division of labour between the different branches, referred to as the 'separation of powers', and this has been influential in the government of many other countries. Social policy in practice tends to focus on executive functions, but before moving too strongly in that direction, it is helpful to consider the legislative framework.

The making of law is central to the activities of government: law is an important part of how a modern state exercises power. Lay people often think of law in terms of 'criminal' law, which is mainly concerned with prohibition and punishment; it is through criminal law, for example, that people are sent to prison, that parents can be punished for neglecting or maltreating children, or that people are protected against fraud and corruption. But this is only a small part of the role of law in society. Law is, much more generally, a system of rules and procedures through which the actions of individuals and people collectively can be regulated and governed. Hart argues that laws can be classified as primary or secondary rules. Primary rules are those which set the terms by which other laws can be determined. They include rules of recognition – systems for recognising formal authority, and the laws themselves; rules of change, which make alteration in the rules possible; and adjudication, which is necessary for application and enforcement of the rules. Secondary laws are the rest.[305]

Law making is important in social policy in four ways.

- *Constitutional law* Laws form the framework through which policies are exercised. The powers of institutions have to be

---

[304] M Weber, Politics as a vocation, in H Gerth, C Wright Mills (eds), 1948, *From Max Weber*, Oxford: Oxford University Press.

[305] H L A Hart, 1961, *The concept of law*, Oxford: Oxford University Press.

defined by law; they have to be given the competence to act. The institutions of the European Union have been working to establish competence in various areas related to welfare, including health, education, gender issues and social security; the Commission is still in the process of attempting to identify a role in relation to elderly people, disabled people, racial minorities, and people who are poor.[306]

- *Rule making* Law is used to establish the rules by which a policy is pursued. Law has been described as a system of 'norms', that is expectations which are coupled with sanctions in order to produce particular effects.[307] So, for example, a law which states that people must send their children to school is a positive norm (requiring people to do something); a law which states that people must not do something, such as renting out houses which are unfit for human habitation, is a negative norm. But legal principles are not confined to what people should and should not do. One of the implications of constitutional law is that different bodies require their roles to be defined, and there is an extensive use in many systems of 'permissive' law, which gives organisations the power to undertake actions at their discretion.

- *Administrative law* Law is used to define executive processes – that is, the means by which services are to be delivered. Social security systems have not, in many countries, developed spontaneously; the usual process has been that at certain points legislation has been used as a means of establishing procedures by which the state could take on a major proportion of the responsibility for social protection. Similarly, and often by the same processes, laws are used to regulate the conduct of the administration.

- *Enforcement* There is often a negative sanction attached to laws, so that people or organisations who disregard them are liable to suffer some kind of penalty. A penalty against an organisation is not necessarily a penalty against the people who work for it, and it is sometimes difficult to think of any penalty which can be effective against a governmental organisation determined to break the rules; 'respect for the rule of law' is often the main method of enforcement available.

---

[306] P Spicker, 1997, The prospect for European laws on poverty, in A Kjonstad, J Veit-Wilson (eds) *Law, Power and Poverty*, Bergen: Comparative Research Programme on Poverty, pp 137–148.

[307] S Benn, R Peters, 1959, *Social principles and the democratic state*, London: Allen and Unwin.

There is a considerable overlap between the establishment of norms and the provision of a means of enforcement. There are, however, many examples of laws which are not enforced, or enforceable. Some laws are exhortatory, encouraging people to act in a particular way. A Japanese law for the welfare of elderly people, for example, states: 'The aged shall be loved and respected as those who have for many years contributed toward the development of society, and a wholesome and peaceful life shall be guaranteed to them.'[308] Other laws offer guidelines rather than firm norms. The European Union has developed a system of what is called 'soft law', consisting partly of recommendations and partly of generalised agreement about principles, which national governments are free to interpret.[309]

Social policy is not only made through the process of legislation. It can be made that way, in so far as laws are passed which set out the policy, but it is also possible for policies to be developed at other levels, by the executive arms of government. Delegation of authority to the executive is fairly common, because much of what happens in social policy takes place at a level which legislators are inclined to think is beneath their notice. These processes are not very different in principle because in a properly constituted government the executive has to be empowered by the legislative authority before decisions can be taken.

Box 7.1: The social policy of the European Union

If a government consists of a set of institutions with a legislature, executive and judiciary, operating in a defined territorial unit, the European Union is a government. Despite strong political resistance to the use of the 'f-word', the structure of European government is federal. Wheare considers several definitions of a federation:

- a system of government where residual legal power is held by the member states, not the central government;
- a union where member states retain their original constitutions;

---

[308] Law no 133 art. 2, 1963: cited in International Council on Social Welfare, 1969, *Social welfare and human rights*, New York: Columbia University Press, p.250.

[309] L Cram, 1993, Calling the tune without paying the piper?, *Policy & Politics* 21(2) pp 135–146.

- 'an association of states so organised that .... general and regional governments both operate *directly* upon the people',[310] and
- two governments which have coordinate powers, exercised independently of each other.

For Wheare, a federation could be formed

> when a group of territorial communities are prepared to co-operate with each other for the regulation of certain matters but for those matters only, and when they are determined at the same time to remain separate and supreme, each in its own territory, for the regulation of other matters.[311]

All the definitions Wheare considers apply to the EU, and the last definition fits the European case exactly. If the member states did not want to create a federation, they needed to ensure that the upper tier – the general, inter-state element of the structure – could not make independent decisions; but they have done the opposite. The Member States have agreed in successive treaties that the European level of government has 'exclusive competence' in a range of areas where national governments have no further right to choose their own laws.

Social policy in the EU initially meant consideration of industrial relations, with some elements of policy relating to gender. The Commission, the executive arm of the EU, has also been committed to a progressive expansion of the 'competences' of the Union – the establishment of authority to act in a range of governmental areas – and over time the EU's role and influence in social policy has progressively extended. The EU has a direct interest in social protection and the rights of workers. Rules governing aluminium in water supplies established the precedent of competence in relation to environmental health; a programme for language teaching established competence in education; proposals for bus passes have established competence in relation to the welfare of older people and public transport. The Green Paper on Social Policy reflected the expanded field of activity; it discusses employment and training, family structure, social exclusion, health

---

[310] K C Wheare, 1946, *Federal Government*, Oxford: Oxford University Press, p 5.

[311] K C Wheare, 1991, What federal government is, The Federalist 1991, vol 33, pp 1–73, www.thefederalist.eu/index.php?option=com_content&view=article&id=28&lang=en

care, education, women's rights, youth policy, public health, racism, the welfare of elderly people and rural development.[312]

European social policy over the last thirty years has mainly been concerned with setting an agenda – a focus less on what the EU actually does than on establishing the EU's right to do it. Following resistance from a number of member states, and an emphasis on 'subsidiarity', in the sense of restricting powers to lower levels, the expansion of powers slowed; the 'Open Method of Coordination', proceeding by discussion and consensus, allowed member states to interpret rules according to their own politics and priorities[313] – and so gave recalcitrant participants every opportunity to cede nothing. The increasing centralised role of the European Bank has shifted the axis again, and the Commission has recently proposed the establishment of a fund to respond directly to extreme poverty.[314] They claim that 'the objective of this Regulation, namely to improve social cohesion in the Union and contribute to the fight against poverty and social exclusion, cannot be sufficiently achieved by Member States but can be better achieved at Union level.'[315]

Governance

There is a common misconception about governments, both in academic literature and in the popular mind, that their actions are primarily dependent on the ability to use force. The 'command theory of law' developed by Austin[316] supposes that government works by telling people what to do. Compulsion works by imposing sanctions (that is, negative consequences or punishments) on people. This is a characteristic part of criminal law. The ability to impose sanctions almost certainly has a wider effect on compliance with a government's wishes. Because governments can require people to do things, they often do not have to. For example, it is compulsory for parents to

---

[312] Commission of the European Communities, 1993, *Green Paper: European Social Policy – Options for the Union*, Com (93) final.

[313] E McPhail, 2010, Examining the impact of the Open Method of Coordination on sub-state employment and social inclusion policies, *Journal of European Social Policy* 20(4) 364–378; C de la Porte, P Pochet, 2012, Why and how (still) study the Open Method of Coordination?, *Journal of European Social Policy* 22(3) 336–349.

[314] European Commission, 2012, Proposal for a regulation of the European Parliament and Council on the fund for european aid to the most deprived, COM(2012) 617 final http://ec.europa.eu/social/main.jsp?langId=en& catId=89&newsId=1704&furtherNews=yes

[315] European Commission, 2012, p 12.

[316] J Austin (1885) *The province of jurisprudence determined*, Cambridge: Cambridge University Press, 1995.

arrange education for their children: in most cases this means that they have to send their children to school. There are relatively few people who fail to do so, and that means that the direct use of coercion, even if it underlies policy in the last resort, is limited in practice. At the same time, some sanctions are widely disregarded: for example, laws about dog licensing in the UK fell into disuse before their abolition because of non-compliance.

The central problem with the command theory is not that governments cannot compel people, even if there are limits; it is that it assumes that what is true for one part of the system is true for every part. Governments do much more than this, and much of what they do has nothing to do with compulsion. To reflect the situation, the language in which government is discussed has increasingly been framed in terms of 'governance', focusing on the range of methods and approaches by which government can achieve its objectives.

Probably the most important role of government, which is implied by the discussion of law, is the establishment of rules and procedures – a framework for social life. The rules established by governments shape people's personal lives – for example, through marriage, family law and property ownership – as well as the structure of organisations, like education and employment. People's ability to function in society depends heavily on their entitlements – Sen argues that entitlements are fundamental to the issue of poverty[317] – and societies where people are excluded from such arrangements, like the societies in Africa where women cannot own property, have commensurate problems. Regulation is the process of establishing a framework of rules; it is fundamental to the process of government.

Constitutional government begins with the proposition that governments are able to do only those things for which they have been expressly granted authority. Beyond that, in the liberal democracies of the West, there is a presumption that any intervention that is made by government should be minimal. Rather than regulating or coercing people, then, most democratic governments will begin with persuasion.[318] Governments can 'nudge' people, through a combination of incentives, persuasion and marketing techniques.[319] They can persuade more directly through government-sponsored education,

---

[317] A Sen, 1981, *Poverty and famines: an essay on entitlement and deprivation*, Oxford: Clarendon Press, Oxford: Clarendon Press.

[318] S Bell, A Hindmoor, F Mols, 2010, Persuasion as governance, *Public Administration* 88(3) 851–870.

[319] R Thaler, C Sunstein, 2008, *Nudge*, New Haven: Yale University Press.

propaganda, advertising and other means of opinion-forming – though it can stretch, potentially, to lies, indoctrination, even state-sponsored religions. Beyond propaganda, governments can seek to encourage or discourage particular sorts of activity in other ways – typically through the use of selective rewards or penalties. Governments subsidise activities they wish to encourage, and they may try to deter other action through taxation. In the context of social policy, this is often described (slightly misleadingly) in terms of 'incentives' and 'disincentives'.[320] An incentive offers a potential gain to people who change their behaviour in a particular way – like a prize for invention or a financial reward for desired behaviour, like marriage. Disincentives, conversely, imply potential penalties or costs. People do not respond proportionately to rewards or punishments,[321] or directly; the effectiveness of this kind of action depends strongly on context and culture.

Governments do not have to confine themselves to trying to influence the actions of other people. In some cases, where they consider the issues are sufficiently important, they do the work themselves. They can buy things for the population, acting as a purchaser; they can run industries; they can provide services. They are major employers – sometimes they are the most significant employer in a national economy. Governments, in the modern world, are economic actors as much as they are political ones. Although some aspects of this kind of intervention have become unfashionable – it is less common than it was forty years ago for governments to act as bankers for industrial start-ups, to manage agricultural production or to develop industrial sectors themselves – it is still fairly common for governments to take direct responsibility for defence, the economic infrastructure (like roads and rail), and of course the social services.

Figure 7.1 outlines some of the principal methods of governance. It is not a complete account of the way that governments operate – I have not even touched on the ways the public sector can shape people's lives – but it serves to illustrate two points. The first is diversity. Governments have a huge range of different options open to them in pursuit of their political aims. The second is the limitations of government behaviour. The diversity of options reflects both a reluctance to use straightforward compulsion and at times the difficulty

---

[320] P Spicker, 2006, Understanding incentives, Annexure 1 of M Steele (ed), Report on incentive structures of social assistance grants in South Africa, South Africa: Republic of South Africa Department of Social Development.

[321] P Jones, J Cullis, 2003, Key parameters in policy design, *Journal of Social Policy* 32(4) pp 527–547.

Figure 7.1: Methods of governance

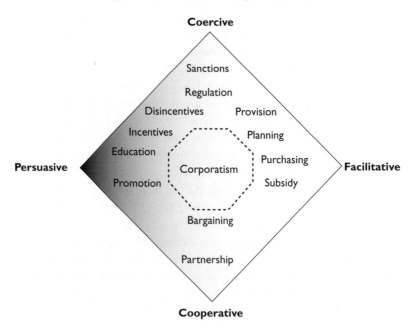

Coercive

Sanctions

Regulation

Disincentives   Provision

Incentives   Planning

Education

Persuasive   Purchasing   **Facilitative**

Corporatism

Promotion   Subsidy

Bargaining

Partnership

Cooperative

which governments have in achieving their ends by any of the means available to them.

In recent years, the emphasis in government has consequently fallen on partnership, negotiation and collaboration, rather than direction and command structures. Governments are being encouraged to accept the limitations of what they can do. This is particularly true of governments in developing countries, and the 'encouragement' is being done by international organisations like the International Monetary Fund (IMF) and the World Bank. In part, this reflects a change in political and economic thinking, which emphasises the importance of independent actors in economic development. It also reflects, however, a more realistic view about the capacity of governments; many governments in the poorest countries have limited capacities, and despite often worthy aspirations, their capacity to act, to establish frameworks and regulate the environment is limited. Ideally, where a government has the capacity, the government will be able to plan services by encouraging and developing patterns of service; several European governments work on a 'corporatist' model, structuring the roles of a range of agencies within the framework of the government's priorities. In developing countries, the process of negotiation and bargaining is more likely to reflect the uneven balance of power between government, non-governmental organisations, international agencies and private enterprise; often governments in developing countries have less influence than other parties.

Box 7.2: Who decides?

In most areas of social policy, there are conflicting arguments about who should have the authority to make decisions. The literature on democratic governance generally begins with the assumption that decisions should be made by publicly accountable authorities, while the assumption behind much of the literature favouring the private sector is that consumers should decide. In the case of education, there are at least eight different potential locuses of authority, where decisions about educational policy might be made. They are:

1. *Central government* Where there is a desire to ensure uniform standards – for example, admission to universal primary education and the promotion of literacy – there is an argument for locating relevant decisions at a national or regional level. The creation of universal basic education in sub-Saharan Africa has depended heavily on central government intervention – even if that intervention seemed at times to go beyond the capacity of the governments to deliver.[322] Several developed countries, including Britain and France, have more detailed and prescriptive national standards; this includes a national curriculum which all maintained schools are expected to follow.

2. *Local government* Local and regional authorities are seen as the democratic representatives of local interests. Localism necessarily implies variation in national standards; in India, which deals with education federally, one effect of localism has been to prevent the establishment of universal basic education, which has to rely instead on voluntary effort.[323]

3. *Interest groups* Although the process of education in schools and colleges is normally protected from outside influence – there are exceptions – a number of interest groups have privileged access. Religious bodies, employers and the armed forces often have special roles, and in some cases exercise delegated authority. Other agencies,

---

[322] R Avenstrup, 2004, *Kenya, Lesotho, Malawi and Uganda: Universal Primary education and poverty reduction*, World Bank, http://info.worldbank.org/etools/docs/reducingpoverty/case/58/fullcase/East%20Africa%20Edu%20Full%20Case.pdf

[323] See National Literacy Mission – India, 2007, www.nlm.nic.in/

such as police, health and social services, may link directly with the educational system to follow their own agendas.

4. *Schools* Schools may be seen as bureaucratic organisations, responding to government initiatives, but they may also be self-governing units controlled by boards of governors. Schools in the independent sector may be governed in accordance with rules established by founders.

5. *Head teachers* Schools may be treated as units of management, where the central authoritative role is held by the Head Teacher as the leader of the school.

6. *Teachers* Within a professional model the responsibility for educational decisions, including objectives, curriculum, is held by teachers. (Despite formal accountability to local government, this was arguably the dominant model in the UK until the 1970s.)

7. *Pupils* Although no national system resides any extensive authority in pupils, there have been long-standing arguments for a more cooperative approach which recognises children's motivation and autonomy. Educational experiments have encouraged pupils to make their own decisions about learning and the curriculum.[324]

8. *Parents* Consumer-based and private-market models tend to see parents, rather than children, as the consumers of education, making choices on behalf of their children.[325]

An educational journalist in the UK comments on the shifting balance between actors:

> When I first became an education correspondent ... we hardly bothered with what the ministers or the civil servants were thinking. That wasn't where the power lay. All the interesting stories were down in the schools – what new forms of assessment, teaching methods or ways of teaching, or of curriculum were being developed in particular schools or local education authorities. Now we have ministers deciding ...[326]

The interplay of a wide range of competing interests might seem to imply that education is a political arena. At times, it is. However, the scope for political discussion is often restricted, depending on the social and organisational context. The idea of 'historical institutionalism' suggests that decisions are

[324] A S Neill, 1968, *Summerhill*, Harmondsworth: Penguin.

[325] P Brown, 1997, The third wave: education and the ideology of parentocracy, in A Halsey, H Lauder, P Brown, A Wells, *Education: culture, economy and society*, Oxford: Oxford University Press.

[326] P Wilby, cited in N Timmins, 1996, *The five giants*, London: Fontana, p 438.

critically affected by agency and political context, but that once the decisions have been made, the institutional structures which have been developed can be difficult to change.[327]

Government and social policy

The field of social policy relates to a complex constellation of policies, institutions and actions. Governments operate and manage a range of practical activities. The broad areas of policy are commonly divided into economic policy, foreign policy and 'domestic' policy. 'Policy' here has to be taken in a fairly general sense; government policy in this sense is whatever government happens to do, or not to do. In those terms, social policy might be seen as a sub-category of domestic policy, along with areas like civil law, culture and environmental policy. This conventional distinction does not work particularly well, however; it seems clear that aspects of social policy cut across all these fields (including economic and foreign policy). Equally, social policy is wider than government policy alone: government plays an important role, but social policy is not just about the work of the state.

The area of activity which is run directly by government is referred to as the 'public sector'. This includes a wide range of activities, including for example direct economic engagement in publicly owned industries, the business of managing government, such as the civil service, and the provision of services to other agencies, like government laboratories or defence procurement. Part of the role of public sector is to provide services, but that is only part.

'Public services' include some public sector agencies, but they also include other kinds of institutional arrangement – they are not necessarily public in the sense of being developed by governments. The provision of medical care in Europe has been heavily influenced by the position of mutual societies and occupational insurance. Public services are 'public' because they are developed for reasons of policy. They are intended in principle to meet the objectives of governments, donors or governing bodies – rather than the aims of purchasers, clients or producers. They are 'services' in the sense that they provide directly for people – roads, schools, libraries and medical care convey a direct personal benefit to the people who use them. (That is not necessarily the same sense they are used in economics, where the provision of a service is distinguished from the production of goods. Many public

---

[327] D Béland, 2005, Ideas and social policy, *Social Policy and Administration* 39(1) pp 1–18.

services are services in this sense – services like education, social work and community development are concerned with intangibles, and service delivery is a process, rather than a specific act of production.[328] However, some public services do provide people with products or goods, like water or medical goods.)

Social services are a sub-category of public services. Conventionally there is a distinction made between public services, like roads, sewers and libraries, and social services, but the distinction is more than a little arbitrary. It is not at all clear why receiving weekly benefit should be thought of as 'welfare', when having the use of a road is not. None of the kinds of explanation which might be given sums the difference up. Public services are available for everyone; but so are some social services, typically including in Europe education and medical care in hospitals. Education is a process, but so is community safety. Both public and social services are usually provided by the state. Public services are sometimes charged for; so are some social services, like public housing. Ultimately, the distinction seems to be purely conventional – it is just the way in which the services have traditionally been referred to. (At the same time, there is an important implication in the idea of a social service, which has to be recognised: it is the assumption that there is something different about the recipients of social services. Public services are for everyone; social services are often thought of, however irrationally, as being for people who have some kind of dependency. Services for old people and children are generally, then, for 'dependent' groups; services which are used by everyone are not.)

The state can provide these services directly, by the financing and employment of different social services. (Some writers, particularly in the US, describe this as a 'welfare state'.) Governments can also provide indirectly through the purchase of services for their citizens. Direct and indirect provision often amount to much the same thing, because in both cases the state can effectively determine the supply of services of effective demand if it so chooses. However, there are some important differences. One is ideological: where governments are convinced that direct provision is intrinsically immoral or unproductive, indirect provision allows a way round. The second is practical: the purchase of services on the private market makes it possible to use the facilities of the market, in particular its responsiveness to demand, and there have been cases (notably in the provision of private residential

---

[328] S Osborne, Z Radnor, G Nasi, 2013, A new theory for public service management?, *American Review of Public Administration* 43(2) pp 135–58.

care for elderly people) where the response rate has been very rapid indeed. Conversely, a government which elects to use the private market is subject to its constraints. It will have limited control of effective supply and demand – what a government is prepared to pay for health care is usually much less than what a private citizen faced with pain, disability or the prospect of death will pay. It can influence supply both by acting as a major buyer and by imposing constraints on suppliers, but it is liable to find itself acting as a guarantor to inefficient suppliers (because most social services cannot simply be allowed to go out of business).

Often, government is the most important service provider; in most cases, it is also the provider of last resort, offering services when no-one else does.[329] Despite the importance of these roles, it has to be emphasised that much of the provision of welfare – and consequently of social policy – does not stem from governments at all. There is a distortion of perspective in the English-speaking literature, because the history of social policy in Britain and the USA does conventionally begin with state action. The English Poor Law was exported to several other countries, including both those that were part of the British Empire and others that were not – there were direct imitations of the Poor Law in some eastern states in the USA. This was not the trend in many other countries. Welfare systems in many countries developed through a combination of independent, mutualist or occupational organisations. In some countries, the trades unions developed systems of support; in others, employers did. The welfare states intervened in social policy fairly late in the day, often with the intention of extending such provision to those who had been left out. For example, the French *régime général* was introduced to include or 'generalise' provision to about half the workforce which did not have social protection. The system of unemployment insurance is still operated by a formal partnership of employers' organisations and trades unions, rather than by the state. In health services, similarly, the benefits provided by the state are supplemented for most people in employment by the *mutualités*, independent friendly societies which offer relatively generous coverage.

There is often a complex interplay between the decisions made by governments and those made by independent providers. The state has a pivotal role in the regulation of welfare; it establishes the rules and settings under which welfare services operate. Moran and Wood, writing about the control of medical care, categorise four types of regulation: regulation of market entry (such as who can become a

---

[329] P Spicker, 2000, *The welfare state*, London: Sage.

doctor and where they can set up), regulation of competitive practices (like advertising), regulation of market structures (through legal rules concerning what can be bought and sold), and regulation of remuneration and prices.[330]

In some cases, governments replace independent provision; in some, they build around it. The state can use the power of purchase; it can decide where to place its resources. There are fiscal controls, through subsidy and taxation; the state can offer financial incentives to undertake certain activities, and conversely it can tax activities which it does not want people to undertake. There are legal controls, for example registration and inspection, which can be used to limit entry to the market; and it can require some firms to offer services as a condition of operating in other fields (for example, by insisting that all employers should offer maternity pay). In political terms, this is sometimes described as 'corporatism', which means (among many other things) a system of interest group representation and state intervention in which the state bargains with other agencies, delegating functions and co-opting them into the structure of power.[331]

The social services

The provision of social services represents one of the ways in which social policy can be pursued; there are many others. If that is so, why are social services thought of as such a major part of social policy overall? The answer is partly historical: the development of social services and welfare states was presented, in Europe particularly in the period immediately after World War II, as the basic means through which social welfare could be improved for everyone. Partly, the answer is ideological; it has to do with the types of collective action and social organisation which people concerned with social policy want to promote. But much of it reflects a concern that the range of public policies often fails otherwise to address important areas of concern. For most of the last two centuries, social policy has been concerned with the failures of other policies – with the people who, for whatever reasons, were left out, people who were poor, socially excluded or dispossessed.

The social services in industrialised countries are usually taken as including social security, health services, housing, education and social

---

[330] M Moran, B Wood, 1993, *States, regulation and the medical profession*, Buckingham: Open University Press.

[331] M Harrison, 1984, *Corporatism and the welfare state*, Aldershot: Gower.

work. It is difficult to give an intelligible explanation of what these terms mean without plunging into details, and learning to make sense of such details is an important part of learning about social policy. Because this book is concerned with general issues, rather than the characteristic features of the social services, I do not propose to go into these features in any detail, but a few words of introduction might be appropriate to clarify what the terms refer to.

Social security generally refers to the system of benefits for income maintenance. The term is sometimes confined to a particular pattern of benefit: in both the US and in European Union law, 'social security' largely refers to benefits for which insurance contributions have been paid, sometimes including health care insurance. But there are many other types of benefit, including means-tested benefits – given to people whose income or wealth falls below a certain level; universal benefits, given for everyone in a particular category like children or old people; discretionary benefits, which usually depend on assessment by a caseworker; and other non-contributory benefits, like benefits for disabled people which have a test of needs but not of contribution or of means. Tax reliefs and tax credits can be difficult to distinguish from other forms of cash benefit. Social security means that people are given money to spend, rather than goods or 'benefits in kind', but at times the distinctions are blurred: in the US, food stamps (now usually represented in the form of electronic benefit cards) are supposed to be limited in their use, while Medicaid is a means-tested benefit for health care.

Health services are something of a misnomer; the term usually refers to medical care and related services. (There are many other ways of protecting people's health, of which the most important are protection of food, water supplies, sewerage, drainage and decent housing; and 'public health', sometimes referred to as 'environmental health', is a major service speciality in its own right.) It is possible to distinguish between care given by doctors and by professions ancillary to medicine, like pharmacy and dentistry, but the dominance of the medical profession is so complete that the distinction helps very little; for practical purposes, the main distinction in the kinds of services which are offered lies between care in hospitals and primary or 'ambulatory' care. In many countries, like France, Germany, or the US, medical care is primarily provided for through the mechanism of insurance; payments for insurers are used to cover people when they are sick. That tends to imply a two or three-tier system where some people will pay privately or draw on funds, some will be covered by insurance contributions, and some will receive means-tested assistance. Some other countries, including Britain, Italy and Sweden, offer medical services without a test of contributions.

Education is unlike most of the other services in that it is likely to be genuinely comprehensive, and not just for those in 'need'; in most countries, it is accepted that everyone should have at least a basic education (a related issue is covered in Box 11.2). The process of education is chiefly identified with schooling, though in theory at least it extends far beyond this, being concerned with intellectual and social development. The main emphasis within this is on children, though there is scope for education for all. Education has been particularly significant as an instrument of social policy, in the sense not only of policies for welfare but also, because of its importance for personal and social development, in policies intended to change the structure of society. It has been used as a vehicle for other types of social policy – health, family policy, social security and employment strategy. Education provides a convenient basis for policy for children because of its universal coverage, the acceptance of responsibility for children's welfare, and because it has been easy to justify welfare measures in educational terms.

Housing is not universally recognised as a social service, because for most people it is provided through the private market. Part of the argument for treating it in these terms is that housing is essential to people's welfare; but the same argument could be applied to food or clothing. The reason, historically, that housing came to be treated as a social service was, in the UK, the slow realisation that the private market could not cope with the problems of public health caused by industrialisation, and elsewhere in Europe the need for reconstruction in the period after the war. As housing conditions have improved, the emphasis in social housing has shifted more towards people who are unable to secure adequate housing in the private market – homeless people, those with special needs, and those in deprived areas. This also means that the concerns of housing policy, and sometimes the methods of work, are like those of other social services.

The 'personal social services' make an odd category. The term came into use in the 1960s to describe the range of social care available outside health, education and social security to deal with people's personal needs. It includes a range of services which might or might not be included in the remit of other services: residential care, for people who have support in specialised accommodation; domiciliary care, for people who receive support or assistance in their own homes; day care, providing services for groups (like old people or people with intellectual disabilities) who can receive support or assistance on an ambulatory basis; and work in specialised settings, like courts, prisons, schools, or hospitals. This is not a particularly distinct or coherent grouping; the services have developed piecemeal as a category of services not provided by other means. There are two main principles of operation. The first is 'social work'. Social workers offer people a range of services which depend on personal contact, including counselling, help with problem-solving, emotional support, therapy, 'brokerage' – acting as an intermediary with others – and advocacy. (Social casework was outlined in Box 4.2). The second is the provision of support and practical assistance to people who have special needs, to make it possible for them to live in their own homes or as 'normal' an environment as possible. This used to be called 'community care' in Britain, though it is not confined to 'the community'; it is more often referred to now as 'social care'.

On occasions the list is extended to include other services, like employment, advice services and policing, but there is no consistent usage. The kinds of activity which are described as 'social services' vary from one country to another. For example, 'social work' does not mean the same kind of activity in different countries (in France there is a range of different professions doing related but often different things); health is not necessarily thought of as a social service (although even in the US, publicly provided services at both federal and State level make up a major part of the pattern of health care); and housing is often left substantially to the private market. Conversely, there are collective activities which in other countries might be thought of as 'social services', such as employment, cultural activities or food distribution. Other services are potentially important, like those covering industrial relations or fuel, but they are more often examined from the viewpoint of particular academic disciplines, perhaps because they do not relate very directly to the other social services. Some other services, like funeral provision or libraries, are not much studied in the field. Areas which are important for society as a whole, like cultural activities or public transport, are more likely to be thought of as public services than social services, but much of what I have written about services and policy in general will apply equally to them.

Comparing policies

When policy-makers or service administrators are trying to review the options for policy, a common first step is to examine what other people have done. Innovation is difficult, often expensive, and fraught with problems; if someone else has worked out how things can be done, it saves considerable time and effort. Major developments, like Bismarck's social insurance scheme or the growth of high-rise housing, were influential because once they were established in some places they offered, or seemed to offer, practical solutions to complex problems in others. Policy transfer tends to be complex, with multiple actors, multiple sources of information and different interpretations of just what is being transferred.[332] In practice, policy transfer tends to be a hit-and-miss affair; the policies that are examined tend to depend on unsystematic approaches, some selective, some pick-and mix,[333] often influenced by opportunities for foreign travel.[334]

The existence of a policy, programme or approach in another country shows at least that the policy is feasible. Several texts in comparative social policy rely mainly on the description of the range of benefits or services provided in different countries, and a number focus on particular services (for example, on social security, child protection or health care finance). Mitchell has identified five approaches to the comparison of welfare in different countries.[335]

- *Comparing explicit policy* The first approach is to compare welfare provision in terms of the explicit terms in which actions are taken. Flora and Heidenheimer review the historical development of welfare in Europe and America. They find that welfare often develops on similar lines, and that it is possible to chart the growth of certain systems – like protection for industrial injury and social insurance – as following certain well-worn paths.[336]

---

[332] D Dolowitz, D Marsh, 2000, Learning from abroad: the role of policy transfer in contemporary policy making, *Governance* 13(1) 5–24.

[333] P Dwyer, N Ellison, 2009, 'We nicked stuff from all over the place': policy transfer or muddling through?, *Policy & Politics*, 37(3) 389–407.

[334] S Ettelt, N Mays, E Nolte, 2012, Policy learning from abroad: why it is more difficult than it seems, *Policy & Politics* 40(4) 491–504.

[335] D Mitchell, 1992, Welfare states and welfare outcomes in the 1980s, paper presented to a conference at the University of York, Social Security 50 Years After Beveridge.

[336] P Flora, A Heidenheimer, 1982, *The development of welfare states in Europe and America*, New York: Transaction Books.

- *Comparing inputs* Inputs are the resources which go into welfare provision. Castles' comparisons of welfare in OECD countries depend primarily on expenditure. [337]
- *Comparing production* The third approach is concerned with the production of welfare – the rules and structures through which services operate. Esping-Andersen defines the positions adopted by different welfare states through evidence on the organisation and delivery of specific services – for example, whether or not benefits are means tested, or whether they are given by discretion or as of right – as the basis for an overall assessment of the characteristics of different welfare systems. For example, he analyses pensions for

> degree of program corporatism (number of status-defined separate pension plans); the étatist bias (expenditure on civil service pensions as a percentage of GDP); the relative importance of private-sector pensions (individual and occupational pension expenditures as a percentage of total pension spending); and what might be called the social security bias (proportion of total pension spending that is neither private nor civil service).[338]

The detailed work in this can be criticised, because he lets a very limited range of indicators determine his classifications,[339] but the basic principle behind it is still important – that the way in which things are done matters in its own right, and is probably the best way of representing the effects of different principles in practice.
- *Comparing operations* Comparisons can be made of the detailed operation of benefits and services – what they do, how they are paid for, and who runs them.
- *Comparing outcomes* The case can be made that what matters about welfare is not what is intended, nor what the process is, but whether or not people benefit from it. Social security policy, for

[337] F Castles, 2004, The future of the welfare state, Oxford: Oxford University Press; F Castles, 2005, Social expenditure in the 1990s, *Policy & Politics* 33(3) pp 411–430.

[338] G Esping-Andersen, 1990, *The three worlds of welfare capitalism*, Cambridge: Polity, p.113.

[339] D Mabbett, H Bolderson, 1999, Theories and methods in comparative social policy, in J Clasen (ed) *Comparative social policy: concepts, theories and methods*, Oxford: Blackwell.

example, has been greatly concerned with the delivery of benefits, and in particular whether benefits are means-tested or not;[340] but there have been arguments for a different kind of assessment. The idea of the income 'package' has been developed to judge whether or not social security is effective; what matters in the package is not so much how it is delivered as whether it reaches the people who need it, and whether it is adequate.[341] This is the basis of the work done by the Luxembourg Income Study in assessing and comparing social security systems in different countries.[342]

These approaches are not completely distinct, and there is no reason why they should not be tackled simultaneously, but they do represent different kinds of emphasis, and they suggest different ways of understanding policy.

Comparisons of this type can be very useful for those looking for new ideas and approaches, but there are important pitfalls. Finding appropriate data for comparisons is not easy. Leichter points to five problems:

1. Policy measures are not directly comparable.
2. Some countries falsify their data.
3. There are peculiarities in the way that data are collected in different countries.
4. Often spending is unreported or hidden. Because of the different distribution of public, private, voluntary and informal welfare in different countries, not everything is likely to be counted.
5. There is variation in the cost of goods and services which makes it difficult to compare inputs.[343]

Some of these problems point to the difficulty of understanding services and policies in different countries. Understanding the operation of maternity benefits, for example, requires more than a comparison of rates and conditions. The benefits have to be set in the context of a

---

[340] see e.g. W van Oorschot, 1995, *Realizing rights*, Aldershot: Avebury.

[341] L Rainwater, M Rein, J Schwartz, 1986, *Income packaging in the welfare state*, Oxford: Oxford University Press.

[342] T Smeeding, M O'Higgins, L Rainwater, 1990, *Poverty, inequality and income distribution in comparative perspective*, Hemel Hempstead: Harvester Wheatsheaf; K Nelson, 2004, Mechanisms of povertyalleviation, Journal of European Social Policy 14(4) pp 371–390.

[343] H Leichter, *A comparative approach to policy analysis*, Cambridge: Cambridge University Press 1979.

range of services, including health services, ante-natal and post-natal care, and alternative benefits, before it is possible to work out what they are really worth. The role of the benefit depends on the conditions of the labour market, including the participation of women and the wages which the benefits replace. And it is difficult to understand the extent to which such benefits protect women or families without knowing the circumstances of families and the position of women.

It follows that this kind of material has to be understood in its context. The effect of treating welfare policies in isolation can be fundamentally misleading as to their potential effects. An adequate base for comparison cannot afford to stop with the operation of services themselves, and a full understanding of welfare systems calls for much more than an understanding of processes and procedures.

ISSUE FOR DISCUSSION

Policy is sometimes represented in terms of what is not done, as well as what is. If a government does not deal with child abuse, or deals with it only in part, is it still responsible for what happens?

CHAPTER 8

Welfare states

The welfare states
Influences on development
Models of welfare
Welfare régimes
Patterns in the development of welfare states
Explanations for development
Beyond the state: globalisation and social policy

The welfare states

The idea of the welfare state is ambiguous. In some writing, it means little more than 'welfare which is provided by the state'; in others, it stands for a developed ideal in which welfare is provided comprehensively to the best possible standards. The term is not, then, just a description of the way in which welfare is organised; it is also a normative concept. The discourse has its origins in Germany, where it came to mean 'The idea that the State should not merely protect the persons and property of citizens(s), but should also endeavour to promote their welfare a model by some more positive action or interference on their behalf.'[344] The normative literature has tended, however, to concentrate on the experience of the United Kingdom, where the 'welfare state' was introduced as a conscious attempt to set welfare provision on a new footing.[345] The Beveridge report in the UK referred to the 'five giants' of Want, Idleness, Ignorance, Squalor and Disease.[346] Though that looks in retrospect like a rhetorical flourish, it caught the popular imagination at the time. The 'welfare state' – not a term which Beveridge himself had used – came to encapsulate the kind of social change which Beveridge was arguing for. It represented an ideal, in which everyone would be able to receive services as a

---

[344] Cohn et al 1894, cited in K Petersen, J-H Petersen, 2013, Confusion and divergence: origins and meaning of the term 'Welfare State' in Germany and Britain 1840–1940, *Journal of European Social Policy* 23(1) 37–51, p 47.

[345] A Briggs, 1961, The welfare state in historical perspective, *European Journal of Sociology* 2 pp 221–58.

[346] Beveridge Report, 1942, *Social Insurance and Allied Services*, Cmd 6404, London: HMSO.

right. In the UK, this was understood by contrast with the Poor Law, which had confined support to those who were destitute, sought to distinguish the position of paupers from workers, and made the services as unpleasant as possible.[347] These principles influenced thinking even in countries which did not have the English Poor Law, including the US and Australia. The welfare state was distinguished from the Poor Law by offering the protection of services to everyone, not just to the poor.

Beveridge's influence was not confined to the UK. His report came in many ways to represent the future the Allies were fighting for; the report influenced both governments in exile in Britain and resistance groups in occupied territory,[348] and it is still referred to in France and Belgium as the basis for their systems of social security – however different they are from the system in the UK. To that extent, the importance of the report, and the idea of the welfare state, was symbolic. When, after the war, the British welfare state was introduced by the Labour government, they took pains to make sure that the main legislation came into force together on the same day, 5th July 1948. It was a way of marking a new beginning.

There are dangers in centring too closely on the experience of one nation. The European welfare states built on a different foundation. The most important models were based on social insurance, which had developed from systems of mutual aid. The German approach, largely based on the lines set up by Bismarck, tied social insurance closely to the labour market, seeing the route to prosperity mainly in terms of participation in the economy.[349] In France, solidarity was taken as the model for further development, with the main aim of policy being to extend solidarity as far as possible.[350] Both these approaches built directly on pre-war experience. At the same time, both had to develop when European countries were engaged in the process of reconstruction, and it has become difficult to distinguish the resulting emphasis on social protection and collective solidarity from the idea of the welfare state in Europe.

---

[347] S Checkland, O Checkland (eds), 1974, *The Poor Law report of 1834*, Harmondsworth: Penguin.

[348] J J Dupeyroux, 1966, *Evolution et tendances des systèmes de sécurité sociale des pays membres des communautés européennes et de la Grande-Bretagne*, Luxembourg: Communauté Européenne du Charbon et de L'Acier.

[349] G Rimlinger, 1971, *Welfare policy and industrialisation in Europe, America and Russia*, New York: Wiley ch 5.

[350] P Spicker, 2002, France, in J Dixon, R Scheurell (eds) *The State of Social Welfare: the twentieth century in cross-national review*, Westport, CT: Praeger, pp 109–124.

T H Marshall argued that the welfare state represented in the twentieth century an extension of the rights of citizenship which had been established in the period following the French Revolution. In the eighteenth century, the rights which were established were civil; in the nineteenth century, political; in the twentieth, social.[351] That was not the pattern everywhere. In much of Europe social rights preceded civil or political ones, and the central development was not down to government. Welfare states developed in Europe through the coming to maturity of the patterns of mutual support and collective action pioneered by guilds, trades unions and friendly societies.[352] In many 'welfare states', the provision of welfare is not actually made by the state. Differences in approach do not seem, however, to undermine the basic principles, and reference to social rights remains one of the main tests by which welfare states might be identified.

Influences on development

The development of welfare in different countries reflects a range of influences. The dynamics of change may stem from the internal situation of a country; they might reflect, no less, external factors.

Internal influences Catherine Jones identifies the social and economic conditions of a country as the 'raw material' on which social policy builds. Social factors include the social structure, elements of social division (like class, gender and racial inequality), and also the demographic structure – that is, the age and distribution of the population, the number of children and old people, family composition and so on. Economic development provides the resources on which welfare services are founded, and further shapes social conditions, like urbanisation and work relationships, in which welfare states operate.

Several reactions are possible. Responses – the policies which are developed – depend crucially on constitutional development and political organisation, which provide the mechanisms through which welfare services are then developed. An understanding of responses is based partly on identifying ideologies, and partly on the political process, through which conflicting interests are mediated. There are important cultural influences; religious influences, for example, have played a considerable historical role.

---

[351] T H Marshall, 1982, *The right to welfare*, London: Heinemann.

[352] P Baldwin, 1990, *The politics of social solidarity*, Cambridge: Cambridge University Press.

Finally, Jones points to results. Social policy affects the social and economic conditions which it is developed to respond to, and there is a constant interaction between these its effects and the 'raw material' on which policy is based.[353]

External influences Welfare states cannot be seen in isolation; the social and economic conditions of one country are often linked with those of another. There may be a common history or geography; countries may be linked by their experience of colonial influence. War (which Titmuss identified as a major influence on social policy[354]) is often a common influence. There may be common cultural influences. External cultural influences can be difficult to identify directly, because they often mirror historical trends – linguistic differences, for example, reflect former patterns of influence – and it is difficult to separate them. Religious influence often developed regionally; the difference between Scandinavia, central Europe and the periphery is reflected in the distribution of Lutheran, Catholic, and Calvinist Christianity.

In an attempt to identify the relative importance of different influences, Wilensky has examined the pattern of expenditure on social security in different countries, relating this pattern to political and social influences. The number of old people is probably the greatest single influence on expenditure, but Wilensky also points to some interesting trends. First, more is spent in systems which were developed earlier; there seems to be a constant pressure to improve benefits. The second concerns the influence of politics; Wilensky finds that since politics often follow the wealth of a country, welfare spending is better explained as a product of resources than it is of political ideals.[355] Castles and McKinlay argue, however, that the political situation most likely to lead to increased welfare spending is where a left-wing government is faced with an active right-wing opposition;[356] and Castle's later work suggests that there are marked differences arising through policy choices.[357]

---

[353] C Jones, 1986, *Patterns of social policy,* London: Tavistock.

[354] R Titmuss, War and social policy, in *Essays on 'the welfare state',* London: Allen and Unwin 1963, ch 3.

[355] H Wilensky, 1975, *The welfare state and equality,* Berkeley: University of California Press.

[356] F Castles, R McKinlay, 1979, Public welfare provision, Scandinavia and the sheer futility of the sociological approach to politics, *British Journal of Political Science* 9.

[357] F Castles, 2005, Social expenditure in the 1990s, *Policy & Politics* 33(3) pp 411–430.

Wilensky's findings are intriguing, but they are open to other interpretations: it has been found, using the same figures, that welfare spending is directly related to how close a country is to Vienna.[358] This is not as strange a finding as it sounds at first: Vienna had claims, at the turn of the century, to be the cultural capital of Europe, and it is possible that the finding probably reflects cultural diffusion. This, in turn, reflects the historical development of welfare in Europe, including patterns of religious influence and the impact of war. In more recent work, Schmitt and Obinger have attempted to trace the influence of neighbouring countries, looking at both geographical and cultural proximity. There is evidence that countries are influenced by what their neighbours do, but it varies with the field of activity and over time.[359]

Welfare in different countries develops through a range of influences and events. Countries which are geographically close to each other often share important links; they adopt similar policies through common historical strands, cultural diffusion (for example, shared religion and shared language), and sometimes direct imitation. The grouping of countries is not just descriptive; they have enough in common to associate particular kinds of principle or ways of operating with the different countries. There is a case for identifying welfare states, not in terms of a particular ideal type, but rather by their resemblance to other states which we think of in the same terms.[360] One of the main justifications for this approach is not simply that they bear some similarities to each other, but that there are underlying relationships which lead to them forming identifiable clusters.

'Black swans' In political science some writers have suggested that policy in any case proceeds in fits and starts – a process of 'punctuated equilibrium',[361] where blocks and veto points slow down responses until there is an opening, and there is a sudden flurry of activity. This, Jensen suggests, is a typical pattern of development in social policy; his evidence is drawn from pensions and unemployment insurance.[362]

---

[358] J Barnes, T Srivenkatamarana, 1982, Ideology and the welfare state, *Social Service Review* 56(2) 230–246.

[359] C Schmitt, H Obinger, 2013, Spatial interdependencies and welfare state generosity in Western democracies 1960–2000, *Journal of European Social Policy* 23(2) 119–133.

[360] P Spicker, 2000, *The welfare state: a general theory*, London: Sage.

[361] P Sabatier (ed), 1999, *Theories of the policy process*, Boulder Colorado: Westview

[362] C Jensen, 2009, Policy punctuations in mature welfare states, *Journal of Public Policy*, 29(3) 287–303.

Frank Castles, however, adds an important cautionary note. The events and issues which shape welfare states are often extraordinary – war, depression, hyperinflation, environmental catastrophes, and so on. While it is tempting to rationalise the influences after the event, the ways in which different countries respond are diverse and hard to classify. That also means that it is difficult to anticipate the likely effects of such events in the future.[363]

Models of welfare

The most fundamental conceptual distinction in the discussion of welfare régimes reflects an historical development – the transition from the English Poor Law (see Box 9.2) to the Welfare State. Wilensky and Lebeaux expressed this in terms of *residual* and *institutional* models of welfare.[364] A *residual* model of welfare is one where welfare is seen as a 'safety net'. In normal circumstances, people should not have to depend on collective welfare provision; what happens, instead, is that they live on their own or their family's resources, and the only people who need to claim welfare will be those who are unable, for whatever reason, to manage on these resources. Welfare in these circumstances is described as 'residual' because it is for those who are left out. The *institutional* model of welfare is one where need and dependency are accepted as normal in society, or 'institutionalised'. Richard Titmuss argued that the 'states of dependency' which people experienced had to be accepted as a normal part of social life. We are all children at some stage, we are all likely to be sick, or to be old; an institutional system is one which recognises social responsibility for these needs and makes general provision accordingly. The residual model of welfare leaves social protection, in most cases, to the resources of the individual; the institutional model is based in acceptance of social responsibility for socially induced conditions of dependency.

Titmuss later fleshed out the distinction between residual and institutional into three models of welfare: residual, institutional-redistributive, and 'industrial-achievement/performance'.[365] The *residual* model remains much the same. The *institutional-redistributive* model of welfare adds 'redistribution', concerned to equalise resources

---

[363] F Castles, 2010, Black swans and elephants on the move, *Journal of European Social Policy*, 20(2) 92–101.

[364] H Wilensky, C Lebeaux, 1965, *Industrial society and social welfare*, New York: Free Press.

[365] R M Titmuss, 1974, *Social policy: an introduction*, London: Allen and Unwin.

between people, to institutional principles. (The institutional redistributive elements are separable in theory, and some writers, like Mishra, use them as the basis for distinct models.[366]) The *industrial-achievement/performance* model was least worked out in Titmuss's scheme. Some social policies could be seen as a way of supporting economic development; education, for example, can be seen as preparing children for work, health care as a way of maintaining the workforce. Probably the best example is the Bismarckian system of social insurance, which ties benefits to contributions in such a way as to reward work effort closely.[367]

Titmuss's models have been a central starting point for much of the work on modelling welfare régimes. Palme's classification is used as a means of classifying different patterns of pensions provision. He identifies pensions as 'institutional', covering needs with a degree of redistribution, 'residual', covering only minimal needs, 'work-merit', in which rewards are geared to occupational status, and 'citizenship', which offers basic security to everyone.[368] Some other work seeks to characterise this kind of division in terms of political opinions. Mishra, for example, distinguishes capitalist and socialist approaches.[369] Esping-Andersen, in probably the best-known classification of models, defines 'capitalist' régimes as 'liberal', 'corporatist' and 'social democratic'[370] – moving from the least to the most committed position in relation to welfare, but still closely related to the residual, industrial achievement/ performance and institutional redistributive models. The models here seem to move from 'right' to 'left', across a familiar political spectrum. At one end, the 'residual' or liberal view can be taken to limit the scope of welfare, while at the other the 'socialist' model guarantees welfare to all as of right. Pinker challenges that kind of divide: he examines collectivism as a model distinct from capitalism or socialism, arguing that the 'welfare states' offer a distinctly different approach to welfare.[371]

The core problem with models of this kind is that they assume connections which may or may not reflect the way that policies work in practice. Titmuss suggests there is a link between institutional welfare

[366] R Mishra, 1981, *Society and social policy*, London: Macmillan.

[367] J Clasen, R Freeman (ed) 1994, *Social policy in Germany*, Harvester Wheatsheaf.

[368] J Palme, 1990, Models of old-age pensions, in A Ware, R Goodin (eds) *Needs and welfare*, London: Sage.

[369] Mishra 1981.

[370] G Esping-Andersen 1990, *The three worlds of welfare capitalism*, Brighton: Polity.

[371] R Pinker, 1979, *The idea of welfare*, London: Heinemann.

and egalitarian redistribution; Mishra, between collective solidarity and comprehensiveness; and Palme, between rewards in the economic market and rewards in the welfare system. The links are often tenuous. Welfare in different countries draws on several different principles and approaches simultaneously, leading to 'mixed' or 'hybrid' systems;[372] in others, there may be no guiding principles at all; and in others again, there is a principle which argues for diversity as something valuable in itself.

Welfare régimes

The models of welfare considered so far are largely based in ideal types, or at least in normative understandings of welfare. The most widely cited presentation has been the work of Esping-Andersen.[373] The main difference between his approach and the other models considered in the previous section is that his analysis and classification of welfare régimes is based on empirical evidence. However, the same evidence can be interpreted in many different ways. Leibfried, for example, describes four characteristic welfare régimes in developed countries (his focus is mainly, but not exclusively, European). These are

- the Scandinavian welfare states, mainly represented by Sweden, Norway, Denmark and Finland, where welfare is most highly developed;
- the 'Bismarck' countries, Germany and Austria, which in his view offer 'institutional' welfare;
- the Anglo-Saxon countries, which include the UK, US, Australia, New Zealand, which he sees as 'residual'; and
- the 'Latin Rim', covering Spain, Portugal, Greece, Italy and perhaps France, where welfare is 'rudimentary'.[374]

As the structure of welfare in different countries, is considered, it becomes more difficult to identify them in terms of Esping-Andersen's régimes. There have been complaints that Esping-Andersen's scheme does not adequately deal with differences between groups of

---

[372] D Bannink, M Hogenboom, 2007, Hidden change, *Journal of European Social Policy* 17(1) 19–32.

[373] G Esping-Andersen 1990, *The three worlds of welfare capitalism*, Brighton: Polity.

[374] S Leibfried, 1991, *Towards a European welfare state?*, Bremen: Zentrum für Sozialpolitik.

countries,[375] that it ignores significant dimensions like gender,[376] and that attempts to apply it to specific aspects of welfare systems tend to founder.[377]

There is much to criticise in the discussion of welfare systems in these terms. They rely on a high level of generalisation; the criteria (like 'institutional' or 'corporatism') are often vague; there are considerable variations within systems; there are different interpretations within countries about what is significant; and they tend to say little about the specifics of policy.[378] As the differences between régimes are examined in more detail, the number and range of models needed to describe them starts to proliferate. Ditch comments: 'The devil is in the detail.'[379]

Most existing attempts to classify welfare states over-simplify, or finish with something of a jumble – which leads Mabbett and Bolderson to conclude that the systems simply cannot be classified.[380] Castles disaggregates spending on welfare into four categories – spending on older people, on people of working age, on health care and other spending – and finds that they are almost completely unrelated to each other.[381] The main justification for continuing with the discussion of 'welfare régimes' is not that it describes what is being done – a much more detailed account is needed for that – but that it helps us to explain why things are done the way they are. The classification of systems is a way of making sense of information that can otherwise seem disconnected and disorderly, and for that reason it has become an important contribution to understanding social policy.

---

[375] W Arts, J Gelissen, 2002, Three worlds of welfare capitalism or more?, *Journal of European Social Policy* 12(2) pp 137–58.

[376] D Sainsbury, 2001, Gendering dimensions of welfare states, in J Fink, G Lewis, J Clarke (eds) *Rethinking European welfare*, London: Sage.

[377] e.g. H Bolderson, D Mabbett, 1995, Mongrels or thoroughbreds: a cross-national look at social security systems, *European Journal of Political Research* vol 28 no 1 119–139; C Bambra, 2005, Cash versus services, *Journal of Social Policy* 34(2) pp 195–213; and see M Powell, A Barrientos, 2011, An audit of the welfare modelling business, *Social Policy and Administration*, 45(1) 69–84.

[378] P Spicker, 1996, Normative comparisons of social security systems, in L Hantrais, S Mangen (eds) *Cross-national research methods in the social sciences*, London: Pinter, pp.66–75.

[379] J Ditch, 1999, Full circle: a second coming for social assistance?, in J Clasen (ed) *Comparative social policy*, Oxford: Blackwell.

[380] D Mabbett, H Bolderson, H 1999, Theories and methods in comparative social policy, in J Clasen (ed) *Comparative social policy: concepts, theories and methods*, Oxford: Blackwell.

[381] F Castles, 2009, What welfare states do, *Journal of Social Policy* 38(1) 45–62.

Patterns in the development of welfare states

Convergence theory Many industrial countries, despite their considerable differences, often seem to follow surprisingly similar paths – which suggests that the impact of ideas, culture or history is relatively limited. This trend is referred to in the literature on comparative social policy as 'convergence'. There are several reasons for convergence:

- *Common problems* Industrialisation is a process which all developed countries have had to go through, and they face common sets of problems in consequence. At the outset, the main issues often concerned the protection of workers, housing, and the urban environment; in more developed countries, nearly all now have ageing populations and falling birth-rates, which means that there are more old people and progressively fewer workers replacing them. This has major implications for health and social security policies. Economic events, similarly, can exert common pressures: a report for the European Commission suggests that 'the recent crisis has speeded up the convergence of the size of social protection expenditure relative to GDP in the EU.'[382]
- *Common approaches* People in different countries and cultures can come to share common approaches through the process of 'cultural diffusion'. In the European Union, the term 'convergence' is principally used to refer to a process of agreeing common values.[344]

  Helgøy and Homme argue that ideologies may diverge even where policy instruments are apparently similar. In the case of education, Britain, Norway and Sweden have used increasingly similar methods for regulation and accountability, but in the UK they have been used to reinforce liberal and elitist models of education, while in Norway and Sweden they have been used to emphasise equality and inclusiveness.[383]
- *Common methods* The way welfare is delivered depends on the methods which are available at any point in time – a point which is sometimes referred to as 'technological determinism'. The dominance of the western model of medicine, for example, has

---

[382] European Commission, 2012, *Employment and social developments in Europe 2012*, Luxembourg: Publications Office of the European Union, http://ec.europa.eu/social/BlobServlet?docId=9604&langId=en, p 199.

[383] I Helgøy, A Homme, 2006, Policy tools and institutional change, *Journal of Public Policy* 26(2) pp 141–165.

led to very similar patterns of hospital organisation, while shared understandings about management have implied similar kinds of service response.[384]

- *Common policy* Countries imitate each other: national insurance in the UK was influenced by national insurance in Germany, while the Beveridge report in Britain became a blueprint not only for the UK government but for European governments in exile.

The empirical evidence about convergence is uncertain. Starke and his colleagues report that while there is some support for the idea that developed countries are becoming more alike, it is limited and not consistently true in different fields of activity.[385]

The welfare state in crisis An alternative account of common trends stresses the 'crisis' of welfare states. Pierson points to four main uses of the idea of a 'crisis'.

- *Crisis as turning point* A crisis can be seen as a period when long-standing problems become particularly severe or aggravated.
- *Crisis as external shock* This can include war and problems in the international economy, like the 'oil crisis' of the 1970s.
- *Crisis as long-standing contradiction* This reflects the concern of Marxists with continuing pressures on the system.
- *Crisis as any large-scale problem.*[386]

Marxists have argued that capitalism must come to an inevitable crisis. Marx had argued that capitalism was intrinsically unstable, and that it must inevitably drive the workers down into such unspeakable misery that they had to revolt. His initial predictions proved to be fairly unsuccessful – later revisions of Marx's analysis, for example by Lenin, offered alternative scenarios – but the idea that there must be such a 'crisis' remained an important element in Marxism, and re-interpretations have continued to emphasise, in different ways, the instability of the financial and industrial system. O'Connor argues that the central threat to capitalism is now a 'fiscal crisis' generated because of the expenditure required for the provision of welfare.[387] Habermas

---

[384] S Uttley, 1988, Technology and the welfare state, London: Unwin Hyman.
[385] P Starke, H Obinger, F Castles, 2008, Convergence towards where?, *Journal of European Public Policy* 15(7) 975–1000.
[386] C Pierson, 2006, *Beyond the welfare state?*, Brighton: Polity, p.145.
[387] J O'Connor, 1973, *The fiscal crisis of the state*, New York: St Martin's Press.

has given this argument its most authoritative form. He writes that capitalism, in order to thrive, needs both to create the conditions in which capital can be accumulated, and to legitimate its actions, through public activities like the welfare state. The cost of legitimation had grown beyond the ability of the industrial system to pay for it, creating a 'legitimation crisis'.[388]

The neo-Marxist argument is reflected in the criticisms of the 'new right', who have also been sceptical of the ability of the industrial system to pay for welfare provision. Bacon and Eltis argued in the 1970s that expenditure on welfare and the public sector has 'crowded out' the expenditure necessary for the productive private sector to flourish.[389] That argument has been revived recently under the mask of 'austerity', but the terms are not equivalent; austerity is about managing with a minimal amount, and transferring responsibility to the private sector is not the same thing. There is little reason to suppose that reducing the size of the public sector does anything to stimulate the economy, and much evidence against it. In the short run, reducing expenditure simply reduces economic activity. In the longer run, there is no direct relationship between public expenditure and the economy; if anything, welfare expenditure tends to be positively, not negatively, associated with a better developed economy (see Box 8.1). There is some reason to believe that the arguments about the 'crisis' of welfare have been at best exaggerated, and at worst misconceived.[390]

Box 8.1: A public burden?

One of the criticisms most frequently made of welfare states is that the effect of providing for social welfare is to hold back the development of the economy. The arguments take three main forms:

- expenditure on welfare imposes high costs. It demands high taxation, reducing incentives to generate wealth, and high labour costs, which reduce the competitiveness of industry, limiting economic growth;
- social protection systems lead to inflexible labour markets, reducing the mobility of labour and leading to unemployment;
- money spent on public activity inhibits the development of the productive, private sector which is essential to economic development.

---

[388] J Habermas, 1976, *Legitimation crisis*, London: Heinemann.

[389] R Bacon, W Eltis, 1978, *Britain's economic problem*, London: Macmillan.

[390] C Pierson, 2006, ch.5; R Klein, 1993, 'O'Goffe's tale', in C Jones (ed), *New perspectives on the welfare state in Europe*, London: Routledge.

These objections were widely made through the revival of the 'New Right' in the 1970s and subsequently in doctrines favoured by the US government under Reagan, the UK government under Thatcher, and the policies of the IMF and World Bank.

These propositions are all subject to question. In relation to the first, welfare in many European countries has developed through contributions rather than state taxation; the association of welfare with taxation is indirect. There is no evidence to show that high taxation limits wealth generation; high taxation is only possible in countries which have higher incomes, such as those in Scandinavia, and countries with higher incomes are generally those which are more economically successful. There is also a confusion in the criticisms between taxation and expenditure. Much of the money used in welfare systems is not 'spent', but transferred – for example, expenditure on pensions is based on a transfer from the working population to the non-working population. Transfer payments are economically neutral, unless the behaviour of the recipient population is different from that of the taxpayer; there is an argument to say that poorer people are more likely to spend, and so that transfers increase economic activity.

In relation to the second, unemployment is primarily conditioned by the state of the economy and the structure of the labour market, which is why it varies markedly when social protection systems stay the same. The unemployment of the 1930s was not created by the social security system, and the full employment of the 1950s and 60s was not prevented by it. As for the third, the idea, that the private sector is productive when the public sector is not, is largely based on ideological prejudice. If expenditure on medical services is in the private sector, it does not implicitly become more 'productive' than if it occurs in the public sector.

The theoretical arguments are not conclusive in either direction. Nor is the empirical evidence. Richer countries tend to spend more on welfare than poorer countries, proportionately as well as absolutely, but they have more to spend. Most of the discussion tends to focus on a limited number of wealthy countries in the OECD; the relationship between welfare spending and national income is shown in Figure 8.1. Because the numbers of countries are limited, the validity of statistical analyses is questionable: many studies, including studies in prestigious, peer-reviewed academic journals, are blighted by common source bias (repeated reference to the same source of information, difficult to avoid when the common source is a country with a uniform national policy) or multicollinearity (variables that are not truly independent). The comparisons are vulnerable to selective interpretation, and indeed to manipulation; leaving some countries out of the statistical process can have a major effect in altering the results. If the figures exclude the former eastern bloc, it looks as if economic performance increases with welfare expenditure; leaving out the less populous countries of Northern and Central Europe can give the impression that economic performance declines with increased spending. As the economist Ronald Coase once wrote: 'If you torture the data long enough, it will confess.' Looked at dispassionately, there is no consistent relationship between welfare expenditure and economic performance,[391] and conversely no clear indication that the welfare state either benefits economies or imposes unsustainable levels of expenditure on developed economies.[392]

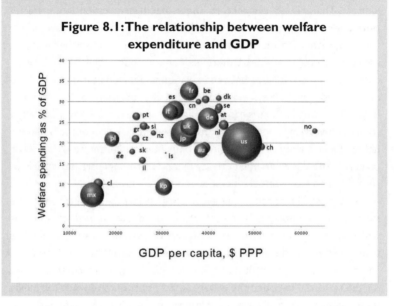

Figure 8.1: The relationship between welfare expenditure and GDP

Periods of development Although they seem to offer conflicting accounts of welfare, convergence and crisis theory are not directly contradictory; both are based on the idea that the welfare state represents, not historical accident, but rather the outcome of a set of social processes associated with industrialisation and economic development. It used to be fashionable to describe these processes in terms of 'periods' of development. One attempt to represent this kind of development schematically was made by Flora and Heidenheimer.[393] They described four stages which welfare states have undergone:

---

[391] See A B Atkinson, 1995, The welfare state and economic performance, in *Incomes and the welfare state*, Cambridge: Cambridge University Press, ch 6.

[392] C Pierson, 2006, *Beyond the welfare state?*, Brighton: Polity.

[393] P Flora, A Heidenheimer, 1981, *The development of welfare states in Europe and America*, New Brunswick: Transaction Books.

- *Experimentation* (1870s–1920s) This period was characterised by industrialisation, policy innovations which attempt to reconcile conflicting political viewpoints, and the gradual introduction of social insurance arrangements.
- *Consolidation* (1930s–1940s) A period of depression, followed by the experience of total war, led to a consensus on the need for subsequent reconstruction.
- *Expansion* (1950s–1960s) Reconstruction, sustained economic growth and full employment led to increasing expectations as well as competition for a share in increased resources.
- *Reformulation* (1970s–date) The pressures of recession and inflation led to political disaffection, a slowing down of the rate of expansion and – largely occurring since the book was written – the 'backlash' associated with the political right.[394]

Carrier and Kendall advise caution about generalised models like this. Theories about the development of welfare states tend to be rather more systematic than the reality merits, and they tend to disguise considerable conflicts in the process of development. 'Periods' and 'turning points' are easily overemphasised; detailed study rarely supports the idea that there are distinct 'watersheds' or dividing lines. Development in practice tends to be piecemeal, and ideas and attitudes do not develop in clear stages.[395]

Explanations for development

The development of policy depends on factors which go beyond explicit policy or political ideas, and there are several competing explanations of the development of welfare states in these terms.

Ameliorism The first is the view that the development of the welfare state consists of a series of progressive improvements. This idea has been referred to by a variety of names – 'social reform', a manifestation of 'social conscience' or 'moral determinism' – but it is a very old idea, and I have used the old word for it. It depends on the view that social welfare is a response to social problems. What seems to happen is that a problem – like poverty, child abuse or bad housing – comes to

---

[394] H Glennerster, J Midgley (eds) 1991, *The radical right and the welfare state*, Hemel Hempstead: Harvester Wheatsheaf.
[395] J Carrier, I Kendall, 1977, The development of welfare states, *Journal of Social Policy* 6(3) pp 271–290.

public attention, and then something is done about it. In principle, if problems are gradually recognised and are responded to, things should get better over time.

This idea has been fairly comprehensively rejected in the modern literature, but before explaining why, it is important to explain why it should ever have been put forward. It contains a grain of truth. In most industrial countries, conditions in relation to children, old people, education and health care have fairly generally improved since 1900, and particularly since 1945; although there may have been setbacks it is not very convincing to suggest otherwise. At the same time, there are compelling reasons for making reservations about the position. It assumes a fairly constant environment: if the environment deteriorates then any amelioration that is due policy may not keep pace. (The main countries experiencing a deterioration in conditions are developing countries with a history of conflict or relatively uncontrolled urbanisation.) It relies strongly on a very simplistic view of the policy process, which does rather more than identifying and responding to problems. And it assumes that policies will have, overall, a beneficial effect; but the benefits of policies are often equivocal, or confined to one sector of the population at the expense of others.

Historicism A second view, no less commonly rejected, is the idea that there are certain 'movements' or trends in history which develop through their own inexorable logic. Karl Popper dubbed this approach 'historicism'.[396] Probably the most famous example has been Marxism: Marx argued that there were certain 'laws' which would lead capitalism inevitably to its destruction. This does not have to be taken too literally – if something is 'inevitable' there is not much which can be done about it. But lesser 'laws', or predictions about society, might be seen as an example of the same kind of argument – indeed, the arguments about the 'convergence' of welfare states are fairly typical of this approach. Similar arguments have been made in the social policy of developing countries – for example, the argument that social protection coverage is linked to the level of development,[397] or that growth leads initially to inequality before improving.[398] These ideas matter, because when people believe that certain social effects can only

---

[396] K Popper, 1986, *The poverty of historicism*, London: Ark.

[397] International Labour Organisation, 2013, Social Protection, www.ilo.org/global/about-the-ilo/decent-work-agenda/social-protection/lang--en/index.htm

[398] M Todaro, S Smith, 2006, *Economic development*, Harlow: Pearson, ch 5.

be achieved through particular routes, it affects the policy decisions they make. The central problem with identifying historical patterns is not that it cannot be done; it is that past trends are not very reliable as a means of predicting what is going to happen.

Functionalism In functionalist theory, a response is 'functional' when it serves a particular purpose, and 'dysfunctional' when it does not. Functionalists argue that things are done in particular ways because that is the way in which they work best; welfare develops, by this argument, by a process of innovation and selection into an effective set of programmes and services. This means, amongst other things, that the pattern of services is likely to reflect both demands for service and constraints on them; services have to adapt in order to continue to work. There is a link between functionalism and convergence theory, because convergence often presupposes the kind of adaptation which is part of functionalist theory.

There is some overlap between functionalist arguments and the belief in progress; indeed, functionalist arguments are often represented in the literature as conservative (because they approve of existing arrangements) and ameliorist (because they assume that changes are for the good). This is a misrepresentation; a functionalist can argue that patterns of activity are dysfunctional as well as functional, or that even if they serve some social purposes they can be morally unacceptable. An example can be found in the anti-fascist and anti-racist stance taken by Talcott Parsons.[399] In other words, social relationships and social policies can mutate under pressure into something which we might not like.

Conflict theory A fourth type of explanation, often linked with crisis theory but separable from it, sees the development of welfare as the outcome of a conflict between different power blocs in society. This position is most commonly associated with Marxism, but it should be noted that there are also Marxists (like Offe[400]) who see welfare in functionalist terms. Marxism is not one belief, but a whole set of different beliefs. These centre on the view that social relationships are shaped by the organisation of the capitalist economy, and that the provision of welfare necessarily reflects the structure of power. This can be taken to mean either that welfare is repressive, because it serves the

---

[399] T Parsons, 1969, *Politics and social structure*, New York: Free Press.
[400] C Offe, 1984, *Contradictions of the welfare state,* London: Hutchinson.

interests of the capitalist classes;[401] that welfare is a concession which has been won by the labour movement in conflict with the capitalist class;[402] or that social welfare reflects the contradictions and power struggles which occur elsewhere in society.[403]

Institutional approaches Social action is not always attributable to the interplay of social forces; there is also a role for agency, where people make decisions and change the world they live in. There have always been histories which explain the development of social policy as the outcome of coalitions of political interest, institutional factors and agency. There is a well-known tendency for social policy to get trapped on the tramlines, a problem often referred to as 'path dependency'; once policy has been started along a particular route, like insurance or state control, it can be difficult to stop.[404] But it is also clear that there are points at which decisions are made, where new policies are introduced, where policies change direction. The combination of institutional constraints, responding to circumstances and pressures, and agency is referred to as 'historical institutionalism'.[405]

Deconstructing development Lastly, it is worth making a sceptical note. Theories about society and social relationships have often been countered by the argument that such relationships are not 'real' in any sense; they are artificial constructs, developed by commentators and observers. The term most often used nowadays for this kind of scepticism is 'deconstruction', a word which sums up the idea of taking apart the constructs that people have built. The welfare state is not, by this account, a 'system' or social structure; it is just a name we have put on a jumble of assorted material. There are no 'trends', no laws, and no patterns except those we imagine are there. This kind of scepticism can be appealing, because it helps to raise very basic questions about the nature of what is being done in the name of welfare.

---

[401] P Day, 1981, *Social Work and social control*, London: Tavistock.

[402] J Saville, 1975, 'The welfare state: an historical approach', in E Butterworth, R Holman, *Social welfare in modern Britain*, Glasgow: Fontana.

[403] N Poulantzas, 1978, *State, power, socialism*, London: New Left Books.

[404] D Wilsford, 1995, Path Dependency, or why History makes it difficult but not impossible to reform health care systems in a big way, *Journal of Public Policy* 14(3) pp 251–283; contrast A Kay, 2005, A critique of the use of path dependency in policy studies, *Public Administration* 83(3) 553–571.

[405] D Béland, 2005, Ideas and social policy, *Social Policy and Administration* 39(1) pp 1–18.

The problem with all kinds of general theory is that they cannot tell us much about the way in which policy has developed in any particular country. To that extent, deconstruction is justified. But it is difficult to sustain the argument that there are no common patterns, and that no generalisations are possible; and the position is not very useful, because it leaves no basis on which to build an understanding of what is happening. Functionalism points to the relationships between society and social policy; conflict theory points to the role of power structures, and the question of whose interests policies serve. Knowing about such theories is helpful, because they point our attention towards issues which might otherwise be forgotten.

Box 8.2: Structural adjustment

Neo-liberal policies became prominent in the 1980s, notably in the USA, the UK and some other countries (such as Chile) dominated by the 'New Right'.[406] 'Reagonomics' and 'Thatcherism' (named for the leaders of the USA and UK) argued for liberal market policies, including laissez-faire – a reduction in government activity, and reliance on the market – and 'marketisation', developing and encouraging markets, privatising activities managed by government, and creating commodities and market mechanisms where they did not exist otherwise. Examples are markets for banking, energy, transport and social care.

These policies were exported to developing countries by the World Bank and the IMF. In the 1950s and 60s, governments around the world had been heavily engaged in economic development, partly to promote economic prosperity, partly to undertake major projects, and partly to support important industrial sectors.[407] In the 1980s, these systems were represented as an obstacle to economic progress, and the international organisations promoted an agenda of 'structural adjustment', based on the 'Washington Consensus'. Neither of those terms was ever clearly defined, but both can be taken to represent the application of market-based solutions to the economic problems of the developing world. Structural adjustment programmes were negotiated between the international finance institutions and debtor countries, including most of the countries in Africa. Their key elements were arguably

---

[406] H Glennerster, J Midgley (eds), 1991, *The radical right and the welfare state*, Brighton: Harvester Wheatsheaf.

[407] SAPRIN (Structural Adjustment Participatory Review International Network) 2004, *Structural adjustment*, London: Zed, p.111.

- policies for economic stabilisation, including measures to reduce inflation, cut government deficits, and limit the use of credit;
- institutional reforms, including changes to the banking, trade and the public sector; and
- policies to promote markets, including privatisation, liberalisation, an end to subsidies and the use of price incentives to govern public policy.

The World Bank claimed at the time that structural adjustment did well, so long as governments cooperated:

> In the African countries that have undertaken and sustained major policy reforms, adjustment is working. But a number of countries have yet to implement the reforms needed to restore growth. And even among the strongest adjusters, no country has gone the full distance in restructuring its economy.[408]

The same report goes on to note that of 29 countries considered in sub-Saharan Africa, six experienced an improvement in policies – not in outcomes – nine a small improvement, and eleven were worse than when they started.[409] Most of the encouraging comments which follow about structural adjustment relate to the best performers; viewed overall, the material findings could be seen as being more negative than positive.[410]

The evaluations of Structural Adjustment Programmes are full of excuses for their uneven performance – local conditions, different political structures, external shocks, imperfect implementation, lack of coordination between donors, economic disruption before the policies started, and so on.[411] The relative success of recent policies,[412] which have taken a different tack, puts that into perspective. Structural adjustment was a failure. The effect on economic growth was erratic, sometimes undermining productive capacity,[413]

[408] World Bank, 1994, *Adjustment in Africa: reforms, results and the road ahead*, Washington: World Bank, p 1.

[409] World Bank, 1994, p 3.

[410] S Schatz, 1994, Structural adjustment in Africa: a failing grade so far, *Journal of Modern African Studies*, 32(4) 679–692.

[411] D Dollar, J Svensson, 2000, What explains the success or failure of Structural Adjustment Programmes?, *Economic Journal* 10 894–917; and see K Donkar, 2002, Structural adjustment and mass poverty in Ghana, in P Townsend, D Gordon (eds) *World poverty*, Bristol: Policy Press.

[412] see e.g. S Radelet, 2010, *Emerging Africa?* Baltimore, Maryland: Center for Global Development.

[413] SAPRIN, 2004, chs 2–3.

sometimes deflationary;[414] economic growth rates in Africa and Latin America were higher before structural adjustment started.[415] The process of privatisation was often open to abuse; liberalisation and deregulation could lead to new monopolies.[416] There were insufficient protections for poor people, and other casualties of the process of adjustment.[417] And the policies were seen as being imposed externally.[418] The policies which have replaced structural adjustment, the Poverty Reduction Strategy Papers, are based on dialogue, commitment, stakeholder engagement and improvements in governance. 'The key point', Radelet argues, 'is that these country-led PRSs – as imperfect as they sometimes are – ... have shifted the balance toward countries establishing key policies and priorities themselves.'[419]

Beyond the state: globalisation and social policy

The development of a global economy has implications for national welfare policies. The nation state is being 'hollowed out', with power being dispersed to localities, independent organisations, and supranational bodies (like NAFTA or the European Union). Mishra argues that globalisation limits the capacity of nation-states to act for social protection. Global trends have been associated with a strong neo-liberal ideology, promoting inequality and representing social protection as the source of 'rigidity' in the labour market. The World Bank and IMF had a particular role in promoting structural adjustment (Box 8.2); they actively promoted a particular brand of economic and social policy to developing countries, and the countries of Eastern Europe, focused on limited government expenditure, selective social services and private provision.[420]

In recent years, however, the role of international organisations has been changing. The 'Monterrey Consensus' supplements market liberalisation with social issues and a much greater stress on

[414] G Mohan, E Brown, B Milward, A Zack-Williams, 2000, *Structural adjustment*, London: Routledge.

[415] S Babb, 2005, The social consequences of structural adjustment, *Annual Review of Sociology* 31 199–222, p 209.

[416] SAPRIN, 2004, ch 5.

[417] T Killick, 1995, *Structural adjustment and poverty alleviation, Development and Change* 26, pp 305–331; SAPRIN, 2004, ch 9.

[418] C Gore 2004, MDGs and PRSPs, *Global Social Policy* 4 277–283, p 279.

[419] S Radelet, 2010, *Emerging Africa?*, Baltimore, Maryland: Center for Global Development, pp 101–102.

[420] R Mishra, 1999, *Globalisation and the welfare state*, Cheltenham: Edward Elgar.

effective governance.[421] The pattern of governance associated with Poverty Reduction Strategies emphasises engagement in dialogue, partnership and self-determination. It is true that there has been retrenchment in many countries, and an increased focus on selective social services. Despite that, most developed countries have moved towards more inclusive social protection policies, and many newly emerging economies are following suit.[422] There has been a greater diversification of the basis of coverage, through a combination of governmental and non-governmental provisions. There is no consistent trend to greater inequality. For some economies, perhaps many, the effect of economic interdependence has been to promote precarious and short-term unemployment; but the same interdependence has also meant the establishment of rights of property and exchange in the market (which Sen refers to as 'entitlements'),[423] and so of greater basic security. There is no simple formula here: there are competing, sometimes contradictory, trends.

ISSUE FOR DISCUSSION

What do welfare states have in common?

---

[421] United Nations, 2003, *Monterrey Consensus on financing for development*, www.un.org/esa/ffd/monterrey/MonterreyConsensus.pdf

[422] A Barrientos, D Hulme, 2009, Social protection for the poor and poorest in developing countries, *Oxford Development Studies* 37(4) 439–456.

[423] A Sen, 2001, *Development as freedom*, Oxford: Oxford University Press.

CHAPTER 9

Principles and values

Distinguishing principles and values
Normative values in social policy
Ideology and social welfare

Much of the discussion of policy up to this point has moved between considerations of empirical evidence and underlying principles. Social policy, unusually in the 'social sciences', is directly concerned with normative issues – that is, with values: not just with what is the case, but what ought to be. Social policy is not just about describing social issues or problems; it tries to change them, and the very fact of trying – the development of services and social responses – means that even if the policy is unsuccessful, things will be different. For Titmuss, values shaped the pattern of social responses, and the pattern of responses shaped the kinds of methods and policies which different governments applied. He argued that 'The definition, for most purposes, of what is a social service should take its stand on aims; not on the administrative methods and institutional devices employed to achieve them.'[424] Institutional welfare was close to Titmuss's vision of an ideal society. [425] It began with ideas like rights and citizenship, and consequently sought to include everyone with a pattern of comprehensive or 'universal' services. This approach led to the National Health Service – public, universal, and free at the point of delivery. Residual welfare was based in a negative, often reluctant approach to welfare, concerned to minimise it to the greatest degree.

Understanding the component elements of these models is partly about principles and values, and partly about the strategies developed to deliver services. This chapter considers the aims, values and principles that guide policy; the following chapter looks at the approaches that are associated with them – approaches like safety nets, redistribution, collective provision and the welfare state.

---

[424] R Titmuss, (1955), The social division of welfare, in Essays on 'the welfare state', London: Unwin, 1963, p 42.
[425] D Reisman, 1977, *Richard Titmuss*, London: Heinemann.

Distinguishing principles and values

Statements of values prescribe how things ought to be done. Values like citizenship, respect for persons or the removal of disadvantage are difficult to justify except in moral terms; whether people accept them depends on their sharing the moral sentiments. Principles are guides to action. That means that they put prescriptions, or statements about what ought to be done, in general terms. They rely on statements like 'thou shalt not kill', 'it is wrong to withdraw from the individual and to commit to the community at large what private enterprise and endeavour can accomplish',[426] or 'housing should be allocated to those in the greatest need'. 'Private markets allow people to choose' is not a principle, because it contains no prescription for action; it can be shown to be true or false. 'Women should be paid the same as men' is a principle; it may be thought to be right or wrong morally, but it cannot be shown to be true or false.

It can be difficult in practice to separate values and principles from the issues with which they are concerned. 'Gender equality', for example, is as much an issue as a principle; 'gender' is the context in which principles (generalised norms governing relationships) are applied. The 'free market' is not itself a principle – the operation of the market is a process, and a context in which norms are applied – but many of its advocates believe that the market embodies the principles they are trying to argue for. Some guides to action are based on judgments about moral principles: 'small is beautiful', for example, is an evaluation based partly in the belief that decentralised, diverse organisations have more to offer than big ones, but also partly in a moral view about the way society should be organised. There is a utilitarian tradition, which argues that the way to tell whether or not a policy is a good thing is to look at its consequences. A principle which states that 'welfare should concentrate on people who are poorest' sounds like a very good idea until one looks at the practical problems: the effect has usually been to offer poor people inferior, stigmatised services and to miss out many of the people who might otherwise have received services. This is reflected in a prominent tradition in social policy, associated with Fabianism but no less important from other political perspectives, which has held that it was not enough to show that something was morally superior; one also had to show that it was economically desirable. The classic example of this is Titmuss's study of blood donation, which not only claimed that it was good for people to be able to give for other

---

[426]   Pius XI, 1931, *Quadragesimo Anno, Actae Apostolicae Sedis* 23, p.203.

people's welfare, but showed that by comparison with blood sold in the private market, blood donation led to more blood being available, with a lower risk of disease.[427]

Principles, in turn, shape administrative practice. The reason why benefit systems for poor people are likely to become so complicated is not that people are trying to avoid helping; it is that principles like equity and charity demand that people who have special needs should have those needs responded to. Compensation for disabled people is complicated for several reasons, but much of it relates to a strongly felt concern that people should be compensated according to their individual circumstances, and that some return should be made where there is a particular injustice. Health services in Britain have to ration services, with waiting lists or diluted services, precisely because they are not prepared to turn people away on the basis of ability to pay.

If the study of normative principles only yielded prescriptions consistent with practical benefits, the principles themselves would not be of much interest. But there are many problems which cannot adequately be understood either in terms of practical benefit, or ideologically. If practicalities were all that mattered, there would be very little reason to protect people with intellectual disabilities abused in residential institutions, to offer poor old people defences against hypothermia or to attempt social casework with families. Decisions about care or control in relation to young people, abortion, or the patterns of treatment of mentally ill offenders, are not simply guided by political principles or practical constraints; they are profoundly moral issues.

Social policy is deeply concerned with the value of actions and the moral nature of different forms of intervention. It is worth remembering, before plunging into the practical detail which characterises so much of the subject, that social policy is a major sphere of moral action, and that one of the reasons for studying it at all is the hope that it might be possible to do something worthwhile with it later.

Normative values in social policy

Considered broadly, the kinds of value with which social policy is concerned fall into six main categories.

1. There are values which affect the circumstances of people individually – concerning issues like the promotion of well-being,

---

[427] R M Titmuss, 1970, *The gift relationship*, Harmondsworth: Penguin.

the definition of need, and the weight to be given to people's interests and choices.

2. There are principles which regulate relationships with other people. These include moral duties, mutual responsibility and solidarity, freedom and rights.
3. There are principles which consider the relationship between the person and society, such as issues of equality and social justice.
4. Some principles govern the relationships between the person and the state: this touches on both freedom and rights again, the role of the state in relation to property, and the provision of welfare services.
5. There are issues which concern the state and its relationship to society, including the responsibilities of the state, the nature of law, democracy, intervention and planning.
6. Finally, there are issues which concern relationships between states, including e.g. global social policy, foreign aid and the role of international organisations.

It is difficult, however, to lay out the values which affect social policy in a comprehensive or systematic fashion. The division between categories is not a firm one; principles which govern individual relationships also limit the role of the state in relation to the individual, and several principles referred to here – freedom, rights and equality – cut across different categories. In the context of a discussion of policy and government, the key principles are those which relate the person to society and the state: freedom, rights, equality, justice, democracy, and those principles are outlined briefly in the section which follows. However, none of these concepts can be explained authoritatively. The principles are multi-dimensional; there are always qualifications, subtleties and problems of interpretation. Many of the concepts have been described as 'essentially contested': there are competing, alternative views. One cannot assume, from a statement like 'this will affect people's freedom', that others will understand the issues in the same way as the person making it. The general rule in discussing such issues is to take nothing for granted.

Freedom In ancient times, freedom was a status; people were free when they were not owned, and not subject to arbitrary authority. In modern times, the idea has come to mean something broader: a freedom to decide and to act. Freedom, Maccallum argues, has three elements.[428] A person must be free from restraint, to do something. Freedom is, then:

- psychological – people must be able to make a choice
- negative – people must not be prevented, and
- positive – people must be able to act.

Individualists argue for a model of freedom where people's freedom depends on their independence. Social welfare and state intervention are seen as undermining independence, and so freedom. A social model of freedom begins from the view that freedom depends on interdependence. To be able to act, people have to have the power to choose in society. In this model, poverty negates freedom. Social welfare empowers people and enhances their freedom.[429]

Rights Rights are rules governing relationships between people; when a person, or a group of people, have 'rights' they can alter the way that other people act towards them. Moral rights are rights which are backed by a moral claim; legal rights are backed by a legal sanction. General rights are rights which apply to everyone in a group, like 'human' rights or rights of citizenship. These have been important for social policy, but they are only part of the story. Particular rights are rights which apply to individuals – for example, the right to have a contract observed. Many of the 'welfare states' are based in particular rights, like rights to protection obtained through insurance or the right to an occupational pension. The scope of these rights has progressively been extended until, in many countries, they have come to cover almost all the population; the final extensions have depended on supplementary or residual benefits.

Equality Equality refers to the removal of disadvantage, but that can be interpreted in many ways – some were referred to in Box 3.1. Equality can refer to

- *Equality of persons* – the belief that there is nothing about human beings, like race or lineage, that justifies one being thought better than another. This is the central principle of the US Declaration of Independence, that 'all men are created equal'. In this sense,

---

[428] G Maccallum, 1967 Negative and positive freedom, *Philosophical Review*, 76, pp. 312–334.

[429] P Spicker, 2006, *Liberty, equality, fraternity*, Bristol: Policy Press.

the idea of equality is very widely accepted in the modern world – though it would not have been for much of human history.

• *Equality of rights* The US Declaration of Independence goes on to say that men 'are endowed by their Creator with certain unalienable Rights, that among these are Life, Liberty and the pursuit of Happiness.' The arguments for human rights are egalitarian, in the sense that they apply to every human being.

• *Equal citizenship* Citizenship can be taken to be the same thing as rights – or at least, the 'right to have rights' – but it is also used to mean membership of a society and a political community. The argument for extending citizenship to everyone, regardless of competence or social status, is that people who are less competent, more marginal or more vulnerable are precisely those who need the rights most. Rawls writes:

> It is as equal citizens that we are to have fair access to the fair procedures on which the basic structure relies. The idea of equality is, then, of significance in itself at the highest level: it enters into whether political activity itself is conceived as a fair system of social cooperation over time between persons seen as free and equal, or in some other way. ... citizens are equal at the highest level and in the most fundamental respects.[430]

• *Access to 'the conditions of civilisation'* Tawney argued for the establishment of a common social infrastructure and foundation of services, providing a common pattern or texture of social relationships. The aim was 'to make accessible to all, irrespective of their income, occupation or social position, the conditions of civilisation which, in the absence of such measures, can only be enjoyed by the rich.'[431]

• *Equality of welfare* Inequality denies people access to the conditions and standards of life which are required in the society where they live. Many concerns about poverty stem from the argument that accept that people's ability to command resources depends on the resources available to others, not just on the absolute value of their income. Because inequality has a direct

---

[430] J Rawls, 2001, *Justice as fairness: a restatement*, Cambridge Mass, Harvard University Press, p.132.

[431] R Tawney, 1931, *Equality*, London: Unwin, 1961, p 122.

effect on welfare, the reduction of inequality can also be seen as a way of furthering welfare in itself.

Social justice There are two competing but very different understandings of justice in society.

- The Platonic view is that justice is what is good and right. John Rawls' idea of justice, for example, is based on what he believes reasonable people would agree to.[432] This is highly contestable; reasonable people may reasonably disagree.[433]
- The Aristotelian view of justice, by contrast, sees justice in terms of proportion: corrective justice is when punishments fit crimes, and distributive justice is when people have resources in proportion to accepted criteria, like desert or needs.

Justice in the Aristotelian sense begins with a presumption of equality; people should not be treated differently without a reason. There may, though, be many reasons. The criteria which have been proposed as the basis for distribution are complex: they have included need, desert, contribution to society, hereditary status, and many others.

Democracy Democracy can refer to

- a system of government. 'Representative' democracy is a system of elected government. Schumpeter argues that democracy consists mainly of a competitive struggle for the popular vote, which makes governments responsive and accountable.[434] Bobbio defines a minimal democracy as characterised by a set of rules about who is eligible to vote, the rights of political parties and free and frequent elections; and a set of rules which establish who is authorised to rule and which procedures to be applied;[435]
- a system of decision-making. 'Participative' or 'direct' democracy gives decisions to the people who are affected by them. Democracy, within this broad set of understandings, is concerned with prescriptions for governance, such as accountability,

---

[432] J Rawls, 1971, *A theory of justice*, Oxford: Oxford University Press.
[433] N Daniels, 1975, *Reading Rawls*, Oxford: Blackwell.
[434] J Schumpeter, 1967, Two concepts of democracy, in A Quinton (ed) *Political philosophy*, Oxford: Oxford University Press.
[435] N Bobbio, 1987, *The future of democracy*, Cambridge: Polity.

participation, dialogue, co-operation, equality and social inclusion. This has been the direction of much contemporary writing;[436]

• a society where people have rights. 'Liberal democracy' accepts majority voting only because a majority is made by the agreement of a collection of minorities.

Welfare provision has grown hand in hand with democracy. Sen claims that there has never been a famine in a democracy; this is because political rights are fundamental to the maintenance of social and economic rights.[437] The UN Research Institute for Social Development points to 'a virtuous cycle linking comprehensive social assistance programmes to electoral competition.'[438]

Box 9.1: Religious values and social policy

'Religion' is not the same thing as faith or belief, though faith may be required in some religions. Religion is a pattern of social organisation, and as such it can be distinguished from the teachings of prophets or scripture. As a pattern of organisation, religious practice has important implications for social policy. The first dimension of religious influence is based in moral teaching. Many religions offer guides to morality, but there may be several strands of moral belief which co-exist.

• *Universalism* is the view that the same principles apply to everyone.
• *Communitarianism* states that we have special responsibilities to some people (such as family members), and that our moral duties define how close we are to others. Many religious institutions – such as charities or waqfs – are founded on a communitarian basis.
• *Individualism* argues that each person is responsible for his or her own actions.

There is no necessary inconsistency between these principles, but different balances imply different social policies.

---

[436] E.g. R Dahl, 1979, Procedural democracy, in P Laslett, J Fishkin (eds) *Philosophy, politics and society*, Oxford: Blackwell; D Beetham, 1992, *The legitimation of power*, Basingstoke: Macmillan; J Cohen, 1997, Deliberation and democratic legitimacy, in R Goodin, P Pettit (eds), *Contemporary political philosophy*, Oxford: Blackwell.

[437] A Sen, 2001, *Development as freedom*, Oxford: Oxford University Press

[438] UN Research Institute for Social Development, 2010, *Combating poverty and inequality*, Geneva: UNRISD, p 299.

A second dimension of religious teaching lies in the extent to which religion is integrated with political institutions. Some religions, and some countries, have made a firm distinction between the secular and religious spheres of their societies – there are examples in Catholic France or the predominantly Protestant USA. Others have established religions and churches, including the formally Christian United Kingdom, the Jewish state of Israel or the Islamic Republics of Iran or Pakistan. Some religious groups are radical, arguing for fundamental political and social change; others are conservative, arguing either for support for established régimes or at least acceptance of the status quo.

Third, there is religion as a means of forging common identity. Ethnicity – though commonly confused with 'race' – is a matter of culture and descent, and it is through culture and descent that religion is principally transmitted. It makes perfectly good sense, in those terms, to describe someone as ethnically Muslim, Jewish or Hindu; the distinction between Protestant and Catholic, Sunni and Shi'ite, is as often a matter of affiliation as of belief. Other religious movements aim deliberately to form a communal identity or sense of membership. Haynes distinguishes movements that are

- culturalist, asserting identity through culture;
- fundamentalist, linking religious, political and social systems;
- syncretistic, drawing strands from different religions to forge an independent identity; and
- community-oriented.[439]

Understanding the role of religious values in social policy often depends, then, on the interplay of these different dimensions – moral responsibility, political orientation and identity. So, for example, the primary issues in the USA lie in the tension between individualist and communitarian interpretations of religious principle; in Turkey they fall between secularism and political Islamism; in much of Africa and South East Asia, they are often based in ethnicity.

Many issues in practice touch on a wide range of moral principles, and it can be hard to separate them. It has been a common experience for people involved in policy making that values do not necessarily come to the fore until some principle has been violated – for example, the realisation that it is not possible to move old people between residences without disrupting rights to quiet enjoyment of their home, or that

---

[439] J Haynes, 1995, *Religion, fundamentalism and ethnicity*, Geneva: UNRISID

medical education does not necessarily justify the removal of dead children's organs. That has to be taken into account along with the contested character of the concepts. It is not possible to anticipate every normative issue, or every possible conflict of values.

Ideology and social welfare

Policies and strategies for welfare are not formed in isolation from their social and political context; they are generally selected according to conventional understandings and representations of issues. Ideas and values are framed within a discourse – a set of common concepts, ideas and a vocabulary. Discourses are identifiable in the terminology, concepts and cultural settings which frame and shape the understanding of policy issues.[440] Even when people disagree, the language they use tends to shape the way the issues are addressed and identified. And, because political argument is based on communication and dialogue, people are pushed into using a common political vocabulary – without it they would not, otherwise, be engaging with the arguments on the other side.

'Ideologies' are patterns of thought within the general discourse. They are inter-related sets of ideas and values, which shape the way that problems are understood and acted on. The way that people think about issues is conditioned by their circumstances. One of the most frequent expressions of this is what people call 'common sense'. People are likely to think about an issue along the lines which others have thought about. Our ideas on economics, for example, are far from straightforward; the idea that economies have to balance budgets year by year, that people respond rationally to incentives and disincentives, or that higher wages lead to unemployment are based in the economic theories of the past, and although some arguments can be made in their favour they are all very disputable. 'Practical men', Keynes once wrote, 'are usually the slaves of some defunct economist'.[441] The same sort of thing is true of views of society: the way we understand responsibilities in families, what we understand as the purposes of schooling, or the value attached to different kinds of work, typically depend on an inter-connected structure of ideas and values. Ideologies affect both how people think about problems and how they can act on them.

---

[440] S Schram, 1995, *Words of welfare*, Minneapolis: University of Minnesota Press; G Marston, 2004, *Social policy and discourse analysis*, Aldershot: Ashgate.

[441] J M Keynes, 1936, *The general theory of employment interest and money*, London: Macmillan, p 383.

Box 9.2: The legacy of the Poor Law

The English Poor Law of 1601 was the not the first system of organised welfare, but it was the first national system; it lasted in one form or another, from 1598 to 1948. The watershed, however, was the development of the 'New Poor Law' – the introduction of a harsher ideological régime intended to rein back the problems generated by industrialisation.

The movement from Poor Law to welfare state has famously been characterised in terms of the models of 'residual' and 'institutional' welfare.[442] The key elements of that distinction are usually understood as covering four dimensions:

- Residual welfare is for a limited number of people (those who are unable to cope in other ways), while institutional welfare is for the general population. The Poor Law was confined to people who were destitute – that is, in extreme need, with no other resources. Institutional welfare would cover people's needs, regardless of financial circumstances, and offer social protection to everyone.
- Residual welfare is given under sufferance, and welfare under the Poor Law was viewed as public burden. Institutional welfare would be based on an acceptance of mutual responsibility.
- The Poor Law was punitive, relying heavily on deterrence to limit liabilities. The institutional model would accept dependency as normal.
- Paupers were deprived of their rights, while the welfare state is founded on the idea of a right to welfare and citizenship.

There are, however, other important aspects of the Poor Law, which have continued to exert an influence to the present day. First, the New Poor Law was liberal (in the nineteenth century-sense of that word), based on individualism and minimal state intervention – the principle known as 'laissez-faire'. The Old Poor Law had allowed considerable variation in the quality and nature of provision. There had been local intervention in the labour market – the reformers were particularly critical of the 'roundsman' system, which allowed employers to use paupers as cheap labour, and the 'Speenhamland' system, which subsidised wages. Ricardo's 'Iron Law of Wages' suggested that these distortions would lead to wages being paid that were below subsistence – that is, what labourers needed to survive.[443] The reformers believed that

---

442 H Wilensky, C Lebeaux, 1965, *Industrial society and social welfare*, New York: Free Press.

443 J Poynter, 1969, *Society and pauperism*, London: Routledge and Kegan Paul.

this kind of intervention depressed wages and threatened the survival of the 'independent labourer'. This was the basis of the idea of 'less eligibility', which tried to make a clear distinction between the position of the pauper and the labourer. In other words, the argument is that state intervention leads to distortion of markets; that if welfare is necessary, it should be kept separate and distinct from the workings of the economy.

Secondly, the arguments for the Poor Law were economistic. The advocates of the Poor Law thought they understood how the economy worked, and what motivated people's actions. 'Nature has placed mankind', Jeremy Bentham wrote, 'under the governance of two sovereign masters, pain and pleasure, It is for them alone to point out what we ought to do, as well as to determine what we shall do.'[444] Benthamites believed in moving people by rewards and punishments. These ideas persist in political and academic debates into the present day – the literature on games and rational choice, resting on the premise that people will always try to maximise their individual gains,[445] is infused with the spirit of Bentham.

Third, the Poor Law was moralistic. The economistic gloss should not disguise the influence of moral judgments, and Offer argues that 'Noetic' beliefs – based in views about the value of work and desirable conduct – were rather more important than the Benthamite ones.[446] One of the main issues which excited the concern of the Poor Law Commissioners was the desire to limit 'bastardy' or illegitimacy – the belief that the Old Poor Law had become a spur to licentious and irresponsible behaviour. Although it was not a major element in the 1834 report, in later years there was a strong distinction between the 'deserving' and 'undeserving' poor; the Guardians were encouraged to distinguish them and directed the 'deserving' towards charity while the 'undeserving' were the province of the state.

These arguments continue to shape contemporary debates on social policy. Jeremy Bentham's stuffed and preserved body is currently displayed in University College London, where he still has voting rights. There's an ill-concealed metaphor in that.

The impact of ideology is commonly interpreted in specifically political terms. Social policy is not the first concern of many people in political debates (though it is not at all clear why it should not be); people

---

[444] J Bentham (1789), *An introduction of the principles of morals and legislation*, Oxford: Blackwell, 1960, p.125.

[445] R Frank, 1994, *Microeconomics and behavior*, New York: Mc-Graw Hill, ch 7.

[446] J Offer, 2006, 'Virtue', 'citizen character' and 'social environment', *Journal of Social Policy* 35(2) pp 283–302.

form their political views and values from a wide range of topics and influences, including for example self-interest, economics, policies on defence, and even the personalities of the politicians who put the ideas forward. When people are asked for opinions on topics which they might not have previously considered – like pensions, home improvement, funerals or scientific education – they are likely to base their comment on a general set of principles, values or concepts to which they can refer. If, for example, one is against the state and for the private market, it is fairly easy to work out a position in relation to these topics – pensions should be for individuals to arrange privately, home improvements are the business of the occupiers, funerals are a private affair and what people learn is up to them. Conversely, someone who believes in collective responsibility through the state can rapidly work out a contrary position: security in old age, housing conditions and education for national needs are a collective responsibility, while funerals, as something everyone has to go through, can be insured or provided for by the state.

Political ideologies

Political positions are commonly identified in terms of a spectrum running from 'left' to 'right'. The description is said to have been drawn originally from where different parties sat in the French national assembly, with the conservative parties sitting on the right and the socialists on the left. The terms are fairly commonplace in writing about politics, but their meaning is fairly hazy; what is thought of as 'left' and 'right' has more to do with convention than with intellectual argument. There is a wide range of opinion on both the 'left' and the 'right': the left includes social democrats, socialists, and Marxists, while the right includes movements as different as Christian democrats, conservatives, free-market liberals, and fascists. An adequate description of the range of ideological views would take a book in itself, but a rapid series of thumbnail sketches will have to do here. An overview of this kind makes it possible, at least, to get some sense of the range of views and some of the major relationships; but it should be recognised that this is also at the expense of some inaccuracy, because within each school of thought there are many further differences and distinctions which should be made.

Marxists see society in terms of a conflict between economic classes. A dominant class (the bourgeoisie or 'capitalist' class) owns and controls the means of production; an industrial working class, the 'proletariat', is exploited by them. The Marxist analysis of welfare concentrates chiefly on its relationship to the exercise of power. The state can be seen either as an instrument of the ruling capitalist class,[447] or as a complex set of systems which reflects the contradictions of the society it is part of.[448] It is often argued that welfare has been developed through the strength of working-class resistance to exploitation.[449]

Marxism is not a unified doctrine; it has come to stand for a wide range of opinions within an analytical framework that is critical of 'capitalist' society. Neo-Marxists argue that the state has two main functions. The first is to improve the conditions for the accumulation of capital – that is, the chance for industries to make profits. The second is to legitimate the capitalist system, by introducing measures (like welfare policies, pensions and health services) which lead people to accept the system as it stands.[450] The requirements of accumulation and legitimation may be contradictory, and the costs of legitimation have led to a 'legitimation crisis'.[451]

Socialism 'There is no such single thing as socialism', Vincent writes. 'There are rather socialisms ... There are multiple definitions of the concept and numerous ways of actually conceptualizing it.'[452] Socialism can be taken to include

- a general movement for the improvement of society by collective action;
- a set of methods and approaches linked with collective action, such as cooperatives, mutual aid, planning and social welfare services;
- a set of arguments for social and economic organisation based on ownership or control by the community;
- an ideal model of society based on cooperation and equality; and
- a range of values.

Some sources confuse socialism with Marxism, which pleases both Marxists, whose importance it inflates, and right-wing critics, who think that the many criticisms of Marxism can be then be levelled at

---

[447] R Miliband, 1969, *The state in capitalist society*, London: Weidenfeld and Nicolson.

[448] N Poulantzas, 1978, *State, power, socialism*, London: NLB.

[449] J Saville, 1975, The welfare state: an historical approach, in E Butterworth, R Holman, *Social welfare in modern Britain*, Fontana.

[450] C Offe, 1984, *Contradictions of the welfare state*, London: Hutchinson.

[451] J Habermas, 1976, *Legitimation crisis*, London: Heinemann.

[452] A Vincent, 1995, *Modern political ideologies*, Oxford: Blackwell.

socialism as well. However, the relationship between Marxism and socialism is limited; the mainstream of socialism in Europe was based in collectivist social movements, it was quite distinct from communism, and its philosophy and approach owe very little to Marx.

Socialism is most clearly identified through its values, not through any fixed set of beliefs.

- Socialism is collectivist: people have to be understood in social context, rather than as individuals. Socialism is often represented in Europe in terms of 'solidarity', which means not only standing shoulder-to-shoulder but the creation of systems of mutual aid.
- Socialism stands for freedom and empowerment. It calls for people to be enabled to do things through collective action. This principle has been central to 'guild socialism' and trades unionism.
- Socialism is egalitarian, in the sense that socialists are committed to the reduction or removal of disadvantages which arise in society. The 'Fabian' tradition, a reformist movement, attempted to achieve greater equality through spending on social services.

These principles – empowerment, equality, and solidarity – are usually described in other terms. They are the 'liberty, equality, and fraternity' of the French revolution, interpreted in collective and social terms.[453] The Party of European Socialists, one of the largest political blocs in the European Parliament, explains: 'Freedom, equality, solidarity and justice are our fundamental values.'[454]

It is difficult to encapsulate the full range of socialist positions about welfare, because these values go to the heart of much of what the provision of social services is about. Socialism tends to imply a commitment to social welfare provision; the main differences relate to method. The state is seen by some (e.g. Fabians) as the principal means through which welfare can be developed; others put more emphasis on collective social movements and mutual support.

Social democratic thought Social democracy, like socialism, is best described as a set of values rather than a developed model of society. Like socialists, social democrats believe in collective action, enabling people to act, and reducing disadvantage. The differences between social democrats and socialists are hazy, because their ideals may coincide in

---

[453] See P Spicker, 2006, *Liberty, equality, fraternity*, Bristol: Policy Press.
[454] Party of European Socialists, 2011, Declaration of Principles, www.pes. cor.europa.eu/pdf/Adopted_PES_Declaration_Principles.pdf

some aspects and not in others, but two are particularly important. First, many social democrats are individualists rather than collectivists; even if they accept arguments for mutual aid or the reduction of disadvantage, they think it important to stress the liberty of the individual, to develop individual rights (as liberals do), and often to restrict the role of the state. Second, some social democrats are not concerned to remove inequality, but only to mitigate its effects through social arrangements which protect people from the worst consequences of a market society. This probably better describes Titmuss's position than the conventional representation of him as a Fabian socialist.[455]

Liberalism Reservations about the role of the state are at the heart of the *liberalism* of the 'new right'. (I am using the word 'liberal' here in the sense in which it is mainly used in Europe; in America the term 'liberal' is often used to mean 'left-wing' or 'in favour of government spending'.) The emphasis on order in traditional conservatism usually means that the state has a clear and strong role in the maintenance of that order. Liberals, by contrast, mistrust the state and argue that society is likely to regulate itself if state interference is removed. Hayek argues that all state activity, whatever its intentions, is liable to undermine the freedom of the individual; that society is too complex to be tampered with; and that the activities of the free market, which is nothing more than the sum total of activities of many individuals, constitute the best protection of the rights of each individual.[456]

Conservatism The traditional right wing is represented, not by liberalism, but by conservatism. Conservatives believe in the importance of social order. This is reflected in a respect for tradition, an emphasis on the importance of religion, and a stress on the importance of inequality – such as inequalities of class or caste – as the basis for structured social relationships.[457] Welfare is a secondary issue, but the sorts of concerns which conservatives have are likely to impose restraints on welfare, with a particular emphasis on traditional values in work, the family, and nationhood. Welfare does raise concern where it is seen to have implications for public order – one British conservative commented, in

---

[455] See D Reisman, 1977, *Richard Titmuss: welfare and society*, London: Heinemann; J Welshman, 2004, The unknown Titmuss, *Journal of Social Policy* 33(2) pp 225–247.

[456] F Hayek, 1976, *Law legislation and liberty*, London: Routledge and Kegan Paul.

[457] S Beer, 1982, *Modern British politics*, London: Faber.

commending the Beveridge report, that 'if you do not give the people social reform they are going to give you revolution.'[458]

Christian democracy 'Christian democratic' thought is closely related to conservatism, but it also has important distinguishing features. Like conservatives, they place a strong emphasis on order; but order is to be achieved, not primarily through state action, but by moral restraints. These restraints have principally in Europe reflected the influence of the Catholic religion. Catholic social teaching has emphasised both the limits of the state and the responsibility of people in families and communities for each other;[459] Christian democrats tend, then, to favour limitations in the role of the state while at the same time accepting moral responsibility for social welfare, solidarity, social cohesion[460] and support for the poor.

The extreme right The extreme right wing is associated with two related but distinct kinds of authoritarianism. *Reaction* is the attempt to 'turn the clock back' to some previous time; reactionary movements have been important in much of Europe, where they have been associated with resistance to liberalism, nationalist movements, and an emphasis on military strength, but they have little direct relevance to welfare. *Fascism* is a form of authoritarian collectivism which argues that the state, the nation or the race is more important than any individual. There are many commentators who argue that fascism has no real ideology.[461] This criticism was based in a political position taken post-war in an attempt to deny the romantic and emotional appeal of much in fascist thought. Fascism appealed to nationalism and racism, and to the values of work, family and country. It had a strong social agenda; in Nazi Germany, the desire to foster racial supremacy included extensive state

---

[458] Quintin Hogg, in *Hansard*, vol 386, col 1918.

[459] N Coote, 1989, Catholic social teaching, *Social Policy and Administration* 23(2), pp 150–160.

[460] See e.g. European People's Party, 2006, For a Europe of the citizens (Rome Manifesto), www.epp.eu/dbimages/pdf/encondoc310306final_copy_1_copy_1.pdf.

[461] S Woolf (ed), 1968, *The nature of fascism*, London: Weidenfeld and Nicolson; S M Lipset, E Raab, 1978, *The politics of unreason*, Chicago: University of Chicago Press.

intervention in society and the economy, with a stress on socialisation (both through schooling and youth movements) and eugenic policies.[462]

The ideologies outlined up to this point represent, more or less, a spectrum moving from 'left' to 'right'. Figure 9.1 shows the ideological positions in terms of two dimensions: individualism and collectivism, and views on equality.

Figure 9.1: Left and right

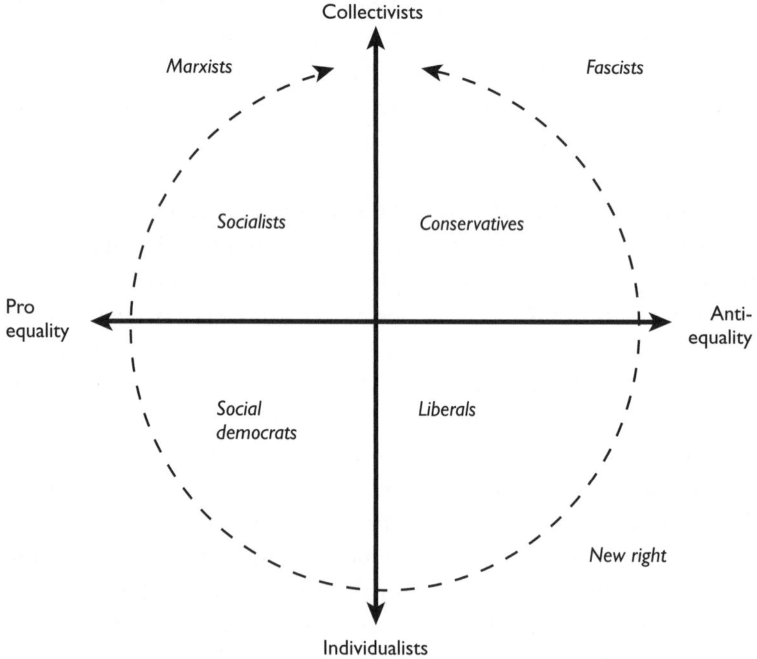

There are other points of view which are not easily described in two dimensions. One such approach is *feminism*, which has as its central values the empowerment of women and the removal of disadvantage. Although these are values more often associated with the left than the right, there is scope for 'liberal feminism', which interprets feminist values within a liberal framework, and 'Christian feminism' which

---

[462] R Grunberger, 1974, *A social history of the Third Reich*, Harmondsworth, Penguin; P Weindling, 1989, *Health, race and German politics between national unification and Nazism 1870–1945*, Cambridge: Cambridge University Press.

asserts the position of women within a Christian moral framework.[463] The most distinctive form of feminism is radical feminism. Radical feminism argues that gender is fundamental to all social relationships, that the relationship of is one of 'patriarchy', which Mitchell describes as a 'sexual politics whereby men establish their power and maintain control.'[464] Gillian Pascall criticises the welfare state on the one hand because it interferes with the private sphere, becoming an instrument of oppression, and on the other because it fails to intervene, leaving women dependent on men. She recognises the potential contradiction.[465]

The second is the '*green*' approach to politics, which is based on the rejection of the mainstream agenda and identification of alternative issues as central – conservation of the environment, the use of natural resources, and the role of humans in relation to other species and the natural world. The agenda of the Green Movement goes far beyond the conservation of natural resources; it is also concerned with different patterns of social organisation, coupling self-reliance with the promotion of communal life and co-operative development.[466] Support for Green politics stretches across the political spectrum, from committed anti-capitalists to conservatives determined to uphold the status quo. Johnston outlines four main positions that people hold about the future of the environment. 'Deep ecologists' argue for a 'natural morality', and a different kind of society based on adjustment to the environment. 'Self-reliance soft technologists' argue for anarchistic, adaptable communities. 'Environmental managers' believe that sustainable development is possible. 'Cornucopians' take the view that environmental problems can be overcome through technological progress.[467] In a political discourse where environmental issues have become increasingly prominent, the traditional concerns of social policy, like the eradication of poverty, redistribution or a belief in progress, have often taken second place.[468]

---

463 M Humm, 1989, *A dictionary of feminist theory*, Hemel Hempstead: Harvester Wheatsheaf.

464 J Mitchell, 1971, *Women's estate*, Harmondsworth: Penguin, p.65.

465 G Pascall, 1986, *Social policy: a feminist analysis*, London: Tavistock, p 27

466 See J Galtung, 1992, The green movement: a socio-historical exploration, in A Giddens (ed) *Human societies*, Cambridge: Polity, pp 325–327.

467 R Johnston, 1989, *Environmental problems: nature, economy and state*, London: Belhaven Press, pp 5–6.

468 But see T Fitzpatrick, 1998, The implications of ecological thought for social welfare, *Critical Social Policy* 54 18(1) pp 5–26.

Left and right

The general distinction of 'left' and 'right' is hazy. When the terms are applied to a subject like social policy the distinction becomes hazier still, because decisions about welfare are not necessarily the basis on which ideologies are formed. Even so, in most English speaking countries – the UK, Canada, New Zealand, Australia and the US – the 'left' is likely to support welfare, while the 'right' considers it has grown too far. It is possible to make some rough generalisations, though they have to be treated with a great deal of caution, and there are some countries where the understanding of 'left' and 'right' is quite different.

The **left wing** is	The **right wing** is
for welfare	against welfare
for public provision	against public provision
collectivist	individualist
for institutional welfare	for residual welfare

It is easy enough to see why these represent two alternative, consistent positions, and it is often helpful to use this kind of classification as a shorthand. Socialists who are in favour of welfare may well support public provision as a means of providing services in practice; because socialism is collectivist, there are few obstacles to recognising a collective commitment through government activity. The sense of society as a collective enterprise also supports the recognition of needs as an institutional part of social life. Conversely, the liberals of the 'new right' are individualistic, support the private market, mistrust state activity and wish to limit the role of the state to the greatest extent possible. Having said this, very few people have such a simple-minded view of the world as these positions suggest. There are some people on the right who want to distribute virtually everything through the private market, but people on the left do not believe that everything should be provided publicly; on the contrary, no-one seriously argues in developed countries for public control of the distribution of food or clothing. People on the right are not necessarily residualist in every respect; many favour general support for education and culture. The 'left' and 'right' are not single, homogenised schools of thought; both are very broad coalitions of interests who agree on some issues and disagree on others. On particular issues, both the 'left' and 'right' may be divided. This is the central argument for looking at people's understandings of particular principles, like freedom, equality and social justice, as well as their general ideological approach.

The political centre There is a 'political centre' distinct from these left-wing and right-wing positions. George and Wilding describe the centre, dismissively, as 'reluctant collectivists',[469] as if they were unable to make their minds up. But there are some consistent beliefs and approaches which can be placed somewhere between the 'left and 'right'. The most important are pragmatism, belief in a 'social market' economy and pluralism.

Pragmatism is often seen as a 'conservative' virtue, but although Burke (one of its most eloquent exponents) is sometimes called 'the father of the British Conservative party' he has also been acknowledged by some as a father of the Labour Party. Conservatives in Britain argued for scepticism about all doctrines, dogmas and principles. The test of whether a policy was beneficial was not whether it fitted preconceived notions, but whether it worked. The way to develop policy, then, was incremental – trying things out, doing a little at a time, seeing what worked and what did not. This places its proponents in the political centre because they are prepared to try things regardless of the political perspective, and because the result is generally an amalgam of different approaches rather than a single, consistent pattern.

Belief in the 'social market' economy is linked with pragmatism – simply, the method of production or distribution which is best is that which happens to work – but there is also a strong theoretical basis for it. Keynes argued that although the private market had worked well in some ways, it did not work well in others. It was not, as the classical economists thought, self-regulating; investment, for example, was too important to be left in private hands.[470] What was needed was a judicious mix of independent action and control. The same kind of argument has been a powerful influence on welfare provision; the status quo is accepted, and the economic system can be seen as the most important factor determining welfare overall, but it is generally thought necessary to moderate its effects through the development of systems of social protection. The idea of the 'social market' has been

---

[469] V George, P Wilding, 1985, *Ideology and social welfare*, London: Routledge and Kegan Paul.
[470] Keynes, 1936.

most clearly elucidated in Germany,[471] where it stands as an alternative model to the idea of the 'welfare state'.

The argument for pluralism is an argument for diversity. Most pluralist arguments are descriptive – they report a diverse range of policies, services and arguments, because that is what is actually there. There is also, however, a prescriptive position – that this is how things ought to be. The pluralist argument is that because no single system is ever likely to be perfect or ideal, a mixed system, which uses a range of different approaches, is more likely to offer a flexibility, responsiveness and security.

ISSUE FOR DISCUSSION

Do people have a right to welfare?

---

[471] G Rimlinger, 1971, *Welfare policy and industrialisation in Europe, America and Russia*, New York: Wiley.

CHAPTER 10

Strategies for welfare

Strategies and methods

A strategy refers to a pattern of decisions, intended to reflect a common approach or purpose. A common purpose can mean that policies are directed towards similar ends – like the relief of poverty, the furthering of economic growth, the promotion of health in a population; or that policies in different fields are guided by similar principles, like the protection of people in a range of circumstances, the reduction of state intervention, or the promotion of equality. Policies might be said to reflect a common approach when the institutions they work through, or the processes they follow, are sufficiently similar – like reliance on a private market, the use of insurance-based systems for service delivery, or the establishment of decentralised local services in preference to national organisations.

Much early work in social policy was concerned not with régimes or whole systems, but with paradigms – patterned approaches that political decision-makers could apply to the provision of welfare, such as the distinction between markets and public provision, or between universal and selective social provision. These issues are sometimes elevated to the level of principle, and there tends to be an assumption in the literature – particularly criticised by Robert Pinker[472] – that different approaches to welfare should be valued not according to what they do in practice, but by the principles they are believed to represent. Although the strategies discussed in this chapter are considered in

---

[472] J Offer, 2012, Robert Pinker, the idea of welfare and the study of social policy, *Journal of Social Policy* 41(3) 615–634.

general terms, at root they are about methods – how welfare might practically be delivered – rather than questions of principle. It is perfectly possible to believe that some services should be based in the market and some not, or that universal and selective benefits might be used in combination.[473] The same methods, and so the same strategies, can be used or adapted for different purposes. This chapter reviews the most common strategies – that is, the main options in welfare provision that are available to decision-makers.

Working with the status quo

Doing nothing is not an option that many people in social policy would want to advocate, but understanding what happens if nothing else is done – the 'null option' – can be important for understanding the difference that policy makes. There is considerable evidence as to what happens in these circumstances, because governments often fail to act; and perhaps surprisingly, the assumption that nothing much will happen in welfare without government intervention is far from the truth. Those who have the resources typically make their own arrangements. Some provision will be charitable. In some cases, people will form mutual aid and self-help groups. Historically, the development of organised mechanisms of support, referred to in continental Europe as networks of solidarity, happened without the assistance of governments, and sometimes despite governments. Some of these arrangements are based in occupations: for example, the pensions available to civil servants or military personnel are commonly available even in relatively poor countries. Some are mutualistic: many forms of insurance are not commercial, but non-profit making associations where people pool risks. Some are co-operative: the building societies in the UK, for example, made funds available to their members, laying the foundations in the process for the development of major financial institutions.

Government rarely begins with a blank slate, and one of the first options that presents itself to governments is to reinforce and encourage independent provision. As networks of solidarity become more developed and elaborate, the hope is that they will gradually fill the gaps, reducing the size of the problem that remains to be tackled otherwise. There are important limitations to this kind of development. One, perhaps obvious, problem, is that richer people are supported long

---

[473] e.g. in R Titmuss, 1968, *Commitment to welfare*, London: Allen and Unwin, p 122.

before poorer people are. In less developed countries, this leads to glaring inequalities, where richer people live in gated communities with access to high-technology medicine and pensions, while poor people live in slums with no facilities. In more developed countries where governments have been relatively inactive – for example, the countries of Southern Europe, or the United States – there is a patchwork quilt of provision, with notable holes in the provision that is available.

The second limitation rests in the complex, diverse, often muddled provision that results. Because provision is based on many different principles, there is little hope of looking for consistent policy. Some people will be protected many times over; others will be left out altogether. If a government is concerned about the impact of social services on the economy, for example, there is little reason why private and mutualistic arrangements should share that concern. Arrangements made for the benefit of contributing members are liable to be rather more conducive to those members' interests than government policies might be. (Often, they are also more expensive.) The geographical distribution of services is likely to be uneven. There will be duplication of some services, and gaps in others. The lack of coherence makes it difficult to develop a coherent, integrated policy overall or to pursue specific policy objectives to the exclusion of others.

Markets and decommodification

The provision of welfare is often represented as an 'intervention' into the existing pattern of an economy. That is a misconception, because economies have no pre-set existing pattern to distort. There are no economies (and probably never have been)[474] where there are not at the same time some other mechanisms of distribution and allocation apart from the economic forces – families, communities, charity or something of the sort. There is always some interplay between patterns of distribution and allocation determined by self-interested, 'economic' procedures – usually described in terms of the 'market' – and other patterns of distribution.

The idea of the market depends in the first instance on the identification of commodities, which are capable of being produced and exchanged, bought and sold. Goods and services are produced in order to make a profit, they are sold to purchasers, and providers have to compete for custom. In *The wealth of nations*, Adam Smith made the case that commercial economies provide goods effectively

---

[474] M Sahlins, 1974, *Stone age economics*, London: Tavistock.

even though they are motivated by self-interest: 'It is not from the benevolence of the butcher, the brewer, or the baker that we expect our dinner, but from their regard to their own interest.'[475] Economic liberals argue that a competitive private market is the best method of arranging the production and distribution of resources According to Arthur Seldon, for example, the price mechanism leads to choice for the consumer; a service led by the consumer rather than by the professions; more efficient services at lower costs (because this increases profitability); responsiveness to need (because their payment depends on it); and the education of people as to the implications of their choices.[476]

The 'radical right' goes further still, and argues that things which have not been part of the market should be commodified, because distribution through the market would be better – like road pricing,[477] or the sale of body parts.[478] The rationale for this is based in economic theories that claim that market distribution is always best. Several economics textbooks claim to prove two 'Fundamental Theorems of Welfare Economics'. The first theorem asserts that every competitive market equilibrium optimises the welfare of the participants; the second, that any desired optimum can be arrived at through market processes. Starr writes:

> The Second Fundamental Theorem of Welfare Economics represents a significant defense of the market economy's resource allocation mechanism. ... any attainable distribution of welfare can be achieved using a market mechanism ... On this basis, public authority intervention in the market through direct provision of services (Housing, education, medical care, child care etc.) is an unnecessary escape from market allocation mechanisms with their efficiency properties.[479]

---

[475] A Smith, 1776, *The wealth of nations*, London: Everyman, 1991 edition, p 13.

[476] A Seldon, 1977, *Charge!*, London: Temple Smith.

[477] Campaign for Better Transport, 2012, *Problems with private roads*, London: Campaign for Better Transport.

[478] e.g. J Savulescu, 2003, Is the sale of body parts wrong? *Journal of Medical Ethics* 29 138–9; R Kishore, 2005, Human organs, scarcities and sale, *Journal of Medical Ethics*, 31, 362–5; B Hippen, 2008, Organ sales and moral travails, *Policy Analysis* no 614, Cato Institute.

[479] R Starr, 1997, *General equilibrium theory*, Cambridge: Cambridge University Press, p 151.

Conversely, distribution by any other means will fail to achieve what markets can.[480]

The proofs of these theorems are wrapped up in pseudo-mathematics and economic jargon, which makes it difficult for non-specialists to engage with them, but they do not do what they claim. They are based on a long series of preposterous assumptions. They confuse welfare with the product of economic processes. They have nothing useful to say about adequacy, inequality or distribution.[481]

The idea that markets provide goods effectively is at least defensible; there are many situations where markets do work. The production of food, clothing or household goods is done through the market, and for the most part it works well enough, even if it is not perfect. One of the objections sometimes raised about markets is that poor people cannot afford to pay for things. The reply to this objection is that this is a case to give poor people more money, not necessarily to provide the service publicly. If poor people cannot afford food, this is taken as a case for better cash benefits, not for a National Food Service.

However, there are also areas where markets do not work well. The main arguments are based, like the arguments on the other side, in economics. The first set of problems relates to the social implications of depending on the private market.

- *Externalities* These are consequences which go beyond the people involved in a transaction: education is worth something to society and to industry, not just to the person who receives it; ill health affects more than the person who is ill, whether as part of an issue in public health or more generally in the fact that society needs healthy workers.
- *Risk* The assessment of risk for a whole society is not the same as the assessment of risk for an individual. It may be reasonable for individuals to take minor risks; it may be less reasonable for society as a whole. A risk of one in 1,000 is very small, but in a society with 60 million people, it would affect more than 60,000.
- *Social choice* Social choices are not necessarily the same as individual choices. The problem comes out, which Galbraith describes in the US, of 'private affluence and public squalor'.[482] If individual customers had to meet the full cost of parks, there

---

[480] L Kaplow, S Shavell, 2001, Any non-welfarist method of policy assessment violates the Pareto Principle, *Journal of Political Economy* 109(2) p 281–7.

[481] P Spicker, 2013, *Reclaiming individualism*, Bristol: Policy Press.

[482] J K Galbraith, 1962, *The affluent society*, Harmondsworth: Penguin.

would probably be no parks. Many people in Britain resisted the introduction of sewers in the 1850s on the ground of personal cost (they were called the 'dirty party' by their opponents).[483] Parks, like roads, sewers – and possibly hospitals – are examples of 'public goods'.

- *Social priorities* Welfare services involve more than the preferences of the people who make the decisions. Welfare services, unlike apples and pears, are not only provided for the benefit of the consumer. They may act as a 'handmaiden' to industry. They may be introduced to redistribute resources. And they may – e.g. in the case of probation or child protection – be a form of social control.

The second set of problems relates to the operation of the private market itself.

- *Economies of scale and efficiency* It may be cheaper to organise a large national service than it is to have smaller competing services. The NHS has been able to reduce the costs of health care, by closing surplus resources, and using its monopoly power to buy in materials more cheaply. The private sector can be argued to duplicate facilities unnecessarily.
- *The geographical distribution of services* The private market does not guarantee a structure of necessary services. Services which are not profitable, because there are too few people needing them, are closed. And the services which do exist are not necessarily in the right place. Pahl gives the example of two ice-cream sellers on a beach. In a planned economy, they would be given a pitch. In the private market, however, they have free choice. This means that the first one sets up in the middle. The next one also has to set up in the middle if he is to get half the custom.[484] The effect is a tendency for competing suppliers to concentrate their efforts in one location. This does work in private welfare, too – which is one reason why major hospitals were concentrated in central London before the NHS, and Harley St. became a centre for consultants.
- *Choice* There are commodities – like health, and possibly education – which people are not well placed to choose, because they have no criteria on which to base their choice. It is in the

---

[483] S E Finer, 1952, *The life and times of Sir Edwin Chadwick*, London: Methuen.
[484] R Pahl, 1975, *Whose city?*, Harmondsworth: Penguin.

nature of the commodity that it is difficult if not impossible for a consumer to judge the quality and value of what is being provided at the time when they need it. People actually have to buy insurance, not health care per se. Social care for elderly people is commonly obtained by relatives or professional advisers. And there are services, like social work and probation, where there may be an element of compulsion – users have no choice.

• *Coverage* The advocates of 'choice' commonly overlook a simple basic point: choice is not just about what the consumer wants to have, but also what producers choose to offer. In any market, some kinds of provision will be not be made. Barr points to issues of 'adverse selection' and 'moral hazard'.[485] Adverse selection occurs when insurance services exclude 'bad risks' – e.g. people with multiple sclerosis, chronic schizophrenics, and elderly people – because the costs of providing for them are greater than the service is prepared to bear. The problem of 'moral hazard' refers to contingencies which claimants might be able to control – like pregnancy or unemployment – and which insurance companies are consequently reluctant to cover.

Economists use the term 'market failure' to refer to a series of special circumstances where the theory of the market cannot apply – for example, where there are externalities, where goods are public and non-divisible like roads, and cases where competition fails through monopolies. The UK Treasury puts great weight on market failure:

> Before any possible action by government is contemplated, it is important to identify a clear need which it is in the national interest for government to address. Accordingly, a statement of the rationale for intervention should be developed. This underlying rationale is usually founded either in market failure or where there are clear government distributional objectives that should be met. Market failure refers to where the market has not and cannot of itself be expected to deliver an efficient outcome; the intervention that is contemplated will seek to redress this. Distributional objectives are self-explanatory and are based on equity considerations.[486]

---

485 N Barr, 2004, *The economics of the welfare state*, Oxford: Oxford University Press.

486 HM Treasury, n.d., Green Book, at www.hm-treasury.gov.uk/d/green_book_complete.pdf

Market failure in this sense is a very narrow rationale for intervention. Markets have much broader limitations. They cannot be expected to cope with every kind of issue or problem – there are areas of human activity which have nothing to do with markets. And they assume that people are able to engage in a market; social and economic exclusion often means they cannot.

The converse of provision and distribution through the market is production or distribution which is not commodified, or commodifiable. Sometimes the issue will be one, like housing, which might also have been distributed through the market; sometimes it will be one, like family care, where markets have only a limited role. Welfare might be 'decommodified';[487] some of the issues that welfare deals with – for example, in relation to issues like freedom, rights and the rule of law – are hardly even expressible in those terms. The most basic argument for decommodification is that where markets cannot deliver welfare, or where they do not, some other process must be found. Those processes include provision in the public sector, the voluntary sector, mutual aid, family and informal support – as well as non-market provision in the private sector. The arguments are discussed in more detail in Chapter 12.

Box 10.1: The limits to market housing

Housing is normally treated as a market commodity which is bought and sold according to the willingness and ability of people to pay. The market is complex, however. Barlow and Duncan point to

- *the impact of space.* Location is acutely important in the housing market; there cannot, because of it, be perfect information and full and free competition.
- *market closure.* Housing markets tend to be localised. This can mean that housing production and finance tend to be dominated by a few major players (in some countries, this may even be true nationally).
- *externalities.* Housing both affects the environment and is affected by it.
- *credit allocation.* The settled housing market tends to be paid for mainly by borrowing, which has to be based on predictions of future value. It is very unlike the market for food.

---

[487] G Esping-Andersen, 1990, *The three worlds of welfare capitalism*, Cambridge: Polity.

- *uncertainty.* Housing is a relatively stable commodity, but its finance is less predictable, and the size of the purchase means that this instability has to be accommodated over long periods of time.
- *market volatility.* Prices are dominated by a limited part of the market – those who are buying and selling property at any time. As a commodity, housing cannot be provided or decommissioned responsively – time lags are inevitable – and immediate adjustments have to take place through the price mechanism.
- *the problem of meeting need.* If profitability is the only consideration, people will be left with needs unmet – most obviously, through homelessness.[488]

This analysis is heavily influenced by the experience of western Europe, though it is generally extendable to most OECD countries. Arguably it misses the importance of systems of land ownership, which is limiting and sometimes exclusive; in some developing countries, where the system of landholding is not clearly established, squatting on unclaimed land, relying on building one's own shelter, may be a normal form of tenure.

Although there is a clear role for governance – regulation and intervention to reduce uncertainty and market volatility – there is only one of these factors which points immediately and directly to a direct role for non-market provision: the problem of meeting need. Residual provision for people in need typically includes provision for homeless people, specialist residential accommodation with support for particular groups of people (such as frail elderly people or people with mental health problems), and disaster relief. And yet provision by non-market sectors is far more extensive than this narrow focus would imply. It includes

- publicly provided housing for communities
- social, voluntary and not-for profit housing to meet general needs, and
- support for particular sectors in the housing market, such as young families or large families.

The development of housing services seems to reflect a range of other considerations. They include

- the view that the market does not provide well for people, and particularly for people on lower incomes. Wherever there is a shortage

---

[488] J Barlow, S Duncan, 1994, *Success and failure in housing provision*, Oxford: Pergamon, ch 1.

of housing, the people who end up without housing, or in the worst housing, are those with the least ability to pay.

- government intervention designed to achieve other objectives – public health, slum clearance, redevelopment, conservation, and so forth. Where governments force populations to move, they take on the responsibility for replacing their accommodation. Where they prevent housing development, they arguably take on an obligation to shield people from the negative consequences.

- the sense of a moral obligation to improve the conditions of the population – a view which has influenced both democratic governments and the voluntary sector. Housing is simply too important to be left to the market alone.

Residualism

The core of the 'residual' model of welfare is the idea that most people can manage through their own or other people's resources; the provision of organised welfare is used residually, for those left over. Another way of representing this approach is as a 'safety net'; the net is only needed for those who fall. This was the model of the English Poor Law, a system which was intended only to help those who were destitute. The association of residualism with the idea of welfare as a 'public burden'[489] has been difficult to shake, and it remains generally true that residual welfare tends to be seen as stigmatising and divisive, and mean. Korpi and Palme argue that benefits which are confined to the poorest tend to be poor benefits: 'the greater the degree of low-income targeting, the smaller the budget tends to be.'[490]

Despite the reservations, residualism appears to have two positive aspects. The first is that residual benefits have proved to be politically rather more robust than their negative image in the social policy literature might suggest;[491] politicians may not like social assistance, but they keep it going when other benefits are being cut. The second is that residual benefits have a particularly strong effect in reducing material deprivation.[492]

---

[489] R Titmuss, 1974, *Social policy – an introduction*, London: Allen and Unwin.
[490] W Korpi, J Palme, 1998, The paradox of redistribution, *American Sociological Review* 63(5) 661–687
[491] M Andries, 1996, The politics of targeting: the Belgian case, *Journal of European Social Policy* 6(3) pp 209–223.
[492] K Nelson, 2012, Counteracting material deprivation: the role of social assistance in Europe, *Journal of European Social Policy* 22(2) 148–163.

Residual welfare does not have to mean that everything is residual. Welfare strategies are about methods, and methods can be used in different combinations. It is possible to take a different view of safety nets. Safety nets have a role in any kind of comprehensive provision, because comprehensive provision, no matter how well planned, is still vulnerable to exceptional circumstances. That means that residual benefits can exist within a comprehensive system of support – and, because there are always gaps and unforeseen circumstances, it is questionable whether any system which does not have any residual benefits can claim to be comprehensive at all.

Selectivity

A selective policy is one which selects the people who are going to receive a service – not just identifying those who ought to receive the benefits, but also those who ought not to. People are subject to a test of means (usually an assessment of income, and sometimes of capital) or needs (for example, an assessment of disability); those who meet the criteria are provided for, and those do not meet the criteria are excluded. The question of who 'ought' to receive benefits is not confined to tests like income or need. The imposition of further restrictions is referred to as 'conditionality', but that term covers several possible approaches. It commonly includes the imposition of rules that are used to administer a system – rules about filling forms, turning up to interviews and providing true information. (It is debatable how necessary such rules are, but typically they shift the burden of administration from the office to the service user.)[493] Then there are eligibility criteria used to control the potential demand, such as age restrictions on benefits for people with disabilities or eligibility rules relating to family size. And then there are additional conditions, imposed for reasons of morality or policy – for example, rules about residence, demanding active engagement from unemployed people, about the avoidance of immoral or criminal conduct.

Selectivity is very widely and commonly confused with 'targeting'.[494] Selectivity is a form of targeting, but it is a very specific form. Targeted

---

[493] See P Spicker, 2011, *How social security works*, Bristol: Policy Press, ch 6.

[494] e.g. P Whiteford, 1997, Targeting welfare: a comment, *The Economic Record*, vol 73 no 220, 45–50; M Matsaganis, 2005, The limits of selectivity as a recipe for welfare reform: the case of Greece, *Journal of Social Policy* 34(2) pp 235–253; D R Gwatkin, A Wagstaff, A S Yabeck (eds) 2005, *Reaching the poor with health, nutrition and population services: what works, what doesn't and why*, Washington DC: World Bank.

services do not have to be selective or exclusive, even when the target is specifically intended to be 'poor people'. Food subsidies can be targeted, for example, not because they are confined to poor people, but because they can be chosen in order to benefit poor people;[495] and soup kitchens do not need to have a test of means to ensure that only poor people use them. But selectivists argue that benefits or services which are distributed without some criteria for exclusion are wasteful; if they were confined to those with proven need, less money would have to be spent, and it could be spent to greater effect. The question of whether money is being saved, of course, depends greatly on the extent of the problem, and the difficulty of identifying it.

The main arguments for selectivity are arguments based in efficiency and equity. Selectivity should in principle be efficient, in the sense of reducing waste, because money does not have to be lost on paying for people who are not in need or on spillovers (that is, giving people more help than necessary, or help for longer than necessary). It should be equitable, partly because the amount that people receive will relate to their circumstances, but also because selectivity is imposing a test of fairness – part of the point of conditionality is to exclude cases which people would otherwise consider unfair. There are four great problems with this.

1. In order to be selected, individuals have to be clearly identified; there has to be some test of means or needs. The experience of such tests is that they are likely to be intrusive, complex or degrading. Townsend argues that in practice selectivity has been associated with second-class services for second-class citizens; it separates people who are poor or in need from the rest of society.[496]

2. There is the problem of defining and holding to the limits. If people receive benefits or services because they are in need, there has to be some way of distinguishing those who are entitled from those who are not. This can create inequities, because people who are just below a line might end up better off than people who are just above it, and because people whose circumstances change might find themselves unfairly advantaged or disadvantaged. This generally means that if people's circumstances improve, the services have to be withdrawn as their need decreases. This

[495] G Cornia, F Stewart, 1995, Food subsidies: two errors of targeting, in F Stewart, *Adjustment and poverty*, London: Routledge.

[496] P Townsend 1976, *Sociology and social policy*, Harmondsworth: p 126.

214

problem is usually called the 'poverty trap' in social security, because the effect is to submit poor people to very high losses if their income increases, but it happens in other situations as well; a person who learns to cope with a disabling condition might lose benefits, or a tenant in public housing might have to leave their home if their situation improves (as has happened in the US).

3. Selective benefits and services often fail to reach people who are part of the target group. People often do not claim benefits, for a number of reasons including ignorance about the services, a failure to realise that they can receive them, the complexity of the procedures to claim and a sense of shame or 'stigma'.[497]

4. There is a potential conflict between efficiency and equity. Efficiency is about reducing waste, and getting the best return for the money. In health services, the principle of 'triage' is used to direct resources to the people who are most able to benefit, not necessarily those in the worse condition. The same principle applies in other services. Keen points to what he refers to as the 'paradox' of targeting: that because people in the greatest need are probably most expensive to respond to, more needs can be dealt with, and more people can have their basic needs satisfied, if the greatest needs are passed over. This might argue for a reduction of the resources in certain cases where people's needs increase.[498] This creates a problem in equity – the pattern of distribution is not necessarily going to help those in the greatest need.

Social protection and solidarity

One of the most widely practised approaches to improving individual welfare frames the issues in a different way. It aims to promote welfare, not by redistributing resources to bring about change, but by offering security against changes in circumstances. The term 'social security' is mainly now related to financial assistance, but the general sense of the term is much wider, and it is still used in many countries to refer to provisions for health care as well as income maintenance. Most of us are likely to be in need at some point in our lives, whether it is as workers, as old people, or during sickness; it is very important to well-being not just that there is some provision, but that we know there is such provision available. Social security is important, not for what it pays, but for what it might pay in the event of need. Health

---

[497] P Spicker, 1984, *Stigma and social welfare*, Beckenham: Croom Helm.

[498] M Keen, 1991, *Needs and targeting*, London: Institute for Fiscal Studies.

care protects people who might break their legs as well as those who have done so. (Although the benefits of security are not themselves material, they do have a monetary value; people in Britain, where there is a National Health Service, are receiving support which people in the US have to pay for through private insurance or a Health Maintenance Organisation.)

Social protection tends to be outlined in the context of developed economies, because that is where it is most directly established, but there has been a remarkable growth of social protection in developing and emerging economies. In recent years social protection has been extended strongly in several developing countries, including major schemes in South Africa, Mexico, India, Indonesia, China and Brazil – Barrientos and Hulme call it a 'quiet revolution'.[499]

Social protection has offered notable benefits to the poor in these countries, partly through direct service, and the reduction of the hardships and risks associated with poorer economies, partly by mitigating the problems associated with unrestrained growth, and partly through its effect on social inequality. The UN Research Institute for Social Development argues that 'Social protection offers an unprecedented opportunity to integrate concerns with livelihood security and poverty reduction within a unified conceptual and policy framework.'[500] However, the terms on which benefits are delivered in developing countries are not necessarily framed on the same terms as schemes in more established welfare states. Leisering notes that

- benefit levels are often very low, below subsistence
- there are marked differences between administrative agencies and areas
- coverage is often narrowly targeted, and
- implementation can be relatively informal, for example involving community groups and schools.[501]

---

[499] A Barrientos, D Hulme, 2009, Social protection for the poor and poorest in developing countries, *Oxford Development Studies* 37(4) 439–456.

[500] UN Research Institute for Social Development, 2010, *Combating poverty and inequality*, Geneva: UNRISD, p 136.

[501] L Leisering, 2009, Extending social security to the excluded, *Global Social Policy* 9(2) 246–272, p 261.

The World Bank describes social protection in terms of 'social risk management',[502] an approach which identifies the concept with the response to risk, vulnerability and insecurity discussed earlier. The benefits and services which are given as social protection often work as insurance benefits. They are there to protect people from the consequences of undesirable events, not just to respond to need. Some of the benefits offer income replacement – ensuring that people will be able to carry on with the life-style they had before. (This may well mean that richer people will get higher levels of support than poor people.) Others are contingent rights; people in certain circumstances, like ill health or maternity, will be able to obtain services and to avoid extra expenditure. Social protection may include 'safety nets', but a safety net is not the same thing; means-tested benefits are there to stop people falling below a certain level, not to protect their previous position.

This principle is understood in much of Europe in terms of 'solidarity'. Social security developed, in much of Europe, from mutual aid societies or trades unions, in which members agreed to pool their risks and share responsibilities for support.[503] The idea of solidarity is seen in many countries as the basis of collective social provision: for example, the French Code of Social Security declares that 'the organisation of social security is founded on the principle of national solidarity. It guarantees workers and their families against risks of every kind liable to reduce or suppress their ability to earn.'[504] But solidarity is not only about mutual aid; it can also be seen as a principle of 'fraternity', which takes welfare as a form of collective activity and so the responsibility of the wider society rather than of individuals.[505] Much of the history of this principle has been about the extension of solidarity to groups which were previously excluded. The central aim of French social policy has been gradually to extend the range and scope of solidaristic networks, a process of 'generalisation'. This has led to a patchwork quilt of services, provided on many different terms but seeking to ensure that nearly everyone is included. The approach to policy, then, has centred on two strategies: trying to identify and

---

[502]   World Bank, http://go.worldbank.org/R8ABRRLKX0; and see World Bank, 2001, *Social Protection sector strategy: from safety net to springboard*, New York: World Bank.

[503]   P Baldwin, 1990, *The politics of social solidarity*, Cambridge: Cambridge University Press.

[504]   Code de Sécurité Sociale, 2007, article L111-1, sourced at www. legislation.cnav.fr/textes/lo/css/TLR-LO_CSS_L111-1.htm

[505]   P Spicker, 2006, *Liberty, equality, fraternity*, Bristol: Policy Press.

work within existing patterns of support,[506] and seeking to integrate or 'insert' people at the margins into the available networks.[507] In the process, a principle which initially referred primarily to insurance has come increasingly to refer to redistribution.[508]

The phrase 'nearly everyone' points to one of the central problems with the idea of solidarity. Networks of community solidarity are exclusive as well as inclusive. They define the people who should not be supported as well as those who should; giving priority to some groups, like the sons and daughters of one's neighbours, works against others, like immigrants or people discharged from long stay psychiatric care. A common arrangement in Bismarckian systems is that the people who are protected are those who are able to pay insurance contributions, while the poorest – those who are unable to contribute – are left out. The same is true in a more extreme way in many developing countries, where the middle classes may have systems of social protection, like pensions and health care, that are not available to the bulk of the population.

Universality

Universality is usually presented as the alternative to selectivity, though – as the range of options here suggests – it is not the only alternative. The idea that services are 'universally' available suggests that everyone should have access to them, and there are many services that are not selective but not genuinely available to everyone. A targeted set of responses which is not dependent on stopping people claiming – like a needle exchange for drug addicts, or redevelopment of a poor area – is not well described as 'universal'.

Although the idea of 'universality' suggests comprehensiveness, universal benefits are often not intended for everyone. They are more likely to cover everyone within a defined category: universal basic education generally means education for children, and universal pensions are for old people. The argument for universality is the argument against selective approaches; the process of selection is inefficient, and inequitable, difficult to administer, and it fails to reach people. By contrast, universal social provision can reach everyone, on the

[506] Baldwin, 1990.
[507] R Lejeune, 1988, *Réussir l'insertion*, Paris: Syros–Alternatives; E Alfarandi, 1989, *L'Insertion*, Paris: Sirey; J Donzelot, 1991, *Face à l'exclusion*, Paris: Editions Esprit.
[508] See P Spicker, 2000, *The welfare state*, London: Sage.

same terms. The degree of uniformity simplifies administration; there may well be cases in which broadly-based indicator targeting proves cheaper than more selective alternatives. But there are also positive reasons for universality. One is the view that everyone has basic needs, and those needs can often be supplied more simply and effectively through general provision to everyone. This is the argument for public water supplies and roads; it was extended during the 1940s to decent housing, education and health services. Second, universality has been seen as a way of establishing a different kind of society – one in which every citizen has a right to basic services, and the basic texture and pattern of social life is one in which people do not suffer unjustifiable disadvantages. This is the root of the 'institutional' model of welfare, outlined in Chapter 8.

Box 10.2: Basic Health Care Packages

Austerity, in the West, is often used as a synonym for cuts or retrenchment – spending less, making the same amount manage for more people, reducing 'waste', and limiting the role of the public sector. That is not what it used to mean, and it is not what it means in much of the developing world. Austerity is about making do with a minimal amount, without excess or luxury, and that often implies increasing the role of the public sector, rather than reducing it. The central problem faced by developing countries is that relatively small amounts of money have to be spread to cope with very high levels of need. The World Development Report 1993 argued that developing countries had to move away from attempts to imitate western-style, high-tech hospital care, focusing instead on how to get the best return from the small amounts of money they were able to afford. This is done most effectively by a focused, universalist response.

> Governments in developing countries should spend far less – on average, about 50 percent less – than they now do on less cost-effective interventions and instead double or triple spending on basic public health programs such as immunizations and AIDS prevention and on essential clinical services. A minimum package of essential clinical services would include sick-child care, family planning, prenatal and delivery care, and treatment for tuberculosis and STDs (*sexually transmitted diseases*).[509]

---

[509] World Bank, 1993, *World Development Report 1993: Investing in health*, Washington DC: World Bank.

Note some of the elements that are not in this list of priorities: cover for serious accidents and traumas, provision for old people, psychiatric care, eye care, dentistry and support for disability among them. It is not that these things do not matter, but long term, intensive intervention is costly, and it does not offer the same returns.

In subsequent years, a range of countries have introduced basic or minimum health care service, also called Essential Health Packages, and several other related terms. Ethiopia's Essential Health Package, for example, includes

- Services for families and children
- Services for dealing with some communicable diseases, including TB and HIV/AIDS:
- Basic curative care and treatment of major chronic conditions
- Hygiene and environmental health
- Health education and communication. [510]

Liberia's Basic Package of Health Services consists of

- Reduce maternal, infant and under-five mortality rates
- Routine immunization
- Nutrition interventions
- Primary Health Care Services
- Malaria treatment
- Sexually transmitted infections, HIV and AIDS
- TB and leprosy control
- Safe motherhood
- Selected social welfare services
- Emergency Preparedness Response (EPR)
- Essential drugs and medical supplies.[511]

Both systems deliver medicine through three tiers of service – primary health care, large health centres and hospitals reached by referral, and a central referral unit for the whole country.

Indicators from developing countries are sometimes unreliable, but between 2000 and 2012, despite a disturbing increase 2007–2009, Liberia reduced under-five infant mortality from 135 deaths per 1,000 children to 73. Ethiopia reduced under-five mortality from 166 per 1,000 in 2000 to 88 in 2011. These

---

[510] www.who.int/healthsystems/topics/delivery/technical_brief_ehp.pdf
[511] www.ilo.org/wcmsp5/groups/public/---ed_protect/---protrav/---ilo_aids/documents/legaldocument/wcms_126728.pdf

are examples of a general trend *The Economist* has called 'the best story in development'.[512]

The welfare state: comprehensive provision

The description of welfare systems in terms of 'models' tends to suggest a coherence and consistency of policy that is rarely found in practice. The decisions that are made and the things that are done in one area of policy are not necessarily based in the same principles as in others. Similarly, the emphasis in the literature on ideologies tends to suggest that there will be patterns and inter-relationships between policies of different types. However, because they develop from a complex, contested political environment, the choices that are made may pull in different directions; policy-makers tend to have a range of different, sometimes conflicting objectives. In any case, what policies can do in practice depend on a series of compromises, depending on resources, external constraints and the demands of other policies. The same reservation applies to considerations of strategy and method.

It is not common, then, for approaches and methods to be adopted as part of a consistent, overarching strategy, but it does happen. The British 'welfare state' was developed as a comprehensive set of systems. Beveridge knew, as every administrator of services for a century had known, that it was not possible to separate services for poverty, health, and housing. (The point was made, for example, in Edwin Chadwick's report on sanitary conditions in 1842.[513]) Beveridge declared that his social security system was based on some 'assumptions', without which the system could not work.[514] They included a national health service, child allowances, and full employment. Why were the assumptions there? It is tempting to dismiss them as propaganda, but they were more than that. Health care was necessarily associated with social security because, as Chadwick and later Poor Law administrators had discovered in the 19th century, ill health was a major cause of poverty. If people were sick, and no other source of support was available, they would have to claim poor relief. The link of unemployment with poverty was self-evident; full employment was necessary both because people would otherwise need to claim benefits and, no less important,

---

[512] *Economist*, 19 May 2012.

[513] E Chadwick (1842), *Report on the sanitary condition of the labouring population*, Edinburgh: Edinburgh University Press 1965.

[514] Beveridge Report, 1942, *Social Insurance and Allied Services*, Cmd 6404, London: HMSO.

people have to be employed to pay into the scheme and to fund it. Family allowances were necessary, in Beveridge's view, to protect the incomes of people in work, because otherwise they may have been better off out of work if they had numerous children. (There were other concerns elsewhere in Europe – in particular, fear that the birth-rate would be undermined if having children became uneconomic. In France, family benefits rather than benefits for the poor were the main systems through which people who were unemployed, sick or lone parents were supported.[515]) The same kind of argument could, of course, be extended to education – because both education and the welfare of children are essential for social reconstruction – and to much else besides.

Much of this vision has been lost since. The separation of the elements of the welfare state into constituent parts has led more and more to separation in the language in which the services are discussed, their methods of operation, and the problems they face. Services operate in 'silos'. Poverty used to be a general, overarching theme which brought together all the services; now it is often treated as a matter for social security. The primary response to ill health is medical care; it used to be thought of as a matter of clean water, decent housing, and income. This can be seen in part as a sign of social advance. Poverty in western and northern Europe has become a question of income because the infrastructure of housing, health care and education seems to many people to be complete. Housing in those countries is less important for health than it was because most of their housing has improved beyond recognition in the last sixty years. At the same time, the issues are inter-related; it is difficult to formulate an adequate strategy against poverty that would not cover health, housing and income maintenance, a strategy for health promotion that does not consider income, housing and the environment, or a policy for community care which ignores medical services, housing and income.

ISSUE FOR DISCUSSION

Systems based in solidarity and social protection are not necessarily available to all. Is it legitimate to cover fewer people if this means better services?

---

[515] P Spicker, 2002, France, in J Dixon, R Scheurell (eds) *The state of social welfare: the twentieth century in cross-national review*, Westport, CT: Praeger.

CHAPTER 11

Policy in practice

Policy analysis
Aims
Values
Goals
Methods
Implementation
Outcomes
Analysis for practice

Policy analysis

Social policy is an applied subject, and any adequate understanding of the subject has to be able to identify the implications of policies for practice. Much of the literature on policy analysis is concerned with explaining what policy is, how it is developed and why it matters.[516] Understanding the process through which policy is made is an important part of understanding social policy overall. But the study of social policy is about much more than understanding what happens; it is important to make judgments and to consider choices for action. To do this, students and practitioners working in the subject area should be able to collate information and to evaluate policy. They need to know what effects a policy is having, whether it is being implemented appropriately and, if necessary, what to do about it. The skills and approaches which are needed to do this kind of work are still referred to as 'policy analysis', but it is a different kind of policy analysis from much of the material found in the academic literature. It is analysis *for* policy, rather than analysis *of* policy.

The central principle of analysis, of all kinds, is that complex issues are broken down into less complex ones. At the outset, the analysis of a policy requires at least three steps:

1. the establishment of criteria for evaluation – how we can know whether a policy is working or not;

---

[516] See e.g. M Hill, 2005, *The public policy process*, Pearson/Longman.

2. the identification of its results or effects; and
3. the comparison of the effects with the criteria.

There is an argument for doing rather more. The literature on public policy refers to an elaborate model referred to as the 'rational' approach to policy making. The rational model is a lengthy list of stages that planners are supposed to go through to make informed decisions. In addition to the steps outlined here, rational policy making begins with an assessment of the initial environment. Policies are presumably supposed to do something; they have aims. Aims have to be operationalised, or translated into achievable goals. Then there needs to be examination of alternative means of reaching goals. The policy has to be put into practice; the rational approach argues for consideration of the process of implementation as part of understanding how a policy

Figure 11.1: 'Rational' policy making

Monitoring and evaluation

Assessment of the environment

Implementation

Aims

Methods

Goals

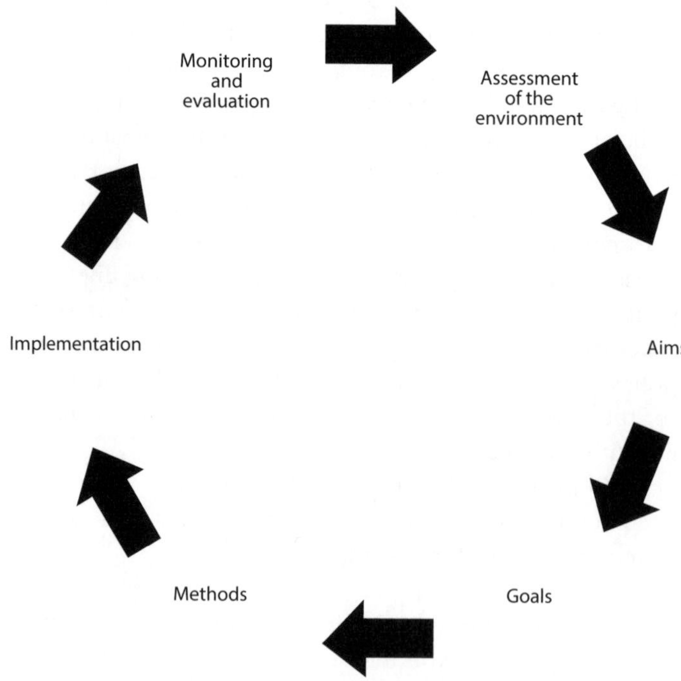

will work. Monitoring and evaluation of effects are equally part of a rational procedure.[517]

The rational model is stated differently in different places: some presentations cover as few as four stages (aims, methods, implementation and outcomes), while others have ten or more (context, aims, objectives, goals, methods, prediction of consequences, selection, implementation, monitoring, evaluation and feedback). The Treasury *Green Book* describes a cycle covering:

1. A *rationale* for policy
2. Identification of *objectives*
3. *Appraisal* of options
4. Implementation and *monitoring*
5. *Evaluation*, and
6. *Feedback*.[518]

Although the language is slightly different, this boils down to much the same kind of approach. It breaks policy-making and practice down into stages that have to be reviewed in turn.

Rational approaches have been extensively criticised, because they do not really describe how policies work in practice. In real life the stages are difficult to separate. Decisions depend on circumstances, negotiation, resources, compromise, pressure, discussion and many other things. The demands of rationality ask more of policy-makers than may be feasible – the examination of alternative approaches and their consequences is time-consuming, expensive and often speculative.[519] But the rational model is a useful starting point for breaking down a large problem into smaller, more comprehensible issues, and it points to some important issues which otherwise might not be taken into account.

---

[517] See e.g. A Faludi, 1973, *Planning theory*, Oxford: Pergamon; N Gilbert, H Specht (eds) 1977, *Planning for social welfare*, Englewood Cliffs NJ: Prentice-Hall, part 2; S Leach, 1982, In defence of the rational model, in S Leach, J Stewart, *Approaches in public policy*, London: George Allen and Unwin.

[518] HM Treasury, *The Green Book*, www.hm-treasury.gov.uk/media/785/27/Green_Book_03.pdf, p.3

[519] Faludi, 1973.

Box 11.1: PRSPs

Rational planning may look like an obscure academic exercise, but the process has gradually taken root in government internationally. It began in American government in the 1960s; it spread from there to other English-speaking countries; it became part of European procedures in the late 90s. One of the chief mechanisms by which the process has spread in recent years has been the Poverty Reduction Strategy Papers (PRSPs) required from governments throughout the developing world by the IMF and the World Bank.[520] The process was announced in December 1999. At the time of writing this section in 2012, 66 developing countries had prepared PRSPs, either interim PRSPs, which identify issues and explain how the procedure will be developed, or full programmes, which are reported on annually and updated every three years. The IMF has engaged rather more countries in related processes, and has suggested in previous reports that the numbers of countries involved will shortly go above 70.[521]

The PRSP approach requires governments to consult with social partners, to encourage participation in the development of the programme, to be explicit about their aims and intentions, and to recognise what they have done or not done. The IMF and World Bank identify the process as

> setting clear goals and targets that are linked to public actions; improving budget and monitoring systems; opening the space for discussing national priorities and policies for poverty reduction and growth; filling country-specific analytic gaps; and aligning and harmonizing donor assistance with national priorities. [522]

With the exception of the last, these are typical objectives of a rational planning process. The link with donor assistance does, however, give the clue to how the process has become so widespread; engagement with the process is essential to the receipt of international funding.

The PRSP process is not prescriptive about policies, but there are detailed guidelines about the sort of activities that governments are supposed to be involved in order to prepare the papers. Governments are encouraged to consult, to engage social partners, to formulate plans of actions, and to build capacity to assess their work. The sorts of issue which the IMF and World

[520] See www.imf.org/external/np/prsp/prsp.asp
[521] International Monetary Fund and World Bank, 2005, 2005 review of the Poverty Reduction Strategy approach, www.imf.org/external/np/pp/eng/2005/091905p.pdf
[522] IMF/ World Bank, 2005, p 87.

Bank identify as 'good practice' include establishing a foundation of data for decision-making; developing consultation and participation; building links through existing institutions; and setting realistic targets.[523]

Some reports, to be sure, fall short of those expectations. Independent organisations have been critical of some governments for their lack of consultation and engagement of civil society in the process.[524] The IMF's approach has been uncharacteristically relaxed; their evaluation reports are long on positive encouragement, and short on negative criticism.

Any direct gains from the process in terms of poverty reduction have been described, not unreasonably, as 'modest';[525] but it is not clear that reductions in poverty are what the policy is mainly about. What the plans actually include has to be decided at national level; it might be plans for economic growth, social policy, or political measures to incorporate different actors into the process of development. The common elements are procedural. The tests which the international organisations are applying – transparency, openness, participation, planning or the development of capacity – are issues in governance rather than poverty reduction. The PRSPs represent one of the most extraordinary exercises in international governance ever undertaken.

Aims

The identification of aims is central to the establishment of criteria by which the success or failure of a policy can be judged. Some criteria are based on principles, or generalised rules – for example, that 'child protection should further the best interests of the child' or that 'benefits should lead to work for those who can'. An alternative approach is to begin with a normative objective, or an end in sight. This may refer to a general end, like the 'abolition of poverty'; it may also refer to some model or pattern, like the 'free market'. In many cases, this amounts to the same thing as judgment by principles, but it is not always the same. There is a general problem in welfare economics of 'second-best' options: a compromise on one point may imply violation of the assumptions which made a particular option desirable.[526] It means that even if option B is less desirable than option A, a compromise

---

[523] International Monetary Fund/International Development Association, 2002, Review of the Poverty Reduction Strategy Paper (PRSP) Approach, www.imf.org/External/NP/prspgen/review/2002/032602a.pdf

[524] Coopération Internationale pour le Développement et la Solidarité/ Caritas Internationalis, 2004, *PRSP: Are the IMF and World Bank delivering on promises?*, www.cidse.org/docs/200404221144166307.pdf

[525] CIDS/Caritas, 2004, 3.22

[526] C Brown, P Jackson, 1978, *Public sector economics*, Oxford: Robertson p.20.

between them – half-way towards A – could be worse than either. For example, abstinence from narcotics might be more desirable than managed addiction, but partially successful enforced abstinence may well be worse than both. Working to a principle and aiming for a specific end can produce very different kinds of result. Working towards ends can be used to justify the means, even if initially people are made worse off. This is a dangerous position: Stalin felt able to legitimise his actions because the end he was aiming for, economic prosperity under socialism, justified the means.[527] In a principled approach, each stage in a process needs to be compatible with other norms and values – values such as human rights, the rule of law or the protection of the vulnerable. At a less elevated level, too, social policies will also have a range of subsidiary aims – commitments to economy, accountability and prudent action – which have to be balanced with other considerations.

Identifying the positive aims of formal agencies is probably the simplest part of the process, in the first place because such aims are often made explicit in policies, and second because by default the improvement of welfare can be taken as a basic test. For example, the aims of a service for elderly people might be to improve the welfare of elderly people; to preserve their independence at home for as long as possible; to offer support to frail elderly people and their carers; and, where it becomes necessary to consider other forms of care, to ease the transition as far as possible. Many services and agencies will explain what their broad aims are; many other aims become explicit when the critical literature is reviewed. These then become the tests by which the service can be judged.

At the same time, there are some important areas of uncertainty. Aims can be positive – in that there are factors which have to be achieved – or negative, in that there are things which ought to be avoided. An example of a 'negative' aim is the idea that people's freedoms should be respected. Policies are often counted as illegitimate if they breach this rule, and legitimate if they do not. Negative aims are more difficult to identify than positive ones, because they are unlikely to be mentioned unless the conditions are breached. So, it tends to be implicit rather than explicit that services should not cost too much; they should meet received professional standards; they should not upset their political masters; the workers should observe the rules for financial propriety; they should be able to report their results in an approved format. Time and again, services have fallen foul of a whole set of rules,

---

[527] A Nove, 1964, *Was Stalin really necessary?*, London: George Allen and Unwin.

often unwritten and unexplained, which mean that they are judged and found wanting.

Another source of ambiguity lies in the normative content of many aims. Criteria which might seem technical (such as whether or not a policy has particular redistributive effects, or whether it is cost-effective) may well conceal normative judgments. An example referred to earlier is the attempt to define poverty. Different tests are liable to yield very different results.

It has to be stressed, too, that the selection of relevant criteria is a political judgment. Decision making in the political arena generally rests in the negotiation of conflicting interests. The reasons why policies are adopted may not be clear. Nor is it always clear whose interests the policies serve; it does not have to be the recipients'.

Values

Policy documents often make explicit statements about values. Examples are statements about empowerment, social inclusion or promoting health. Values are usually intended to guide an agency's actions. Describing something as a 'guide' carries the implication that it is unlikely to be paramount; it will be taken into account as one factor among others. Even when values are strongly emphasised, there is little room for absolutes: people might say, for example, that they put the needs of their clients above everything else, but every agency has to consider other issues – even if it's only where the money is coming from.

Values which are expressed as part of a policy are generally expressed positively: they represent what the policy is trying to achieve. Examples are health, welfare or social justice. Many of these are specific to particular types of agency or policy. In a democratic society, however, there are also some general principles which run across service boundaries. The character of 'democracies' differs, but they share a common approach to institutional governance. The core elements include

- principles of *beneficence* – public services are there to serve the public. Public services are supposed to do good – for example, to improve people's welfare, to improve their health, to protect the vulnerable, or to reduce disadvantage. Bryson recommends an 'ethical analysis' grid with explicit consideration of the relative seriousness of effects, the vulnerability (or potential damage) to people affected, the possibility of compensation and the compatibility with overall objectives.[528] His approach is extraordinarily prescriptive, but it has to be better to make these issues explicit than to take them as read.

- principles of *citizenship* – public services belong to the public. Many are based in concepts of right or entitlement. (The main exceptions are criminal justice and penal institutions, where people may be held to have forfeited rights; but even in these cases there is often a presumption that the user's interests must be safeguarded.)
- principles of *procedure*. It may seem odd to elevate procedure to the sphere of values, but procedure is fundamental to the way that public services operate in a democracy. No less than electoral restraints, democracies are founded on the rule of law. In every public service, without exception, there are institutional constraints, financial, administrative or legal, regulating the behaviour of agencies.
- principles of *accountability*. 'Democratic accountability' is usually interpreted in terms of the structure of authority: even if officials are not elected, the authority for taking decisions derives from an electoral process, and officials in the public sector are ultimately accountable for their actions to people with that authority. The practical implications of the idea are discussed further in Chapter 13.

Many principles are negative, rather than positive; they do not say what people should do, but they do say what they should not do. Negative guidelines are just as important as positive ones, but they can be difficult to identify. Often they are implicit, rather than explicit. It is unusual for all values to be identified directly: many of them are default positions which only become relevant when they are breached. Policies should not need to say that they are done honestly, impartially and without thought of personal reward for the officials who implement them, but clearly, when this does not happen, it can be taken as a legitimate basis for criticism. It is not usually considered necessary for a local authority in the UK to declare itself to be opposed to nepotism or swearing at members of the public, because, even if they happen, they are relatively rare. And positive guidelines may disguise further negative ones. When an agency describes itself as 'empowering people', we cannot be sure what they will do, but it should at least mean that locking service users

---

[528] J Bryson, 2004, What to do when stakeholders matter, *Public Management Review* 6(1) pp 21–53.

in solitary confinement should not be on the agenda. (This is not an imaginary example: it is what happened in the use of 'pindown' in residential care for children during the 1990s, a disciplinary approach which depended on isolation, humiliation and confrontation.[529])

Umberto Eco once commented that if you want to know what the problems of an agency are, you should look at their rules and assume the opposite.[530] This happens because the issues which people feel are important enough to make statements about are often those which are in doubt. For example, community care plans do not say much about managing fraud, demanding bribes or physical abuse, not because they do not happen, but because these are not the areas that planners feel the need to make statements about. The plans do, however, have a lot to say about treating people as individuals, giving them a voice and ensuring a joined-up service. When you read this, you can be certain that people are being made to fit into pre-conceived categories, that users' wishes are being overridden, and that all sorts of different services are coming in to deal with them at different points. Eco's rule may be a little cynical, but it's not wildly off-target.

Goals

Aims can be expressed in very general terms – for example, that 'this policy should offer value for money' or 'this policy should foster people's independence in their own homes'. But they can also be very specific, such as the statement that 'benefits should be calculated accurately in at least 95% of cases'. For convenience, the first class of objective is usually referred to as an 'aim'; the second type is a 'goal' or 'target'. (That distinction ought to be treated with some caution, because there is no agreement on what these terms really mean.) The important difference between the classes is that the second type is 'operationalised', or translated into terms which can be acted on. Operational goals usually have some kind of general principle lurking behind them, and the usual guidance given in texts on planning is that both aims and goals ought to be clarified. The process of operationalisation – translating general ideas into specifics – is crucial for policy making, but often it is obscured by a failure to recognise the distinction between the initial principles and the practical details.

---

[529] See e.g. L Bell, C Stark, 1998, *Measuring competence in physical restraint skills*, Edinburgh: Scottish Office.

[530] U Eco, 1987, *Foucault's pendulum*, London: Secker and Warburg.

The process of operationalisation is often seen as a technical issue, but it is dangerous to leave it at that. The problem is that issues change in the process; an initial concern with unemployment, poverty or homelessness can be subtly altered into something else. Services which set out to deal with 'poverty', for example, often begin with a concern about living standards, but generally come to concentrate on low income – because low income is the best available indicator of the problems of poverty. This is liable, in turn, to lead to a redefinition of the issues. Poverty in the nineteenth century was primarily perceived as an urban problem; the social surveys of Booth were focused on the distribution of urban problems, but the debates on his work centred instead on the question of budgets and minimum income.[531] Rowntree built on this topic, and in doing so shifted perceptions so that the question of poverty became very much a question of income.[532] When in the 1960s and 70s the issue of urban deprivation became a serious issue, one of the most devastating criticisms was that poverty was not geographically centralised.[533] That is undoubtedly true, but it did not follow that poor areas should not be considered in themselves a matter of concern; it shows the extent to which the understanding of 'poverty' has come to be dominated by the methods we use to measure it.

It may seem strange that goals should be operationalised before methods have been chosen. The idea of specifying desired outcomes – 'management by objectives' – has been part of an important shift in the pattern of governance. The implication is that the goal might be achieved flexibly by a range of methods. The Millennium Development Goals (Box 6.1) are arguably an example – but while they are welcome as a statement of intent, and as criteria for evaluation, it is debatable whether they have led directly to much of the improvement which has happened. The outcome figures are dominated by one country (China) which has not shown much interest in the goals. The World Bank used to specify desirable approaches and institutional structures closely; it has moved to a different model of governance, suggesting that countries can work out for themselves how the goals can best be achieved. The same is true within the British government. The UK government's advice is that targets should be 'SMART' –

---

[531] P Spicker, 1990, Charles Booth: the examination of poverty, *Social Policy and Administration* 24(1), pp 21–38.

[532] B Rowntree, (1901), *Poverty: a study of town life*, Bristol: Policy Press, 2000.

[533] S Holtermann, 1975, Areas of deprivation in Great Britain, *Social Trends* 6 pp 43–48.

- specific,
- measurable,
- achievable,
- relevant, and
- time-bounded.[534]

This sounds initially reasonable, but it should be not be taken for granted. Vague targets can indicate the direction of movement without being too specific on how far one has to go. Aiming, for example, to cut deaths from cancer, or to recruit as many people as possible from minority ethnic groups, makes perfectly good sense, and it does not have to be tied to a fixed target. If a goal is very specific, it tends to imply not just that we know what the policy ought to achieve, but how it should be done. The idea that goals must be 'achievable' before they are set conceals assumptions about method and approach. If SMART targets are set, there is at least a risk they are being set in the wrong order.

Specific objectives are not only geared to results; they can be concerned with the process and management of a service. Ambrose, writing about urban regeneration, distinguishes three types of performance indicator. Some are concerned with *structure* – the organisation of services or programmes. Some are concerned with *process* – the way in which policy is put into practice. And some are concerned with *outcomes,* or the results of policy.[535] There is a literature concerned with the development of valid, reliable measurements of performance,[536] but that is a will-o-the-wisp; part of the problem is the usual confusion about what indicators are capable of showing, part is uncertainty about which aspects of process are of value.

There are many disadvantages in precise targets. Probably the best-known problem is that the targets take over policy, and that less tangible objectives are sacrificed in the determination to achieve the targets at all costs.[537] An example is the attempt to reduce lengthy waiting lists for hospital care. The policy to reduce waiting time has had many beneficial

---

[534] HM Treasury, The Green Book, at www.hm-treasury.gov.uk/media/785/27/Green_Book_03.pdf, p 13.

[535] P Ambrose, 2005, Urban regeneration: who defines the indicators?, in D Taylor, S Balloch (eds) *The politics of evaluation*, Bristol: Policy Press, pp 48–50.

[536] see G Boyne, K Meier, L O'Toole, R Walker (eds) 2006, *Public service performance*, Cambridge: Cambridge University Press.

[537] A Etzioni, 1964, *Modern organizations*, Englewood Cliffs: Prentice Hall, pp 8–10.

effects. But it has also changed service priorities: one reason why some people were waiting a very long time was that their condition was considered less urgent, or less dangerous, than some other conditions. Throughput – the number of cases treated – has been more important than the quality of service. Alcock comments on the same problem in another context: targets in area-based initiatives have tended to 'steer' the management of policy in the direction of inputs and outputs, rather than outcomes.[538] 'Indicators', he comments, 'do not just become a proxy for real social change, they become a substitute for it.'[539]

A second problem has been 'gaming', or manipulation of the figures. There have been controversies where service delivery or practice has been distorted in order to present the figures in the best possible light. The Commission for Health Improvement suggests that

> One of the reasons for long delays in A&E [accident and emergency] departments accepting patients from waiting ambulances may be their own need to achieve a target that no patient should wait more than four hours from arrival in A&E to admission, transfer or discharge. This illustrates how targets set for one service may act against cooperation between services.[540]

In another example, a report on an English police service found redirection of police activity to the pursuit of crimes that were relatively easy to resolve, like shoplifting and minor drug offences, coupled with incorrect classification of more serious, more time-consuming offences such as rape, burglary and crimes of violence, which were treated as 'no crime'. The inspectors attributed this conduct to 'an historic culture of chasing targets'.[541]

The third problem is that too much is expected from the objectives. Long lists of targets, Wildavsky argues, become a way of providing excuses – 'mechanisms for avoiding rather than making choices.'[542] Agencies focus on the tasks they can achieve and jettison the ones they

---

[538] P Alcock, 2004, Targets, indicators and milestones, *Public Management Review* 6(2) pp.211–229.

[539] Alcock, 2004, p 221.

[540] S Boseley, 2003, Ambulance queues highlight A&E crisis: targets blamed as patients left waiting hours for handover, *Guardian* 16 September, p 7.

[541] Her Majesty's Inspectorate of Constabulary, 2013, *Crime recording in Kent*, London: HMIC, www.hmic.gov.uk/media/crime-recording-in-kent-130617.pdf.

[542] A Wildavsky, 1993, *Speaking truth to power*, 4th ed., New Brunswick, NJ: Transaction Books, p 29.

---

cannot. But, at the same time, 'everyone knows that the objectives of many public agencies are multiple, conflicting and vague'[543] – which means that short lists are unconvincing and inappropriate. He writes:

> the attempt to formalize procedures for choosing objectives without considering an organisation's dynamics leads to the opposite of the intended goal: bad management, irrational choice and ineffective decision making. It is not that sophisticated analysts do not realize the pitfalls but that, having dug the pits themselves by semantically separating objectives from resources, they are surprised when client organizations fall into them.[544]

Fourth, the issue which is being dealt with might not be one which lends itself to operationalisation in terms of simple, practical targets – in which case planners may be tempted to substitute a more manageable, less 'wicked' problem. 'The poor' are not a consistent, predictable group of people; many people are vulnerable to poverty, and many people experience the problems of poverty for limited periods of time. That means that decision-makers cannot spend money on the problems of poverty and be confident that the problems they are dealing with will become smaller, that the numbers of people apparently in poverty will fall, or that the people who are being helped will be identifiable as poor in three years' time. Money for 'poverty' tends to be spent, at the local level, on 'communities' and redeveloping housing estates: the houses are easy to count, improvement is visible, and the houses can't get up and walk away. The need to make goals achievable and politically acceptable can determine what sort of problem is likely to be addressed.

Michael Scriven complains that planning and management based in the specification of aims, values and goals can lead to bad policy:[545]

- the process is biased in favour of the perspective of service management, against service users. If users have a different perspective, a tight focus on aims will not leave room for it. This is an important potential criticism. The main way to forestall it is to ensure that the aims which are identified have been based, at the outset, on some degree of consultation or participation.
- aims and goals need to change; they cannot be set once for all, but have to be interpreted flexibly, as policy develops;

---

[543] Wildavsky, 1993, p 30.
[544] Wildavsky, 1993, p 29.
[545] M Scriven, 1991, *Evaluation thesaurus*, London: Sage, pp 37–8, 178.

- the tests of good policy have to go beyond explicit aims, to other, unpredictable dimensions. There may be negative, concealed aims – things which a policy is supposed not to do (such as costing the earth, generating embarrassing problems in the media, or antagonising users of alternative services) but which only become apparent when it has done them.

In practice, agencies are often vague about the criteria they want to apply. Patton and Sawicki add a health warning, however: aims and criteria which are added only at the end of a process of review are often used as justifications of policy, rather than genuine tests of the success or failure of policy.[546]

Methods

A substantial part of the study of social policy has been devoted to the ways in which policy is devised and implemented, including the role of government, the institutions and agencies which are used to bring about social ends, and the constraints under which services operate. It is basic to policy-making that these measures and approaches should be intended to do something, so it does not call for a great intellectual leap to realise that the means employed should be consistent with the aims and objectives. At times, however, the link between aims and methods can be tenuous. A government wants to reduce racial unrest, so it renovates housing. It may want to improve housing conditions, but decides instead to pay people a cash benefit. It wants to reduce juvenile crime, so it provides social work to families. Or it wants to prevent obesity, and devises a programme of competitive sport. (None of these examples is made up.)

There are several reasons for this kind of disjuncture. The first is that the declared aim may not be the genuine one. The US 'War on Poverty' was not really about poverty as such; it was a way of responding to racial issues, and in particular a way of promoting participation and engagement in political processes. Second, policy making can be influenced by factions who have a commitment to particular approaches or ideas, and who use the opportunities created by the political environment to further their cause. With this shift, priorities change. Public health in Victorian England was initially a matter of engineering, rather than medicine; the medical profession

---

[546] C Patton, D Sawicki, 1993, *Basic methods of policy making and planning*, Upper Saddle River, NJ: Prentice Hall, p 58.

asserted their influence and the process became their province in the 1870s.[547] The personalisation of social care services has been advocated in times of prosperity as a way of furthering choice, and in times of recession as a way of saving money. The development of policy for 'social inclusion' in Scotland was captured by an established lobby for urban regeneration. Third, the patterns through which policies are developed are heavily influenced by ideologies, preconceptions and assumptions about the process. There are presumed, 'common sense' links between sport and exercise, between racial conflict and urban conditions, or teenage pregnancy and sex education, which largely disappear when the evidence is examined, but the influence of prejudice in shaping policy cannot be underestimated. And fourth, the process of policy making is an area for discussion, bargaining and compromise. It should not be surprising if the process leads to some non-sequiturs.

The rational model argues for a review of all the possible alternative measures, considering their costs, and their implications. This is not really possible – it would be hugely time consuming and expensive. What happens, instead, is that policy-makers have to review a range of plausible alternatives. The sorts of consideration which have to be made include the costs and benefits of different measures, both now and in the future. Appraising what is likely to happen, as well as what does, makes the reliability of any decision uncertain. Decisions which commit decision-makers or the future are often unsafe decisions. One of the tests is 'robustness' – the ability to change tack if something goes wrong.

Implementation

Whenever policies are introduced, they have to be implemented in practice. It is rare that policies simply go into the machine at the top, and the intended effects come out at the bottom – a process of 'perfect administration'. Something happens in between; the process of implementation and service delivery changes the character of policy. In some cases, the policy becomes diluted, as compromises are necessary in practice. Governments may want to build houses, but constraints like the availability of land, negotiation of planning restrictions and the capacity of the construction industry may limit what is actually happening. Decentralised administrations have to delegate decisions to local level, creating a series of points at which

---

[547] R Lambert, 1963, *Sir John Simon 1816–1904 and English social administration*, London: MacGibbon and Kee.

policies can be delayed or forestalled.[548] In other cases, the policy changes in character – sometimes subtly, sometimes substantially. Agencies are influenced by a range of constraints, including finance, the practical problems of dealing with the public, the size of their operation, and the external environment. They have to make choices about where their time, effort and resources will be devoted. Faced with the pressures of practice, community regeneration might become housing improvement; employment programmes might become personal development programmes. Agencies are influenced in these choices by professional standards, administrative conventions and 'service ideologies'. The effect of providing nursery places in schools is different from providing them in social care centres; schools tend to emphasise educational criteria, while social care centres tend to emphasise child protection. Community development is likely to be handled differently if it is the responsibility of departments dealing with housing, community education or economic development.

Box 11.2: Universal Primary Education in Uganda: the Big Bang

Every child, the Ugandan constitution states, has the right to an education. Uganda, like many developing countries, faced the problem that low numbers of children were receiving an elementary schooling. In 1995, there were more than four million children who did not go to school. Universal Primary Education, despite is name, was not designed to be completely universal; it made it possible for a family to have up to four children in school without having to pay fees. But that was general enough to lead to an explosion of entitlement. Between 1997 and 2003, the numbers of children enrolled went from 2.7 million to 7.3 million.

It is one thing to declare a policy; it is another to deliver it. Making provision for over four million extra children calls for practical issues to be addressed – issues like who will teach tem, where they will sit, where they can write, whether there are enough pencils and paper to go round, where there is any water for them to drink, where they will go to the toilet. Most schools are able to provide one teacher for 60 pupils, and books are even scarcer – a report estimates there is one book for each 175 pupils.[549] In 2004, more

---

[548] M Hill, P Hupe, 2003, The multi-layer problem in implementation research, *Public Management Review* 5(4) 471–491.

[549] F Juuko, C Kabonesa, 2007, *Universal primary education in contemporary Uganda*, Kampala: Makarere University Human Rights and Peace Centre, www.huripec.mak.ac.ug/working_paper_8.pdf

than 700 schools used drinking water from river or lake water. The World Bank gives one example from a primary school, whose enrolment increased from 573 children to 2,598. There were 17 classrooms; that averages 153 children for each classroom. Subsequent support from the World Bank has reduced class sizes since to 94.[550] But the problem is worse than that suggests, because in practice some classes are five times bigger than others[551] – the largest class in developing countries is usually the first grade.

'Big Bangs' have been attempted in several other countries – Ethiopia, Kenya and Malawi among them. A report from the World Bank and UNICEF is critical:

> If poor children were the most vulnerable to the imposition of fees and the existence of other economic barriers, they could also, ironically, be the most vulnerable to unplanned or underplanned attempts to remove these barriers. ... Quality was compromised by dramatic increases in class size and a loss of school-level funding, far too frequently leaving the children of the poor no better off than before.[552]

The argument that children are 'no better off' is disputable; much of the evidence is based on the deterioration of school quality in Malawi, and that can happen while coverage and attainment are increasing. At the same time, the big bangs have put millions of children, and particularly girls, in the way of having some education, instead of having none. Few policies display such a stark contrast between policy and implementation. But is it better, we need to ask, to do something small well, than to do something big badly? Probably the best answer, which the World Bank leans toward, is to do the big thing, but to do it better – planning the process, introducing the policy in phases and making sure that systems are in place to support the implementation.

Much of the process of policy analysis is concerned with the activity of agencies. This can be difficult for social scientists, whose training does not always prepare them to take an organisational perspective: many of the models used in social science are based on studies of individual subjects rather than collective ones. Institutions cannot think or feel; they do not 'act' in the way a person acts. Nevertheless, there are

---

[550] World Bank Independent Evaluation Group, n.d., *Fall out from the 'Big Bang' approach to Universal Primary Education: The case of Uganda*, www. worldbank.org/oed/education/uganda.html

[551] World Bank/Unicef, 2009, *Abolishing school fees in Africa*, Washington DC: World Bank, www.unicef.org/publications/files/Aboloshing_School_Fees_in_Africa.pdf p 14.

[552] World Bank 2009, p xii.

both behaviours and attitudes of people in organisational settings, and organisations do in practice 'act' in order to produce certain effects. Agencies can be examined by reviewing their formal policies, but that has the limitation that what agencies intend, and what they do, may be different. The practice of an agency can be reviewed by examining its records, looking at its processes, and perhaps by focusing on 'critical incidents' – the points where policy goes wrong. This can be done by recording the results of actions or by questioning service users and other stakeholders.

There are difficulties in interpreting such results. The actions of officers are not necessarily the actions of the agency – officers are individuals and may act differently. The effects of a policy or set of practices may be unintended, and even unnoticed. The results which are identified may be the result, not of the actions of the agency, but other external factors – if service users are disadvantaged, and the actions of an agency are neutral, they will still be disadvantaged when the policy is put into practice. Most difficult, organisations are not simply the sum of their parts. A large organisation full of well-intentioned, dedicated individuals can still act to disadvantage people through poor communication, lack of co-ordination, bureaucratic delays and failure to identify the consequences of a series of actions.

One of the most fundamental questions in designing any policy is to ask: 'what can go wrong?' Some policies hardly consider implementation at all. Visionaries whose eyes are focused on distant horizons seem at times not to notice the swamp under their feet. But many policy analyses focus almost exclusively on the process of implementation, under the name of 'audit'.[553] The governments who fund audit are not usually looking to be told that their policies are ill-considered, but they do want to know whether or not agencies are performing in the way they are being funded to perform. 'Process evaluation' similarly is concerned with the question whether agencies are behaving in appropriate, or expected, ways; often this is done for newly established agencies, which have not been in place long enough to achieve clear results, in order to establish whether they are well run. A fuller discussion of process will make much more sense after consideration of administration in practice, and the issues raised by implementation are returned to in Chapter 17.

---

[553] see e.g. Audit Commission, 2005, *Approach to service inspections*, www. auditcommission.gov.uk/Products/NATIONAL-REPORT/78F62C1A-D68F-4ce0-8276-631A8BAC1B47/ApproachToServiceInspections.pdf

Outcomes

Although policy is intended to produce effects, the effects can sometimes be difficult to identify. There are cases where the outcomes are relatively clear, like examination results from schools, but these tend to be cursory and liable to misinterpretation – examination results say more about the initial social position of the schools than they do about the quality of the schools themselves. What tends to be considered instead is either inputs – that is, a measure of the resources used, like the amount of money spent – or outputs, the services which the resources are used to provide – e.g. accommodation provided, or the number of beds. An input is what goes into a service – like the number of doctors per head of population or the cost of support for unemployed people. (Extra resources devoted to a service are easy to measure; the benefits of such resources may not be.) An output is what the service makes available, like the number of day care places, or the proportion of the population which receives education. An outcome is the result – the effect of what has been done. In some cases, the output will be the outcome – the number of houses built or the creation of a road, or the money which is redistributed through social security. In principle, though, outcomes could include other kinds of benefits, including improved health, social contact, personal development or happiness.

Services are typically evaluated by considering whether or not the outcomes are the sort envisaged in their aims or goals. This is the test of effectiveness: a service is effective if it succeeds in achieving what it was supposed to achieve. In order to assess outcomes it is necessary to consider not only what the policy seems to do but what might otherwise have been true. It is difficult to judge what the impact of health services is unless there are some indications of what would happen without them; improvements in public health have often reflected other issues (like sanitation, diet or even economic development).[554] Transport systems directly affect where people live and work, and there are implications for housing and employment opportunities which are difficult to assess directly. A policy which is already in place cannot always conveniently be compared with some prior state; critics of rent control, for example, try to argue what the situation might have been like without it,[555] but where rent control

---

[554] J Riley, 2001, *Rising life expectancy: a global history*, Cambridge: Cambridge University Press.

[555] P Minford, M Peel, P Ashton, 1987, *The housing morass*, London: Institute for Economic Affairs, ch 2.

has existed for any length of time there is no effective point for such a comparison. Where there are changes, it is not always clear that they result from the policies, rather than from some other social factor. The same problems affect comparison with other societies: there are too many possible explanations for differences.

Effectiveness is not the only test of outcomes, because there may be unexpected and undesirable effects. Faced with the problem of cholera in nineteenth-century London, the secretary of the Poor Law Commission, Edwin Chadwick, argued for the development of sewers. Following a strand of medical opinion at the time, Chadwick believed that cholera was caused by 'miasma' or air-borne particles, and that the important thing to do was to shift sewage away from where people lived. This is what the sewers were designed to do – and they shifted the sewage to the nearest stretch of water, the river, which unfortunately was also a major source of drinking water. People died in their thousands.[556] The policy might be thought to be 'effective', in that it achieved precisely its operational objectives. In the short term, it was ineffective in terms of its general aims, which were to reduce liability to cholera; in the longer term, of course, people realised they could no longer drink the river water, and the sewage system became one of the main defences against disease.

Conversely, there may be unexpected effects which are desirable. Compulsory education has had the important side-effect of providing child-minding for families; provision for homeless people has offered an escape route, however limited, for women subject to domestic violence; sickness and invalidity benefits have helped to fill gaps in provision for unemployed people. Desirability is, of course a matter of interpretation – it might have been better if these gaps had not existed. Many issues in social policy deal with a range of different interests, and measures may be desirable for some at the expense of others. 'Community care' may improve the lifestyle of dependent people at the expense of their carers; policies for positive discrimination may favour some groups over others.

Analysis for practice

Although this chapter discusses the elements of policy analysis in general terms, the rationale for including those elements has a more specific application. Policy analysis is a set of techniques for identifying a series of interrelated issues that should be considered to make sense of policy

---

[556] S E Finer, 1952, *The life and times of Edwin Chadwick*, London: Methuen.

in practice, and the stages considered here provide a method of breaking down a complex process into a series of more manageable steps.

1. *Aims* The first step is to consider the aims and goals of a policy: what the policy is supposed to do, and how it will be possible to know it has done it.
2. *Methods* The second step is to review what can be done: to consider what are the options, constraints and resources, and to consider whether the methods are consistent with the aims.
3. *Implementation* The policy has to be put into practice, and a policy analysis has to consider whether the process of putting the policy into practice is consistent with the intentions and the aims.
4. *Outcomes* Lastly, there needs to be a review of the effects of a policy – what the effects are, how they relate to the intentions, what the costs and benefits are, and whether or not the aims have been met.

Those four steps are central to the analysis of policy in practice; there is more about them in Chapter 19.

ISSUE FOR DISCUSSION

'Wicked' problems are subjects that are complex, constantly changing, or uncontrollable; their nature is often disputed and the goals of policy may be contradictory. Examples are poverty, health inequalities, interpersonal violence or teenage pregnancy. How does one go about developing policy to deal with such issues?

PART 3

SOCIAL ADMINISTRATION: THE ORGANISATION AND DELIVERY OF WELFARE

CHAPTER 12

Welfare sectors

The social division of welfare
Welfare pluralism
Governance: partnership and agency

The social division of welfare

An emphasis on politics, public policy and the role of the state tends to suggest that the state is central to the organisation and delivery of welfare. This is a half truth at best. The state is central to the establishment of policy, both because the state establishes a framework for the formal organisation of welfare, and because only in the state is there a locus through which conscious decisions can be taken to change or maintain the direction of welfare policy across a whole society – the ability to take such decisions being part of the definition of what a state is. But the state also has important limitations. In the first place, there are limits to the authority of any state; the political process requires a degree of negotiation between parties, and compliance is not necessarily assured. Second, the state is not necessarily the sole, or even the main, provider of welfare services; there are many other routes through which welfare is provided.

Titmuss identified several different kinds of redistributive process, arguing that it was not possible to understand the distributive impact of social policy without taking them fully into account. He referred to a 'social division of welfare', including three types of welfare:

- 'social welfare', which represented the traditional 'social services';
- 'fiscal welfare', which was distributed through the tax system; and
- 'occupational welfare', distributed by industry as part of employment.[557]

Titmuss's concerns represented at the time a major extension of the traditional field of social administration, and the essay was enormously influential in broadening the definition and understanding of the subject,

---

[557] R Titmuss, 1955, The social division of welfare, in Essays on '*The welfare state*', London: Allen and Unwin, 1963.

but the rationale behind it has never been wholly clear. If the 'social division' he described was intended to explain the channels through which redistribution might take place, it was far from complete.[558] The category of 'fiscal welfare' could be taken to include two very different types of redistribution. The first concerns subsidies, or measures which are intended to have an effect on people's behaviour. Examples are housing subsidies and tax relief on personal pensions. The second is income maintenance, which is intended to redistribute income and protect people's living standards. Occupational welfare, similarly, is not a single homogeneous category. It includes perks, which are part of a contractual relationship and not really 'welfare' at all; redistributive measures, provided by employers as a 'handmaiden' to enhance their productive functions, like sick pay or employee crèches; and private insurance, which is sometimes provided by employers, but may also be purchased by individuals. There are, besides, other avenues through which welfare is distributed. They include legal welfare, which is compensation through the legal system (particularly the courts); and, probably most important of all, the voluntary and informal sectors.

The reference to 'sectors' leads to one of the most important categories in the contemporary study of social policy: the distribution of welfare services through a range of social mechanisms beyond the state itself. There are four main sectors through which welfare is provided: public, private, voluntary and informal – though, as the previous discussion suggests, there is a case for considering more. The public sector consists of services provided by the state; the 'private' sector, through commercial activity; the voluntary sector, action by non-profit-making organisations (though in some countries 'private' activity is also considered to be 'voluntary'); and informal care is provided by friends, neighbours and families – or, more usually, by women in families.

The role of the public sector

The public sector is financed and managed by the state – including government, local authorities and quasi-autonomous government organisations or 'quangos'. In some of the literature this is closely identified with the idea of the 'welfare state', though this usage does not necessarily convey all the moral ideas which are associated with the term.

---

[558] P Spicker, 1984, Titmuss's social division of welfare, in C Jones, J Stevenson (eds) *Yearbook of social policy in Britain 1983*, London: RKP.

The public sector has come to dominate social policy in many countries. The systems in many countries began, however, with a range of services beyond the state – charities, religious foundations, mutual aid associations, employment based provision, trades unions and so forth; governments came to the field belatedly. One of the principal pressures for state involvement has been the demand for residual welfare – a safety net, for people who are unable to deal with the contingencies in other ways. Once a government accepts a role of provider of last resort – a role accepted even by right-wing opponents of state welfare, like Hayek[559] – it binds itself to act when every other route has failed. In practice, governments which have taken on that role have found it impossible to limit what they do only to the last resort, partly because of the difficulty of defining the boundaries, but also because very selective provision is expensive, there are economies of scale, and governments can perform more efficiently and effectively if they accept a broader remit.[560] The area of debate concerns not whether state welfare should exist, but what its scope and extent should be, and on what terms it should be delivered.

A number of arguments for delivery of welfare by the state – such as issues of social protection or control – have been considered in the course of the book. State services can be seen, simply, as the means through which state policies can be pursued. The most important question to resolve is whether the public sector is the best or most appropriate medium through which such policies might be achieved. The arguments are strongest in three cases:

- where there are minimum universal standards to maintain, requiring either a general régime or residual provision to plug the gaps. Only the state has the capacity to legislate generally for everyone.
- where there are elements of control being exercised by the service, such as the enforcement of criminal justice or the protection of children in social work. There have been experiments with private provision in these fields, but there is a fundamental ethical problem: limiting people's liberty can only be done within the rule of law, and that is necessarily the province of government.
- where there are social objectives to be met, and there are substantial economies of scale or effort in meeting them through

[559] F Hayek, 1944, *The Road to Serfdom*, London: Routledge and Kegan Paul, pp 89–90.
[560] P Spicker, 2000, *The welfare state: a general theory*, London: Sage, Part 3.

a unified system, rather than through fragmented services (for example, the considerable economies achieved by national health services). If the public sector is more effective, better quality or cheaper than the alternatives – as it sometimes may be – the arguments for distributing services through the private sector come to look rather weak.

There is an argument, too, for the state to step into the breach when other sectors fail, but that may be a reason for bolstering the other sectors rather than replacing them. None of the arguments about the public sector can be considered in isolation, because necessarily they refer to the performance of the state relative to the alternatives.

The public sector has been the subject of strong criticism from the 'radical right' and the advocates of private sector solutions. Government is criticised for being paternalistic,[561] inefficient,[562] slow to respond[563] and for not doing what markets would do instead.[564] Many of those comments are tendentious – either they pick on bad practice while ignoring counter-examples, or they simply assert that governments do the 'wrong' things. But there are also cases where public services do fall down by their own criteria, typically because their aims are self-contradictory. Hood points to three main sets of values:

- 'sigma type values', emphasising frugality and the reduction of waste,
- 'theta type values', emphasising rectitude, fairness and legitimacy; and
- 'lambda-type values', emphasising resilience, robustness and security.[565]

These can pull in different directions. Saving money works against robustness; accountability and legitimacy can be wasteful, and obstruct effective processes; it is difficult to be resilient and to follow strict procedural rules at one and the same time.

---

[561] A Seldon, 1977, *Charge!*, London: Temple Smith; M Friedman, R Friedman, 1981, *Free to choose*, Harmondsworth: Penguin.

[562] C Winston, 2006, *Government failure versus market failure*, Washington DC: Brookings, pp 2–3.

[563] A Seldon, in Tullock, Seldon and Brady 2002, p ix.

[564] J Le Grand, 1992, The theory of government failure, *British Journal of Political Science*, 21(4) 423–442.

[565] C Hood, 1991, A public management for all seasons? *Public Administration* 69(1) 3–19.

The private sector

The private sector is usually associated with the principles of the economic 'market'. In principle, that implies that private services are independently owned and run, engaged in commercial activity, and motivated by profit or personal reward. The arguments for and against market provision were considered in Chapter 10. The central question is, once more, which approach offers the best way to promote welfare and achieve the objectives of policy.

The identification of the 'private sector' with the 'market' carries with it a risk of over-generalisation. The private sector is far more complex than market-based theories suggest: there are many different patterns of provision, and the process is often negotiated within a framework of regulation, contract and public purchasing. Beyond commercial provision, where commodities are exchanged for money, the private sector engages in social welfare provision through:

- occupational welfare, the provision of services to employees. Examples include health provision for employees and occupational pensions.
- delegated welfare activity, where the private sector acts as the agent of government. (In several countries, private firms are also required to collect taxes on behalf of government.)
- engagement in policy-making and processes of government, for example by participating in lobbying or partnerships; and
- corporate social responsibility, where private firms act to improve welfare in the wider society. This includes both philanthropic activity and compensation for external costs imposed by firms, such as cleaning up pollution.

'Public-private partnerships' (PPPs) have become part of the process of welfare provision, but there are many different interpretations of what this might mean. In the USA, Goodin comments, PPP means the delivery of public services by private firms working for profit, chosen by service users and paid for by a capitation fee or fee for service. In the UK, it typically means the engagement of private finance in the development of public works. In Australia, it means contracting out services to private firms through a block contract. 'Obviously', Goodin writes, 'these are three fundamentally different policies, travelling under similar names.'[566]

Box 12.1: Health care in the USA

The USA is often thought of as a model of a 'private' health care system, but this is misleading. The system is largely based on insurance – 90% of the population have some kind of insurance cover, and the aim of health care reforms has been to extend coverage to those who are left out. The coverage depends on a 'mixed economy', not solely on private market provision.

The private sector in the US is also referred to as 'voluntary'. Some voluntary hospitals are non-profit; some are philanthropic, which is not quite the same thing. The voluntary sector commonly combines private work with charitable aims and a degree of public funding, in the same way as health care in Britain before the NHS. A US hospital will often have private rooms, private wards, and public wards – with clear status divisions between the classes as a result. Public provisions include:

- *Medicare* This is public assistance to elderly people for hospital care. For other forms of medical care, there is additionally Supplemental Medical Insurance.
- *Medicaid* This is means-tested public assistance with health bills for people who are poor. At the discretion of the authorities, students and people who are chronically sick (like kidney patients) may also be included.
- *State services* The term 'state' may be confusing here. The 'United States' is a federation; there is a central government, but there are also State governments, each with their own legislative, executive and judicial functions. Psychiatric care, in particular, is often provided for at State level. Two States, Minnesota and Hawaii, have services that are sufficiently extensive to be considered equivalent to a National Health Service. The State Children's Health Insurance Program offers supplementary federal funding to states supporting insurance for families with children.
- *TRICARE (the military health system) and the Veterans' Health Administration* Services personnel, ex-servicemen and their dependants are covered by special arrangements. These services have a wide coverage, currently over 72 million people.

---

[566] R Goodin, 2003, *Democratic accountability, the third sector and all*, JF Kennedy School of Government, http://papers.ssrn.com/sol3/Delivery.cfm/SSRN_ID418262_code030624590.pdf?abstractid=418262&mirid=1

There are other more minor federal provisions, including services for the President and the Indian Health Service for native Americans; and most public servants in regular employment have health care paid for by their employer, which is again the government. Effectively, government in the US pays for most of the medical provision in the country.

However, these provisions are only partial. At the time of writing, 50 million people in the US do not have health insurance and many more are not insured adequately to cover major illness.[567] The Patient Protection and Affordable Care Act 2010 aims to extend the scope of insurance by ensuring that everyone not covered by employment-based insurance or a public system should obtain insurance.

The voluntary sector

The voluntary sector – sometimes called the 'third sector' – is extremely diverse, ranging from small local societies to large, very 'professional' agencies. It covers a wide range of different types of activity, typically focused on health, social services, housing and community development, environmental, cultural and international aid agencies. Kendall and Knapp suggest that the definition of the voluntary sector can be expanded to include independent educational institutions, business and trade associations and sports clubs.[568] In the US and some European countries, the 'voluntary' sector is closely identified with non-profit associations; in some cases it may simply refer to non-governmental organisations. A 'voluntary' hospital may simply be an independent one.

Much of the work done by the third sector is professional and commissioned by public authorities; the issues of coverage and governance are similar to other public services, while issues relating to delegated authority and diversity are similar to other independent provision. To some extent, the role of the voluntary sector is simply supplementary to statutory services; in England and Wales, the National Society for the Protection of Cruelty to Children does, in large part, what would otherwise have to be done by social workers. But it can also be seen as complementary, in a number of ways: the initiation of new approaches and techniques, the development of specialised expertise, and the establishment of 'partnerships' or contracts between

---

[567] C DeNavas-Walt, B Proctor, C Smith, 2011, *Income, poverty and health insurance coverage in the United States: 2010*, Washington DC: United States Census Bureau, p 77.

[568] J Kendall, M Knapp, 1996, *The voluntary sector in the UK*, Manchester, Manchester University Press.

voluntary and statutory agencies. Voluntary agencies can do things which statutory agencies could not do: for example, they can work with people (like people with drug dependencies) who might reject any statutory service; they can criticise state services; and they can help people dealing with state services, as in welfare rights work.

There is a further dimension to the voluntary sector, which calls for consideration in its own right: voluntary activity, where people donate their labour without payment. This can refer to a wide range of activities. Jones, Brown and Bradshaw classify the different types of volunteering as including direct service giving; running voluntary organisations (like the 'voluntary housing sector); participation or self-help groups; fundraising; public service (which is often unpaid); and pressure group activity.[569] They detail some of the disadvantages of reliance on volunteers. There are problems with staffing; the dominant ethos of charitable work in Britain has tended, Gerard once commented, to be 'sacrificial' rather than professional,[570] and despite substantial changes in the sector in subsequent years there is still an element of truth in that. The selection of volunteers is not always strict; things may be done judgmentally; many volunteers are unwilling to do administration. There are also problems in responsiveness to need. Services are provided not necessarily where they are needed, but where people want to give them; voluntary agencies founded to meet the needs of one period can outlast their usefulness; and agencies with a single aim can be inflexible in their use of resources. However, many of the same criticisms could equally be levelled at statutory agencies.

Mutual aid

There is a particular part of the third sector which deserves special notice, because it has quite distinctive characteristics: this is the class of services which are based on mutual aid or solidarity. There is a good case to consider this category as a sector in itself, because the organisation and behaviour of solidaristic groups is quite different from that of other non-profit organisations. Historically, mutual aid was one of the main foundations of welfare organisations, through trades unions, professional associations and friendly societies;[571] in many countries, solidaristic services of this kind have continued to be one of the primary

---

[569] K Jones, J Brown, J Bradshaw, 1978, *Issues in social policy*, London: RKP.
[570] D Gerard, 1983, *Charities in Britain*, London: Bedford Square Press.
[571] H Raynes, 1960, *Social security in Britain*, London: Pitman; J-J Dupeyroux, M Borgetto, R Lafore, 2008, *Droit de la sécurité sociale*, Paris: Dalloz.

focuses through which welfare is provided.[572] The relative neglect of such arrangements in the English-speaking literature is difficult to explain – Beveridge certainly understood 'voluntary action' in these terms[573] – though David Green has argued that solidaristic approaches offer an alternative both to the state and to the commercial sector.[574]

The central principle of mutual aid has been voluntary collective effort, which is both self-interested and supportive of others. People who enter such arrangements make some kind of contribution – such as paying a subscription, offering labour, or participating in management – and receive support on a mutual basis. The most common model is probably a system of voluntary insurance, usually for income maintenance or health care, which offers social protection in return for a basic contribution. But there are many other examples, including co-operatives, self-help groups, and the trades unions themselves.

The scope of mutual aid is considerable – the mutualist arrangements for health care in Israel covered nearly 90% of the population before the government decided to break it up.[575] The main limitation is that solidarity cannot be comprehensive: some people have a limited ability to contribute, and others are likely to be excluded by the conditions of membership.

The informal sector

The 'informal sector' consists of communities, friends, neighbours and kin. The discharge of people from institutions and maintenance of individuals in the community has led to a greater emphasis on the role of carers. The trends are not straightforward: evidence relating to older people with intense needs in the UK showed that in the late 1980s and early 90s, older people were moving into formal care and relying less on informal carers, and in the period from 1995 to 2000, they were moving from formal to informal care. There has been a

---

[572] P Baldwin, 1990, *The politics of social solidarity*, Cambridge: Cambridge University Press; J Clasen, E Viebrock, 2008, Voluntary unemployment insurance and trade union membership, *Journal of Social Policy* 37(3) 433–452.

[573] W Beveridge, 1948, *Voluntary action*, London: Allen and Unwin.

[574] D Green, 1993, *Reinventing civil society*, London: IEA Health and Welfare Unit.

[575] Y Zalmanovitch, 1997, Some antecedents to healthcare reform: Israel and the US, *Policy & Politics* 25(3) pp 251–268.

more general trend, too, for the proportions of people receiving very intensive care to fall over time.[576]

The experience of community care has been to stress the limitations of the state and the public sector. Michael Bayley made the argument, in respect of people with intellectual disabilities, that most care was not being provided by the statutory services, but by informal carers. The role of the state is, realistically, to supplement, relieve or reinforce the care given by others.[577] This approach has led to a range of criticisms. The social costs to carers ought to be considered, while the economic costs are underestimated because they are not charged. Feminist writers have criticised the burden imposed on women. 'When the word 'community' is used,', Elizabeth Wilson writes, ' ... it should be read as 'family'. Furthermore, for 'family' we should read 'women'.'[578] Pascall suggests that if a woman is present, the services will not offer support.[579] This is not strictly true; services reduce support if anyone else is present in a family, male or female.[580] But where there is more than one potential carer, both male and female, it will in practice normally be the female who incurs the extra responsibility of care. The situation is arguably no better from the point of view of recipients. Service to dependent individuals is often unexamined; there is no guarantee that informal carers will offer the best care.

Welfare pluralism

The study of different sectors makes it clear that the state does not operate in isolation; rather, it acts in conjunction with a number of non-statutory organisations. In the days before 'welfare states', charities and the voluntary sector were not necessarily as independent as they might have appeared; the state often had an active interest in regulation and support of their activities.[581] The commitment of post-war states to welfare may have given the impression that these relationships had been, or were in the process of being supplanted, but in most industrial

---

[576] L Pickard, 2012, Substitution between formal and informal care, *Ageing and Society* 32(7) 1147–1175.

[577] M Bayley, 1973, *Mental handicap and community care*, London: RKP.

[578] E Wilson, 1982, Women, community and the family, in A Walker (ed) *Community care*, Oxford: Blackwell.

[579] G Pascall, 1986, *Social policy: a feminist analysis*, London: Tavistock.

[580] S Arber, N Gilbert, M Evandrou, 1988, Gender, household composition and receipt of domiciliary services, *Journal of Social Policy* 17(2) 153–176.

[581] J Barry, C Jones, 1991, *Medicine and charity before the welfare state*, London: Routledge.

countries there is a complex set of relationships between the state and the other sectors of welfare, which has to be regarded as the normal pattern through which welfare is organised and distributed.[582]

This has prompted arguments about 'welfare pluralism', which is the provision of welfare services from many different sources. The idea of the 'mixed economy of welfare' emphasises the diversity of the provision of welfare in society. Table 12.1 was originally based on work by Judge and Knapp; I have developed it further from an earlier version.[583]

Table 12.1: The mixed economy of welfare					
	Provision				
Finance	*Public*	*Private*	*Voluntary*	*Mutual aid*	*Informal*
Public	Social services depart- ments	Private homes for elderly people	Delegated agency services	State- sponsored mutualist régimes	Foster care
Private corporate			Occupa- tional welfare	Philan- thropic founda- tions	Employer- sponsored workers' organis- ations
Charges to consumers	Residential care for elderly people	Private health care	Housing association rents	Building societies	Child- minding
Mutualist (subscriptions/ contributions)	National insurance	Health mainten- ance organis- ations	Union pension funds		
Voluntary	Hospital friends	Purchase of services by voluntary organis- ations	Religious welfare organis- ations	Self-help groups	Family care

[582] P Spicker, 2000, *The welfare state*, London: Sage.
[583] K Judge, M Knapp, 1985, Efficiency in the production of welfare, in R Klein, M O'Higgins (eds) *The future of welfare*, Oxford: Blackwell; P Spicker, 1988, *Principles of social welfare*, London: Routledge.

There are three basic, and powerful, arguments for welfare pluralism.

- *Diversity* The range of services offered, the kind of things which can be done, is wider with the contribution of different sectors than without them.
- *The welfare society* The second is a moral argument for the type of society we want to live in. Conservatives have emphasised the pluralistic nature of welfare; traditional conservatism stresses an 'organic view' of society, as a series of interconnecting relationships, and the role of family and duty. Similar sentiments are shared by those on the left: Titmuss argued that the voluntary sector also has an important social role; it allows people to be altruistic.[584] We had to become not only a 'welfare state' but a 'welfare society'.[585]
- *The recognition of reality* The state does not, and cannot, provide all the welfare in a society. In practice, what the state does may be relatively minor in relation to the burdens of care experienced by informal carers, and the state's task is to complement and supplement this kind of care to the greatest degree possible.

At the same time, some reservations should be made.

- *Comprehensiveness* A pluralistic welfare society might not be able to respond comprehensively to need. The extension of solidarity suffers from a basic flaw; that the definition of people to whom we hold responsibility also has the necessary effect of defining others as falling outside that area of responsibility.
- *Equity and social justice* Solidaristic networks are highly differentiated, which means they work very much more favourably for some people than they do for others. Where there is a concern with social equality – that is, the removal of disadvantages – there is the problem that those who are poorest and least able to protect themselves are also those who are least likely to be adequately supported by other social networks. The effect of trying to complement and supplement provision, rather than to redress the balance, may be to commit such people to an inferior and stigmatised form of residual provision.

---

[584] R Titmuss, 1970, *The gift relationship*, Harmondsworth: Penguin.
[585] W A Robson, 1976, *Welfare state and welfare society*, London: Allen and Unwin.

Governance: partnership and agency

Chapter 7 introduced the idea of 'governance'. The process of government is not simply a matter of governments deciding what to do, issuing commands or doing things themselves; there is a process of regulation, planning, partnership and coordination. The provision of welfare depends on a range of actors, many of whom will not be part of the 'state'. Regulation was explained before as the process of establishing a framework of rules. Planning is a process of identifying objectives, methods and the means of implementation. When governments are trying to plan for the provision of welfare, they have to recognise and respond to circumstances.

Co-ordination and partnership

Hudson identifies three approaches to co-ordination: co-operative strategies, incentive strategies and authoritative strategies.[586] Authoritative strategies mean that people are instructed to work together. (The creation of formal co-ordinating bodies is not always welcome – Marris and Rein, in one of the few studies brave enough to explain where things went wrong, describe one agency which was perhaps unsurprisingly rebuffed when it offered to co-ordinate others.[587]) Incentive strategies involve some kind of inducement for agencies to work together. Agencies can be given financial incentives or disincentives for particular types of action – either relating to individual cases, or by offering funding with a requirement for co-ordination before the funds can be unlocked.

In co-operative strategies, people try to work together by mutual agreement. At the level of management, working in partnership is seen as a way to achieve 'joined up thinking' and coordinated services. Partnerships are believed to increase the capacity of partners, through

- 'synergy' – the added value that comes when a partnership can do something that individual partners cannot do separately;
- 'transformation', because partners learn new ways of working from their engagement; or

---

[586] B Hudson, 1985, Collaboration in social welfare, *Policy & Politics* 15(3) 175–182.
[587] P Marris, M Rein, 1974, *Dilemmas of social reform*, Harmondsworth: Penguin.

- budget enlargement,[588] because people working together should be able to pool their resources. Often they are able to gain access to funds they cannot achieve individually.

'Partnership' has become a norm of governance. Governments throughout the developing world have been encouraged by international organizations to re-think their approach to governance, working jointly with commercial and non-governmental organisations.

McDonald distinguishes 'strategic' and 'communicative' partnerships.[589] Strategic partnerships are instrumental; they are intended to achieve particular results, such as the delivery of a service or to tackle a problem. Communicative partnerships are justified mainly in terms of the act of cooperation; they work as a forum for discussion, and a way of developing networks between organisations. Many practitioners are suspicious of 'talking shops', not without reason. It is difficult to say whether communicative partnerships actually help service delivery – but that is not what they are there to do. What should be true, in principle, is that the development of networks should help to identify mechanisms for the times when problems do arise – provided, of course, that the agencies involved, and perhaps the personnel, are reasonably stable.

Contracts for public service

An alternative approach to the co-ordination of services has developed through imitation of the private market. In the private market, services often duplicate each other; they compete for the custom of users, who are able to choose between different competing organisations. There is not then usually one organisation which might do a task, but a range of organisations. One way of bringing about this form of competition is what Gilbert and Terrell refer to as the 'purposive duplication' of services[590] – services are deliberately set up, or at least encouraged to set up, in competition with others. The same effect can be achieved by fragmenting existing services, so that independent

---

[588] Mackintosh, cited by M Powell, B Dowling, 2006, New Labour's partnerships: comparing conceptual models with existing forms, *Social Policy and Society* 5(2) pp 305–14.

[589] I McDonald, 2005, Theorising partnerships, *Journal of Social Policy* 34(4) pp 579–600.

[590] N Gilbert, P Terrell, 2002, *Dimensions of social welfare policy*, Boston: Allyn and Bacon.

hospitals or independent social security schemes then have to compete with each other.

The development of competition might suggest that the difficulties of co-ordination would be magnified; but that is not, for the most part, how a private market system works. Firms which hope to have some kind of service performed can approach a number of organisations, and where they are able to undertake the work more effectively or efficiently the firm commissions work from them. Supermarkets do not usually have their own builders to create new developments; they commission builders to develop units for them, and pay them for their services. The organisation of the social services is not quite like the organisation of a supermarket, but there are arguments for seeing some of the functions of social services in a similar way. At the simplest level, this has been the argument behind the 'privatisation' of a range of functions previously tackled in the public sector, like office cleaning, catering and building services; but the same rationale can be applied to many other kinds of work. A social services authority does not necessarily have the resources and the specialised staff to offer a régime appropriate for a young offender with severe emotional problems who also requires resocialisation and control; what has become commonplace is for one social service, or a voluntary organisation, with particular expertise to act for others, receiving payment for the service. Co-ordination, then, rests not on the willingness of people to co-operate, but in the functional differentiation of distinct organisations.

Agency arrangements are based on a distinction between principal and agent. Policy is made by a decision-maker (the 'principal'), but the implementation of policy is based on a contract between the policy-making body and the organisation which carries it out (the agent). Common and Flynn identify four types of service contract. These are

- *Service contracts* These are detailed specifications describing the process that will be undertaken.
- *Partnership contracts* Purchasers and providers collaborate to design a mutual agreement.
- *Service agreements* Providers are contracted to provide a service, rather than to conduct a specific process. This is commonly used with in-service units and long-standing voluntary organisations.
- *Informal agreements* Arrangements are made between local managers for ad-hoc provision.[591]

---

[591] R Common, N Flynn, 1992, *Contracting for care*, York: Joseph Rowntree Foundation.

The agency model is capable of generating a wide range of different approaches to service delivery. However, the nature of the contract tends to be strongly geared to the achievement of explicit goals, usually understood in terms of service output – the number of patients treated, the number of clients advised, and so forth. The guidance given to health authorities, for example, allows for three types of contract:

- block contracts (for provision of a service),
- cost–per–case (for services to individuals), or
- a combination of cost and volume.[592]

Contracts in the UK generally seem to be made on block contracts with the voluntary sector, but cost per case in the private sector (e.g. residential care for elderly people). The UK government has been experimenting, too, with 'black box' contracts that offer payment for results, without supervision of the intermediate process. To date, the effect of such contracts has been to obscure what is being done, because it removes from the sub-contractors the responsibility to account for their actions in the way that public governance demands. There are incentives for providers to do what will best deliver them returns rather than to provide a comprehensive service, and it is very questionable whether these contracts are capable of delivering the intended benefits.[593]

If policy-making has to pass through a series of stages, and it alters at each stage, what comes out may look very different from what happened at the start.[594] Ashworth et al identify five problems in agency arrangements:

- resistance, where the contracted agencies seek to follow their own agenda;
- ritualistic compliance, where the agenda is distorted by slavish compliance to specified targets;
- performance ambiguity, where because aims are vague, it is not clear what is being done;

[592] G Foster, J Wilson, 1998, National Health Service Financial Management, in J Wilson (ed) *Financial management for the public services*, Buckingham: Open University Press, p 241.

[593] House of Commons Work and Pensions Committee, 2013, *Can the Work Programme work for all user groups?*, London: TSO, HC 162.

[594] M Hill, P Hupe, 2003, The multi-layer problem in implementation research, *Public Management Review* 5(4) 471–491.

- gaps in data, where reporting is made impossible by lack of information; and
- capture, where the principal begins to comply with the agent.[595]

There are, of course, parallel problems in the management of public service agencies.

There tends to be an assumption in analyses of principal-agent relationships that the motivations and behaviour of public and private agencies are pretty much equivalent.[596] That is partly true – in both cases the objectives of the principal can be subverted by the self-interest of the agents. It can also be misleading, because the pattern of behaviour of agencies undertaking public service is not equivalent to the pattern of behaviour of sub-contractors working on private sector projects. Simply put, a private firm commissioned by government to run a prison is not in the same relationship to its principal and others as a plumber commissioned by a builder to fit a bathroom into a house under construction. There are three main differences. The first lies in the structure of accountability. The public sector has developed a pattern of working based on accountability and reference to authority (considered further in Chapter 13), and in many cases private contractors have to conform to that. The second rests in the continuing provision of a service, rather than a single act of production. Where there is a continuing process, there has to be continuing monitoring and reporting, and that calls for the contractor to be subject to the same kind of régime and framework as a public agency would be. The third is a relationship to service users – in the case of a prison, to various agencies, including the system of criminal justice, and to prisoners themselves. That places the private contractor in a similar position politically to public agencies, where roles and understandings have to be negotiated. It follows that private contractors are subject to similar constraints to public agencies.

Quasi-markets

Since the 1980s there have been increasing attempts to bring the activities of public sector agencies into line with the behaviour of private sector organisations. Some part of this is ideological; the 'new

---

[595] R Ashworth, G Boyne, R Walker, 2002, Regulatory problems in the public sector, *Policy & Politics*, 20(2) pp 195–211.

[596] A Bertelli, 2012, *The political economy of public sector governance*, Cambridge: Cambridge Univertsity Press.

right' believes that the private sector is intrinsically more efficient, because of the constraints of competition, than the state. In part, it reflects some of the arguments of economists who see the implications of scarcity as inevitable, and consequently argue that public sector firms can be analysed in terms of economic theory in the same way as private sector ones. The recognition of welfare pluralism has also had an impact in its own right; if the state is not a sole provider, but is one of several potential providers, then the kinds of consideration which affect the behaviour of suppliers are likely to be similar to those which affect firms in the private market, including consumer demand, the performance of competitors, and relative efficiency.

Services were prepared for this kind of structure by a process of 'agencification', based on a distinction between the component parts of a service. If each part of a service can be treated as a different unit or agency, it becomes possible to review the management of each separately, and to consider whether that unit would operate better in the public or private sector. The same principle can be simulated in large, complex organisations through cost-centred budgeting. Every part of a firm is expected to make money; if it does not it is likely to be closed down or sold off. If a task can be performed more efficiently or cheaper by a sub-contractor, it should be. The effect overall is to minimise costs and maximise output. (There are some reservations to make about this theory. A classic example is of a restaurant which only breaks even on its food, but makes the largest profit on wine and coffee. In theory, it should stop serving food and offer drinks instead; in practice, if it did so there would be no demand for the drinks at the price offered. Similarly, it is all very well to tell a hospital that it should have a cost-centre for pharmaceutical provision, but it cannot necessarily stop having a unit to dispense pharmaceuticals and continue to function effectively as a hospital.) A more appropriate comparison for many social services is the development of corporate management. Galbraith argues that private firms have had to adapt to complex technologies by increasing the number of specialists who have to work in a multi-disciplinary team.[597] The effective cost-centre becomes the team, rather than the functional speciality. The theory behind cost-centring may be valid, but it is essential to define such centres appropriately to the functions which the agency is performing.

One of the implications of this approach has been that the provision of welfare has fragmented between the different services. Policy and planning remain with a central authority, but the responsibility for

---

[597] J K Galbraith, 1972, *The new industrial state*, Harmondsworth: Penguin.

service provision can be shared between a number of autonomous organisations. A hospital which wishes to discharge patients rapidly might rely on other social services; it may employ its own staff to do so; but it also has the option of commissioning an independent organisation to undertake the work. A pensions agency may maintain its own computer staff, or it may sub-contract the work to specialists. The image which emerges of welfare systems becomes less that of an ordered hierarchy than of a network of providing organisations, with a diversity of rules and methods of proceeding. Co-ordination of effort takes place from the top, because a planning authority is attempting to use its resources to steer the pattern of provision, and from below, in that consumers (or professionals acting on their behalf) are purchasing a range of services which are appropriate in individual cases.

Box 12.2: Packages of care

The foundation of the 'welfare state' in the UK led many to think of the state as the crucial actor in the provision of services. Bayley's work on the position of people with learning disabilities challenged that position: the primary role in the provision of social services was taken, not by statutory services, but by the families; the statutory services had to be seen at best as contributors to a network of services. The provision of services became, then, not a matter of the state providing comprehensively for each individual, but the development of a range of alternative services. From this range, each individual could be offered a programme selected for that person. Bayley refers to this process as 'interweaving' state services with community support.[598]

The Griffiths report on community care took forward this idea in the concept of 'packages of care'.[599] If there was a range of services, it would be possible to select the services that were most appropriate to a person's needs, 'tailoring' services to the needs of individuals.[600] Griffiths argued:

> care and support can be provided from a variety of sources. There is value in a multiplicity of provision, not least from the consumer's point of view, because of the widening of choice, flexibility, innovation and competition it should stimulate. The proposals are therefore aimed at stimulating the further development of the 'mixed economy' of care.[601]

[598] M Bayley, 1973, *Mental handicap and community care*, London: RKP.
[599] R Griffiths, 1988, *Community care: agenda for action*, London: HMSO, 1988, p 1
[600] Griffiths, 1988, para 6.5
[601] Griffiths, 1988, para 3.4

The same approach is reflected in contemporary arguments for 'personalised' services.

> Personalisation places an emphasis on providing social care services tailored to the individual needs of the user, rather than fitting people into existing services that may not deliver the right kind of support for their particular circumstances.[602]

Both the idea of the package, and the related idea of personalisation, are essentially quasi-market approaches; they are an attempt to duplicate the choice, flexibility and responsiveness of the private market in contexts where traditional markets have found it difficult to operate.

In practice, any gains in practice have been patchy, and heavily dependent on context, even though the operation has selected those most likely to benefit.[603] Some of the problems stem from the difficulties of operating like a market in circumstances where people are vulnerable and their alternatives are limited. Decisions are constrained;[604] service users and carers often feel that decisions have been made by other people.[605] There is a visible tension between the promise of individual choice and the role of professional assessment. That is true partly because of the imbalance of power, but it is also true because personal choice and professional assessment lead to different outcomes – if they did not, there would be little reason to bother with a professional assessment.

Beyond that, these approaches also have the same disadvantages as market-based provision. The first, and most obvious, is the scarcity of resources. Choice does not mean that people get what they want; it means that they are able to take a preferred option from a necessarily limited range. There is always an opportunity cost – the sacrifice of something else that might have been desirable, but is less to be preferred. Then there are limits to how many options providers will offer. Choice in the market is not only exercised by consumers; it is also exercised by providers. Circumstances which are difficult or uncommon, people who are isolated or geographically

---

[602] J Harlock, 2010, Personalisation: emerging implications for the voluntary and community sector, *Voluntary Sector Review* 1(3) 371–8, p 371.

[603] P Spicker, 2012, Personalisation falls short, *British Journal of Social Work*, doi: 10.1093/bjsw/bcs063

[604] I Allen, D Hogg, S Peace, 1992, *Elderly people: choice, participation and satisfaction*, London: Policy Studies Institute; B Hardy, R Young, G Wistow, 1999, Dimensions of choice in the care and assessment process, *Health and Social Care in the community* 7(6) 483–91.

[605] H Arksey, C Glendinning, 2007, Choice in the context of informal care-giving, *Health and Social Care in the Community*, 15(2) 165–75.

remote, lead to restricted choices at best. And then there is the scarcity of resources and options at the time when they are needed. It is all very well telling people they have a choice; there may be nothing appropriate to choose. [606]

Quasi-markets are like markets, but they are not the same as markets.[607] Agency arrangements are quite different: the purchaser is the principal, not the consumer, and the provider is an agent, not an independent supplier. If public services are run for reasons of policy, so are the contracts they commission. Public services operate within a conventional structure of governance and delegated authority. The contracts they issue have to be framed within those constraints, and that typically means that private firms that are providing services on an agency basis become subject to the same constraints. The advocates of the market sometimes complain that government does not act like a business. That is perfectly true, and just as perfectly it misses the point. Public services are not meant to operate like businesses, and if private sector firms are commissioned within a structure of delegated authority to operate public services, they cannot expect to operate like businesses either.

There are important differences between public services and private enterprises. Social services organisations have other aims besides profit and loss. At the individual level, people who it is inefficient or uneconomical to treat have still to be dealt with; they cannot effectively be excluded, as they might be by private insurance. Private firms need, in the constraints of the private market, to be efficient. This means that they will produce units at the lowest unit cost. If they exceed their capacity for efficient production, unit costs start to rise and profits fall. Social services, by contrast, cannot limit production at the point where unit costs are lowest, in most cases because this will imply that some people are left without service. The private sector can hold its costs down by avoiding problematic cases. This implies, of course, that when other things are equal private firms will be more efficient than public services, because the public services are trying to do something different. But it also means that agency contracts are not going to be efficient, either.

---

[606] C Needham, 2011, *Personalising public services*, Bristol: Policy Press.

[607] J Le Grand, W Bartlett, 1993, *Quasi-markets and social policy*, Basingstoke: Macmillan.

Exit from the market is not an option for the public sector. Building firms frequently go out of business, sometimes with work half finished; a housing agency which is trying to provide a service for its tenants cannot permit that to happen. Nursing care for elderly people cannot be discontinued because an operator goes out of business. People cannot be released from prison because a private operator cannot afford to continue operations. If a contractor's performance is poor, the public authorities may have no choice but to carry on. As one witness told the inquiry into one of the NHS's worst hospitals:

> [Witness] These contracts, okay, you can argue they're legally binding, but the reality is that how do you implement a contract when you've got a service like [this] hospital ...? The ultimate sanction is you either close the hospital or you take significant funds away. Neither is an option....
>
> [The Chairman]: Does it amount, then, to an acceptance that to some extent, not completely, the concept of commissioning by contract is a little bit of a fiction?
>
> [Witness]: My own personal view that in these circumstances ... the contract could be described as a fiction, because if it has no teeth, how do you implement the penalty that drives the contract?[608]

What happens effectively is that the state, implicitly or explicitly, accepts losses on such activities when they are undertaken within the public sector, and underwrites public services activities when they are commissioned from the private sector. There is a strong case, even where activities might be done cheaper elsewhere, for maintaining them in the public sector.

ISSUE FOR DISCUSSION

What effect does the source of provision have on the character of a service? Does it matter who provides services?

---

[608] R Francis (chair) 2013, *Report of the Mid Staffordshire NHS Foundation Trust Public Inquiry*, vol 1, 7.338, HC 898-1, London: TSO.

CHAPTER 13

The organisation of public services

The public services
Welfare bureaucracies
Organisational roles
Divisions of labour

The public services

Administration is not a subject to excite the passions and set the pulse racing, and there is a tendency in some of the literature to ignore issues of administration because intentions, motives and power relationships are simply more interesting. A common flaw in analyses of policy is the assumption that ideologues, reformers or governments have simply to agree what they want and they will get it. There may be times when this is true, but it is wrong as often as not. Whatever governments decide, policies cannot simply be set in motion; policies have to be translated into practice. The effect of policies may be very different from what is expected, and the administrative process plays a major role in this. In sociology, explanations for policy and process are often based on a distinction between 'structure' – the social relationships and conditions which set the framework for action – and 'agency', or human action. That distinction tends to miss a third dimension, the influence on policy of the institutions and organisations which carry out policies. The recognition of the influence of administrative organisation has been called a 'new institutionalism', though as with many things that claim to be new, there is nothing new about it.

Public services have three characteristic methods of operation, which lead to them operating quite differently from commercial organisations. First, they serve the purposes of public policy; they are there because somebody, a government or a founder, has commissioned them to do what they do. Second, they are redistributive: the person who pays is not the person who benefits. Whether funding comes from taxation, from charitable donation or mutual subscription, there is not a simple exchange of money for services. And that leads to the third feature of the operation of public services: they are generally operated as a trust.

In a charitable trust, one person pays, a trustee operates the service, a third party benefits. For services provided by government, similarly, the government acts in trust, for the benefit of citizens. Because public services are formed to pursue public purposes, because they are not governed by demand in the market, and because they operate as trusts, there has to be some other mechanism by which they can be led to meet their objectives. There has to be a system of accountability.

Accountability takes several forms. *Professional* accountability implies that people in public services guarantee levels of competence and quality of service, and can be held to account for failure by their peers. *Administrative* accountability implies that officials will be accountable to others who have the responsibility to supervise their actions. Financial accountability, which is a sub-category of administrative accountability, is usually a reference to a distinct set of systems, requiring administrators to open financial accounts to scrutiny. *Legal* accountability arises because, where people can make legal claims against an agency, agencies have to be prepared to explain their actions in relation to any individual case. *'Democratic* accountability' depends on systems which make public services ultimately accountable to elected authority. To be legitimate, the actions of public services have to be developed through a legitimate process, where the authority to act is delegated to them, and they are accountable to the higher authority for what they do. This is often explained in terms of the electoral process, but the principles apply much more generally in the public services than a focus on elections might apply; it is at the root of constitutional governance, and it applies in third sector as much as it does in the public sector (Box 13.1).

The characteristic pattern of work in the public services is that public servants have to expect to be accountable for their actions, and organise processes and procedures in order to meet those requirements. This means that relationships between providers and service users are not simply governed, as free market theorists think it should be, by the spontaneous interaction of producer and consumer. Public services depend instead on a reference to structures of authority and rules of accountability which can legitimate their actions.

Box 13.1: Constitutional governance and accountability

'Democratic accountability' is usually taken to mean that officials in the public sector are accountable for their actions to an elected government. Much of the discussion of the idea focuses on the element of 'democracy'; but the second part – accountability – is critical.

In principle, every action of a democratic government can be traced back to an ultimate source of authority – often the electorate, or an elected parliament, but sometimes a legal system. This source is sometimes referred to in terms of 'sovereignty'. In a constitutional government, like the United States or Germany, the limits of authority are defined in terms of the constitution. In the United Kingdom, where there is no written constitution, the source of authority may be more obscure – it is often taken to be the elected House of Commons – but the same principle holds: government, the executive and public bodies are able to do only what they have expressly been given the authority to do. Local authorities, in turn, derive their authority from Acts of Parliament. For ninety years, the main legal precedent limiting the powers of local councils was AG v Fulham Corporation, where the London Borough of Fulham was forbidden to provide laundry facilities for poorer people.[609] Following a change in the law granting a general power to promote well being, several London boroughs have been permitted to form a mutual insurance company.[610]

Constitutional governance implies that the powers of any public agency have to be exercised in terms, and within the limits, of the authority that the agency has been given. There is a 'golden thread' of accountability, running all the way through the actions of government. Every agency with delegated authority is accountable for the use of that authority, and accountability means, not that the agency is subject to command or control, but that actions that have been legitimised by an authority are reported to that authority. The standard pattern in recording minutes of meetings is that referrals from superior bodies and actions taken by subordinate ones are recorded so that each body can see a record of what the other has decided – though often the way this is recorded can be mysterious, calling for readers to follow through a chain of authorisations before it is possible to work out what has been decided and what has been done. In practice, authority in most public sector organisations is delegated and diffused throughout the structure, and policy is made at a range of levels, including the actions of agencies, officials and 'street-level bureaucracy'.[611]

These patterns of accountability are not confined to government organisations. Voluntary organisations, charities and social enterprises typically have constitutions and actions have to be justified in terms of powers specified by trustees, a board or a committee. While there may be external regulation which imposes a structure of accountability – for example, rules related to accounting practice, or charity regulation – constitutional

---

609 Attorney General versus Fulham Corporation, 1921.
610 Brent LBC & Ors v Risk Management Partners Ltd [2011] UKSC 7.
611 M Lipsky, 1980, *Street level bureaucracy*, London: Sage.

governance is more firmly established in the third sector than that would suggest. Bob Goodin suggests that the accountability of third sector organisations relies heavily on a public service ethos, bolstered by networks, values and a focus on reputation. [612] That seems to raise the question why the third sector should work to the same constraints as the public sector. The question may have it backwards; the third sector has been operating in this way for centuries. Historically, many religious charities and schools were subject to constitutional foundations – the wishes of the founders often being seen as paramount. The public sector often learned how to operate from the voluntary sector.

Welfare bureaucracies

Public services are not 'command structures', where someone at the top gives orders and everyone in the structure is subject to those orders. The structure of accountability works in a very different way. Each officer in a public service has a degree of delegated power to undertake a specified task. Each officer is accountable for the use of that power and the performance of that task. This is the root of the model of bureaucracy.

The idea of bureaucracy is most usually referred to the work of Weber, who outlined an 'ideal type' or rational organisation. Weber's model of bureaucracy identifies several elements:

- people have specified tasks: 'the regular activities required for the purposes of the organisation are distributed in a fixed way as official duties'.[613] Officials have to possess a particular expertise or knowledge relevant to these functions.
- there is a hierarchy of authority, with a chain of command stretching from the top to the bottom. The progress of an official's career consists of promotion through the hierarchy.
- the system is governed by rules, which are framed in abstract terms and can then be applied to specific cases.
- the system is impersonal; outcomes are decided according to the rules, rather than personal relationships, and there is a strict separation of personal affairs from official conduct.

---

[612] R Goodin, 2003, *Democratic accountability, the third sector and all,* JF Kennedy School of Government, http://papers.ssrn.com/sol3/Delivery.cfm/SSRN_ID418262_code030624590.pdf?abstractid=418262&mirid=1

[613] H H Gerth, C Wright Mills, 1948, *From Max Weber,* London: RKP.

The presentation of an 'ideal type' invites a theorist to embellish the bare bones, and that can lead to the inclusion of some less essential issues. Weber suggested that officials had to have full time appointments, and that they should have no financial stake in the organisation. He probably included these factors to distinguish the work of a bureaucracy from historical patterns of public service, and from other kinds of industrial organisation. But this is a valuable model from the point of view of welfare, because it points to a number of features which characterise welfare agencies. The first point concerns the functional division of labour. People in bureaucracies have particular roles, which means that to get something done one has to identify who has responsibility for the task. The structure of authority in bureaucracies is related to the functional tasks the agency performs.

The second argument is that there is a hierarchy. Each person in a hierarchy has some kind of delegated function, for which they are responsible to someone above them. The structure of such an organisation is like a pyramid. The person at the top is able to direct people immediately below, who in turn direct their subordinates, and so on down the pyramid. Officials are directly accountable only through the hierarchy, and not personally. (So, civil servants in the UK make decisions in the name of their minister; they are anonymous functionaries. In a traditionally run local authority, junior officers have no authorisation to make decisions. Letters are signed in the name of the head of department; in order to trace where the letter actually comes from, the reference code will usually note the initials of the letter's author, and the head of department's signature will be initialled by the person who actually signs it.) Consumers may be able to exercise sanctions through formal mechanisms for accountability, but they do not have a direct sanction against officials. Since the actions of government are nominally taken through a form of legitimate authority, and it is necessary for subordinates to be clearly and visibly accountable to elected authority, this approach is the one most commonly found in the executive branches of government.

The major advantage of such a structure is that it concentrates effective control at the centre – or at least, that it appears to: appearances are very important in the establishment of legitimate structures, because control must not only be exercised but must be seen to be exercised. The main disadvantage is that control can only be exercised by fettering the discretion of people working in the lower tiers.

In practice, the structure of welfare organisations is rarely simply hierarchical. Hierarchical lines of accountability are cross-cut by inter-relationships which demand negotiation, contact and collaboration.

Networked organisations can have multiple leaderships, and rely on a corporate structure in which colleagues exchange expertise.[614] Galbraith describes this pattern as the dominant model in high-tech industries, which rely on a strong division of labour between people with specialised expertise.[615] This is a better description of, for example, hospital management or university education, than a simple bureaucratic model would be.

Understanding the principles by which contemporary services manage their responsibilities is more difficult; there is often some distance between the formal statements of an agency's mission and what actually happens. There are not many works which have given much thought to the ways that social service agencies are actually organised, so I am going to go back to a classic study from thirty years ago. David Billis's discussion of welfare bureaucracies is an attempt to identify the division of responsibilities within social services organisations. He outlines five basic 'strata' or levels at which services operate.[616]

5. *Comprehensive field coverage*

   This is the level of policy-making and planning. The concern is to create a framework of services to meet a range of needs. Much is done at central government level; there is also corporate planning in local authorities, and much of this work is now done through partnerships of agencies.

4. *Comprehensive service provision*

   This is the organisation and direction of a complete service, like a housing department, a children's services department, a hospital or a social security office. Billis emphasises the broad territorial focus – an area in which a range of responses are possible, and in which specific responses are not prescribed.

3. *Systematic service provision*

   This is a responsibility for providing particular service units, dealing with a defined range of issues rather than individual cases: examples are residential care homes, police stations or the specialities within a hospital supervised by consultant surgeons.

---

614 A James, 1994, Managing to care, Harlow: Longmans, ch 7.

615 J K Galbraith, 1972, The new industrial state, revised ed., Penguin, Harmondsworth.

616 D Billis, 1984, Welfare bureaucracies, Aldershot: Gower.

2. *Dealing with problems as situations*

> This is generally the level at which professionals work; the test is that the professional is able to define the problem and the response. Doctors, social workers, health visitors, area housing managers and police officers work at this level.

1. *Dealing with problems as demands*

> This is a reactive approach, where service is provided in response to a specific demand; the response made is prescribed for the person who makes it. Receptionists or social security clerical officers are examples.

People within the agencies do not necessarily work exclusively at one level; some of the work is at one level, some at another. For example, a family doctor may be involved at levels 2 and 3, and sometimes at level 1. A practising social worker is unlikely to go outside levels 1 and 2. Community care managers mainly work at level 3, though some work at level 2 may be necessary. Housing management cuts across all the levels.

The levels are hierarchical in a sense, but while there is some prestige in working at higher levels, the hierarchy is not clearly about status. A family doctor generally has a higher status than a social worker, but the work that doctors do will bring them into contact much more often with social workers and health visitors rather than with planners or researchers at level 4. A hospital consultant at level 3 may well have higher status than a senior housing manager, but the housing manager will be a member of level 5 partnerships when the hospital consultant is not. A novice practitioner in social policy may well be pitched straight into work at level 5. What is being described is a different kind of system, which reflects the functional demands on an organisation. People working at different levels are doing different types of work, and need different competences to do it. Knowing how to prepare a community plan is not a qualification for running a residential care home, or vice-versa. There will generally be people at each level who occupy a different status in the hierarchy, and the lines of accountability will not run up through the levels, but in different directions.

This also reflects on some contemporary ideas about public management, many of which are drawn from a model of entrepreneurship in the private sector rather than the complex networks of public service. The tasks that are being undertaken at each level are different from the other levels. It cannot be assumed that people working at lower levels are subject to the direction of people at higher levels. The family doctor working at level 2 may employ a practice manager to undertake the level 3 work; level 5 work is sometimes done by middle-ranking managers delegated by level 4 managers. Equally, there is no reason to suppose that people at higher levels 'lead', motivate, inspire or determine the pattern of work of people at lower levels – it is not certain that they will even come into contact with them. Planning and oversight at levels 4 and 5 commonly often call for dialogue, negotiation and brokerage, rather than command and control.

Organisational roles

There is considerable variation in the organisation of social service agencies; the structures, conventions and lines of accountability differ between services, and agencies often specify different roles within their organisations. The key roles are occupied by *bureaucrats*, who perform official functions; *professionals* (and semi-professionals), who have the power to make independent decisions about responses to clients; and *managers*, who have delegated power to run sections of an organisation. These roles often overlap in practice, but considering them separately helps to understand some of the differences in the structures of accountability than people work with.

Bureaucrats

The conventional model of bureaucracy lays great emphasis on the exercise of rules. A centralised bureaucracy should, in principle, be able to establish rules to determine the behaviour of officials in every case. The obvious problem with this kind of centralised service is that where a service is designed to deal with the public, no system of rules can possibly legislate for all circumstances. In theory, subordinates must seek authority for their actions in difficult cases. This is true even where the agency has discretion: in a rational hierarchy, giving authority to the organisation does not mean that individuals at the bottom of the hierarchy have the power to make decisions. In practice, however, the complexity of circumstances leads to imperfect understanding of the rules,[617] leading to errors, some conservatism in the use of judgment, and decisions made without authority – in a classic study, Hall identifies the role of receptionists as crucial.[618] Bureaucrats are functionaries.

---

[617] P Spicker,. 2005, Five types of complexity, *Benefits*, February; National Audit Office, 2005, *Dealing with the complexity of the benefits system*, HC 592 2005–06.

[618] A Hall, 1974, *The point of entry*, London: Allen and Unwin.

They are able to exercise judgment – because someone has to decide whether a case fits the rules – but they are not allowed discretion, in the sense of a free decision in those cases where rules do not seem to apply. (The distinction between discretion and judgment is made by Davis.[619])

Weber's emphasis on the limits of personal influence reflects this concern. There is almost always some scope for such influence to be exercised, but the purpose of hierarchical organisation is to reduce this scope to the greatest degree possible. It has been argued, in the literature of public administration, that public sector workers act, like others, to maximise their status, power or income.[620] Weber's formulation outlines common constraints, but people will seek to work around these constraints; it would be naive to suppose that public bureaucrats respond solely to a conception of the 'public interest', or the interests of their agency, without reference to their personal circumstances.

Box 13.2: Social security – the bureaucratic model

The UK social security system is an extreme example of 'top-down' decision making – a bureaucratic system operating on centrally determined rules. In the days of the Poor Law, financial assistance was provided at a local level, and subject to the discretion of the Guardians of the Poor. The system which replaced it was intended to be as different from the Poor Law as possible. Benefits were to be given as of right, and the officials administering the system were not to be given any latitude about the decisions they made.

The system which resulted was consequently as centralised as it possibly could be. In the immediate post-war period, there were two main branches: National Insurance, administered by the Ministry of Pensions and National Insurance, and National Assistance, administered by the National Assistance Board. They were combined into the Department of Social Security in 1966, and the Department of Health and Social Security (DHSS) in 1968. The local offices of the DHSS were administered in accordance with national instructions. Every officer of the DHSS was a civil servant, and subject to the rules of the civil service. All decisions were taken not by individuals, but in the name of the minister. All the actions of the DHSS were governed by the Official Secrets Act. Civil servants were entitled to be anonymous. The organisation of the offices, and the pattern of service delivery, including forms, filing systems, even the design of office counters, was determined nationally in London. Wherever there were problems

---

[619] K Davis, 1966, *Discretionary justice*, Louisiana: Louisiana State University.
[620] M Hill, 2005, *The public policy process*, Harlow: Pearson/Longman.

which could not be clearly interpreted locally, those problems were referred upwards for decisions. Over time, the combination of decisions, precedents and the need to issue guidance and clarification became progressively more elaborate and complex. This made it the largest centralised bureaucratic system in the UK; arguably, it was the largest centralised system in Western Europe.

The system has undergone successive reforms since, including conversion to delivery by agencies, computerisation, and repeated attempts to change the culture. Claimants are intermittently referred to as 'customers', benefit administration has been combined with employment services and shifted away from local agencies. The process of administration, however, remains bureaucratic in form. The task of benefit officers is to operate a huge, complex system as efficiently as possible. Most of the work is done by people working at clerical and executive grades. In the days of the DHSS, claims were processed through a conveyor belt process or 'stream' within each office. The process of computerisation has led to most procedures being redesigned on different principles, but there are still divisions of labour between stations; initial calls are handled by first contact, cases are passed to local Jobcentres for interaction, and benefits go to Benefit Delivery Centres which process claims, reviews and payments. That means that several people are typically involved with the processing of each person's claim, and depending on what needs to be done about the case it will be passed to different places for processing. The Department for Work and Pensions' (DWP) diffusion of responsibilities and functional division of labour reduces the scope for judgment by individuals, and consequently helps to ensure conformity with centrally determined rules.

The bureaucratic approach tends to receive publicity only when it goes wrong – for example, during the DWP's notorious computer crashes. It receives very little attention at all when it does things right. The UK social security system has been destabilised by successive reforms, but at its peak it was remarkably effective. The average office dealt with thousands of claimants every week. Most benefits are processed within a very short period, generally a target of 14 days. This might be contrasted with other régimes: in France, the calculation of pensions begins two-and-a-half years before retirement, and some claimants may not have been paid six months after stopping work. When responsibilities have been transferred from social security offices to other administrations, the other administrations have hardly been able to cope. The transfer of responsibility for Housing Benefits to local authorities, in 1982/3, was described in its day as 'the greatest administrative fiasco in the history of the welfare state';[621] the local authorities were overwhelmed by the sheer volume of the work. Something similar happened in the development of Child Tax Credit under the aegis of the Inland Revenue: it took the best part of a year before the Revenue was able to process many routine claims. What the social security system lost in responsiveness to individual circumstances, it gained in effective service delivery.

Professions and semi-professions

In the provision of welfare, the position of the ideal 'bureaucrat' is not typical. The problem is that rule-based administration is not necessarily practical in all circumstances. The clearest example is probably medical care, where doctors exercise professional judgment about treatment rather than working to pre-established rules; but the same principles apply to many other workers who have to make judgments in relation to circumstances, including social workers, health visitors, counsellors, community workers, teachers, advice workers, nurses and housing managers. These are referred to as 'semi-professions', because their professional role has to be understood within a management hierarchy. The position is usually discussed in terms of their 'professional' roles, as opposed to bureaucratic ones – though it is important to recognise at the outset that the exercise of such roles also takes place within a hierarchical structure.

The 'professions' refer to certain classes of occupation which give people a distinctive place in their society. In the past, the terms mainly referred to doctors, lawyers and the clergy; Jones et al also identify the professions with higher educational qualifications, which are part of the process.[622] Among the many criteria which have been proposed as criteria for professional conduct are skill based on theoretical knowledge; the provision of training and occupation; tests of the competence of members; organisation; adherence to a professional code of conduct; and altruistic service.[623] These kinds of criteria have been criticised for their looseness. In the discussion of social welfare work there are few areas in which the description would not apply; since all social services can be represented as having an altruistic ethic, all governmental activities have some code of conduct, and the

---

[621] The Times, cited R Walker, 1986, 'Aspects of administration', in P Kemp (ed) *The future of housing benefits*, Glasgow: Centre for Housing Research, p 39.

[622] K Jones, J Brown, J Bradshaw, 1978, *Issues in social policy* London: RKP, p 60.

[623] Jones et al, 1978, p 6.1

only thing which seems to distinguish 'professionals' from others is the process of qualification after a test of competence.

Probably the most important characteristic of the professions in practice is their use of discretion. Every application of rules, whether it is in a bureaucratic hierarchy or by an independent operator, requires some use of judgment. Discretion concerns the procedures which apply in cases where rules do not; it implies the use of autonomous judgment, where the rules do not offer guidance. Professionals reserve areas in which they can act autonomously – the 'clinical freedom' of doctors, the social work relationship, or the conduct by teachers of their classes. There are tensions here to be resolved; the need for flexibility and responsiveness has to be balanced against the agency's concerns to develop consistent practice, and professional claims are mediated through a process of constant negotiation.

The 'professional' role of welfare workers requires some modification of the nature of the 'rational' hierarchy. It is difficult to say whether this is a consequence of professional claims for independence, or whether the independence of professionals reflects the functional necessity of delegating decisions to people. The test of competence required as part of professional activity can be seen as a way of protecting the profession's claim to specialised knowledge, but it can also be seen as a means of protecting their clients from incompetent handling. What is generally true is that the hierarchy has to be able to accommodate some independence of action, and that this changes the nature of the hierarchy. It is scarcely possible to delegate the power to make decisions while at the same time holding only central authority to be accountable for its actions. What happens is that authority for some decisions is maintained at the centre, with some framework of rules, while other decisions are delegated to practitioners. Professionals who have wished to maintain a greater degree of independence, like doctors and dentists, have tended to prefer 'arm's length' arrangements in which they are contracted for services rather than salaried, but from the point of view of the service agency the principle is the same; some independence has to be allowed as a precondition for work to be undertaken.

Management

The idea of 'management' in social services has been imported from literature on the private sector. This reflects the growing importance of private sector initiatives – and, one has to say, of political dogma – in modern welfare states. The idealised 'manager' is a specialist, not in the provision of a service, but in its organisation. Like bureaucracy, management is organised hierarchically, but the role of the manager is different from the bureaucrat:

- The work of the manager is not specialised, but generic; managers have a general responsibility for all the functions taking place below them in a hierarchy.
- The management hierarchy is governed not primarily by rules of conduct, but by performance criteria – in the private sector, by profit, and in the public sector, by measures of outcomes and performance.
- The behaviour of the manager is governed by incentives (including financial rewards) and disincentives.
- The manager motivates staff, through 'leadership'.

This is an ideal type, rather than a reflection of the way that firms area actually organised, and it has been pointed out that it really applies to only a limited number of private firms – for example, firms involved in food distribution, rather than firms dealing with high technology.[624] The model is linked with the development of quasi-markets partly for ideological reasons, and partly because linking the role of the 'manager' with the performance of specific units or cost-centres is seen as a way of achieving the best performance from each unit.

The primary justification for this approach to management comes from a literature which is outside the area of social services, and it is difficult to know how effectively it can be applied in this context. There are some reservations. One problem concerns the nature of the work: if there are circumstances in which social services cannot work in the same way as a market, nor can their managers. There are limits, too, to how far certain tasks, like medical or community care planning, can be subject to generic management. Typically, workers in health services are simultaneously part of three structures – a professional structure, a multi-disciplinary team and a service setting (like a hospital or health centre) – each of which has its own lines of communication and accountability. There have been criticisms in nursing and social work of the impact of 'managerialism', policies developed in the belief that systemic problems have to be responded to by clearer performance criteria and more prescriptive supervisory direction. This approach, Lees and her colleagues argue, generates anxiety, impaired relationships

---

[624] R Loveridge, K Starkey (eds) 1992, *Continuity and crisis in the NHS*, Buckingham: Open University Press.

with service users and defensiveness – all to the detriment of the service provided.[625]

A second problem rests in the idea of 'leadership'. It refers, in different contexts, to the role of managers in general; to the aspects of their role relating to relationships with subordinates; to their personal attributes or traits; to the task of motivating and influencing staff; to the situation of being in charge; to methods for the achievement of tasks; or to a pattern of behaviour.[626] In social services the term is also used to mean strategic planning, the coordination of teamwork and responsibility for achieving goals. The term is, then, extraordinarily ill-defined – Wright's review of the literature shows it to be by turns authoritarian, considerate, laissez-faire, empowering, problem-solving, charismatic, self-directed, instrumental or anything else that people think it could mean.[627] The concept has been pressed into service to justify almost any behaviour that managers might want to engage in. At the same time, it places no weight on understanding issues, familiarity with process or administrative competence.

Table 13.1 summarises the main points from these three models.

Table 13.1: Systems of authority			
	Bureaucrats	*Professionals*	*Managers*
Role	Functionally differentiated administrative tasks	Specialised competence	Leadership
Motivation	Public service	Professional commitment	Incentives
Accountability	Responsibility to superiors	Professional standards	Performance criteria
Decision-making	Rule based	Discretion	Quasi-autonomous

Radical alternatives

There are alternatives to these models, though they are less important than the others. Hierarchical modes of operation have been prominent in social service welfare delivery for a long time, and unsurprisingly they have engendered not only modifications but a range of counter-

[625] A Lees, E Meyer, J Rafferty, 2013, From Menzies Lyth to Munro: the problem of managerialism, *British Journal of Social Work* 43(3) 542–558.

[626] See P Spicker, 2012, 'Leadership': a perniciously vague concept, *International Journal of Public Sector Management* 2012 25(1) 34–47.

[627] P Wright, 1996, *Managerial leadership*, London: Routledge.

reactions. Gilbert and Terrell refer to an 'activist' role, which offers an alternative approach to professional and bureaucratic organisation.

> The egalitarian/activist orientation, the polar opposite of the professional/ bureaucratic model, rejects professionalism and embraces an open-system perspective of organisation. Neither the organisation nor the professionals are to be relied on: one must turn to different sources of legitimacy, wisdom and policy. These sources may be alternative institutions, such as free clinics and cooperative schools ... or they may be the recipients of services – the people, the community, the poor.[628]

Although this is not very clearly developed as a model, it does point to something that matters. Several organisations, particularly but not exclusively in the voluntary sector, are suspicious of the role of officials in the public services and see a potential in that role for the abuse of power. 'Radical social work', for example, has developed both as a critique of the role of social workers and as a means of developing alternative patterns of practice.[629]

It is difficult to point to a common pattern of work, because there is so much variation, but at the same time there are characteristic approaches.

- The approach to decision making is collectivist, and emphasises team work. The group, not the individual worker, is responsible for decisions, and decisions are made collectively and non-hierarchically.
- The principle of non-hierarchical decision making extends beyond the workers as well as between them. There is a strong emphasis on participation by clients and advocacy on their behalf.
- Because the approach is motivated by principle, it is strongly associated with a high-minded, potentially moralistic, approach to service delivery.

The rejection of formal structures and hierarchies can circumvent some of the problems which stem from the emphasis on hierarchy and expertise – such as denying junior workers and recipients a voice in the organisation. It has the disadvantage, however, of removing protections

---

[628] Gilbert and Terrell, 2002, p 150.
[629] R Bailey, M Brake, 1975, *Radical social work*, London: RKP.

which allow people to function in a working environment despite their differences, and group working can be difficult to sustain where the workers' beliefs lead them in different directions. Charles Handy argues that so much time can be spent negotiating functions and boundaries that the agency can be disabled: 'Dreams without systems (and hard decisions) can become nightmares as the transaction costs of a group exceed its output.'[630]

Collective organisation used to be fairly characteristic of feminist groups, reflected for example in Women's Aid, and it was also found in some social work organisations. In recent years, however, it has become less common, reflecting pressure from external funders to be able to identify people with specific financial responsibilities.

Divisions of labour

Describing welfare services in terms of a 'system' implies that there is some kind of inter-relationship between the different parts. There has to be a division of labour between different services – if every service tried to be comprehensive and 'holistic', they would spend much of their time duplicating effort and dancing on their partners' toes. But there does not have to be any standard, simple relationship between them. In practice, the way that services are organised is unlikely to be rational or cohesive; many services have 'just grown', often starting with pilots or local initiatives, and often there are problems of co-ordination and liaison between the different parts.

The differences between different kinds of service are fundamental; it cannot be assumed that a neighbourhood advice office, a residential home and a national social security organisation will share objectives and methods of work. There are four main distinctions between different types of services: functional, professional, client-based, and area-based.

Functional divisions The first, and most obvious, distinction between services is based on what they do – such as health, housing, social security, social work and education. This is usually referred to as a 'functional' distinction – that is, a distinction based on the kind of work they are set up to do. It works reasonably well, for the most part, but the boundaries between services are indistinct. Child guidance, for example, can be seen as education, social work or a form of health

---

[630] C Handy, *Understanding voluntary organisations*, Harmondsworth: Penguin 1994, p.134.

care. Supported housing for elderly people can be housing or personal social service. Provision for medical care can be seen as a form of social security as well as health provision. The reasons why services are blurred in this way are not simply technical; they follow from some of the issues considered earlier. If housing is justified because of its effect on public health, health care because of its importance for social protection, or social assistance as a form of personal assistance related to social work, there is no intrinsic reason why administrative boundaries should be maintained.

Services are sometimes thought of as 'silos', keeping their roles distinct and separate despite the interactions between them. A 'silo mentality' is often criticised, but it comes down to focusing on core tasks, which may well be good practice. The problems tend to occur at the boundaries, the points either where no-one is clearly responsible, or where more than one service is.

Professional distinctions Sometimes the divisions of labour between services will be reflected in different professional approaches. The professions involved have different methods of work, language, and standards of professional practice. In housing, for example, the appropriate management of cases is usually interpreted as a rationing process giving priority to those in greatest need. Social work is concerned with risk and vulnerability. In medicine, the emphasis falls on professional judgment to respond appropriately to the needs of each person. The central problem, however, is institutional: agencies have different aims, and different criteria by which to measure success or failure.

Client groups Some services might respond only to specific groups of people – old people, children, or unemployed people. A specialist service for old people might be doing much the same kind of thing as a service for younger physically disabled people; however, because they are dealing with distinct groups, there may also be some specialised knowledge, particular insights into the needs of the people, and the possible advantage of bringing together people with similar needs into social groups. The distinctions made between client groups are not necessarily functional, though; they might also depend on distinctions between people which are not directly related to the service's functions or methods of operation. The groups may have different political priority for resources, or a different history of service development. There are 'separatist' services, which deliberately duplicate the pattern of other services in order to meet the needs of a particular group who might otherwise be disadvantaged – like voluntary housing for minority groups. In the Netherlands, the traditional 'pillars' of society were represented in distinctions between services for Catholics, Protestants, and others.[631]

A classification that straddles functional, client-based and professional divisions of labour is the distinction between generic and specialised work. A 'general practitioner' is a family doctor who is expected to offer continuing medical care across the full range of medical problems in the community; a 'specialist' concentrates on particular types of ailment or sets of problems, like 'anaesthetics' (a functional specialisation) or 'medicine for the elderly' (a distinction which is client based but is also partly functional). There are similar distinctions in the role of social workers: the specialised worker relates specifically to a particular client group, whereas the generic worker tries to exercise skills which are transferable between different classes of client. Genericism has been criticised in social work on the basis that generic workers are unlikely to have all the skills and knowledge necessary for work with certain groups, and the general trend in recent years has been for services to children and families to be separated from the provision of social care.

The main problems here are again to do with who is responsible for what. If the main services dealing with general needs work to different administrative structures, different authorities, different budgets, or different boundaries, then the transfer of a person from one agency to another can have important financial implications. Moving an old person out of an acute ward, which is often essential for efficient use of medical resources, means that some other agency is going to have to pick up the tab. A person with intellectual disabilities who ceases to attend school becomes the responsibility of some other agency in the community. A psychiatric patient who is discharged from hospital will have to be supported by another agency in the community.

Area-based divisions The fourth main division of labour between services is geographical: services are responsible for what happens within a particular area or location. Unlike functional, professional or client-based divisions of labour, territorial distinctions are not based on any fundamental difference in objectives or purpose; they may be made within the same service, operated by like-minded officials, working with similar purposes. In a sense, almost all services recognise some kind of area-based division of labour, because almost all services are formed at least on a national basis; but commonly within services,

---

[631] M Pijl, 1993, The Dutch welfare state, in R Page, J Baldock (eds) *Social Policy Review 5*, Kent: Social Policy Association; but see M Vink, 207, Dutch 'multiculturalism' beyond the pillarisation myth, *Political Studies Review* 5(3) 337–50.

the basis of a service might be by region, county, district, or a small community, and wherever that happens, there needs to be some kind of arrangement to determine who will be served and where. The area covered by a service shapes its response in two main ways. One is that certain functions are possible only with a sufficient level of resources, demand or need to make provision possible; specialised functions are difficult to design at a very local level. The other is that the kind of area which is covered – urban or rural, narrow or diffused – affects decisions about whether services should be centralised or decentralised, in fixed or mobile locations. The most important argument for geographic centralisation is the equalisation of standards and principles: Hölsch and Kraus suggest, for example, that more centralised social assistance is better at redistribution than decentralised systems.[632] Another justification for centralisation has been economies of scale – larger units can avoid duplication of support activities, such as management, finance and procurement. At the same time, centralisation has disadvantages; it is often felt by advocates of decentralisation to be unresponsive, unaccountable and inefficient. The main arguments for decentralisation are local accountability and responsiveness to local needs. Decentralisation can be criticised for tending to favour some people over others (notably local residents over outsiders), for placing the greatest responsibility on those units which have the least resources to meet their needs, and for proliferating organisational complexity. In so far as welfare provision depends on the pooling of risk, larger units are better able to deal with risks that are extraordinary, or particularly expensive. The effect of decentralised budgets can be to make local units on tight budgets unwilling to take on high costs or extended responsibilities. Decentralisation alters the character of local political debates, and there can be a tendency for decentralised services to reinforce views of welfare as a 'public burden'.[633]

The emphasis on markets and quasi-markets in recent years was based partly in a belief that the processes of distribution, allocation and delivery could be managed without explicit coordination. Markets rely on a common framework of signals, and people who act independently are supposed to respond in common, predictable ways. The 'new public

---

[632] K Hölsch, M Kraus, 2004, Poverty alleviation and the degree of centralization in European schemes of social assistance, *Journal of European Social Policy* 14(2) pp 143–164.

[633] R van Berkel, 2006, The decentralisation of public assistance in the Netherlands, *International Journal of Sociology and Social Policy* 26(1/2) pp 20–31.

management' of the 1980s and 1990s led, then, to formal arrangements for joint approaches and planning being abandoned. The idea that it would be possible to manage without such arrangements has proved largely illusory, and in recent years there has been a renewed emphasis on co-ordination, partnership and 'joined up thinking'.

One of the clichés of inter-service co-ordination is that it relies on good will, and people forging good working relationships. As a generalisation, that should be treated with some suspicion. Good relationships can sometimes be used to get round the problems of an obstructive organisation; but the problems will still be there. It is not good enough to suggest that poor personal relationships could lead to a bad service – an effective system should work regardless of the personal relationships of the officials involved in it. And one might hope that where structures are effective, good relationships should follow.

'Joined up thinking' has been associated in some policy developments with service unification. At the professional level, there has been an increasing trend towards the sharing of professional tasks, such as the development of common assessments (performed by anyone at hand) in social care.[634] But this is a false trail; in a professional structure, each professional is individually responsible for their decisions, and effective cooperation depends on each professional performing their own expert role, not on them doing the jobs of others.[635] A better alternative is to clarify responsibilities and establish a division of labour. One of the most effective options for dealing with individual cases has been the establishment of workers tasked with specific aspects of co-ordination – for example, distinguishing key workers with primary contact, who work most closely and directly with service users, and role-coordinators, who collate information and refer it on to those who need to know it. Successful co-ordination depends on working with, rather than against, divisions of labour.

ISSUE FOR DISCUSSION

What kinds of service rely on co-ordination, and what kinds of service do not need it?

---

[634] Scottish Executive, 2001, *Guidance on single shared assessment of community care needs*, circular CCD 8/20001; M Macadam, 2008, *Frameworks of integrated care for the elderly*, Ontario: Canadian Policy Research Networks.

[635] R Rushmer, G Pallis, 2003, Inter-professional working: the wisdom of integrated working and the disaster of blurred boundaries, *Public Money and Management* 23(1) 59–66.

CHAPTER 14

Value for money

Managing resources
Cost-effectiveness
Efficiency
The distributive impact of policy

Managing resources

For the most part, the provision of services implies the distribution of scarce resources – scarce in the sense that needs and demands generally exceed the capacity of services to meet them. Research into different areas of need has tended to throw up a vision of welfare as a bottomless pit, into which no amount of resources thrown could hope to satisfy every claim. It has become a cliché of some right-wing commentaries on welfare provision that the effect of providing items free to users is that there will be over-consumption.[636] This is not necessarily true: the demand for thoracic surgery is not unlimited, and there are no conceivable circumstances in which it might be. Some services carry considerable non-monetary costs for the consumer: having to live in residential care is something which many of us would wish to avoid, and it is fairly easy to envisage circumstances in which the demand for residential care would fall radically. What is true is that 'needs' represent, not a fixed set of conditions which have to be met, but a range of claims; as more urgent claims are met, lesser claims may come to have greater prominence. On that basis, we can say that there will always be a shortage of finance for services, even if particular services may be over-provided relative to others.

Services have to be limited, therefore; there have to be systems for the financial control. Public expenditure has proved difficult to control in practice, for a number of reasons. Public spending on any social service depends, Glennerster argues, on six factors:

- the ideology of governments
- the cost of various demands

---

[636] See e.g. A Culyer, K Wright, 1978, *Economic aspects of the health services*, Oxford: Martin Robertson.

- the structure of taxation
- the balance of power between government departments
- the prevailing economic wisdom, and
- the state of the economy.[637]

To this we might add another factor which seems to have considerable influence in practice – the previous cost of services, for it is difficult to make changes immediately. Capital expenditure (on buildings and equipment) is fairly easy to change rapidly, which is why housing tends to suffer in times of economic hardship; but revenue expenditure, of which the largest component is expenditure on labour, is difficult in practice to manage.

Public service agencies have to budget. The Chartered Institute of Management Accountants defines a budget as

> A quantitative statement, for a defined period in time, which may include planned revenues, expenses, assets, liabilities and cash flows. A budget provides a focus for the organisation, aids the coordination of activities, and facilitates control.[638]

The main approaches to budgeting include:

- *Financial planning systems* These predict expenditure on the basis of past expenditure plus allowances for inflation (increased costs) and growth, or minus proposed cuts. A typical approach is to say something like, 'every department should plan to cut 5% of expenditure.'
- *Bidding* Constituent agencies or cost centres estimate their needs and bid for the allocation of funds. The figures are put together and allocations are made. This system has been used by central government to make allocations to local authorities in housing and education. The system tends to encourage over-bidding, and often rewards higher spenders.
- *Planned programme budget systems (PPBS)* This was the dominant approach in UK central government for nearly thirty years, but it has fallen out of favour. PPBS works by identifying expenditure

---

[637] H Glennerster, 1979, The *determinants of public expenditure, in T Booth (ed)* Planning for welfare, Oxford: Blackwell.

[638] Cited J Williams, A Carroll, 1998, Budgeting and budgetary control, in J Wilson, *Financial management for the public services*, Open University Press, p 62.

in terms of programme objectives (e.g. 'services to old people', rather than 'area teams') and planning changes in funding over a number of years, using a rolling programme.

- *Zero-based budgeting* This is a 'rational' approach, requiring planners to start from scratch and work out how to meet needs.

The difficulties of controlling expenditure in the public sector have led some critics, not unnaturally, to suggest that it may be more controllable in the private sector. It should be true that if the state has contracted for a particular service from an independent operator, it will know exactly how much that service will cost; this is not always the case when it undertakes the operation itself. It is not true, however, that the private sector has intrinsically superior systems of financial control: private firms, like the public sector, also have difficulties making assessments of its costs, and in the private sector there are many operators who make their money by reviewing the miscalculations of others, and buying or selling accordingly. Particular problems arise when there is a rapid, unpredictable turnover or changes in circumstance – the kinds of problem which many social services have to deal with continually.

The management of public finance differs from the private sector in several ways:

- The public sector works to fixed budgets, and the private sector often does not. In principle, if a private sector firm does better, there will be more demand for the service, and more income. The public sector, by contrast, generally has to work to the income that is allocated. Ranade points out that fixed budgets lead to some inappropriate incentives. Services which deal with more needs increase their costs, but not their income; services which perform well attract more work, but no more rewards; inferior services, conversely, have less to do without being penalised for it.[639]
- The private sector is able to carry losses or profits forward from one accounting period to the next. The public sector, by contrast, has to spend exactly what has been allowed for. If it spends too much, central control is lost; if it spends too little, it risks having its budget cut for the future. Commonly this means that at the end of a financial year money is likely to be spent so as not to be lost.
- Public expenditure is often committed in advance, while private expenditure can usually be treated as being committed on a rolling basis. The private sector can pull the plug on its commitments in

---

[639] W Ranade, 1994, *A future for the NHS?*, London: Longmans, pp 56–57.

a way that, for political reasons, the public sector usually cannot (though there are exceptions: Israel has experienced 'strikes' by local authorities which have closed down local services when money ran out, and in 2013 the US Federal Government shut down when its budget was not approved). This all implies a much greater limit to flexibility in the public than in the private sector.

- The private sector is able to balance its books in other ways than the control of expenditure; there is usually the option of supplementing income through diversifying activities, taking loans, adjusting payments to owners and where necessary terminating loss-making activity. The options in the public sector are much more limited and any of these possibilities may be barred.

- In the public sector, frugality and the avoidance of waste are liable to be treated as a virtue in their own right. Private enterprises balance the issues of short-term profitability with a range of other considerations[640] – their practice is designed, for example, to attract and hold employees, to create an environment that will impress clients and encourage confidence, and so on. There is a long-standing tradition of services in the public sector that are mean and mean-spirited – a tradition reinforced by public protest in circumstances where government is considered to be extravagant.

Budgeting is not just an administrative mechanism: it sets restraints within which services have to operate. If budgets are set before the establishment of priorities within a service, it generally follows that financial and economic considerations are the first to be considered in the political process of establishing social policy objectives. The reason is that social priorities then have to be negotiated within the constraints of economic priorities. It may be possible to challenge economic priorities, pleading for more money in order to undertake a particular kind of objective, but it is a rare government that is prepared – like the Brazilian government in the construction of Brasilia – to damn the expense and forge ahead regardless. If money has to be found, it typically comes from borrowing, taxation or at the expense of other governmental activity. There are, of course, other possibilities – governments can, for example, run commercial enterprises to raise revenue – but they are less frequently pursued. Effectively, budgeting

---

[640] see A Griffiths, S Wall, 2007, *Applied economics*, Harlow: Pearson Education, ch 3.

restricts the potential expenditure on particular service activities, and priorities have to be negotiated within the total budget.

Cost-effectiveness

There are three main ways of understanding costs. The first, 'common sense' approach is to look at costs as an 'average' – that is, the mean for each item, derived by adding up the sum of all costs and dividing it by the number of items. If an advice agency costs £150,000 a year, and it deals with 3,000 enquiries (about 60 per week), the average cost for each enquiry is £50. So, in evaluating Pathways to Work, the DWP programme to return people with long-term sickness to the labour market, the National Audit Office writes:

> We estimate that Pathways as a whole, including delivery of New Deal for Disabled People in Jobcentre Plus Pathways areas, has cost £451 per programme start or £2,942 per job achieved for claimants starting Pathways up to the end of March 2009.[641]

This is the starting point for many basic evaluations. The approach is extremely simple, but it goes straight to the heart of the issue.

The second approach is to review the marginal cost – the cost of adding further items. If an agency has spare capacity, dealing with extra queries will bring down the average cost. Because many of its costs are already committed, like salaries and accommodation, it may be able to do the extra work with very little extra money. For practical purposes, many of the decisions which have to be made are about changing direction rather than the existence of the organisation, and marginal costs are consequently just as important as average costs.

An idealised production function is shown in Figure 14.1. As production increases, average costs tend to fall slowly, then start to rise. Marginal costs tend to be below average costs when production is limited, but they rise rapidly when obstacles are reached.

The third type of cost is the economic concept of 'opportunity cost'. This is the cost of not doing something else with the money. This does not appear in balance sheets, and it is much more difficult

---

[641] National Audit Office, 2010, *Support to incapacity benefit claimants through Pathways to Work*, London: NAO.

Figure 14.1: Average and marginal costs

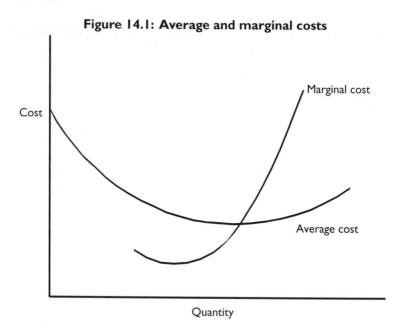

to assess, but it is part of any sound appraisal of the costs and benefits of undertaking different programmes.

Cost-effectiveness is the central test of how costs are employed. A policy is effective if it meets its aims. It is cost-effective if it meets its aims at the lowest price possible. The NAO identifies 'sustainable value for money' with 'the optimal use of resources to achieve the intended outcomes.'[642] This is not the same as saying that it is cheap, because cheapness can often only be achieved by compromising the objectives. There is a risk that when people are vague about aims, it might be reduced to little more than an emphasis on cost reduction. There is equally a risk that the costs to the agency are all that are considered, when there are other forms of cost: it is often possible to save expenditure on social services by making clients travel to the service, but the costs to the clients (and the impact on service effectiveness) have also to be considered. Further, as the previous section suggests, what is counted as a 'cost' is not straightforward. Costs can include average costs, marginal costs or opportunity costs. The NAO's approach adds a further dimension, which is 'sustainability' – not whether the policy is environmentally friendly, but the question of whether value can be

---

[642] National Audit Office, 2011, *The Efficiency and Reform Group's role in improving public sector value for money*, London: The Stationery Office, HC 887, p 4.

maintained over a longer period of time. Cost-effectiveness is likely, then, to be open to discussion.

The emphasis on cost-effectiveness has a profound effect on the character and procedures of the public services. Cost-effectiveness is not equivalent to economy, but services are not cost-effective if more is being spent than necessary. This is usually described as 'waste', and the elimination of wasteful expenditure – coupled with the need to account for every part of the operation – is part of the DNA of the public services. (It was mentioned in Chapter 13 as one of the three sets of values identified by Hood,[643] and I have already noted that it can come into conflict with other values – public services can insist on cutting waste even if the lack of flexibility sometimes means that net costs will be higher.) The public services may for example be enjoined to accept cost-effective tenders, rather than to obtain a service they judge to be more secure or better run. (That applies to non-profit making trusts, too; the trustees have a fiduciary duty to obtain best value.) Private sector firms can afford to budget for 'slack', allowing for changes in circumstances, as long as they can make a profit; public services cannot. The insistence, for example, that hospital beds have to be fully occupied[644] leads to constant problems – inflexibility, bottlenecks and 'bed blocking' (when services cannot respond to fresh needs because all the beds are full).

Saying that a policy is cost-effective is not a judgment about whether it was worth doing in the first place; it is saying that the aims have been achieved at the minimum cost. More commonly, cost-effectiveness is assessed in terms of a comparison. If two methods yield the same results – or at least, if there is not much to choose between them – the cheaper method is the one to go for. This is the basis of 'cost-effectiveness analysis', or CEA. CEA works by comparing the relative costs and effectiveness of alternative methods. CEA has been widely used in health care,[645] but it is now more common in a specialised form: the cost of each 'quality adjusted life year', or QALY. The QALY is one of the standard measures used by NICE, the (English and Welsh) National Institute for Health and Clinical Excellence, in its assessment of the relative value of different health care treatments (see Box 14.1). The

---

[643] C Hood, 1991, A public management for all seasons? *Public Administration* 69(1) 3–19.

[644] T Dalrymple, 2000, It's not the flu that ails our NHS, *New Statesman* 17th January.

[645] See F Sloan, H Grabowski (eds) 1997, The impact of cost-effectiveness on public and private policies in health care, *Social Science and Medicine* 45(4) pp 505–647.

WHO has taken to using a related measure – the DALY or disability adjusted life year.

Box 14.1: QALYs

In welfare economics, preferences are expressed largely in terms of trade-offs – people tend to want more, but they will usually take less of one thing to get more of another. There are certainly trade-offs that policy-makers do make, whether or not they admit to them. They may say that the value of life is beyond price; they may well mean it, especially if the life is their own; but when push comes to shove, there is a practical limit as to how much they are ready to spend in the attempt to keep someone else alive.

A QALY is a 'quality adjusted life year'. The concept makes it possible to judge, for different forms of medical treatment, whether or not a treatment is effective. The QALY is based on two impacts. The first is the length of time a person will live after the treatment. The second is the 'adjustment'; a year of healthy, active life is more to be wished for than a year of suffering. So, while a year of good health counts for 1, a year of anxiety, moderate pain and discomfort might count for 0.22, and a year bedfast in extreme pain counts for –0.43.[646] (The minus sign is contentious, because it suggests that the last of these states is worse than being dead.) The calculations mean that problems with longer duration are weighted far more than acute problems and that children tend to count for more than old people. The method could imply that measures to help people who are terminally ill count for less than measures which keep people alive.

NICE, the UK's National Institute for Health and Clinical Excellence, uses the QALY to judge the relevant effectiveness of health care treatments. It is possible to work out, for each treatment, a cost per QALY. This is a form of cost-effectiveness analysis (CEA), but it has also been described as 'cost-utility analysis'. There are two main reasons for doing it – to determine which measures represent the best value for money in treatment, and to compare outcomes for different treatments for different conditions in a way that makes it possible to identify priorities. In the NHS, there is an implicit limit to how much the service will spend for limited benefit – estimated, in 2002, as somewhere in the region of £30,000 for each QALY gained through medical intervention, though the figure is probably higher for terminal care. In 2012, it has been suggested that that guideline – which was still around £30,000, despite inflation – might be reduced to £13,000.[647] The headline

---

[646] www.medicine.ox.ac.uk/bandolier/painres/download/whatis/QALY.pdf
[647] www.pulsetoday.co.uk/nice-threshold-could-be-reduced-to-13000-per-qaly/13948182.article#.UKE6n2c3_Ug

---

figure is slightly misleading, because it has always been the case that where one treatment offered a better cost per QALY than another for the same disease, that option would be preferred. The figure of £13,000 does, however, reflect the actual cost of treatment for a range of conditions, including cancer, circulatory, respiratory and gastrointestinal problems, and it tends to come in at less than that.

The reason why these measures are used is simple enough – someone, somewhere has to make a decision, even if the decision may seem distasteful when it is looked at coldly. Alan Williams, one of the leading advocates of QALYs, argues: 'Nature abhors a vacuum. These people have to make decisions and they will make the decisions. Out of their decisions, wittingly or unwittingly, there will come to be a pattern of activity.'[648]

The main problems in assessing cost-effectiveness come from decisions about marginal costs – the cost of doing a little bit more. This leads us on to the related issue of 'efficiency'.

Efficiency

Efficiency is often confused with cost-effectiveness. Sir Peter Gershon's report *Releasing resources to the front line*[649] used the term 'efficiency' to refer to a range of cost-savings and increased outputs. The definitions include

1. 'reduced numbers of inputs ...whilst maintaining the same level of service provision';
2. 'lower prices for ... resources' ...
3. 'additional outputs ...'
4. 'improved ratios of output per unit cost of input', and
5. 'changing the balance between different outputs' .[650]

Most of these are examples of cost-effectiveness rather than efficiency. A process is cost-effective if it meets its objectives at the lowest possible cost. It is efficient if produces goods or services at the lowest possible

---

[648] A Williams, in A Towse, C Pritchard, N Devlin (eds) 2002, *Cost-effectiveness thresholds*, London: King's Fund, p 40.

[649] P Gershon, 2004, *Releasing resources to the front line: independent review of public sector efficiency*, London: HM Treasury.

[650] Gershon, pp 6–7.

cost per unit, and that is not the same thing. Gershon's first and second definitions are about cutting costs, 'economy' or 'cost minimization'. Economy and frugality are part of the practice required of public organisations; they may be part of efficiency or cost-effectiveness, but they are not enough to guarantee either. The third definition is concerned with improved achievement of aims, which is probably about greater effectiveness – though it could also, arguably, be an example of doing more rather than doing things better. Only the last two definitions are about efficiency.

The difference between efficiency and cost-effectiveness is most easily explained graphically. Figure 14.2 shows a model production function.

Figure 14.2: Efficiency and cost-effectiveness

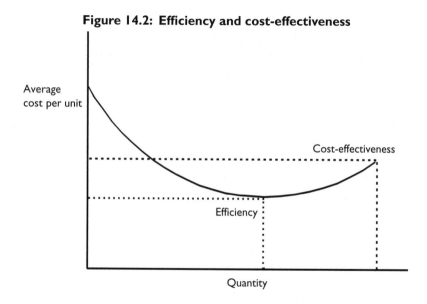

Efficiency is maximised at the bottom of the curve. The most cost-effective approach, by contrast, depends on what the service is supposed to achieve. If it is supposed to cover the whole population – like the fire service, the postal service or access to medical care – the quantities to be provided will be set, even if it costs more to reach everyone. Cost-effectiveness for a generalised public service is typically found somewhere towards the right-hand edge of the curve, where average costs are higher, but aims are achieved to the maximum degree. (The calculation of cost-effectiveness is liable to be a little vaguer than this suggests. As the number of people served increases, the costs rise. The service may well need to take a view about the maximum cost that is permissible, and is likely to ration – to limit what is done – as costs approach that level.)

Efficiency improves when the ratio of costs to outputs is improved. The 'cost efficiency' targets of the NHS are intended to cut unit costs of treating each patient. Cost-efficiency targets are based on reference costs for a range of NHS hospital activity. Unit costs are identified by taking the total number of costs and dividing by the number of cases treated. Dawson and Jacobs explain: 'The only way to achieve an "efficiency gain" is to increase the number of patients treated per pound of the budget.'[651] A policy to bring down average costs substantially would need a much more radical rethink of the management system – decisions, for example, about business processes (e.g. reception and filtering), triage (selection of significant cases), rationing (e.g. the reduction of staff time spent on each case) or the allocation of resources (reviewing the staff complement). There is a combination here of cost reduction, productivity gains and reduction in service. The purpose of triage, for example, is to reduce responsiveness to cases where services are less likely to make a difference. This approach has been used in the NHS, for example in the initial sorting of primary care cases on the basis of telephone contact. The NHS cannot, however, opt to treat only the less problematic patients, and ignore the more problematic ones, even if that is more efficient.

The prospect of reducing services is a major part of what distinguishes efficiency from cost-effectiveness. Unit costs depend on how expensive each case is to deal with. Achieving every aim may be inefficient, because some aims are more expensive and difficult than others, and because costs are likely to rise when agencies are straining to meet targets. Because the pursuit of profit creates an incentive for efficiency, private services may well act differently from public ones.

- *Adverse selection* Private sector firms have a choice, whether or not to serve particular customers. If some customers are more expensive to serve than others, it makes sense not to devote resources to them. That choice – 'adverse selection' – will make production more efficient. So, for example, private firms may decline to serve people in remote and rural areas; many residential care homes are reluctant to take on people with mobility problems.

---

[651] D Dawson, R Jacobs, 2003, Do we have a redundant set of cost-efficiency targets in the NHS?, *Public Money and Management* 23(1) p 71.

- *'Creaming'* and *'parking'* In the same way, private sector providers may select recipients who are likely to produce the best returns. A public service contract, intended to reach everyone, might be subject to 'creaming' – choosing to serve those who will best respond – or 'parking', where services are minimised or not given at all.
- *Playing the odds* Some large private sector firms minimise input costs rather than optimising outcomes, in the expectation that processing sufficient numbers will yield satisfactory returns. For example, utility companies may seem litigious in relation to debtors, but that is because few actions are costly or complex, or even contested; they can afford to lose a few. The Work Programme in the UK, introduced to get unemployed people into work, was designed to pay private providers by results. There were initial fears that there would be an incentive for creaming and parking, but the behaviour of private providers actually revealed a different pattern. The Parliamentary Committee which has been monitoring the programme reported the comment that 'too often the providers played a pure "numbers game", "randomly" pushing jobseekers towards vacancies in the hope that "a few stick".'[652] If that is right, the providers are not carefully selecting who to encourage and who to ignore, but the reverse; they have reduced the level of service given and looked instead for outcomes overall. (This strategy may not last; outcomes have been poor, and prospective employers are complaining about their time being wasted.)

In economic theory, productive efficiency is one of the outcomes of competition, and attempts to introduce commercial factors, marketisation and competition into the public sector are generally concerned with promoting efficiency in this sense. From the perspective of the public sector, by contrast, achieving productive efficiency requires some sacrifice of service objectives. Public services are often accused of being less efficient than private services. That is probably right. There is often a trade-off to be made between efficiency and cost-effectiveness. When that happens, public services are supposed to choose the best way to meet their objectives, not to compromise

---

[652] House of Commons Work and Pensions Committee, 2013, *Can the Work Programme work for all user groups?*, London: The Stationery Office, HC162, para 71.

them. Public services are supposed to be cost-effective. They are not meant to be efficient.

(There is another use of the term 'efficiency' in economics, which is 'allocative efficiency'. Allocative efficiency occurs when the balance of production matches demand. Demand in economics is mainly understood in terms of individual preference, expressed through the mechanisms of the market. In public sector provision, however, 'demand' is mainly expressed in other ways – through the assessment of need, the exercise of choice, and user empowerment – and the interpretation of demand is strongly subject to social and political aims and values. For that reason, the idea of 'allocative efficiency' is not much used in this context.)

Box 14.2: Cost benefit analysis

A standard means of determining the appropriateness of a policy is to establish whether it offers sufficient benefits to outweigh its costs. The basic technique is called cost benefit analysis, or CBA. CBA requires all costs, and all benefits, to be taken into account.

This approach is beset with problems. Much of the literature is concerned with technical issues. The technical problems include:

- Identifying the nature of costs (as considered before).
- Identifying what constitutes a benefit (on the same basis).
- Allowing for inflation, or changes in the value of money.
- Discounting for the future. The further away the benefits are, the more uncertain they become. Many capital projects are built for a thirty-year life or beyond; it is conventional gradually to discount future values by taking off a proportion of costs. The UK Treasury's Green Book recommends a discount rate of 3.5% per annum. At that rate, £1000 now is worth £709 in ten years' time.[653]
- The valuation of intangibles, such as a person's time, or the value of life. Time is a crucial element in the determination of the benefits of transport projects. A person's life has to be valued because people are likely to be killed in major construction projects. A modified version of CBA is planning balance sheet analysis, which puts costs and benefits into columns while leaving intangibles unquantified.

---

[653] H M Treasury, n.d., The Green Book, www.hm-treasury.gov.uk/media/785/27/Green_Book_03.pdf, p.26

There are also two important issues of principle. The first issue concerns redistribution: those who pay are not necessarily those who benefit. Technically, CBA assumes that the winners could benefit the losers (the 'Kaldor-Hicks' criterion[654]); but this is not the same as saying that they will actually do so. The second issue concerns the use of money as the basis of valuation. Cash values are taken are as given, but cash values can reflect questionable standards. In cash terms, a house which is worth £300,000 is worth six times a group of five flats each worth £50,000. That means that given the choice between putting a road across the site of a £300,000 house occupied by one household, or a block of low-priced flats occupied by five households, it is the flats which will be knocked down. The central difficulty of using CBA in a more general way, then, is that it has little to say about the distributive implications of policy, and distributive issues are fundamental to social policy.

CBA and its variants get extensive coverage in the literature. Partly, this is because it is a useful illustration of general principles, but it is mainly because it is one of the very few applied methods that Economics has given to the world, and economists have made a lot of it. In the UK, some problems, like road-building, have lent themselves to the process, and CBA is fairly routine in major construction projects. By contrast, in relation to most social policy, CBA is rarely applied in its unvarnished form. The main application of the techniques takes the form of cost-effectiveness analysis (CEA), which was referred to before. Because the aims are given, CEA is mainly focused on costs, and the trade-off between costs and outcomes is made explicit. Because effectiveness is defined by the aims of the policy, it is possible within a CEA to ignore some of the intangibles, which are the same for each of the competing methods. Once the application stretched beyond those confines, CBA tends to raise more questions than it answers.

The distributive impact of policy

One of the most basic tests for determining whether a policy uses its resources well is the question of whether it is well targeted – whether it benefits the people it intends to benefit. The basic concepts used in the analysis of redistribution were outlined in Chapter 3, and some of the ambiguities of the process – understanding, for example, whether distribution is horizontal or vertical, or whether it should be viewed statically or dynamically – were introduced at that point. The questions this kind of exercise raises are far from straightforward. One problem is that the same redistributive effects can be interpreted in different ways.

---

[654] R Layard, 1972, *Cost-benefit analysis*, Harmondsworth: Penguin Education.

The effects of redistribution across the life cycle may be that apparently horizontal redistribution turns out to have unexpected vertical effects. Payments for pensions seem vertically redistributive, but if the design is solidaristic then their impact on redistribution between better-off and worse-off sectors of society may be limited. Conversely, payments for older children at school seem regressive, because this is often a point of peak earnings for families, but if the issue is seen across the life cycle such payments may seem relatively neutral.[655] This illustrates an important principle: the way the problem is thought about is likely to affect not only the criteria by which outcomes will be judged, but also the judgment about what the outcomes are.

The second problem is knowing where to start. Many analyses begin with salaries as if they represented some kind of natural order, and then look at the way that initial pay is altered by taxation, benefits and services. But many of the initial salaries are there only because of the public services – that is true both of people who are directly employed, like police, teachers or nurses, and others who are indirectly employed, such as firms carrying out contracts for the public sector. The OECD maintains figures for 'employment in general government and public corporations' as a proportion of the labour force; in the Nordic countries that figure runs at something between 20% and 30% of all employment.[656] If there were no government, the initial distribution might look very different – but where is there no government?

Third, redistributive impacts are difficult to measure. This is partly because it is not always clear where the benefits of particular services fall – who benefits from the probation service? – and partly because some benefits are not based on the receipt but on the possibility of receipt. Where there is a National Health Service, people are receiving a benefit – health coverage – for which people in other countries have to pay, and they would be receiving this coverage even though they do not actually use the service. Le Grand, in a discussion of redistribution and equality, points to several different measures:

- public expenditure – whether people have different amounts of money spent on them

---

[655] J Falkingham, J Hills, C Lessof, 1993, *William Beveridge versus Robin Hood: social security and redistribution over the life cycle*, London: LSE/Suntory-Toyota Centre for Economics and Related Disciplines.

[656] OECD, 2011, *Employment in general government and public corporations*, http://statlinks.oecdcode.org/422011011P1G067.XLS

- final income – whether the amount of money spent has an equivalent effect on the recipients
- use – whether people are able to use the service to an equivalent extent
- cost – whether people suffer equivalent costs as a result of their problems
- outcome – whether people finish in equivalent positions.[657]

There is, for example, a considerable literature examining the distribution of health care and resources, in which different assumptions about the appropriate measures leads to very different conclusions about the impact of health services.[658]

Fourth, there is a problem that the analysis of redistribution has in common with other assessments of outcomes: to understand the effects of a policy it is necessary to consider not only what the policy seems to achieve, but what might otherwise have been true. If health services appear to have no effect on inequality, it does not necessarily mean that they have failed – it is possible that inequalities would otherwise have widened.

Table 14.1 comes from work by Glen Bramley, reviewing the distributive implications of local government expenditure in the UK.[659] Bramley's work is suggestive: if it is possible to attribute distributive impacts to particular services, then it should also be possible in principle to target resources by selecting services which are better placed to serve people on lower incomes. The idea of targeting was discussed earlier, in the context of the focus of policy. If a policy is intended to redistribute resources, or to direct resources to a particular group, then the distributive impact may be one of the criteria on which services are distributed. Even if that is not one of the central aims, an awareness that a policy has distributive consequences may reasonably be taken into account in its development.

There is a trap to avoid here. In the specific context of considering the distributive impact of services, targeting is equitable if it directs

[657] J Le Grand, 1982, *The strategy of equality,* London: Allen and Unwin, pp 14–15.

[658] See e.g. P Townsend, N Davidson, M Whitehead, 1988, *Inequalities in health,* Penguin; Department of Health, 1998, *Independent inquiry into inequalities in health,* London: TSO; . M Bartley, 2004, *Health inequality,* Brighton: Polity.

[659] G Bramley, G Smart, 1993, *Who benefits from local services?,* LSE/STICERD; G Bramley, 1998, *Where does public spending go?,* London: Department of the Environment.

Table 14.1: The distributive effects of local services				
Strongly for the better off	**Moderately for the better off**	**Neutral or ambiguous**	**Moderately pro-poor**	**Strongly pro-poor**
Higher education Education 16–19 Adult education Car and road use	Waste tips Car parks Markets Libraries Museums Sports Swimming Arts Enter-tainments	*Neutral:* Secondary schools mental illness Playgrounds Environmental services *Ambiguous:* Nursery schools School meals Careers Youth services Special transport Consumer advice	Social care for older people: day care meals home care Services for disabled people Buses Bus passes Community centres Primary Education Further education Special education Community regeneration	Social housing Housing advice Welfare rights Social services for children

resources to people who should have them rather than those who should not. It is efficient if it yields the greatest benefit for the target group at the least possible cost, wasting as little as possible. The arguments for selectivity are based in the belief that excluding people who should not receive benefits is the way to deliver services more efficiently. The problem with that position is that the process of exclusion can create more problems, and generate more costs, than it resolves. Selectivity raises some well-known issues: the creation of barriers to access for those who it is supposed to reach, the expense and complexity of managing the administrative tests, and the difficulty of identifying and maintaining the boundaries. Three other problems can reduce efficiency of targeting:

- *deadweight.* People receive the service or benefit, whose circumstances are not materially improved by it.
- *spillovers.* People continue to receive help after the help has ceased to make a difference.
- *failure to reach the target group.* The effects of barriers to access or low take-up imply that the policy does not touch the people it was supposed to help.

Effectiveness – whether a policy achieves its aims – is compromised mainly by the third problem, poor coverage. Although the first two affect efficiency (how much a policy costs, and how much is wasted), they do not necessarily mean that the policy is failing. The third does.

ISSUE FOR DISCUSSION

When is it acceptable, in the interests of efficiency, to leave some needs unmet?

CHAPTER 15

Service delivery

The production of welfare
Priorities
Rationing
Equity and procedural fairness
Managing the demand for services
Delivering services

The production of welfare

The process of providing public services is sometimes referred to as the 'production' of welfare. 'Production' is an umbrella term, covering many different kinds of service: social services are not necessarily involved in the same kind of activity. Some of the services which social policy is concerned with, like social security and housing, involve the distribution of material goods; this means that 'production' is strongly identified with the goods provided, that is money and housing. Others, notably social work and education, are mainly provided as personal services, which require the appointment of someone who carries out the function; 'production' is mainly measured in terms of the numbers of people involved (often, in education, through class sizes). Medical services are largely personal but have a considerable material element. Production in the social services, however, is not much like production in businesses – or at least, not like the sort of businesses that commonly feature in textbooks of management and economics. In many circumstances, the social services typically offer services – such as continuing health care, community safety, social care – rather than goods. These are processes, rather than transactions. And that, Stephen Osborne argues, means that the relationship is quite different from the way that production is conventionally understood. The service user is part of the process: services cannot be delivered, or 'consumed' – the service cannot be 'produced' – if the service user is not there. The interaction between the provider and the service user is part of the process of service delivery.[660]

---

[660] S Osborne, Z Radnor, G Nasi, 2013, A new theory for public service management?, *American Review of Public Administration* 43(2) pp 135–58.

Even in the field of services, public and commercial services approach things differently. Commercial enterprises offer goods or services to 'customers'. Customers, in a commercial setting, have a contingent contractual relationship with a business. It is contractual because it is based in voluntary agreement and exchange; it is contingent because either party can withdraw. The relationship between public services and service users is quite different. Public services are not provided to meet economic demand; they are provided for public purposes – that is, for reasons of policy. The relationship between producers and consumers is not based on the exchange of resources; the services are generally redistributive. Nor are they necessarily based on choice. The providers have to provide; they can be prevented from withdrawing, because they have statutory duties, or their users have rights. Some service users may be driven by necessity to use benefits or social care; some are compelled by law. Even if service users are able to opt out of provision by health services or education, they will still be covered in the event of unforeseen circumstances. And people cannot withdraw from provision by police, roads and street-lighting, the courts or child protection services.

Priorities

Priorities indicate some degree of preference or precedence; something is a 'priority' when it commands attention before other issues. When people talk about 'priorities', it can mean several things.

- It can mean simply that something is important – saying that something is 'not a priority' usually means that it does not matter very much.
- It can refer to relative value: priority setting often works by attaching different weights to different options, and allocating resources accordingly.
- It can refer to precedence – some issues make a stronger claim than others. When housing is allocated, the person with the highest priority gets the first house, the person with the second highest priority gets the second, and so on. If homeless people have the highest priority, no-one gets housed until cases of homelessness have been dealt with. (That is not how things work in health care – saying that people with cancer have priority over people with respiratory problems means that people with cancer get seen quicker, not that no-one with respiratory problems is dealt with.)

- It might also refer to the order on an agenda – precedence in terms of timing rather than of importance. If cleaning has to be done before surgery is possible, cleaning comes first.
- A priority might be a special status, like a ring-fenced budget for dealing with disability issues.[661]

The ambiguities in the language of priorities mean that it is difficult to know, when people talk about their priorities, just what they intend – or how they will eventually deal with competing claims.

The essential message here is that, whenever priorities are being considered, there are competing claims vying for attention, and it is not self-evident how they will be dealt with. A 'claim' in this sense can refer to any kind of call for resources, from any source – including policy-makers and administrators as well as consumers; claims differ in their strength and their content, but they have to be decided on as part of the process of allocating resources. The main determinants of the strength of a claim are legitimacy and support: support because the claim has to be negotiated in a political context, legitimacy because the claim has to be accepted within the policy-making process. The setting of priorities is a political process, then: it generally involves the negotiation and arbitration between different interests.

Arguments about 'need' have to be understood in part as a form of claim-language; conflicts between different understandings of 'need' are often conflicts between different claims, rather than disputes about the meaning of the word.[662] A claim of 'need' may be an effective part of a claim for resources, but needs are not necessarily the only, or even the main, elements of a claim: some needs are not responded to, while others which seem relatively minor may be respected. 'Needs' have to be understood in relation to the resources which are available. Gilbert Smith's studies in social work led him to comment as follows:

> 'Need', as used by welfare professionals, is not simply a single concept but rather a set of interrelated notions and assumptions about what is to be viewed as the proper object of social work activity. It is helpful to view this body of ideas in terms of a professional 'ideology' about the nature of need.[663]

---

[661] P Spicker, 2009, What is a priority?, *Journal of Health Services Research and Policy* 14(2) 112–6.

[662] P Spicker, 1993, Needs as claims, *Social Policy and Administration* vol 27 no 1, pp 7–17.

[663] G Smith, 1980, *Social need*, London: RKP p 112.

In social work, emotional problems (which are intangible) are often seen as more important than material ones, and an assessment of 'risk' – the dynamics of a situation – is probably more important than immediate, 'presenting' problems. In the allocation of social housing, by contrast, needs which are definable and measurable are treated as being more legitimate than those which are not, and existing needs are treated as being more important than potential needs. The conditions which housing officers have to work with – the limited supply of houses, the need to fill vacancies, and the problems of balancing pressures from different sources – provide the framework within which the demand for the service is expressed.[664] Priorities are not only set explicitly, because (as happens in the case of budget-setting) the administrative process can itself have an effect in determining priorities. In practice, the priorities which are established are conditioned by other administrative requirements, like the need to make sure that houses are occupied quickly, or the requirement to collect information before acting – because people cannot easily be evicted after allocation, the criteria for allocation have to be thoroughly satisfied first. The essential point is made by Rein. It is not always the case that concepts and ideals determine the way in which a service operates; it is just as likely that norms in policy are shaped by administrative structures and the conditions in which a service works.[665]

Rationing

In order for people to receive services, services have to be provided; the recipients have to gain access to them; their eligibility for receipt of services has to be determined; and the supply of services has to be matched to the requirements. This can be restated, in economic terms, as a problem of relating the supply of the services to the demand. The problem of balancing supply and demand outside the mechanism of the market is a process of 'rationing'. Where services are scarce – which they are always likely to be – some kind of rationing procedure is inevitable; come what may, someone is going to be left without a service, or the people who do receive it are going to get less. Rationing limits the service received. Figure 15.1 outlines the main processes. Rationing procedures are complex; several, like delay or deterrence, potentially have multiple effects, changing the behaviour of both

---

[664] P Spicker, 1987, Concepts of needin housing allocation, *Policy & Politics* 15(1) pp 17–27.
[665] M Rein, 1983, *From policy to practice*, London: Macmillan.

Figure 15.1: Rationing processes

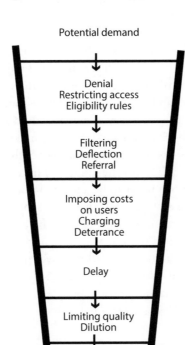

Potential demand

Denial
Restricting access
Eligibility rules

Filtering
Deflection
Referral

Imposing costs
on users
Charging
Deterrance

Delay

Limiting quality
Dilution

Effective
demand

providers and service users. Scrivens offers a useful framework to discuss the issues. Rationing, she suggests, can be done either by limiting the supply, or by inhibiting the demand. In this chapter, I plan to focus on issues of supply; issues of demand are considered in the next chapter, along with other issues relating to users. Within the options for limiting the supply, Scrivens identifies two main forms of restriction: restrictive or dilutant rationing. Services are restricted when people are prevented from receiving them. This can be done by denial – restricting access and eligibility rules; delay; and filtering through deflection and referral. Dilutant rationing implies some kind of reduction in the service, through accessibility, limiting the quality, or limiting the duration for which a service is given.[666]

---

[666] E Scrivens, 1980, Towards a theory of rationing, in R Leaper (ed) *Health wealth and housing*, Oxford: Blackwell.

Denial: restricting access Simply denying access is an odd way to restrict service delivery, but there are cases where it happens: hospital wards have remained closed because there is no money to open them, public services have laid off workers when there is no money to pay for them. What is far more common is that there is some kind of selective denial – some people are let in, and others are not. In theory, this can be done randomly. A lottery can be held which will let some people in while others are barred. This is not very widely practised, but there are some examples: Elster, who has collected many remarkable illustrations of different allocation procedures, gives examples of the allocation of visas and the selection of soldiers for the draft.[667] I have known both public housing and job opportunities to be allocated out of a tombola drum. But this can produce strange allocative effects, because it implies that some people will be randomly included at the expense of others. In the Netherlands, students who qualify for entry to medical education are selected by a weighted lottery, which gives more chances to those with higher grades but also allows the admission of students on lower grades.[668] This must mean that some people are excluded who might have passed, while others are included only to fail.

Eligibility qualifications Selection at the point of entry implies the use of eligibility qualifications: people who meet the qualifications are allowed in, and others are not. The criteria which are used for admission or restriction are enormously variable. It seems fairly evident that services for disabled people should depend on people having disabilities, that child care should be for children, or that old age pensions should be designed for old people. But there are problems in definition and testing eligibility; it is much less clear that medical care should be confined to people who are sick, or that benefits intended to help poor people should be confined to those who are demonstrably poor, because either rule may exclude those for whom the service is intended.

Eligibility criteria are not simply about directing services, however; they are also important for managing claims. Even if services for people with physical disabilities should only be used by disabled people, there may be too many disabled people in a position to claim. It is possible to limit services to a particular level of disability: several

---

[667] J Elster, 1992, *Local justice*, Cambridge: Cambridge University Press, pp 59, 30.

[668] O Ten Cate, 2007, Medical Education in the Netherlands, *Medical Teacher* 29 752–757.

countries have systems that refer to percentages of disability, such as '80% disabled'. It may be decided to limit coverage to particular types of disability: the rules for mobility benefits in the UK used to be limited to disabilities with an attributable organic cause, which cut out many developmental disabilities. Alternatively, other kinds of rule may be applied: limiting services for physical disability to those under 65 conveniently excludes the majority of disabled people, and this represents a considerable saving on the potential cost of a service.

Criteria are sometimes applied which have little directly to do with the subject of the service being provided. Elster again provides a wide range of examples: such issues as age, race, religion, gender, family status and sexual orientation have often been used as a criterion for acceptance or rejection.[669] Direct discrimination on the basis of gender has become much rarer – in the European Union, it violates Community law – but there are many examples. Elster points to the presumption that mothers should have custody of children in divorce, and the exemption of women from military service. Family status may be a criterion for allocation: India has penalised large families in the allocation of housing while Israel has given them priority.[670]

It is worth pointing out that the formal use of eligibility criteria is not the only way in which such criteria might be used to restrict access. If some test has to be conducted before people can be considered eligible, then one of the ways of limiting access might be to limit access to the test itself. In the days of mass clearance in England and Wales, public health officers were commonly limited in the number of houses they could declare unfit, because the classification contained a commitment to future action. In the Cleveland inquiry into the sexual abuse of children, there was a rush of referrals to the doctors, as professionals realised that here were two consultants prepared to make the diagnosis. The Director of Social Services asked the doctors who were diagnosing sexual abuse to slow down the rate of diagnosis, because his department was not able to deal with the problems rapidly enough. The doctors refused, on the basis that their task was to provide the best information for future treatment, and managing priorities for child protection was up to Social Services; they were criticised for doing so by the inquiry.[671]

---

[669] Elster, 1992, pp 76ff.
[670] Elster, 1992, pp 78; 98–99.
[671] Cm 412, 1988, *Report of the inquiry into child abuse in Cleveland 1987*, London: HMSO.

Filtering Referral and deflection are systems for separating out people who have needs from others, without actually denying them service. General practitioners, for example, refer cases on to specialists; receptionists deflect cases from the social work office by sending them somewhere else, like social security. Screening people, requiring them to undergo some kind of professional assessment before they can receive specialised treatment, or advising them that another service could be more appropriate for their circumstances (e.g. welfare rights advice rather than social work) might be seen as a form of eligibility qualification; they are ways of shielding higher levels of service from inappropriate demand. At the same time, the services which are doing the filtering are performing a valuable function in themselves. General practitioners in medicine are monitoring people's health care and advising them. Screening offers people important reassurance as well as access to a service when necessary. Giving people information, from a referral point, allows them to receive appropriate service.

Delay Delaying the delivery of service – making people wait – is one of the most common forms of rationing, simply because it is what is going to happen if other decisions about rationing are avoided. Once a service is performing to its full capacity, there will be room for further cases only when some other activity ceases and space is created; this implies that someone will have to wait.

The simplest form of structure for waiting is a queue – where the first come is the first served. This is easily understood, and it is often upheld in housing and health services as being 'fair'. But neither housing nor health services can actually maintain a strict principle of allocation by date order. The problem is that some people have greater and more urgent needs than others. What happens is that there has to be some priority system. People who use that system can be seen as 'jumping the queue' – an accusation often levelled both at homeless people and at private patients – but the truth is that there is no 'queue'. The difference between the two circumstances is that homeless people are being taken within a priority system, according to certain rules, and private patients are avoiding the system of priorities – which is why the first is fair and the second is not.

An emphasis on date order can have in itself important allocative effects. In research on the allocation of council housing, Clapham and Kintrea found that the effect of giving some priority in an allocations scheme to people according to how long they had waited was greatly to alter the prospects of rehousing for those in need. People who were in lesser need on the waiting lists were generally on higher incomes as well as in better conditions; they were more able to wait. People in worse conditions were also poorer and less able to wait. The ability to hold on was crucial to the quality of housing that people were offered; people in less need were able to refuse, while people in greater need were not. The effect was that people with more priority for waiting time got better housing, while those with more priority for need got worse housing.[672]

Dilution The other main way of inhibiting supply is the dilution of services. This means that less is given of a service, in terms of quality or duration. Diluting the quality means that people get less – for example, time with a less qualified worker, less money, fewer checks and tests, less personal attention, or a quicker termination of service.

Dilution is less common than other forms of rationing. One reason is that professionals are reluctant to do it knowingly; giving people standards which are deliberately lower runs counter to professional ethics, and if there is the alternative to exclude someone altogether in order to maintain standards for others, it tends to be preferred. There are also, it should be noted, disincentives to professionals who wish to dilute the services they offer; doctors who offer lots of people a rapid interview probably have to work rather harder than those who take their time with fewer patients. Second, some services cannot easily be diluted. It is usually difficult to offer less by way of an operation or rehousing.

Box 15.1: Allocating social housing

Housing allocations are intended in principle to determine who should have priority for social housing properties, as and when the properties become available. People apply on a housing list or register, their circumstances are recorded, and they are ranked in order of priority. Because people cannot share the allocated properties, there are no equal priorities; there must always be some way of ranking one person above another. In most of the documents produced by housing organisations, allocations are presented in terms of one of four types of policy:

- 'points' schemes, which give priority according to a set of priorities;

---

[672] D Clapham, K Kintrea, 1986, Rationing, choice and constraint, *Journal of Social Policy* 15(1) pp 51–68.

- 'date order' schemes, where people are treated on the basis of 'first-come, first served';
- 'merit' schemes, where cases are treated 'on their merits'; and
- 'group' schemes, where a range of categories are treated by different rules.

This classification is very misleading. There are actually five sequential stages in the process of allocations.[673]

1. *Access to the housing list* Prospective tenants have to identify themselves, and they have to be accepted onto the list before their application can be dealt with.

2. *Determination of categories of applicant* People who have applied for rehousing are placed into categories, mainly according to the location and size of property available. People who want four-bedroom houses are not considered to be in competition with single people looking for flats. Most social landlords run a large number of different lists.

3. *Identification of priority groups* Some categories of people have a special status and are treated differently from others on the list – for example, homeless people, people with special medical needs or resident staff. Every scheme is a 'group scheme' to some extent.

4. *Assessment of priority within groups* Once the groups are established, it has to be decided which person has the greatest priority. This is commonly done by 'date order', 'merit' or 'points schemes'. Date order has been shown to have serious disadvantages – the people who are most able to wait are generally those in less need – and the general trend in recent times has been to try to avoid the sense that this is a 'queue'.

5. *Matching of applicants with available property* Even if a particular case appears to have priority, the process of matching individual people to particular properties commonly involves some further considerations. The considerations most often taken into account are the choices and preferences of applicants and the need to balance other management considerations.

The pattern of housing allocations has developed to deal with a range of practical constraints. I have mentioned one before, the size and location of properties. But there are several others, which can be just as important.

---

[673] P Spicker, 1988, *Allocations policy: a housing information brief*, London: Institute of Housing.

- *The management of the housing stock.* Allocations are more a means of finding tenants for existing property than a way of finding property for people. Early research on allocations found that irrespective of what allocations policies said, the people who were likely to be housed were those whose households were the right size for two or three bedroomed houses: the ones who waited longest were people who wanted smaller or larger properties than that.[674] Most social housing in the UK is good housing physically, but some of the properties available to let are in undesirable areas. Suppose, for example, that a landlord has 3,000 good properties, and 200 socially undesirable properties. In a typical year, there will be 4% vacancies in the good properties, or 120 vacancies, and 20% vacancies in the undesirable area, or 40. Each of the undesirable properties might be offered to three people; each of the desirable properties will go immediately. That means that there will be as many offers going on 200 undesirable properties as on 3,000 desirable ones. It also means that landlords have to find tenants desperate enough to accept the least desirable housing. Usually these will be people with no choice – people who are homeless, and people who are disadvantaged.
- *Fairness.* Housing allocation is highly contentious, and often politicised. (It has largely been forgotten, but the flashpoint for the civil rights marches and troubles in Northern Ireland was discrimination in housing allocation.) The best defences for harassed officials are open transparent procedures, following strict published rules.
- *Response to public pressure.* The pressures are huge. The issues around dealing with members of the public, many of whom are desperate to improve their lives, are considerable. For decades, housing managers used unofficially to 'grade' applicants according to standards of cleanliness and the likelihood they would be well-behaved as tenants: the practice allowed them to head off problems both from applicants who would be insulted by being offered 'bad areas' and from existing residents who would object to them rehousing the wrong type in their area. This does not happen any more – at least, as far as official policies go. But there may still be restrictions on people believed to be liable to anti-social behaviour, criminal activity or rent arrears.

  Public housing provision is, perhaps to a surprising extent, a sort of 'market'. In the market, people who are more able to exercise choice are better able to command resources. In systems where some people

---

[674] P Niner, 1975, *Local authority housing policy and practice: a case study approach*, Birmingham: Centre for Urban and Regional Studies.

317

> are able to wait, to bargain, to negotiate, those people are able to get better housing. People who are not able to negotiate – people in precarious situations, people with few rights, and those who are desperate – get the worst housing.[675]

Equity and procedural fairness

The principle of 'equity' or fairness is an important issue in the delivery of scarce services. Equity means that like cases are treated alike. Where there are differences, those differences are reflected in differences of treatment; where there are none, distinctions between cases are unfair and arbitrary.

Substantive fairness Substantive fairness is concerned with the fairness of outcomes or results. The idea of equity is linked with 'distributive justice'; people are treated 'fairly' when they receive services or resources commensurate with their circumstances.[676] There is a presumption of equality where circumstances are equivalent, and of difference where they are not. There are many different principles which might be held to guide the idea of equity: the relevant circumstances which distinguish people might be differences in their needs, but they might also be differences in their entitlements, their deserts, their previous contribution, or their status.[677] Benefits for need include those which cover financial hardship or the functional problems of disability; benefits which recognise desert include war pensions; social insurance benefits (and, arguably, industrial injury benefits) are based on contribution. Health care is based on needs in so far as it responds directly to sickness; it reflects contribution to society when it is made specifically for members of the armed forces, or veterans; it reflects entitlement when it is based on insurance cover or statutory rights. Health care based on status is unusual, but the South African system, which formerly distinguished between people on the basis of race, might be an example.

Procedural fairness is a prerequisite for substantive fairness. In order to achieve a fair result, there has to be a fair procedure. The central demand of a fair procedure is consistency – because like cases cannot otherwise be treated alike. This implies the need for impartiality, because prejudice, bias or favour towards some people will lead to

---

[675] Clapham, Kintrea, 1986.

[676] J Thomson (ed) (1953) *The ethics of Aristotle*, Harmondsworth: Penguin.

[677] D Miller, 1976, *Social justice*, Oxford: Oxford University Press; P Spicker, 1988, *Principles of social welfare*, London: Routledge, ch 11.

inconsistent actions otherwise. It has also been argued that procedural fairness requires openness; if a procedure cannot be seen to be fair then its fairness remains open to doubt. Similarly, the opportunity to have decisions reviewed is of great importance, because otherwise unfairness cannot be corrected.

Procedural fairness is not, however, enough in itself to guarantee substantive fairness. Lotteries are fair procedures on their own terms, but they do not necessarily lead to fair results. Similarly, making people queue is widely thought of as a fair procedure, but the effect is to put those who cannot afford to wait at a disadvantage. Consistent procedures may well lead to consistent unfairness when they have failed to take into account relevant considerations, like need or urgency. For equity to be substantive, there has to be some means by which priorities can be identified and responded to.

Box 15.2: Limiting the demand for health care

The process of rationing health care is often represented as a trade-off between health and economy. Things are rarely so simple. Where health care is expensive and effective, most developed economies have found ways to make funding available. It also happens, however, that intensive treatments have diminishing returns: that as a person's health fails, there is scope for more and more invasive, possibly futile, intervention, leading to a combination of crushing expense with ineffective, and possibly counter-productive, treatment.

Modern pharmaceuticals have suffered from a combination of competition with established approaches, increasing regulation and the growing complexity of medical practice. 'Imagine', Scannell et al argue, 'how hard it would be to achieve commercial success with new pop songs if any new song had to be better than the Beatles ... We suggest something similar applies to the discovery and development of new drugs.... An ever-improving back catalogue of approved medicines increases the complexity of the development process for new drugs, and raises the evidential hurdles for approval, adoption and reimbursement.'[678] To justify the introduction of a new drug, there are many issues to resolve apart from its cost: they include the effectiveness of the treatment, its reliability relative to established alternatives, and the risk of harm. Many of the drugs being developed are potent, and they can have devastating effects when they are misapplied. Wherever this is true,

---

[678] J Scannell, A Blanckley, H Boldon, B Warrington, 2012, Diagnosing the decline in pharmaceutical R&D efficiency, Nature Reviews: Drug Discovery, 11 191-200 doi:10.1038/nrd3681.

what should happen is that successive tests are used gradually to refine the definition of the potential recipient group, so that each drug is used appropriately for people who stand to benefit, and avoided for those who are most at risk.

For people who are desperate for a cure, these constraints may be difficult to accept. In a court case in the UK, a woman took her health authority to court for refusing to prescribe a much-touted 'wonder drug' prior to its approval. The drug in question had appeared in trials to have benefits for some – actually rather less than was claimed – but for others it carried a risk of congestive heart failure.[679] The litigant was convinced that not receiving the drug was tantamount to a 'death sentence', and she made several emotive appeals to the press before winning her case in court.[680] By that time, the Secretary of State for Health had already intervened to direct that she should receive the drug. The political intervention consequently overrode the process of testing undertaken to protect the public.

This is indicative of a general problem. When people think they are faced with a choice of life or death, the normal constraints on expenditure do not apply; they will bear almost any cost for a chance of life, if the alternative is none. Unfortunately, public services cannot function on that basis. A powerful illustration comes from the case of Jaymee Bowen, 'Child B', a child who was diagnosed with cancer and refused treatment by the local health authority in Cambridge. Jaymee was given a 1% chance of responding to treatment. One has to ask whether this can be justified with such a low rate of survival. The health authority decided it could not. A spokesman for the health authority made the mistake of referring to cost, but the decision was not about money; it was about effectiveness. Treatment is painful, distressing and has unpleasant side effects. The clinician responsible for Jaymee's care told the court deciding the case that

'I took the view that it would not be right to subject Jaymee to all of this suffering and trauma when the prospects for success were so slight.' [681]

From the point of view of Jaymee, and her father, one chance in a hundred was better than no chance at all, and they campaigned to be allowed treatment. The court, which was bound to consider the issues from the individual's point

[679] M Piccart-Gebhart and 31 others, 2005, Trastuzumab after adjuvant chemotherapy in HER2- Positive Breast Cancer, *New England Journal of Medicine* 353:1659-1672.

[680] D Batty, 2006, Woman wins Herceptin appeal, *Guardian* April 12th, http://society.guardian.co.uk/health/news/0,,1752310,00.html

[681] Cited C Ham, S Pickard, 1998, *Tragic choices in health care: the case of Child B*, London: King's Fund, pp.20–21.

of view, agreed. From the point of view of the health authority, by contrast, one chance in a hundred is not a decision about one individual. It is saying that for every 100 people they treat in the same circumstances, 99 will die, with greater discomfort and pain than would otherwise be the case, and one will survive. Jaymee did receive the treatment, and she died.

Managing the demand for services

The 'demand' for welfare services is not the same thing as the sum of the claims which are actually made on them. The concept of 'demand' is used by economists to refer to the amount of service which would actually be used if the service was supplied at a particular price. It is possible to distinguish 'potential demand' – demand which might arise under certain conditions – from 'effective demand', which is the demand that actually exists under the conditions that currently apply. People can claim services for which they do not qualify; conversely, they can have rights for services they are not prepared to use, or fail to express the needs they have.

Ellie Scrivens, in classifying rationing processes, points out that they are not only concerned with the restriction of supply; it may also be possible to ration by inhibiting demand.[682] In order to restrict demand, the supplier has to be able to change the behaviour of the people using the service. This is mainly done through increasing the cost of claiming services, relative to the benefits. Such 'costs' are not only financial; they may include limitations on access, obstacles to be overcome, or stigma. Because inhibiting demand depends on the balance between costs and benefits, supply rationing plays a part in the process; but there are further restrictions which can be imposed. The most important are charging for services, limits on access, and deterrent procedures.

Charging for services is the standard way that demand is inhibited in the market; a high enough price reduces effective demand and can 'clear the market' of people waiting for service. Waiting lists are very unusual in the supply of private goods, simply because if they exist the supplier can increase prices until the waiting list disappears. This also means that those who are put off are likely to include those who cannot afford the service, and that is one of the main objections to the use of charges in social policy. If, for example, charges for home

---

[682] E Scrivens, 1980, Towards a theory of Rationing, in R Leaper (ed) *Health, wealth and housing*, Oxford: Blackwell.

helps mean that old people do not use them, the kinds of social care and monitoring which home helps do is not going to be undertaken.

Limiting access can be done in various ways. Access can be made more difficult, for example by closing offices, or by only offering services in particular locations. This sounds a bizarre way to select clients, but it does happen in some voluntary agencies – for example, there are housing associations who 'close' their waiting lists to enquiries for part of the year. Often this is done by default: a small agency may know it cannot over extend itself, so it begins working wherever it can, and only when it gets further resources will it expand its remit. The scope for limiting access is considerable. If people have to pass several stages in order to gain access, it follows that they can be encouraged if these stages are made easier to pass, and discouraged if they are made more difficult. Lack of information, complex procedures and time limits on claiming can all have an effect on demand overall.

Deterrence is an important issue in its own right. Demand might be restricted by making a service deliberately awkward to reach, onerous to claim, unpleasant or humiliating. Specific examples of explicit deterrent policies are unusual, but there are several. Probably the most famous was the 'workhouse' of the English Poor Law, which was intended to offer a discipline 'intolerable to the indolent and disorderly'.[683] At one stage, in order to deter people from using hospital care, an instruction went out that hospital patients had to be brought through the grounds of the workhouse so that they would know just where they were.[684] Another example is the deliberate holding down of benefits for unemployed people, in the belief that otherwise the benefits will create a 'disincentive to work'. The fear is that people will find living on benefit more attractive than working; cutting benefits is a way of making them relatively unattractive. 'Workfare', developed in the US, requires claimants to do some labour as a condition of receiving benefit;[685] but

---

[683] S Checkland, O Checkland, 1974, *The Poor Law Report of 1834*, Harmondsworth: Penguin, p.338.

[684] B Abel-Smith, 1964, *The hospitals 1800–1948*, London: Heinemann.

[685] N Park, R van Voorhuis, 2001, Moving people from welfare to work in the United States, in N Gilbert, R van Voorhuis (eds) *Activating the unemployed*, New Brunswick: Transaction; E Dahl, 2003, Does workfare work? *International Journal of Social Welfare* 12(4) 2003 274–88.

---

some of the arguments seem more focused on increasing the penalty for claiming, so as to encourage people not to claim.[686]

The difficulty here is distinguishing deterrent effects which are deliberate from those which are not. One of the problems in identifying deliberate deterrence is that other deterrent effects are so prevalent: the stigmas associated with claiming psychiatric care, poverty benefits or special education are strong, and they can only be reduced by special efforts to the contrary. If social security offices are generally depressing and sparsely furnished, is it because there is a deliberate attempt to make them unpleasant? Or is it just that public services are generally fairly dowdy and drab unless someone makes a deliberate effort to change them? If homeless people are offered the worst public housing, is it because the housing officers are trying to put them off or is it because the officers have to find someone who is desperate enough to accept the housing they have to offer? Are medical receptionists designed to help doctors work more efficiently, or to keep out patients who would otherwise be a nuisance? It is true, however, that there are circumstances where deterrence is liable to be introduced in local offices. Officials who are faced with excessive demand for services, and who have very limited control over policy, and who cannot determine the supply or production of services, have to manage the situation somehow. There may be little else they can do.

Brian Smith links the arguments about restricted access with those on the structure of welfare bureaucracies. A number of organisational practices, he argues, lead to problems in access, and so to disadvantage. These include the compartmentalism that creates multiple gates for people to negotiate; the tendency of agencies to favour success, which encourages the 'creaming' of cases which are more likely to yield it; and, in systems geared to equity on the basis of individual cases, the vulnerability of those systems to negotiations which middle-class people are generally better equipped to deal with.[687] In other words, the problems of access to welfare are not solely the product of deliberate policy decisions; they also reflect structural issues in the organisation of services.

---

[686] A Deacon, 2002, *Perspectives on welfare*, Buckingham: Open University Press.

[687] B C Smith, 1988, *Bureaucracy and political power*, Hemel Hempstead: Harvester Wheatsheaf.

Delivering services

The allocation of services to individuals takes place only at the end of a complex set of processes. It is not enough to say that services have been provided; they have actually to be delivered. This passes through a process of implementation, which is sometimes short – because spending time being assessed by a doctor or social worker constitutes receipt of a service in itself – but can equally be long and tortuous.

An example of the process might be the delivery of services to elderly people being discharged from hospital. People who have been receiving treatment in an acute ward could, of course, simply be told to go away. But the situation they have come from may not be tolerable. Some may have fallen or burnt themselves because they are effectively unable to cope at home; the admission is a signal that something needs to be done. There can be domestic problems: relatives who have been caring for an elderly person often realise at the point where an old person has had to come into hospital that they are unable to cope any more. There can be material problems: time in hospital can lead to problems in the tenure of property and the receipt of social security benefits. New problems may have come to light. People with dementia may have succeeded in functioning in their home environment, but the point of admission to hospital can reveal the extent of mental deterioration, because they are unable to adjust to the change in their situation. And being in hospital may create problems in itself. If a person is fully recovered, then in theory discharge should not leave someone much worse off than when they entered hospital. This is not necessarily true.

From the hospital's point of view, there are further considerations. Full recovery from many procedures can take some time; but it does not necessarily call for the kind of facilities found in an acute ward, and indeed there are strong arguments for saying that acute wards are fairly bad places in which to recuperate. Elderly people are at risk of deterioration. The hospital can respond in part by providing rehabilitation or convalescence wards, but it is in the nature of rehabilitation that it takes time, which makes it expensive and also means that large numbers of places are required. There will still be some patients who are not likely to recover and who will require long-term residential or nursing care. While people are waiting for such care to become available, there is a risk they will 'block' acute beds. There may be some generic response which might be made to everyone in this situation, but it seems inappropriate; people might be forced to wait in hospital beds because of the state of their health, because of problems at home, because of a lack of hospital facilities, or because of a lack of alternative kinds of facility in the community. The situation requires, then, some kind of assessment, and some kind of allocation, or at least management, of resources in order to facilitate discharge.[688] What is happening, then, is that some judgment has to be made in order to match services to demand, and the pressure comes at least as much from the services themselves as from the needs of the client.

The outcome of this process will vary in different circumstances, and it is difficult to offer generalisations about it, but there are some points which might usefully be made. One is that the outcome is not necessarily going to be in the best interests of the client – simply because the needs of the agency are an important driving force behind the impetus for discharge. Actions taken in the interests of the client are constrained; if someone is stuck on an acute ward, and there is an insufficient range of alternatives, the agency will have to refer that person to something else both because its own priorities require it and because the patient may deteriorate if left waiting. So, where the options for referral are limited, people who are referring 'bed-blockers' on will look for whatever options are available; they may have to settle for services which are 'second best' (e.g. nursing care in place of rehabilitation). Second, the problem as presented is not the problem of every part of the agency; it most specifically affects one section, the acute wards. What may happen, unless there are agreed objectives and an appropriate distribution of resources, is that that part of the service unloads its problems onto other parts. So, for example, old people might be referred to continuing care (one of the most expensive decisions which can be made) because of the absence of medium-term rehabilitation.[689]

This is illustrative of a deeper process, and one which is characteristic of many social services. Deliberate policy plays only a limited part in the determination of outcomes for services and for their recipients. The process of implementation is complex, and in this process rules have to be interpreted, practices develop, and judgments have to be made, which in themselves constitute a major part of social policy in practice. Lipsky has christened this process 'street-level' bureaucracy,[690] because many of these decisions are made at the lowest official level. Street level bureaucrats, Lipsky argues, 'make policy in two related respects.

---

[688] J Glasby, 2003, *Hospital discharge*, Abingdon: Radcliffe Medical Press.

[689] P Spicker, J Hanslip, 1994, Perceived mismatches between needs and services in the health care of elderly people, *Scottish Medical Journal*, 39(6) 172–174.

[690] M Lipsky, 1980, *Street level bureaucracy*, London: Sage.

They exercise wide discretion in decisions about citizens with whom they interact. Then, when taken in concert, their individual actions add up to agency behaviour.'[691] I started my career in social housing, where there was a huge difference between the formal published rules and 'management practice'; the process of managing a diverse housing stock, responding to need and negotiating with applicants and tenants called for a range of policies that had never been formally considered. It might be argued that something of the kind is happening at each and every level of a bureaucracy, where discretion is called on to fill the lacunae left by the absence of policy rules. Policy-makers set guidelines and constraints; officials have to work out some way to implement them. That formulation suggests, however, that a central policy which is more complete and specific might reduce the scope for street-level bureaucracy, and that is uncertain – it might only increase the pressures that lead to street level workers having to adapt their practice. Reviewing the experience of recent failures in child protection, Marinetto argues that attempts to improve services from the top down are doomed to failure: 'The normal, daily and informal routines of professional workers are integral to how the child protection system operates. These very same routines may inadvertently culminate in systemic failures that result in child protection tragedies.'[692]

The judgments which officials have to make are made under constraints – constraints which include, not just the structures imposed from those directing the service, but relations with the public they serve. Service ideologies – received patterns of thought and approaches to practice – are constructed under such constraints. Officials do not simply make up policies as they please; they have to develop methods of working which fit in with the circumstances of the agency. These methods become enshrined in the working patterns of officials, and are passed from one person to another. The 'common sense' which people learn in agencies consists, in large part, of the developed practice of the agency.

This process can lead, over time, to formal policy, as well as informal, being made from the 'bottom up'. Officials try to work out practical ways of responding to issues; their practice is imitated by others; the approach is taken up by decision-makers at local or national level; the practice becomes general policy. Examples in the UK include the introduction of deterrent workhouses, pioneered in Nottinghamshire in

---

[691] Lipsky, 1980, p.13.
[692] M Marinetto, 2011, A Lipskian analysis of child protection failures, *Public Administration*, 89(3) 1164–1181.

the 1820s – George Nicholls, the overseer at Southwell, became a Poor Law Commissioner on the strength of his work; the use of short-term loans to help families in need, developed under powers made available to social workers in 1963[693] and incorporated into the Social Fund between 1988 and 2013; or the development of GP commissioning within the NHS, which grew from voluntary cooperation between practices for the purchasing of services.[694]

ISSUE FOR DISCUSSION

Is rationing by price preferable to rationing by delay, dilution or deterrence?

---

[693] M Jackson, B M Valencia, 1979, *Financial aid through social work*, London: RKP.

[694] R Singer (ed), 1997, *GP Commissioning: an inevitable evolution*, Abingdon: Radcliffe.

CHAPTER 16

Receiving welfare

The receiving end

The picture the previous chapter conjures of the service available to welfare recipients is a depressing one. The experience of claiming welfare is not a question of having one's needs identified and met; recipients have often to overcome a series of hurdles, and when they do they are often subject to intrusive inquiries, deterrence and a low quality of service.

I referred earlier to the arguments of Osborne and his colleagues about social services. Because the services being provided – education, health care, social work, employment support – are not 'products', because there is no provision or production that is separate from consumption or use, and because the relationship continues over time, the delivery of social services depends on a relationship between the service and the service user.[695] Radnor and Osborne describe this in terms of 'co-production', but then they go on to explain what this term includes: 'a surgical procedure is influenced just as much by the individual pathology of a patient as by the skills of the doctor'.[696] The idea of co-production seems to suggest active engagement; the truth may be rather more passive and rather less consensual. It is difficult to relate the language of co-production to punitive sanctions imposed on

---

[695] S Osborne, Z Radnor, G Nasi, 2013, A new theory for public service management?, *American Review of Public Administration* 43(2) pp 135–58.

[696] Z Radnor, S Osborne, 2013, Lean: .a failed theory for public services?, *Public Management Review* 15(2) 265–287, p 278.

benefit recipients,[697] the treatment of people with dementia in ways that undermine their dignity,[698] or a system of child care where children 'are moved frequently and often suddenly, miss too much schooling, and are left to fend for themselves at too early an age.'[699] But what is certainly true, regardless of the terminology, is that the service users are intrinsic to the process of service delivery, and that process can hardly be understood without considering their actions. Service users discuss, they bargain, they change the pattern of service delivery, they often do part of the provision themselves.[700] And they may resist, renegotiate or redefine the terms on which services are delivered.[701]

Despite the central position of service users, it is all too easy in studies of social policy to lose sight of the people who receive benefits and services. There are legitimate reasons why this should happen. Social policy which is oriented towards the recipient can be seen as emphasising the negative aspects of policy, like individual dependency. There is a good argument that welfare services should be like drains – boring, safe, taken for granted and used by everyone. Ideally, there should be no more reason to discuss the individual situation of someone receiving social security or health care than there is to talk about people who use roads, take out library books or watch a public service broadcast on television. But this is not the way of the world, and the recipients of social services are not thought of in the same way as other people. They may not have much else in common, but they are all at the receiving end of the sort of process described up to this point; that of itself implies some important issues about their experience.

Claims: demand, needs and rights

In Chapter 4, I made the case that needs call for a response – a statement of need is a claim for services. The 'demand' for social services discussed in Chapters 14 and 15 has some similarities to the concept of 'need': it refers mainly to problems which people have, which call for particular types of response. 'Need' and 'demand' are not exactly equivalent,

---

[697] P Larkin, 2007, The 'criminalisation' of social security law, *Journal of Law and Society*, 34(3) 295–320.

[698] T Kitwood, 1997, *Dementia reconsidered*, Buckingham: Open University Press.

[699] House of Commons Children, Schools and Families Committee, 2009, *Looked after Children*, London: The Stationery Office HC111, p 15.

[700] Osborne et al, 2013.

[701] D Prior, M Barnes, 2011, Subverting social policy on the front line, *Social Policy and Administration* 45(3) 264–279.

however. Demand can exist where there is no need: a universal service, like a family allowance, may be claimed by every family even if they do not need the money, and people can have needs which are not recognised as constituting effective demand. It has been argued that the idea of 'need' is superfluous; for practical purposes, it is demand rather than need with which services are concerned.[702] The problem with this position is that the ways in which 'need' is translated into potential demand would then be concealed. There may be no 'demand' for many services for elderly people from people below retirement age, because they are excluded from the assessment; but the need is probably there, and where people are giving the opportunity (as in schemes for early retirement) they often take it.

Bradshaw's 'taxonomy of need' is the best known classification of needs of different types. He distinguishes four categories of need: normative, comparative, felt and expressed.

- *Normative need* is need which is identified according to a norm; such norms are generally set by experts. Benefit levels, for example, or standards of unfitness in houses, have to be determined according to some criterion.
- *Comparative need* concerns problems which emerge by comparison with others who are not in need. One of the most common uses of this approach has been the comparison of social problems in different areas in order to determine which areas are most deprived.
- *Felt need* is need which people feel – that is, need from the perspective of the people who have it.
- *Expressed need* is the need which they say they have. People can feel need which they do not express, and they can express needs they do not feel.[703]

Bradshaw's classification is concerned with the way in which needs are defined, with who defines them, and so with the type of claim that is being made. Different kinds of need can occur in different combinations, and the strength of the claim reflects the way the need is framed and understood.

---

[702] A A Nevitt, 1977, Demand and need, in H Heisler,(ed) *Foundations of social administration*, Basingstoke: Macmillan.

[703] J Bradshaw, 1972, *A taxonomy of social need*, New Society March 640–643; also in R Cookson, R Sainsbury, C Glendinning (eds) 2013, Jonathan Bradshaw on Social Policy, York: University of York, http://bit.ly/BradSW

'Demand' and 'need' are not the only kind of claim which might be made for services. The provision of parks and libraries, and support for the arts or sport, have less to do with a concept of 'need' than the belief that welfare is positively enhanced when such things are available. The strength of a claim rests on the moral judgments that back it up, rather than its importance for welfare; people can suffer greatly from unemployment or ill-health without feeling any sense of entitlement, but they can become indignant about something they have bought, because there they are confident they have rights.

Rights, in this general sense, can also be seen as a sort of claim.[704] There are some rights that are not claims, because they do not require other people to act differently – for example, there are 'rights' attached to liberties, which do not seem directly to claim anything; but many rights do act as demands for service, for example for social security benefits, health care or education. Sometimes the claim of rights is moral: moral rights are intended to give people a sense of entitlement and legitimacy. Marshall wanted the 'right to welfare' to be understood as a basic right for everyone, as part of a new understanding of citizenship.[705] The ideal of the 'welfare state' may seem remote at times from the practical problems of claimants, but it has an important persuasive role: perceived legitimacy is important in maintaining a sense of social honour, and where people feel a sense of shame or humiliation in receiving services, advice workers do refer to general principles of this kind.

Positive rights are those which are backed up by law, and 'claim-right' is the term for the type of legal right that allows someone to enforce a claim.[706] Typically claim-rights are linked to some kind of sanction, such as redress through a system of judicial review. Some claim-rights are universal, in the sense that they apply to everyone in the same position, but many are not. Some are contingent, which means that they apply only when certain conditions are met – examples are rights to war pensions, or provision for widows. Other claim-rights are particular, which means only that they apply to specific individuals; people gain a particular right if someone has a personal obligation towards them (for example, as the result of a promise, a contract, or an injurious action). On the face of the matter, particular rights look as if they ought to have only a limited role in social policy overall, but there are

---

[704] M Rein, 1983, *From policy to practice*, London: Macmillan.

[705] T Marshall, 1981, *The right to welfare*, London: Heinemann,.

[706] W Hohfeld, 1920, *Some fundamental legal conceptions as applied in judicial reasoning*, New Haven: Yale University Press, obtained at archive.org.

several countries where particular rights have become the main means through which welfare is delivered. Pensions, in much of continental Europe, are not based in the general rights of the population; they are tied closely to each person's work record, and the contributions which people make while they are working give them a contractual right to receive benefits in due course. However, this kind of arrangement can never provide comprehensive coverage of a population, and the same systems which in Europe protect a substantial majority of the population have proved difficult to extend in the relatively informal economies of the developing world.[707]

The process of claiming

The 'claims' referred to so far are mostly claims in a general, 'thin' sense; they can be made by anyone, and they are best understood as aspects of the demand for services. 'Claims' are also used in a 'thick' sense – that is, a sense which is more specific and more developed even if it is narrower – to refer to particular applications for service. People 'claim' benefits when they fill in a form and hand it in to the appropriate office. They 'claim' medical care when they present themselves to a doctor for assessment. 'Claiming' has become an important part of the administration of services; it places the initial responsibility for receiving services on the 'claimant' or client, rather than an agency which is failing to reach people.

There are some services which do not require a 'claim' to be registered in this way. Medical care is usually initiated by the patient, but in cases where the patient is not able to do so – for example, after a road accident – it will be initiated by someone else. Social work is not always undertaken with the consent of the parties involved, let alone on their initiative, and the equivalent of the 'claim' in social work is the 'referral', where someone informs workers that their intervention might be appropriate. That 'someone' might be the client, a member of the family, someone who had come into contact with the client (like a fuel supplier or a police officer) or another professional in welfare services. By contrast, social security is almost always dependent on the registration of a claim by the prospective recipient – which is arguably unnecessary, because in a universal system it is fairly simple to make the payment of age-related benefits automatic. 'Claiming' is sometimes defended on the basis that it respects the choice of individuals: there

---

[707] R Beattie, 2000, Social protection for all: but how?, *International Labour Review* 139(2) 129–148.

is a view that people only have true 'rights' if they are able to choose whether to exercise them or not.[708] There are some grounds to support this in the case of medical care, where the implication otherwise would be that people would have to have compulsory medical treatment. However, the argument sometimes seems suspect: if people have money paid to them automatically they can still choose whether to use it or not.

This points to an important issue about demand. The effect of placing the burden of claiming on the recipients of welfare is that some people will not use the service. People may not use services because of a positive choice. For example, people may not want to go into residential care because they do not like the kind of life-style that it offers. Some medical operations are unpleasant and possibly frightening; for example, people often delay seeking help for cancer both because of pessimism about what can be done and because the treatments are generally unpleasant. The issues are rather more complex than the issue of 'choice' implies. There is a major problem of 'non-takeup', where people who are entitled to benefits, and for whom it is intended that they should receive the benefits, do not get them. For many years, this was described as a problem of 'stigma', because some claimants felt humiliated by claiming, but the problem is rather more complex than this suggests. Reasons for non-takeup include ignorance about benefits, the complexity and difficulty of the process, previous problems in attempting to claim, limited marginal benefits and the costs to the claimant of proceeding.[709] The financial advantage to be gained by claiming some social security benefits may be outweighed by the time, trouble and negative experience involved in claiming. Weisbrod, in a short working paper, outlined a central principle which has become one of the most important insights in this area: that the decision whether or not to claim can be understood as a balance between costs and benefits.[710]

When demands are formed, people have to balance the costs and benefits of their actions. they have not only to exercise their formal entitlements but also to overcome a series of practical obstacles. Kerr

---

[708] H L A Hart, 1955, Are there any natural rights?, *Philosophical Review* 64 pp 175–191.

[709] C Davies, J Ritchie, 1988, Tipping the balance, London: HMSO; P Craig, 1991, Costs and benefits, *Journal of Social Policy* 20(4) pp 537–565.

[710] B Weisbrod, 1970, *On the stigma effect and the demand for welfare programmes*, Madison, Wisconsin: University of Wisconsin Institute for Research on Poverty.

outlined a series of stages, which he intended to apply to social security benefits but which might equally apply to others.[711]

1. People must feel a need, or at least they must want to have what is being offered.
2. They have to find out that the service exists. Few people have had reason to hear about orthotics (which provides devices such as corrective footwear), and that means that even when they have the problems they do not necessarily know to ask about the service.
3. They have to know they are likely to receive the service; a service for 'poor people' is not certain to be taken up by people who do not think of themselves as poor.
4. They have to feel that the benefit is worth claiming. This is mainly influenced by the size of the benefit, but there are also hidden costs – such as the problem of travelling to an office or surgery, and the time that claiming is likely to take.
5. There are the beliefs and feelings of potential recipients: someone who believes that benefits are degrading is less likely to claim than another person who thinks they are an entitlement.
6. It is important that people should recognise their situation as being stable. People with debilitating illnesses are unlikely to think of themselves as 'disabled' until either they know the condition is likely to last, or that it has lasted a long time. A newly separated mother may be unsure that her situation is going to last, and may delay claiming before the position becomes clear.

Kerr intended his model to represent a series of 'thresholds': in order to make a claim, a person has to negotiate each obstacle in turn. In practice, the divisions are rather less well defined than this might suggest: someone with negative attitudes towards a service may well know less about the service (because such a service is 'not for people like us'), while people may not get to work out whether a benefit is worth claiming until they have worked out how long their circumstances are going to last.[712] Besides, when the focus shifts to other services besides social security, there may be important differences. Filling forms is one of the banes of social security administration; it is not a major part of claiming health care in a universal system. By contrast, it is possible to deal with many social security claims remotely – the current policy

---

[711] S Kerr, 1983, *Making ends meet*, London: Bedford Square Press.
[712] Davies and Ritchie, 1988.

in the UK is that administration should be 'digital by default' – but health care usually relies on visits to particular locations, even if the initial access begins remotely.

Problems like this visibly affect many social services. The problem of 'non take-up' is interpreted differently in different services. In health care, the problem seems to be that people who are most in need are least likely to receive appropriate levels of health care. People in lower social classes have greater health needs, but they are less likely to receive services.[713] There are two main explanations for limited access. Cultural explanations locate the problem in the behaviour of people in the lower classes, who are said to be less able to explain complaints to middle-class doctors, less able to negotiate for resources, and more willing to tolerate illness. Practical problems concern the difficulties of obtaining access: doctors' surgeries tend to be in more salubrious, middle-class areas, while people in lower social classes are less likely to have access to a telephone and less likely to have cars, and besides are less free to take time off work without losing pay.[714]

Box 16.1: Means testing

Means testing is the process of determining entitlement for benefits or services according to a person's means. This is usually interpreted as the person's income, though there may also be a test of capital – whether the person holds certain types of asset as wealth. It is one of the main methods used for selectivity, the process of deciding who will receive benefits according to need, and many of the objections to means testing are also objections to selectivity: the difficulty of defining boundaries fairly, the problem that comes because benefits are withdrawn if a person ceases to qualify, and the general experience that selectivity excludes people that it is supposed to include, because of ignorance about the rules, complexity and stigma. Means testing is widely assumed to have all these problems,[715] though some means-tested benefits seem to have overcome them – the means-tested pension in Australia does not seem to suffer from any general stigma,[716] and nor did the student grants system that used to exist in the UK.

---

[713] P Townsend, N Davidson, M Whitehead, 1988, *Inequalities in health*, Harmondsworth: Penguin; Department of Health, 1998, *Independent inquiry into inequalities in health*, London: TSO.

[714] M Morgan, 2003, Patients' help-seeking and access to health care, in M Gulliford, M Morgan (eds) *Access to health care*, London: Routledge.

[715] W van Oorschot, 1995, *Realizing rights*, Aldershot: Avebury.

[716] C Mood, 2006, Take-up down under, *European Sociological Review* 22(4) 443–458.

Means testing has, however, problems of its own.[717] They include problems of fairness:

- how to identify the 'thresholds', the points at which people will become entitled
- how to treat different forms of capital, such as owner occupation, inheritance, and possession of goods, and
- how to ensure equity of treatment between households with different compositions. One example is the treatment of children of different ages relative to adults, the problem of 'equivalence'; the other problem is how to treat a couple compared to two adults, the problem of 'cohabitation'. Wherever couples are treated differently from two adults, there has to be some rule to distinguish them. Often it centres round sexual relationships. In the UK officials are instructed not to ask questions about sex, which leads to interactions that are only a little less awkward and embarrassing than if they did ask the questions.

Then there are complicating elements which are part of the process of assessing means:

- how unearned income should be treated
- what happens when people receive other benefits (which are, of course, a form of income)
- how to treat people in the household who are not dependants or part of the family
- what to do with self-employed people
- how to treat occasional work, and
- how to deal with fluctuations in income. In cases where benefits are paid to people in work, they can be slowly reduced or 'tapered' as income increases. This approach has become more widely used, but it makes benefits exceedingly complicated – it can be difficult to know when entitlement stops or starts, or how much it should be – and because income fluctuates, it tends to make benefits unpredictable too.

From the point of view of claimants, the problems of means-tests include the assumption that they know what their financial position is, that they can answer directly and accurately, and that they can provide the evidence. People are routinely asked about their personal details, domestic circumstances and household composition, employment history, special needs, sources

---

[717] See P Spicker, 2011, *How social security works,* Bristol: Policy Press.

of income and capital. It is not unusual in the UK for there to be more than a hundred questions. Some people do not know what their income is going to be before they receive it. Many people, especially those in small businesses, do not know what their income is from month to month – it takes time (and sometimes expertise) to make annual tax returns. When the Tax Credit scheme was introduced in the UK, overpayments left some claimants confused – and liable to repay large sums of money they did not know they were not entitled to. The Parliamentary Ombudsman commented:

> There are many for whom the experience has been, and indeed remains, highly distressing. Whilst they may be only a relatively small proportion of the overall numbers claiming tax credits, they are a significant number, and the impact on the customers concerned, typically those on the very lowest incomes who are amongst the most vulnerable in society, is huge.[718]

That report questioned 'whether a financial support system which included a degree of inbuilt financial insecurity could properly meet the needs of very low income families and earners.'[719]

The costs of claiming

The benefits of claiming services are usually self-evident. Services which provide medical care, housing or education are offering a particular kind of service, and the nature of the service is the simplest explanation for why people should claim. The costs are much less obvious, because they are not necessarily material, and often they are not measurable.

The costs which might be considered are of four kinds.

- *Access* This sort of issue has been considered in the preceding sections: it refers to problems like giving up time, travelling, consulting, and overcoming obstacles.
- *Use* In order to be recipients of different kinds of care, people often have to go without some of the things which others have. The long-term consequences of receiving psychiatric care can include unemployment and poverty, because people who enter care have to leave the labour market. People living in residential

---

[718] Parliamentary and Health Service Ombudsman, 2007, *Tax Credits – getting it wrong?* HC 1010, p 43.
[719] Parliamentary and Health Service Ombudsman, 2007, p 5.

care are restricted in their freedom of movement, and their ability to live as they want in their homes; they often have limited choices about when they can eat or when they can go to bed.[720] At the extremes, people can be subjected to neglect, brutality and dehumanising treatment.[721]

- *Stigma and loss of status* The extent to which people feel a sense of 'stigma' – loss of status, shame, humiliation – is much disputed, but if there is such a sense, that is a cost too.

- *Exit* Once someone has begun receiving a service, it may be difficult to stop. This may happen simply because the benefits of the services are likely to be lost. In social security, it has been claimed that there is an 'unemployment trap', in which people might be better off receiving benefit than working for a low wage.[722] Problems also arise following changes in circumstances in other services: for example, young people leaving residential care are often particularly vulnerable to problems of unemployment and homelessness.

  In some cases, there are further costs associated with exit. Lone parents looking for employment commonly have the cost of child care to consider, if this is not provided freely by the state. Being discharged from hospital is a difficult situation for the person who has been in an institutional environment for a long time, which combines the loss of service with all the problems of being able to establish oneself in the world outside.[723]

The precise effects of these costs are difficult to establish, because they have to be measured against the benefits. The attitudes of people who fail to claim services are often markedly different from those who do claim – which is to be expected if some have been deterred while others have not – but it is not necessarily the case that those who have claimed are not in some way affected by the costs.[724] Similarly, the existence

---

[720] See W Wolfensberger, 1972, *The principle of normalisation in human services*, Toronto: National Institute for Mental Retardation.

[721] R Barton, 1959, *Institutional neurosis*, Bristol: Wright (3rd ed 1976); J P Martin, 1985, *Hospitals in trouble*, Oxford: Blackwell.

[722] House of Commons Committee on Work and Pensions, 2007, *Benefits simplification*, London: TSO, HC 463–1.

[723] P Bean, P Mounser, 1993, *Discharged from mental hospitals*, Basingstoke: Macmillan; P Spicker, I Anderson, R Freeman, R McGilp, 1995, Discharged into the community: the experience of psychiatric patients, *Social Services Research*, 1995–1 pp 1–9.

[724] P Spicker, 1984, *Stigma and social welfare*, Beckenham: Croom Helm.

of costs at the point of exit may delay the process, but the existence of costs of claiming, and further benefits in not doing so, may outweigh this effect. The problem with generalising about people's behaviour on the basis of incentives or disincentives – the kind of argument made by Charles Murray in *Losing ground*[725] – is that we know very little about the extent to which people will actually respond to such stimuli. This responsiveness (economists refer to it in terms of 'elasticity') might vary enormously according to circumstances, and generalisations can only be supported through empirical evidence.

Choice

The picture which all this tends to conjure of service delivery is one in which the people who receive welfare have their behaviour conditioned and determined by the services. But recipients still have to balance costs and benefits, it is usually their decision to claim, and the choices made by recipients are an important constituent part of demand. The analysis of choice is mainly the province of economics, and in particular of welfare economics; choice is the mechanism through which utility, and so welfare, can be maximised. In the operation of social welfare services, however, the opportunity to exercise choice has often been limited.

The case for choice has mainly been expressed through arguments for considering the delivery of welfare in terms of a market, in which the recipients of welfare services are consumers (or even 'customers'). The central principle is that decisions are made by the person who is likely to receive the services, rather than a professional or bureaucrat on their behalf. In the operation of an economic market, consumers have the opportunity to use resources to purchase goods and services. The priorities which are determined, and so decisions about rationing, arise from the interaction of many people rather than the policy of some central authority. Part of the rationale for marketisation and the development of the 'quasi-markets' considered earlier is that markets create opportunities for choice, and so for the maximisation of welfare for consumers according to their own lights.

This argument is a strong one; and, despite the reservations considered previously about the operation of the private market, it is very widely accepted on both right and left. When people are short of food or clothing, few people would argue for distribution by the state; the argument is much more commonly made that people need

---

[725] C Murray, 1984, *Losing Ground*, New York: Basic Books.

to have the money to pay for such items. Indeed, the idea that poor people might be subject to a régime in which they are unable to choose what they eat or what they wear is usually seen as a sign of repressive paternalism, rather than liberation from the constraints of the market. Greener and Powell point to an important ambiguity in the debates: the idea of 'choice' is not used consistently. In discussing education, choice is taken to imply diversity; in health, it is about responsiveness to service users; in housing, it is about personal responsibility and control.[726] Arguments for 'personalisation' (Box 12.2) have been used to make a similar case in the provision of social care.

Arguments for social security or income maintenance are generally arguments for the private sector – to give people the money to choose rather than giving them what they need. The arguments against choice consequently respond by pointing to the inefficiencies and constraints on choice which arise in the private sector. The problem is not simply that people have unequal resources – that would be an argument for redistribution of cash instead[727] – but that the process of exercising choices leads to inequities or inappropriate distributions. Part of this is attributable to the problems of exercising choice meaningfully – people who are desperate are not in a strong bargaining position; part, in health care, is the problem of knowing and understanding what is being purchased; but the major part, too, is that the process of exercising choice itself leads to serious problems of disadvantage. It is not just the consumer who has a choice; producers do, too, and they can choose to exclude people who are needy, isolated or difficult to reach. In housing and education, the effect of choice is to produce a stratified system with profound social consequences.

The effect of permitting choice in the structure of non-market services may be to duplicate some of the inequalities of the private market. The recipients of welfare services tend to be disadvantaged, and they have fewer options from which choices can be made. In these circumstances, the opportunity to exercise choice may simply aggravate existing disadvantages. Box 15.1 describes how public housing allocation responds to reflect the pressures of people with competing claims for better housing. In education, parents who can afford to move into the catchment areas of the better schools are able to buy a considerable social advantage for their children. The problem with limiting choice is that it does not necessarily guarantee that

---

[726] I Greener, M Powell, The evolution of choice policies in UK housing, education and health policy, *Journal of Social Policy* 38(1) 2009 63–82.

[727] A Seldon, 1977, *Charge!*, London: Temple Smith.

disadvantages will be redressed. The real aim is not to obstruct choices and opportunities, but to ensure that those who are poorest and most disadvantaged will be able to exercise such opportunities.

Rights

Allowing people rights as individuals is crucial to protection in the circumstances where they are vulnerable. Welfare recipients can be denied rights in practice. The worst cases are those of people who have impaired abilities, like people with intellectual disabilities or dementia. The effects are devastating; they include the use of drugs to control their behaviour, admission to institutions without their consent, and even, in the case of people with intellectual disabilities, compulsory sterilisation. People need special protection if their social competence is limited, because they are vulnerable to exploitation and abuse, and because they may suffer serious harm without the necessary safeguards. But this is an argument, not to reduce or limit protection given them, but to increasing it; the people who are least able to exercise rights freely are precisely those who need them most.

Positive rights – rights which are backed up by some kind of sanction or redress – can be substantive or procedural. Substantive rights are rights to a good or service which is claimed. They can be enforced through procedures for the redress of grievances – for example, internal review, or structures for appeal. Although there are many substantive rights in social services, particularly to social security benefits, they are not generally applied, for reasons which were discussed when considering the role of professionals in service delivery: wherever professional discretion is to be applied, the effect of a substantive right would be to deny the professional scope for manoeuvre. Interestingly, many of the formal rights which apply in social services are not 'claim-rights' at all, but liberties – protections against intrusion or treatment without consent.

The procedural rights include rights to information, and to rights which make the redress of grievances possible – including rights to be heard and to be represented, to be judged impartially, and to have recourse to judicial procedures when other means fail.[728] Procedural rights are prerequisites for the redress of grievances; they are not enough to guarantee redress, but they are necessary.

---

[728] See J Alder, 2011, *Constitutional and administrative law*, pp 403ff.

There are often important limitations on the procedural rights available to people who receive social welfare services. First, decisions may be made solely on an individual basis; for substantive rules to be developed, there has to be some system of precedent, so that people can refer to judgments in other cases as support for their own. Second, professional or administrative discretion can drive out rights of this kind, as well as substantive rights, although it would still be true that professionals who exercise discretion are expected to do so by the standards of their profession, rather than through personal prejudice. Third, the problems which people experience are not always individual; they may be collective, like the effects of pollution, inadequacies in the education service, or a refusal to cover some contingencies for insurance. The law in the United States permits 'class actions', where people can sue as a group, and the 'Brandeis brief', which allows the social implications of an action to be taken into account in a legal judgment. Neither used to be possible in the United Kingdom, but there has been an incremental development of comparable processes, along with a trend for legal actions to be taken by groups and representative organisations.[729] Lastly, and perhaps most important, legal redress is worth very little if people cannot gain access to it: there has to be some mechanism which allows people to afford the legal costs, or alternatively a structure for the redress of grievances, like the use of administrative tribunals, which allows such costs to be circumvented. Legal aid in the UK has largely been supplanted by contingency fees, where lawyers take a percentage of winnings. For people whose social capacity or functioning is impaired, there has to be an effective route through which arguments can be made by them or on their behalf.

The gap in social protection left by the inaccessibility of legal redress has led to the development of a set of strategies usually referred to as 'welfare rights'. 'Welfare rights' refers to a range of activities in which citizens are advised and supported in their claims for social welfare services, and in particular for social security benefits. There are four main types of activity which are considered to be part of 'welfare rights':

- advice and support given to individuals who have problems with specific services.

---

[729] C Harlow, 2002, Public law and popular justice, *Modern Law Review* 65(1) 1–18.

- agencies dedicated to advocacy and specialised advice, which is intended not only to assist individuals but to challenge and test the work of agencies in the welfare field, and to establish precedents in practice.
- publicity, extending awareness of the nature of the rights.
- the political and campaigning arm of welfare rights work, which draws on information gained from practice to argue for legal and administrative changes in the treatment of recipients.

These are different approaches, but they are mutually reinforcing; campaigning work is often dependent on the authority established by a foundation of practically-based knowledge and action, while casework throws up issues which require other avenues to be explored beyond the immediate scope of legal redress.

Empowerment

Countering these problems is increasingly seen as an issue of 'empowerment'. The idea of 'empowerment' means that people who are relatively powerless are able to gain more power. The term has only recently come into widespread use, and it tends to reflect its origins in social work practice. Solomon, in one of the earliest uses of the term, defines empowerment as

> a process whereby the social worker or other helping professional engages in a set of activities with the client aimed at reducing the powerlessness stemming from the experience of discrimination because the client belongs to a stigmatised collective.[730]

This has subsequently been extended to refer to 'the mechanism by which people, organisations and communities gain mastery over their lives'.[731]

At the individual level, empowerment might be seen as a form of freedom; people are empowered when they are able to decide issues for themselves. Arguments for 'normalisation' overlap with those of empowerment when 'normalisation' is seen as a route to autonomy.

---

[730] B Solomon, 1976, *Black empowerment*, New York: Columbia University Press, p.29.
[731] Rappaport 1984, cited L Holdsworth, 1991, *Empowerment social work with physically disabled people*, Norwich: University of East Anglia Social Work Monographs, p.3

Pinderhughes thinks of power primarily in terms of social interaction, with the result that facilitating social skills and communication can be seen as a form of empowerment.[732]

At the collective level, empowerment can be taken to be a response to a lack of power; the powerlessness of stigmatised groups reflects the place of disadvantaged groups in the wider society. The movement to 'participation' in the late 1960s and early 1970s was rooted in concepts of direct democracy, the idea that collectively people could exercise joint authority in the decisions which affect them. It was encouraged by a number of influences, including imitation of trends in the US, public interest in conservation, and the recognition of planning as a political activity. The same principles were directly extended to social housing, where they have become an accepted part of housing management. Some views of the impact of participation on local government practice have been pessimistic; the experience falls far short of direct democracy, possibly because the structures of local government are incompatible, possibly because they are resistive, because they are too complex to be moved easily.[733] It is questionable, however, whether direct democracy is what participation is supposed to achieve; empowerment within a process is a much more limited objective. One of the arguments for participation was that it was thought to enhance the personal abilities of the participants. This made it a desirable strategy for community workers and others concerned with the position of disadvantaged groups. Another argument was that it facilitated decision making, by providing information and permitting negotiation with service users. In other words, participation has been a means of incorporating different groups within the policy process. The established position of participatory mechanisms has made them a model for subsequent strategies concerned with empowerment.

A collectivised approach to empowerment is often realised within the structures of local communities. The strategies commonly pursued within local government and services focus on disadvantaged groups and communities. Broadly speaking, there are four main strategies defined in the literature:

---

[732] E Pinderhughes, 1983, Empowerment for clients and for ourselves, *Social Casework* 64(6) 331–338

[733] D McKenna, 2011, UK local government and public participation, *Public Administration* 89(3) 1182–1200.

- *Community social work* focuses on individuals and their social interactions in order to increase their potential within a social context.[734]
- *Neighbourhood work* consists of attempting to develop the networks and relationships in a community, by strategies of outreach and access, in order to facilitate social action.[735]
- *Community education* is concerned with developing the social skills and collective potential of disadvantaged people.
- *Community organisation* (also referred to as 'community action' and 'community development') is concerned with political mobilisation and collective action. This drew inspiration from models in the US (e.g. Alinsky's *Rules for radicals*[736]) which saw the roots of social problems as lying in the structure of power in society and set out in order to redress the balance.

These categories are not discrete, and several strategies can be adopted simultaneously.

The emphasis on empowerment at the collective level reflects an important ideological commitment among certain communitarian socialists. It rests in part on the assumption that there are collective groups: there is a strong connection with 'identity politics', of the sort which has been most effective for feminist and gay groups; it can be seen for example in the extension of the model to the 'disability movement'.[737] There are two problems with the approach. The first is that identity is often uncertain: many people with disabilities do not identify themselves in those terms.[738] Attempts to extend identity politics to people with experience of poverty have similarly proved difficult;[739] there is not one experience of poverty, and the exclusionary character of poverty tends to work against identification. That points

---

[734] National Institute of Social Work, 1982, *Social workers: their role and tasks,* NISW.

[735] P Henderson, D Thomas, 2001, *Skills in neighbourhood work,* London: Routledge.

[736] S Alinsky, 1972, *Rules for radicals,* New York: Vintage Books.

[737] M Oliver, 1990, *The politics of disablement,* Basingstoke: Macmillan.

[738] Department for Work and Pensions, 2013 *Disability statistics,* from the ONS Opinions and Lifestyle Surve: January to March 2013, https://www.gov.uk/government/uploads/system/uploads/attachment_data/file/210030/q1-2013-data.xls

[739] G Roets, R Roose, M de Bie, L Claes, G van Hove, 2012, Pawns or pioneers? The logic of user participation in anti-poverty policy making in public policy units in Belgium, *Social Policy and Administration* 46(7) 807–822.

to a second, more fundamental problem: that the people who are most disadvantaged are also liable to be disadvantaged in their ability to present their case individually or collectively. Some psychiatric patients participate very effectively in collective organisations, but many do not; those who are homeless, in particular, may not only have lost their friends but have no residual family contact.[740] Disruption of communication, the loss of social contact and atomisation have profoundly disempowering effects.

Box 16.2: Empowerment and dementia

Welfare services have often suffered from the assumption that people who are dependent are unable to make decisions for themselves. Over the course of the last thirty years, there has been a growing movement to empower service users and to affirm their capacity to make decisions. The arguments for empowerment have been made for people with intellectual disabilities, people with psychiatric disorders and children. In the case of older people with dementia there is still an assumption that sufferers are unable to make decisions – that the person with dementia has become, somehow, an empty shell, lacking the capacity for feeling or understanding, and that decisions have to be made by carers in their behalf.

Dementia is not one disease, but a range of conditions associated with a pattern of experience. Roth defines dementia as 'a global deterioration of the individual's intellectual, emotional and conative faculties in a state of unimpaired consciousness.'[741] The deterioration of intellectual faculties implies that sufferers become progressively less able to retain new information, and so to absorb it. They become gradually cut off from their environment. The term 'conation' refers to a person's will and directed activity, and the loss of conation means that the person with dementia becomes unable to behave autonomously. The deterioration of emotional faculties shows itself in behavioural disturbance, emotional over-reactions, passivity and inappropriate responses – though all of these might be a reaction to the loss of abilities otherwise experienced in dementia.

Dementia is a difficult condition – difficult for sufferers, for carers, and for professionals. None of that means that a person with dementia should be assumed to be unable to express a view. Dementia is a degenerative

---

[740] N Crockett, P Spicker, 1994, *Discharged: homelessness among psychiatric patients in Scotland*, Edinburgh: Shelter (Scotland).

[741] M Roth, 1981, 'The diagnosis of dementia in late and middle life', in J Mortimer, L Schuman, *The epidemiology of dementia*, New York: Oxford University Press, p 24.

process: people start with capacities, which they slowly lose. People with dementia still, in general, have the ability to speak; they have often formed preferences and decisions, for their own reasons. Kitwood makes a strong case that people with dementia are responsive to their social environment and still show a degree of social awareness, while in other cases there may be 'rementia' or a positive regain of abilities through social interaction.[742] Researchers who have made the effort to communicate have found that communication is possible. Killick comments:

> To see the struggle for expression on people's faces, to hear the sounds tumbling over themselves in an effort to become words, phrases, sentences – this is painful. But when communication has been achieved, when the individual has leaped across the barrier to attain an utterance which embodies an insight – this is inspiring, often for both parties.[743]

The arguments for empowerment are not less strong in cases where people's ability to express their views is impaired. On the contrary, these are the circumstances where it becomes more important to ensure that people's rights are protected, and that they have a voice in what happens to them.

Developing user control

The development of user empowerment, Means and Smith suggest, has focused on three strategies. These are rights, 'exit' and 'voice'.[744] The idea of 'exit', which is associated with market approaches, emphasises the importance of choice; if people are able to take their custom elsewhere, providers are to that degree accountable. The theory of the private market, from which the idea of 'exit' is drawn, also assumes competition between many providers, and responsiveness to demand through a profit motive. When these conditions are not met, there is no guarantee that services will be responsive to particular demands or claims, especially those considered to have low priority.

---

[742] T Kitwood, K Bredin, 1992, Towards a theory of dementia care, *Ageing and Society* 12(3) 269–287; T Kitwood, 1999, *Dementia reconsidered*, Buckingham: Open University Press.

[743] J Killick, 1997, Confidences: the experience of writing with people with dementia, in M Marshall (ed), *State of the art in dementia care*, London: Centre for Policy on Ageing.

[744] R Means, R Smith, 1994, *Community care: policy and practice*, Basingstoke: Macmillan, ch 4; A Hirschman, 1970, *Exit, voice and loyalty*, Cambridge Mass: Harvard University Press.

'Voice' implies that views are represented and can be put somewhere within the process. This is sometimes linked with ideas of participation and direct democracy, though its scope is limited; giving people a say is not the same as giving them a degree of control. There is a stronger link with the idea of 'deliberative' democracy, identified with governance based in negotiation and discussion, the representation of interests or the legitimisation of dissent.[745] 'Voice' is part of this process. At the level of the individual, giving each person an opportunity to contribute allows that person to raise issues that matter, to have a sense of participating, and to have some sense of a stake in the process.

Arnstein describes a 'ladder of participation' (Figure 16.1);[746] the process of listening to people is sometimes no more than a pretence. I think that underestimates the importance of voice. Having a say is clearly better than having none, and mechanisms for voice have some

Figure 16.1: Arnstein's Ladder of Citizen Participation

| Citizen control |
| Delegated power |
| Partnership |
| Placation |
| Consultation |
| Informing |
| Therapy |
| Manipulation |

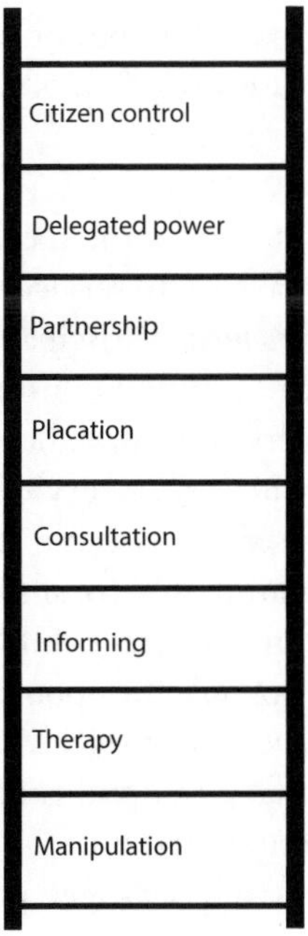

[745] J Cohen, Deliberation and democratic legitimacy, in R Goodin, P Pettit (eds), *Contemporary political philosophy*, Oxford: Blackwell 1997.

[746] S Arnstein, 1971, A ladder of citizen participation, *Journal of the Royal Town Planning Institute* 57(4) pp 176–182.

value even if they cannot hope to shift the balance of power. Voice is an important aspect of empowerment, and for those who are disadvantaged in their ability to exercise a voice, like people with intellectual disabilities or psychiatric patients, an advocacy movement has been developing.

There are also practical reasons for enabling voice. One of the simplest arguments for consultation is that it makes it possible for people to express different, or contradictory, opinions from others. The people who respond to consultations, for whatever reason, have a range of points of view. Some of them – even one of them – may just be right. Another is legitimation. Public agencies which consult generally claim that the consultation makes their final decision more legitimate. Usually they will find some way of establishing that their view has been supported. But they are not wrong to make the claim: other things being equal, a process which has been subject to consultation is more legitimate than one which has not been.

A focus on voice can help in the process of empowerment, but clearly it falls short of giving users control over the services they receive. Deakin and Wright suggest that a number of other criteria have to be examined to ensure that the users of services have an adequate degree of control. They propose six tests:

1. *Accountability* There has to be some mechanism through which services can be made to answer to service users for their decisions.
2. *Representation and participation* Participation in decision making implies not only that the views of consumers are expressed, but also that their views carry some weight.
3. *Information* People who use a service must have access to information about that service, because lack of such information denies them the opportunity for comment or control.
4. *Access* Services have to be accessible because the effect of inaccessibility is to deny people the opportunity to use the service.
5. *Choice* The ability to exercise choice is an important aspect of user control, because a lack of options means in itself that users are unable to control outcomes.
6. *Redress* Obtaining redress of grievances, and even having concerns addressed, is important to limit the use of control by agencies as well as to give users the formal opportunity to raise concerns.[747]

---

[747] N Deakin, A Wright (eds) 1990, *Consuming public services*, London: Routledge.

Most of these criteria are procedural, rather than substantive, but in practice the distinction is hazy. The tests which seem most directly to be concerned with procedures, notably accountability and representation, are generally defended because they limit the actions of agencies while opening avenues for the users of services to exercise some degree of control.[748] In so far as the relationship between producers and consumers is concerned with power, the effect of limiting the producers is often to increase the relative strength of the user. There is something wrong, Øvretveit observes in passing, with the very idea of 'user involvement' or 'participation'. 'We forget', he writes, 'that most people choose to involve services in their lives.'[749] If we begin from the perspective of the service, then the issue is expressed in terms of 'participation' or 'involvement'. If, however, we are concerned with services as being services for people, the focus shifts to them rather than the perspective of the service.

The recipients of social services are not only disadvantaged in terms of their relationship with producers; their lack of power reflects a more general social position. The stigmatisation of recipients, their lack of resources and status, and their vulnerability pose important problems for the social services. The development of formal mechanisms for protection, and substantive rights, offers a means by which the people who receive services are not solely dependent on decisions made by the producers of welfare; these rights represent one of the most important means through which recipients can be empowered. But the social disadvantages remain; people who are poor, disabled, mentally ill or unemployed cannot be expected to overcome the problems they face simply because they have more effective control over services. There are then limits to what it is possible to achieve in the narrow context of service delivery. It is important, too, not to overestimate the potential effects of this kind of procedure. Dwyer lists some of the chief objections to user-based approaches. There are conflicts of interest between users of different types; users are often in competition for scarce resources with others; user groups can lose touch with their grass roots; and the process as a whole can contribute to the exclusion of marginal groups.[750]

---

[748] Deakin and Wright, 1990; A Richardson, 1983, *Participation*, London: RKP; B Smith, 1988, *Bureaucracy and political power*, Brighton: Harvester Wheatsheaf.

[749] J Øvretveit, 1993, *Co-ordinating community care*, Buckingham: Open University Press, p.166.

[750] P Dwyer, 2004, *Understanding social citizenship*, Bristol: Policy Press, pp 59–60.

ISSUE FOR DISCUSSION

Service recipients are often in competition for scarce resources. Is it right to empower people, if it furthers the claims of some groups only at the expense of others?

CHAPTER 17

The administrative process

The art of the possible
Administration in practice
Analysing complex processes
Keeping track of implementation

Administration is an intrinsic element of service delivery. Every policy has to have some kind of administration; every administration has to find ways of operationalising policy – translating it into practice. The same issues which lead to divisions of labour between services also imply further divisions of labour within them. But the same divisions imply further issues of coordination, and more gaps between policy in theory and policy in practice.[751]

Some models of administration represent it as a process of learning; some as an incremental or experiential process, a sort of 'evolution'.[752] 'Evolution' means that things that work survive, and things that do not work have to be dropped. There are often adaptations to circumstances. An example is the development of 'service ideologies'. One of the reasons why service ideologies develop is because officers are exposed to common pressures. Social work departments tend to focus on 'risk' rather than service quality because their officers are more liable to be held responsible for extraordinary events that go radically wrong than they are for generally poor outcomes. Housing providers are most subject to pressure from service users and community organisations, which has led to a much greater emphasis within housing services on equity and procedural fairness than on risk assessment. At the same time, it would be unwise to assume that everything that is done is there because it is needed. Public sector organisations tend to be fairly conservative institutions, where people often take it for granted that the ways things are done is the obvious or only way to do them. A recurring mantra is, 'if it ain't broke, don't fix it'. That comment

---

[751] M Hill, P Hupe, 2003, The multi-layer problem in implementation research, *Public Management Review* 5(4) 471–491.

[752] J-E Lane, 2000, *The public sector,* London: Sage, ch 4.

should be handled with caution; what works for some people is not necessarily what works for others.

Administration is also a political process. The administration can be seen as an arena where different factions, interest groups and approaches compete, deliberate and negotiate approaches. A lot of the literature on public administration is written by political scientists, and perhaps unsurprisingly they tend to find political elements in every part of the structure. Some have described the process in terms of coalitions of interests, some as a structure with a series of actors, some as a symbolic political process.[753] The idea of the 'rational', self-interested bureaucrat draws on economic theory to predict outcomes. Other models have emphasised different motivations in bureaucratic practice, including a belief that the service is making a contribution to society.[754]

Overlapping with both these views is the idea that administration is a policy process in its own right. It has all the elements of policy-making – a structure of decision making, the contribution of different actors, and the problems of translating policy into practice. Several approaches to administration treat it as a 'perspective', either treating it as a process, or reading backwards from outcomes to identify the motivations, process and effects. For practical purposes, it is difficult to avoid this. Administration has to be seen both as a part of policy making, and as a way of generating policy in practice, which has to be mapped and checked to work out what is happening.

The art of the possible

The central issue in selecting methods is effectiveness – the extent to which a method achieves the aims of the policy. Politics, Bismarck famously said, is the art of the possible. The approaches that are open to agencies have to be appropriate to the aims. But they also have to be feasible – capable of being put into practice.

Legal competence The kinds of action which can be taken depend on the powers and competence of the organisation which does them. Central government in the UK is legally unrestricted in most of the actions it can take (though there are treaty obligations, particularly relating to the European Union, which limit the potential course of action). Central government in many other countries, like the United States or the Federal Republic of Germany, is limited by a constitution or basic law: governments can only do what they are permitted to do.

---

[753] Lane, 2000, ch 4.
[754] B G Peters, 2001, *The politics of bureaucracy*, London: Routledge, 5th ed.

Constitutional and administrative law defines what it is possible to take into account, and what is not. There may be constitutional limitations on the power or authority of public services: powers (or 'competences') have to be granted legally. Many of the debates in social policy in the European Union have been about establishing the powers of the Union in areas like public health or social exclusion. Establishing the principle has often been more important than the specific issue: it has led to bitter debates about bus passes for pensioners (competence in the welfare of old people and in public transport), language teaching in schools (competence in education) and the effect of aluminium in water supplies on workers needing renal dialysis (competence in environmental health).

Most autonomous and quasi-autonomous public sector organisations have, in the same way, a constitution or definition of powers which defines the legitimate range of action open to the agency. Third sector organisations have a greater scope for manoeuvre than government, but even those are limited by their constitutions and by the fiduciary duties of trustees. (As a volunteer in housing aid, I was able to help people who were in rent arrears; as a committee member of a housing association, I have had to agree to evict people for non-payment of rent.)

Beyond the constitutional restrictions, there is a host of other legal restrictions. In the UK, the kinds of legal constraints that are likely to have an influence are limitations (real or feared) about Data Protection or Human Rights legislation, and specific rules introduced to govern policy areas. There are general principles of administrative law. One of the legal principles that every administrator ought to be aware of is 'natural justice'. Natural justice has two central elements: that decisions about disputes have to hear evidence from both sides, and that because decisions have to be seen to be fair, arbitrators have to be free of compromising interests.[755] These principles run through lots of issues in practice: they govern issues like dispute resolution, disciplinary hearings and the declaration of interests by decision-makers. Another important principle, more recently introduced than natural justice but no less important for administrative practice, is promissory estoppel.[756] Subject to the powers of the agency, it says that if an official makes a statement, and that people act on the strength of that statement, the agency is bound by the consequences. Natural justice and promissory

---

[755] W Wade, C Forsyth, 2000, *Administrative law*, Oxford: Oxford University Press, 8th edition.
[756] Wade, Forsyth, 2000, pp 242–244.

estoppel are core principles, and even if some agencies or administrators choose to ignore them, the courts won't.

Political feasibility Values and ideology play an evident role. Some methods are likely to be discounted out of hand, possibly because they are considered and rejected as unacceptable, but possibly because patterns of thought are so firmly set that other options are not even thought about. It took years before health professions were ready to consider that child abuse might occur within families, and years later before any policy-maker was prepared to link the issue to the corporal punishment of children.[757] Bachrach and Baratz coined the term 'non-decision' to refer to the issues that are not on the table, and to decisions that are not even made because they are so obviously unthinkable.[758]

A further set of constraints lie in policies which have already been adopted for other purposes. It is not uncommon for governments to adopt general policies, with the intention that they should be used as a test for later decisions. Examples are environmental policies, such as Agenda 21 and environmental impact assessments,[759] or mainstreaming policies on gender.[760] This sort of approach is unlikely in itself to lead to material changes in policy, but it does give advocates of the issues within decision-making bodies the opportunity to raise concerns formally. It follows that they are more likely to act as an obstacle to inconsistent actions than a positive force for change.

Administrative issues Then there are the operational constraints. Administration ought to be workable, and the observation that an agency does not have the capacity to implement the policy ought to be viewed as a serious objection. Policy-makers ignore this at their peril; several major administrative fiascos have happened largely because decision-makers chose to disregard the warnings. The computerisation of social security has led to repeated, predictable problems because of the determination to produce an all-singing, all dancing computer programme that would do everything. There are obvious difficulties in doing this – most of these schemes founder on the problems of storing

[757] M Sheppard 1982, *Perceptions of child abuse*, Norwich: University of East Anglia.

[758] P Bachrach, M Baratz, 1970, *Power and poverty: theory and practice*, Oxford University Press, Oxford.

[759] A Jonas, A While, D Gibbs, 2004, State modernisation and local strategic selectivity after Local Agenda 21, *Policy & Politics* 32(2) pp 151–168.

[760] A McGauran, 2009, Gender mainstreaming and the public policy implementation process, *Policy & Politics* 37(2) 215–233.

incompatible media, coordinating different systems, information sharing or managing changes – but beyond all that, there is a problem with the conception. Any computer system, no matter how wonderful, can only be as good as the information that goes into it, and in circumstances where people's circumstances change rapidly, they do not have the information, or they do not know how to answer, there is no chance that computerisation will resolve the problems. The Child Support Agency in the UK, another example in a similar field, tried to replace a previous, unsatisfactory system with an assessment that relied on an impossibly complex means test – requiring information about the income, household circumstances and relative liabilities of two parents living in different households. Any of these elements would be difficult; balancing all six made the task unworkable. Nearly fifty years ago, Richard Titmuss launched a blistering attack on 'computermania', and particularly the vice of 'expecting the computer to solve the problems which human beings have not yet adequately diagnosed'.[761] I have recently been making much the same argument in relation to the UK government's absurdly presumptuous plans for a Universal Credit.[762] At times it seems we learn nothing.

Financial constraints Finance is central to many decisions. Almost every decision has an opportunity cost – there is something else that could be done with the same resources. If a measure costs too much, or if it does not seem to deliver value for money, the decision is likely to be reviewed and trimmed.

Path dependency The problem with beginning with a view about what is possible is that it tends to dispose policy-makers towards a conservative frame of mind – rejecting what is supposed to be unrealistic, often without examination (because discussing impossible things is, almost by definition, a waste of time.) Some thinkers have pushed forward with programmes to 'think the unthinkable', and some bizarre fantasies have emerged – such as Milton Friedman's proposal to deregulate quack doctors and leave things to the market,[763] Arthur Seldon's suggestion for putting machines in cars to allow individual billing for road use,[764] or

---

[761] R Titmuss, 1968, Universal and selective social services, in *Commitment to welfare*, London: George Allen and Unwin, p 114.

[762] P Spicker,, 2012, Universal Credit: simplification or personalisation?, *Local Economy* 27(5–6) 496–501.

[763] M Friedman, 1962, *Capitalism and freedom*, Chicago: University of Chicago Press.

[764] A Seldon, 1977, *Charge!*, London: Temple Smith.

the electronic tagging of criminals, which seems to have been inspired by a Spider–Man comic.[765]

The way things have been done is a major constraint on the ways that things can be done in the future. This tends to be seen as a form of inertia, and there is some truth in the idea that policy which is not deliberately changed will carry on unless some other force intervenes. This has been translated, in political science, into the idea of 'path dependency': that policy travels on tramlines, and once things have started, they can be difficult to stop. An example might be pensions. Pensions are not policies for a single point in time; they are based in the past, the present and the future. In the past, people will have made contributions, and have gained entitlements. In the present, current pensioners have needs and problems, conditioned by previous policies, which any policy has to address. Current contributors, meanwhile, are changing their behaviour, and gaining entitlements, which will affect their position in the future, and commit agencies which will deal with them.

Path dependency can be interrupted by major events, like wars, natural catastrophes or economic collapse, but policy cannot be planned on that basis. Changing policy for pensions is a long-term operation. It requires consideration of established entitlements, current needs and future expectations. Transitional arrangements may have to be put in place. It may take twenty years or more to bring about major changes.

The attitudes of administrators and officials There are many ways in which reforms can be 'tripped up' by officials. Stoker refers both to 'exploitation' or opportunistic behaviour – taking advantage of administrative change to bring about shifts in approach, function or policy – and to direct antagonism. [766] If officials really do not want to do something, they can say 'no' in more languages than the continent of Africa. Some of the reasons for not doing things are listed by Perri 6 and his colleagues:[767] they include

---

[765] e.g. A Vitores, M Domenech, 2003, From inhabiting to haunting, in M Hard, A Losch, D Verdicchio (eds) *Transforming spaces*, obtained at www.ifs. tu-darmstadt.de/fileadmin/gradkoll//Publikationen/transformingspaces. html

[766] G Stoker, 1999, *The new management of British local governance*, Basingstoke: Macmillan, pp 10–11.

[767] Perri 6, D Leat, K Seltzer, G Stoker, 2002, *Towards holistic governance*, Basingstoke: Hampshire, p 122.

- lacking the authority, including legal constraints, contractual agreements, data protection, and so on;
- lacking legitimacy, on the basis that policy isn't delivering tangible benefits, or the proposal comes from an unrepresentative source;
- lacking the capacity, including resources, management capacity, and so on;
- low priority, because existing tasks are more important;
- fear of loss of control, including the effects on professional power and career opportunities;
- bargaining, where agreement is conditional on other steps being taken;
- jeopardy, where it is argued that there are risks and dangers in the policy;
- inconsistency with objectives, including the accusations that policy is contradictory and which won't work; and
- difficulty, because of the problems of methods, implementation or practicality.

I pointed a little earlier to the dangers of disregarding administrative experience. In fairness, that has to be set against the possibility that administrators might just be finding ways of putting obstacles in the way. David Donnison observes wryly that when the civil servants in the benefits administration were reduced to objecting that there weren't enough filing cabinets to do the job he wanted, he knew he had them on the run.[768] Perri 6 and his colleagues comment: 'it became clear from our case studies that when it is hard to do something, it is more usually because they do not want to rather than because they cannot. ... In general, "can't" turns out to mean "won't."'[769]

Administration in practice

Organisations matter. Things often work, or do not work, because of the way that the administration is set up. Hogwood and Peters compare the analysis of organisations to medical pathologies. Some of the problems they describe are malfunctions, through inadequate information, poor specification of objectives or adaptive responses to constraints; but others are based on internal dynamics, like empire building (when an official tries to gain status and influence through taking on more responsibilities or appointing more staff), obesity (the

---

[768] D Donnison, 1981, *The politics of poverty*, Oxford: Martin Robertson.
[769] Perri 6 et al, p 124.

impact of gradual expansion, taking on new programmes or otherwise over-extending) or hyperactivity (the effect of over-commitment and the proliferation of procedures).[770] The way things are done can be explained away either by the social structure and context, or by the behaviour of the individuals who work in an organisation.

Some factors have a huge effect on the size, shape and pattern of the operation. They include

- *contact with the public.* Agencies which deal extensively and directly with the public have different needs for accommodation and personnel from those which do not. Personal contact affects access to buildings, reception areas, interview facilities, security arrangements and methods of recording. Extensive correspondence and the length of records have a major effect on information management. Where there are home visits, car parking for staff – always a vexed issue – becomes acutely important.
- *accommodation.* Accommodation has a huge effect on management systems, staff relations and relations with the public. Some public agencies operate from converted houses on depressed estates; others work from purpose-built civic centres. Architects for public buildings often seem to pay more attention to a building's impact on the skyline[771] or the ability to defend buildings from rioters[772] than they do to the impact of buildings on the services that occupy them. On the other hand, C Northcote Parkinson once suggested that the point where an agency got the perfect building was the point at which it tumbled into terminal decline.[773]
- *information management.* The central test of information management is that it should be fit for purpose. Major problems have been caused for administrations which have ignored simple basic precepts and practices. The Child Support Agency compounded its early problems by failing to keep case files in alphabetical order. The Victoria Climbié inquiry, to take another

---

[770] B Hogwood, G Peters, 1985, *The pathology of public policy*, Oxford: Clarendon Press.

[771] Commission for Architecture and the Built Environment, 2000, *By design: urban design in the planning system*, Department of Environment, Transport and the Regions,

[772] J Coaffee, D Wood, 2006, Security is coming home, *International relations* 20(4) 513–517.

[773] C Parkinson, 1958, *Parkinson's Law*, London: John Murray.

example, comments that in one authority 'the case recording throughout was grossly inadequate and the likelihood of cases drifting or being lost was high',[774] while in another authority it commented on the 'haphazard and chaotic nature of the administrative system':

> Victoria managed, during the time that her case was open in Brent, to acquire five different 'unique' identification numbers on the various systems that were designed to ensure that the progress of her case was effectively monitored.[775]

Information management used to mean little more than 'filing', and it was a major part of the floor space of public offices until the advent of computers. Times have changed: the computer has taken over everywhere. Computers have many virtues. They can perform repeated calculations rapidly and accurately; they allow cross-referencing and sharing of information; they have improved the presentation of documents immeasurably. But they also have vices. They do not handle correspondence well, and basing files on computers operated by different staff usually means that files are held in more than one place. Centralised systems are vulnerable to crashes. Custom-designed programmes are error-prone and difficult to maintain. Modern public offices have been blighted by the purpose-designed computer programme, intended to offer comprehensive responses to impossibly complex circumstances.

After the practical constraints, there are the constraints imposed by policy decisions outside the agency. They include:

- *the level of funding.* Many public sector operations are done on a shoestring, reflecting widespread pressure to be accountable for the use of funds. This is not always the most economical way of doing things: public officials can find they are wasting time, which is expensive, because they have not been allowed to order in enough materials to keep their work going.
- *peripheral activity.* The bulk of public funding in most agencies is devoted to the mainstream, or 'core', operations. However, temporary funding, often for three year periods, is commonplace.

---

[774] H Laming, 2003, *The Victoria Climbié Inquiry: Report*, Cm 5730, p.67
[775] Laming, 2003, p.104.

The emphasis on evaluation and justifying the expenditure means that work with agencies on this sort of funding represents a disproportionate amount of the work that policy analysts are asked to do.

- *responsibilities to service users.* Although some services have taken to referring to service users as 'customers',[776] the relationship is not much like the relationship of producers and consumers in a private market – I pointed to some of the differences in Chapter 15. There are circumstances where users and services are tied to each other; the pattern of service delivery, and the structure of the services, has to reflect that relationship. Some provision has to be continuous; hospitals and residential care establishments have to take responsibility for making alternative provision in order to discontinue relationships. Some services, like social work, probation and the police, have to have mechanisms to track and chase uncooperative users. (The Probation Service in England has moved to referring to its users as 'offenders' instead of 'clients'.[777]) Other services, like education, have had to introduce quasi-judicial mechanisms for the termination of relationships, including exclusion of children from schools and the withdrawal of children from formal education.

The third set of influences are the conventions of administrative practice. These include

- *accountability.* Public services in a democratic culture have to be able to explain what has been done, and why. This leads to a substantial emphasis on 'paper trails' – the ability to show in writing what has been done, when and by whom.
- *the conventional patterns of public service.* The British Civil Service has been based largely on the conventions of the most senior staff, the 'First Division'. Those conventions include
  - ○ the view that actions of the civil service are taken in the name of the Minister, not by a specific named official.
  - ○ the guarantee of anonymity given to every officer making decisions. (This does not apply in local authorities but does apply in central government agencies like the Department for Work and Pensions.)

---

[776] N Flynn, 2012, *Public sector management*, London: Sage, ch 8.

[777] J Newman, S Nutley, 2003, Transforming the Probation Service, *Policy & Politics* 31(4) pp 547–63.

○ an emphasis on confidentiality. (This has recently been made subject to Freedom of Information legislation, but is still strong in many services, especially the National Health Service – in areas going well beyond medical confidentiality.)

Although these approaches have their origins in the highest levels of the service, they have been very widely applied: the administration of social security has generally depended on the application of similar rules, including for example the requirement that social security officers (and some people visiting social security offices) sign the Official Secrets Act.

- *accounting practice*. The public sector works to some common financial standards. Typically in the UK this includes

  ○ programme budgeting on an annual basis. Although central government has now introduced 'accruals accounting', which is more flexible, public sector agencies still have very limited ability to save or transfer money between years or between budget heads.

  ○ accounting for gross expenditure and income. All income is reported without deducting expenditure, and income which is earned cannot be used to offset expenditure.

  ○ preserving 'audit trails' through meticulous recording of petty expenses.

- *service ideologies*. This has been explained before: different services have different accepted norms of conduct, the 'common sense' of the field of activity.

- *ethical rules*. In some places, ethical rules are tightly prescribed and officials are required to comply with them. For example, it is not legitimate to use the power which stems from a role in public service for personal gain, such as bribery, or to show favouritism to one's family. The problem here is that no list of rules can ever be long enough and full enough; something will always get left out. The main way to deal with this is to emphasise the professionalism and moral character of the official, rather than explicit codification of every rule, and most ethical codes in the OECD are based in integrity rather than compliance[778] – relying on the moral conduct of the official, rather than the avoidance of specific ills.

---

[778] S Gilman, 2005, *Ethics codes and codes of conduct as tools for promoting an ethical and professional public service*, Washington DC: World Bank, obtained at www.oecd.org/mena/governance/35521418.pdf

The 'seven principles of public life' promoted in the UK are selflessness, integrity, objectivity, accountability, openness, honesty and leadership.[779] There are difficulties with this approach. The principles are vague and open to different interpretations. Some are contingent – officials may have to be discreet rather than open, or be required to advocate specific positions rather than acting objectively. And the list is necessarily selective – for example, the principles do not call for respect for human rights, restraint in the use of power or even benevolence. What the approach points to, however, is a strong tradition of probity – a combination of moral conduct and openness to personal scrutiny, designed to ensure the scrupulous application of authority.

The generalisations made in this section are defensible, but they should be treated with caution. Patterns of administration vary between services, and even to some extent between offices. Very few general observations apply consistently. A social policy analyst, materialising for the first time in a strange agency, cannot rely wholly on previous experience or book knowledge to decipher the codes of the organisation. There should be a record of decisions and authority somewhere – a paper trail – but even well-laid trails can be difficult to make sense of if implicit assumptions have not been made clear. Interpretation calls for an anthropological approach – talking, observing, and getting a feel for the culture.

Box 17.1: Identifying institutional racism

The idea of 'institutional racism' has been attributed to Stokely Carmichael, who used it to refer generally to a widely-held, systemic presence of racism in society.[780] In the UK, although the term has been used to refer to systemic racism in British society,[781] it has come to be used in the narrower, more closely focused sense of racism expressed in the actions of institutions. The Stephen Lawrence Inquiry defined it as 'the collective failure of an organisation to provide an appropriate and professional service to people

---

[779] Committee on Standards in Public Life (chair: Lord Nolan), 1995, *Standards in public life*, London: The Stationery Office, Cm 2850.

[780] S Carmichael and C Hamilton, *Black Power: the politics of liberation in America,* New York: Vintage Books, 1967 pp. 2–6, excerpted at http://smccd.net/accounts/wrightg/race.doc.

[781] Scarman report, 1981, p.11, cited Cm 4262–1, 1999, *The Stephen Lawrence Inquiry* (The Macpherson report), London: TSO, www.archive.official-documents.co.uk/document/cm42/4262/4262.htm, para 6.7

because of their colour, culture or ethnic origin.'[782] Similarly, the Institute for Race Relations has suggested that institutional racism 'covertly or overtly, resides in the policies, procedures, operations and culture of public or private institutions – reinforcing individual prejudices and being reinforced by them in turn.'[783] That focus makes it an appropriate case study for consideration of implementation.

The Stephen Lawrence Inquiry (also called 'the Macpherson Report', after its chair) focused on a boy who was murdered in a racist attack. Stephen was left to bleed to death. At the outset, police failed to do anything to save his life; subsequently they failed to pursue or apprehend the murderers, or to obtain necessary evidence, while his parents were fobbed off. (It also appears from later evidence that when Stephen's parents persisted, they became targets for investigation themselves.) In the view of the inquiry, the failure of the police to respond appropriately was not attributable solely to racism on the part of officers; that racism was compounded by incompetence, insensitivity, poor management and patterns of conduct which acted to reinforce racial disadvantage.

Institutional racism can arise through a variety of processes. They include

- overt or covert prejudice;
- direct discrimination;
- discriminatory processes; and
- the production of disadvantage.

Prejudice Expressions of prejudice are probably the easy things on this list to identify: a spoken quotation or a written comment can be sufficient. The Macpherson report notes several examples of 'unwitting' racism, including 'insensitive and racist stereotypical behaviour' and 'the use of inappropriate and offensive language'.[784] This is described as 'unwitting' because the officers themselves were unable to see that what they were saying was prejudiced.[785]

Direct discrimination Direct discrimination depends on both prejudicial intent and the translation of that intent into policy or practice. This is probably the most difficult issue to identify in practice; it can require a level of proof which is unlikely to be forthcoming or confirmed by the perpetrators. The Lawrence Inquiry gives several examples of discriminatory behaviour

---

[782] Macpherson report, 1999, para 6.34.

[783] A Sivanandan, cited Guardian, 24th February 1999, *What is individual racism?*, www.guardian.co.uk/lawrence/Story/0,2763,208688,00. html#article_continue

[784] Macpherson, 1999, para 46.28.

[785] Macpherson, 1999, para 6.2

motivated by prejudice, including e.g. jumping to conclusions, failure to take statements and brushing complaints aside..

Discriminatory processes A discriminatory process is one which, if practised generally, would have discriminatory effects. The clearest example of a discriminatory process in the Macpherson Report is the police's 'inadequate' treatment of racist incidents, which they suggest is the root cause of the under-reporting of such incidents.[786]

This has proved to be a difficult area to monitor in practice. Individual disadvantage can be evidence of a discriminatory process, but there are individual circumstances where some discrimination can be justified in specific contexts – for example, whether someone subject to religious dietary restrictions can work as a food taster. Disadvantage might be produced in aggregate, but it may reflect other issues besides the process itself (such as problems a minority group has in society). Judgments about processes have tended in consequence to be guided by assumptions about 'good practice'.[787] Unfortunately, the field of equal opportunities has been bedevilled with ill-informed approaches – like 'equal opportunities' interviews which impose common structures on job applicants (which is the reverse of equal opportunity, because only those who fit the preconceived structure will do well), or racial quotas, which provably act to limit the opportunities they are supposed to create,[788] and were consequently made illegal in the 1975 Race Relations Act, and yet which are still being advocated by those who ought to know better.[789]

The production of disadvantage Demonstrating disadvantage is largely a matter of identifying outcomes. Criticisms of the police service's use of 'stop and search' are based on the differential outcomes, which show that the policy is used disproportionately against minority groups.[790] Often disadvantage may be assessed through 'ethnic monitoring', but judging outcomes in terms of statistical representation works badly for locations where minority groups are diffused (which is true of many of the places in Scotland where I work), or in small-scale operations. The most successful studies have been those which

---

[786] Macpherson, 6.45.
[787] see Commission for Racial Equality, 2005, *Good practice*, at www.cre.gov.uk/gdpract/index.html
[788] See J Elster, 1992, *Local justice*, Cambridge: Cambridge University Press.
[789] e.g. in Commission for Racial Equality, 2005, *The police service in England and Wales*, London: CRE, p.49, at www.cre.gov.uk/downloads/PoliceFI_final.pdf.
[790] Macpherson, 6.45.

have looked intensively at problems, like the detailed studies undertaken by the Commission for Racial Equality,[791] or the Lawrence Inquiry itself.

Systemic disadvantage Showing that disadvantage is systemic – that is, that it occurs throughout a system – can be shown if the disadvantage is the product of deliberate policy, if it is cumulative, or if it is recurrent. Deliberate disadvantage occurs where policy makes discriminatory distinctions. The Macpherson Report explicitly exonerates the Metropolitan Police of any suggestion of deliberate disadvantage, but argues that it is institutionally racist on other grounds.[792] Cumulative disadvantage arises where the effect of a series of smaller processes is to add up to substantial disadvantage. This has been consistently demonstrated in the allocation of council housing, where progressive filters reduce the prospects of rehousing for minority ethnic groups.[793] Recurrent disadvantage is disadvantage evidenced by repeated examples over periods over time, e.g. in police recruitment, use of 'stop and search', or the treatment of racial incidents.

Analysing complex processes

Analysis works by breaking down complex operations into smaller, less complex parts. Once that has been done, it should be possible to identify relationships between the elements. In analysing the process of service delivery, there are four main approaches. The first is to identify a series of independent variables, looking for ways that those variables can affect performance and outcomes. This approach is used in many conventional forms of social science; some of the best work of this kind uses multivariate analysis to identify the contribution of different elements,[794] but it is also effectively what writers on organisations are doing whenever they claim that particular factors – leadership, incentives, decentralisation and so forth – have particular effects. I pointed to the difficulty of this kind of analysis in Chapter 6: the elements are difficult to count sensibly, the issues are multidimensional, and the very process of selecting factors can lead to a

---

[791] Commission for Racial Equality, 2005, *Inquiries and formal investigations*, at www.cre.gov.uk/publs/cat_fi.html
[792] Macpherson, 6.46–6.48.
[793] D Smith, A Whalley, 1975, *Racial minorities and public housing*, London: Political and Economic Planning; P Spicker, 1988, *Allocations*, London: Institute of Housing; R Skellington, 1992, 'Race' in Britain today', Buckingham: Open University Press.
[794] G Boyne, K Meier, L O'Toole, R Walker (eds) 2006, *Public service performance*, Cambridge: Cambridge University Press.

distorted perspective. Everything depends on whether the initial selection of the variables is appropriate, and that is uncertain.

A second approach looks at processes sequentially, for example by identifying a series of stages within the process of implementation. This might involve examining illustrative cases, and checking what happens at each point along the route; an example is 'business process engineering', which identifies the stages and proposes ways of shortening chains, circumventing problems or parcelling out parts of the operation.[795] A modified and wider-reaching version of this approach is represented by 'Lean', a method originally drawn from motor manufacture. Lean seeks to identify the stages of production as a 'value chain' and asking what value is added at each stage of the process. In the public sector, the focus of Lean has tended to fall on participative discussions with employees in order to find ways to improve the continuity of processes, eliminate waste and to improve outcomes at each stage of service delivery.[796] In both methods, implementation is described as a sequential or linear process, and methods of dealing with policies or processes are tracked so as to find out what actually happens. This kind of approach works for some kinds of topic but not for others. The sort of issue it works for are processes which have a sequence and identifiable outcomes, such as housing maintenance, or consideration of a patient's pathway prior to discharge. An example of the kind of issue it does not work for might be debt prevention. There may be a sequence of events which follows a person's request for help, but there is no single process which describes how that person got to the point of needing help in the first place.

Third, it may be possible to apply a framework or theoretical model – something which says, for example, that 'there are X key elements in this problem, each of which needs to be examined distinctly'. Some frameworks consists of lists of criteria – for example, ISO 9000,[797] the International Standards Organisation's guidance for public sector

[795] e.g. B Harrington, K McLoughlin, D Riddell, 2001, Business process re-engineering in the public sector: a case study of the Contributions Agency, in G Johnson, K Scholes (eds) *Exploring public sector strategy*, Harlow: Pearson.

[796] Z Radnor, P Walley, A Stevens, G Bucci, 2006, *Evaluation of the Lean approach to business management and its use in the public sector*, Edinburgh: Scottish Executive; Z Radnor, S Osborne, 2013, Lean: a failed theory for public services?, *Public Management Review* 15(2) 265–287.

[797] International Standards Organization, 2008, *ISO 9000– Quality management*, www.iso.org/iso/home/standards/management-standards/iso_9000.htm; ISO, 2012, Quality management principles, Geneva: ISO, www.iso.org/iso/qmp_2012.pdf

management, or the WHO Quality Rights Tool Kit, which specifies standards for mental health and social care.[798] Others are based on theoretical structures outlined in the academic literature: examples include descriptions of organisations in terms of hierarchies, teams or networks – and of course, the distinctions made earlier in this book between bureaucracy, professional structures and management. Whether there is a pre-existing model available depends on the literature on the subject, and how well it fits is a matter of judgment.

A fourth technique is systems theory, also called systems analysis. This is a method for working out what the elements of a complex set of issues are. It has gone out of fashion, partly as a result of the indigestible jargon that went along with it, and partly because of a rather questionable assumption that it was somehow functionalist, but the method is still used very widely and it is worth knowing how to do it. The key points about systems theory are that:

- complex systems can be understood in terms of sub-systems;
- sub-systems are important because of their relationship to each other;
- sub-systems can in turn be broken down and understood as sub-sub-systems.

This may look daunting, but it is much simpler than it appears at first. The approach is widely used in everyday situations, such as car maintenance, building, and medicine. A car has distinct subsystems for suspension, braking, electrics, and so forth. A house has distinct systems for plumbing, electrics, roofing and so on, and these can also be broken down further into sub-systems: so, plumbing deals distinct sub-systems dealing with water supply, storage, heating and waste disposal. The human body has a circulatory system, a digestive system, a musculo-skeletal system, and so on. The same principles, and much the same methods, can be used to break down complex issues in social policy. To understand how a social security system works, one might begin with the whole system of benefits, looking at the way that different benefits combine to offer an 'income package'.[799] But then there are systems within the overall structure – different benefits for different groups, further sub-systems of mechanisms used for the delivery of

---

[798] World Health Organization, 2012, *WHO Quality Rights Tool Kit*, Geneva: WHO.

[799] L Rainwater, M Rein, J Schwartz, 1986, *Income packaging in the welfare state*, Oxford: Oxford University Press.

these different benefits, and complementary systems that impinge on service delivery (such as employment support or medical assessment).

Using a systems approach makes it possible to look at the elements to be considered separately and then together, looking at the way the different components interact. Systems theory prompts analysts to look in different places from other approaches. In most circumstances, whether people are following a theoretical model, a sequence or the influence of a central variable, they will be looking straight at the core of an issue – finding out what is happening at defined stages of a process. Systems analysis points to the edges: what matters is not just what happens within defined areas or sub-systems, but how those areas relate to each other. In the example I have just given, the way to look at both employment support and at benefits relating to employment might well be to look at the connections between them – such as the method used for sanctioning benefits when people fail to comply with the directions of the employment agency – because that will tell us more about how they work than looking at them as if they were separate. The people who have most information about the interaction between sub-systems – also the people who can say the most about processes or organisations – are not necessarily those in charge (whose role is often concerned with reporting outwards and upwards), or even those who have the most central roles; they are the people who bridge different sub-systems, often people who work at the sharp end, or service users themselves.

The choice of methods – using analytical variables, theoretical models, sequence, or systems – is usually quite easy to make. If there is a standard theory that applies, it will be referred to in comparable studies; if there is a sequence to follow, the pattern should be clear enough; if there are too many moving parts to keep track of, then systems theory is probably the way to go. So, for example, a review of disciplinary procedures in a public sector organisation will usually be tested against standard criteria outlined in published guidance.[800] Administering contributory pensions is a sequential process, and not one that has been subject to much theoretical discussion; it is a straightforward candidate for examination in stages, and it has indeed been the subject of 'business process engineering'.[801] Social work with families is not a sequential process, it has lots of moving parts, and people who insist on model theoretical approaches (like one well-known lawyer who, chairing a

---

[800] e.g. ACAS, 2009, *Code of practice 1 for disciplinary and grievance procedures*, www.acas.org.uk/CHttpHandler.ashx?id=1041

[801] Harrington, McLoughlin, Riddell, 2001.

child abuse inquiry, criticised the social workers in it for not reading the same paperback on child abuse that he had read[802]) are positively dangerous. Analysing social work processes in terms of systems makes much more sense than general theory does, and a systems approach makes it possible to come to a range of different conclusions about the processes.[803]

There may, however, be some circumstances where several approaches are possible. An example might be the provision of social care for older people. Looked at sequentially, it is possible to follow through the process as it affects a person in a specific situation, such as support after discharge from hospital. The process might include

- Assessment and identification of needs
- Identification of options for service
- Selection of options, and
- Service delivery.

As a theoretical model, social care depends on the idea of welfare pluralism, or the 'mixed economy' of welfare. This points attention to

- The sectors providing welfare – carers, statutory services, voluntary and independent providers
- Service planning and delivery through 'interweaving' packages of care, and
- Coordination from the perspective of the individual service user.

Looked at as a system (and as a series of sub-systems), the process would consist of

- Identification of actors – the old person, carers, medical support, social care, housing, etc. (Each of those is of course a system in its own right.)
- The purchasing of services – social services management, budgeting and financial constraints, contracting with providers, etc., and

---

[802] L Blom-Cooper, 1985, *A child in trust: the report of the panel of inquiry into the circumstances surrounding the death of Jasmine Beckford*, London: Brent Council.

[803] B Compton, B Galaway, B Cournoyer, 2005, *Social work processes*, Belmont: Brooks/Cole.

- The provision of services – the providers, the services offered, and so on.

Keeping track of implementation

Implementation is fundamental to the success or failure of policies. Some of the issues about what is possible come into discussions about the identification of methods: identifying constraints is part of determining which options are conceivable. Other aspects of the issues belong here, because the analysis of the administrative process depends on identifying conflicts, contradictions between policy and method, and the ways in which the process of implementation channels and diverts policy from its intended course. The main tasks in examining processes are to find out what is going wrong, what could go wrong, and what might be done better.

What is going wrong In principle, it should be possible to identify problems by a detailed audit and assessment of processes and the informed judgment of an expert analyst. But policy analysis is a political activity. It does not usually have much effect when analysts rely on their own arguments and reasoning to make a judgment about whether or not a policy is a good idea. There are some notable exceptions to that rule, such as the criticisms of the NHS made by Roy Griffiths[804] and Alain Enthoven,[805] but those reports had their influence because they were commissioned to take a position in a favourable political environment. Effective criticism generally requires both evidence and support from within the commissioning organisation.

The most common technique for identifying what is going wrong is simply to ask people about it. Key actors and service users often have an acute sense of what is wrong with an organisation. Provided that questions are framed in ways that make it possible to avoid inter-personal criticism and self-incrimination, it is usually possible to draw out issues and concerns. However, there is a significant difference here in management practice in the private sector and the public sector. In the private sector, agencies which are underperforming have a strong tendency to put a favourable gloss on their performance. The way to attract resources and investment is to emphasise success; the price of failure is closure. In the public sector, by contrast, the opposite may be

---

[804] R Griffiths, 1983, *NHS Management Inquiry*, London: DHSS.
[805] A Enthoven, 1985, *Reflections on the management of the National Health Service*, London: Nuffield Provincial Hospitals Trust.

true. The way to argue for resources is to emphasise the deficiencies of the operation. Enoch Powell, a former Minister of Health, once wrote:

> One of the most striking features of the National Health Service is the continual, deafening chorus of complaint which rises day and night from every part of it, a chorus only interrupted when someone suggests that a different system altogether might be preferable ... The universal Exchequer financing of the service endows everyone providing as well as using it with a vested interest in denigrating it.[806]

Since the 1980s, the NHS has often tried to restrain criticisms by threatening employees, and there are parts of the service where officials are consequently reluctant to say much,[807] but it is still true that health services stake the strongest claim when they say how badly they do things.

Another standard way of assessing implementation is to use 'critical incidents' – case studies of issues where procedures have gone wrong.[808] Inquiries, inspections, audits and complaints can provide important insights into problems.

Box 17.2: Learning from complaints

A 'critical incident' is a significant event, one that challenges an organisation. In principle, a critical incident could be a special event, like a natural disaster or major accident, where services are put severely to the test; but more usually, an incident is critical because something has gone seriously wrong. Critical incidents are not 'typical', because something special must have happened to bring them to attention; but they are particularly valuable for learning about processes, and drawing lessons for future activity.[809]

Complaints about services offer an example. The International Standards Organisation defines a complaint in these terms:

---

[806] J E Powell, 1963, *Medicine and politics*, London: Pitman Medical.

[807] R Francis (Chair) 2013, *Report of the Mid Staffordshire NHS Foundation Trust Public Inquiry*, vol 3, ch 22, HC 898–3, London: TSO.

[808] J Flanagan, 1954 The Critical Incident Technique, *Psychological Bulletin* 51, 327–357.

[809] J Flanagan, 1954, The Critical Incident Technique, *Psychological Bulletin* 51, 327–357.

> A complaint is an expression of dissatisfaction made to an organization, related to its products, or the complaints handling process itself, where a response or resolution is explicitly or implicitly expected.[810]

Complaints provide essential feedback about the operation of a service, particularly in difficult circumstances where they test the effectiveness of service responses. The general sentiment is summarised by the Scottish Public Services Ombudsman:

> Complaints are valuable. ... Adopting good practice in complaints management has real benefits for public bodies. As well as providing an efficient, effective and understanding way for users of public services to get their issues addressed, complaints offer a chance for public bodies to gain an accurate picture of the level and quality of service they offer from the perspective of the user. They provide free feedback on service delivery and provide a means for the user to have an input into the continuous improvement of an organisation.[811]

That, at least, is the principle. People complain about services because they have been disappointed or dissatisfied, but most people who are dissatisfied do not go on to make the extra effort to bring the incident to the attention of the service. For that to happen, there has to be some spur – for example, annoyance, serious inconvenience, or outrage. Often there is an 'informal' complaint at first, and it is only if the dispute is not resolved that it is elevated to become a 'formal' one.[812]

It can be difficult in practice to view a process that is mainly concerned with the resolution of a dispute as a form of management information. One example is the management of complaints about the police, which traditionally is closely bound up with the principle of citizen oversight and controls set on the abuse of power. Police officers are licensed to use necessary force against citizens, but there are many examples of those powers being used excessively or abused. In the USA, much of this relates to the use of firearms by police, but examples in other jurisdictions include the use of baton rounds ('rubber bullets'), CS gas and tasers. The use of tasers includes cases of a student tasered for trying to use the library without an ID,[813] a deaf man

---

[810] International Standards Organisation, *ISO 10002–2004*.

[811] Scottish Public Services Ombudsman, 2010, *Valuing complaints*, at www.valuingcomplaints.org.uk/valuing-complaints/

[812] J Gulland, 2011, Taking complaints seriously, *Social Policy and Society*, 10(4) 483–493.

[813] M Bobb, M Barge, C Naguib, 2007, *A bad night at Powell library*, Los Angeles: Police Assessment Resource Center.

tasered for not coming out of a toilet in response to a verbal order,[814] a great-grandmother tasered for arguing with a traffic policeman,[815] and a blind man tasered for carrying a white stick.[816] The fundamental difficulty is that, as long as the use of force is accepted as legitimate, there will inevitably be circumstances where its use is misjudged or abused, and while the existence of some route of redress may give officers pause, no administrative safeguard can guarantee that an officer's response in a confused situation will never be excessive.

Complaints about medical care point to another set of issues. The NHS's complaints procedure seems exemplary on paper, with its emphasis on acknowledgement of problems, mediation, conciliation and learning.[817] The procedure is designed to deal with the difficult, sensitive cases that occur in medical crises, the sort that otherwise might lead to litigation. At that level, however, it is uncertain whether it can achieve any resolution. Some problems are beyond reconciliation or remedy – where there is an avoidable death, harmful treatment or even unanticipated ill-effects, patients and relatives are liable to be distressed, and understandably some people will not be consoled or reconciled. Where the complaint is more straightforward, too, it is not certain that mediation and reconciliation are really what is needed. The Ombudsman has commented, with some exasperation:

> It is incomprehensible that the Ombudsman needs to hold the NHS to account for the most fundamental aspects of care: clean and comfortable surroundings, assistance with eating if needed, drinking water available and the ability to call someone who will respond.[818]

The NHS procedure is supposed to be about 'making experiences count'[819] and 'listening, responding, improving.'[820] It has fallen sadly short of that

---

[814] Guardian, 2009, *US police use Taser and pepper spray on disabled man*, www.guardian.co.uk/world/2009/jul/28/usa

[815] Examiner, 2009, *Texas cop tasers great grandmother*, at www.examiner.com/x-536-Civil-Liberties-Examiner~y2009m6d2-Texas-cop-Tasers-greatgrandmother.

[816] BBC, 2012, *Police use Taser on blind man after stick mistaken for sword*, www.bbc.co.uk/news/uk-england-lancashire-19979184

[817] Department of Health, 2007, *Making experiences count*, London: DoH; NHS complaints procedure, obtained at www.nhs.uk/choiceintheNHS/Rightsandpledges/complaints/Pages/NHScomplaints.aspx

[818] Parliamentary and Health Service Ombudsman, 2011, *Care and compassion?*, London: TSO, p 10.

[819] Department of Health, 2007.

[820] Department of Health, 2009, *Listening responding improving – a guide to better customer care,* London: DoH.

aspiration. A recent report on hospitals with high mortality rates commented: 'There was a tendency in some of the hospitals to view complaints as something to be managed, focusing on the production of a carefully-worded letter responding to the patient's concerns as the main output.'[821] The experience of the scheme in practice is that NHS trusts are seen as unduly defensive, public trust is low, and some of the issues complained about reflect deep-seated concerns with the quality of service.

What could go wrong There is a principle in engineering, sometimes called Murphy's Law, that 'anything that can go wrong will go wrong.' It is more than a joke: the reasoning behind the principle is that repeated iterations will find out any fault. If the odds of something going wrong are one in a million, and there are ten million iterations, it will probably go wrong ten times. The same principle applies in public administration. Whenever human beings enter the consideration, which is rather difficult to avoid in the public services, someone, somewhere will gum up the works. Some services deal with hundreds of thousands of people, some with millions. The reason why residual systems for social security are so complicated is that people's lives are complicated, and no matter what contingencies have been anticipated, there will always be someone whose circumstances do not fit the existing rules.

Some of the techniques used to determine what might happen are the techniques of prediction, considered in Chapter 6. Some are arguments from analogy. Where there have been problems of a similar type in the past, those problems can happen again. Examples are the all-too predictable problems when protections against fraud are removed, when double-entry book-keeping is replaced by a new computer program, or when the frequency of inspections is reduced. The general understanding of 'good practice' in many fields reflects collective experience; it needs to be viewed critically, but it is not wise to disregard it.

One of the primary criteria used in analysis in this stage is not whether things will actually go wrong, but what the safeguards and alternatives are if they do. Many decisions taken in the public sector are dogged by uncertainty; it is not possible to be sure whether a policy will work, how it will work, or how the conditions around it will change. Sensible policies allow for the possibility that the decisions taken may just conceivably be wrong. The idea of 'robustness' has been used at

---

[821] B Keogh, 2013, *Review into the quality of care and treatment provided by 14 hospital trusts in England*, London: National Health Service.

several points in this book: a robust decision is one which is capable of being changed, or which allows later options to be developed. Too often, policies are adopted with a wholly misplaced confidence in the quality of the analysis and the rightness of the solution. Allowing for uncertainty is not just a practical necessity; it is an ethical one.[822]

What could go better Recommendations for improvement are subject to much the same kinds of political constraint as findings of fault; they have the added disadvantage that, unless they have been piloted within a small part of the operation, they are rarely based directly in evidence from the organisation itself. The strongest arguments for adopting new practices are based on analogies with practice elsewhere – work done in similar agencies, or in response to similar constraints. This is one of the reasons why many agencies tend to imitate the practice of neighbouring agencies – there are often regional patterns in the delivery of local authority services like education, housing and personal social services. (Policy transfer tends to be reinforced by the exchange of personnel between neighbouring authorities, who bring related practice along with them.) Unless they are accepted and endorsed by the agency, recommendations are unlikely to be effective in practice.

ISSUE FOR DISCUSSION

What can be done to eliminate the production of systemic disadvantage in an agency's work?

---

[822] Policy Evaluation, 2001, *Ethical policy analysis*, 7(1) pp 15–17.

PART 4

THE METHODS
AND APPROACHES OF
SOCIAL POLICY

CHAPTER 18

Research for policy

Policy research
The research process
Ethical issues in research
Criticising research methods

Policy research

Research is an essential part of the study of social policy. Understanding social conditions, and the effects which responses have on them, depends strongly on being able to draw on good information about what is happening. People working in social policy in practice are expected to be able to interpret research material; and those who hope to develop policy need to appreciate what the effects of that policy might be, and how to find out what they really are.

Having said that, the practice of research in social policy is quite different from the way that research is usually presented in textbooks about social science. The core activity in policy research is problem-solving – policy-makers outline the problems, researchers attempt to offer some answers. Some typical activities in social policy research might be:

- to find out what is happening in a process
- to identify and record the contribution made by different agencies to a policy
- to establish the views of key stakeholders
- to see what people make of a service, or
- to evaluate the work of an agency.

Ritchie and Spencer identify four general categories of applied research:

- *contextual*, reviewing experiences, needs or the relationships between parts of a system;
- *diagnostic*, looking for reasons and explanations of current issues;
- *evaluative*, examining whether aims have been met or issues in service delivery; and

- *strategic*, considering alternative approaches and options for improvement.[823]

There tends to be an assumption in textbooks about social science that research should be generalisable – and so, that it should be designed to reveal insights about more than the subject being studied. There are times when this is looked for – when policy research is done in the hope that what is being found out can be applied somewhere else – but policy research is often not like that. The kinds of problems that social policy practitioners deal with tend to be particular – specific to circumstances, to the needs of a defined population, to an agency, or to the operation of a process. It follows that much of the material in the textbooks about theories of knowledge or the generalisability of results is beside the point.

The second assumption is that research is being done in the interests of social science, when the converse is more likely to be true – the purpose is usually to press social science into the service of the policy area being researched. Social scientists are supposed to begin their research with a range of theoretical understandings, a set of information, and they work from there to advance the state of knowledge. Nigel Gilbert, for example, suggests that researchers will want to employ or construct theories; to test the theory, or falsify predictions; to develop measurements that are valid and reliable; to draw on other studies.[824] Policy research may occasionally fit that model, but it is far from typical. Sometimes analysts are asked to establish what is happening, in a field that neither they nor the commissioning authority knows much about. Sometimes they are asked to find out what has gone wrong. They might need to work out what relations or roles in an agency are. They may be asked to identify problems in order to help government establish an agenda. They might be asked how to save money. This can sometimes be stated in general terms, but the process of research typically comes before any generalisation: the central task of the researcher is to find things out.

A third assumption is that social scientists should be working from a disciplinary perspective. Social research, Gilbert argues, is 'an activity conducted within a research community'.[825] That is often true of

---

[823] J Ritchie, L Spencer , 2002, Qualitative data analysis for applied policy research, in M Huberman, B Miles, *The qualitative researcher's companion*, Thousand Oaks CA: Sage.

[824] N Gilbert, 2008, Research, theory and method, in N Gilbert (ed) *Research social life*, London: Sage.

[825] Gilbert, 2008, p 37.

research in university departments, but policy research is more typically conducted in a policy community, which is something quite different. The expectations of practitioners are not necessarily those of a research community. They are concerned with what research finds, not with process of how it is done. This tends to imply that policy research does not necessarily comply with the demands of the academic disciplines. Anthropologists, as a profession, are supposed to treat the interests of research participants as paramount;[826] in the context of policy, that would be absurd (and politically indefensible). Sociologists are told they have responsibilities to protect the good name of their discipline and to safeguard the interests of later researchers.[827] They are also told that they should only do work of good quality, which poses social policy researchers with particular problems. A lot of work in policy analysis is 'quick and dirty'. Agencies want results they can interpret, cheaply and in good time. They want useful information, not necessarily something that a peer-reviewed journal would publish.

Social policy research is not just an academic exercise. It is done for a purpose – typically, because policy-makers need it to be done. In some cases, the purpose is routine: the use of public expenditure has to be justified or the performance of agencies needs to be monitored. In some cases, the research is instrumental – assessing the demand for a service, finding out what people think about policy proposals, checking whether actions meet certain standards. Sometimes it is investigative – finding out what is happening or why something has gone wrong. And occasionally, but only occasionally, it will be about what lessons can be drawn, what works, or what policy ought to be. A report for the Joseph Rowntree Foundation found that internally generated research – either done within an organisation, or commissioned by it – is much more likely to be used and to have an influence than research from outside. The impact that research had was most likely to be small scale, modifying practice rather than leading to major policy changes. It is most likely to have an impact if it meets a specific need, it is locally relevant and it gives clear evidence. It helps, too, if research has a champion – someone within the agency who can take things forward.[828]

---

[826] Association of Social Anthropologists of the Commonwealth, n.d., *Ethical guidelines for good research practice*, www.asa.anthropology.ac.uk/ethics2.html, s.1.1.a.

[827] British Sociological Association, 2002, *Statement of ethical practice for the British Sociological Association*, www.sociology.org.uk/as4bsoce.pdf

[828] J Piercy Smith, 2002, *Promoting change through research*, York: Joseph Rowntree Foundation.

Textbooks in social research are not written for the sort of applied research that people in social policy do, and they have to be approached sceptically. Nevertheless, students and practitioners in social policy research are likely to be asked to find out things that will be useful for policy – identifying what the issues are, working out what is happening, collecting information and presenting it. The methods that are used to find out evidence are much the same as the methods that social scientists use to collect evidence, and it follows that people working in the field of social policy routinely use the concepts, skills and techniques associated with research in social science. The application of research to practice is why research techniques are so useful, and so important for social policy.

The research process

The process of conducting research generally calls for a number of stages, outlined in Figure 18.1. It is necessary to select and then frame the issue or problem which is to be researched. Methods have to be chosen. Data have to be obtained. The results have to be collected, sifted through and interpreted.

Figure 18.1: The research process

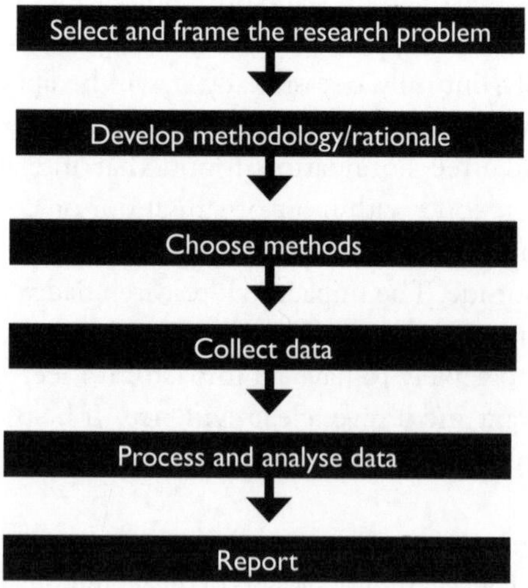

Select and frame the research problem

↓

Develop methodology/rationale

↓

Choose methods

↓

Collect data

↓

Process and analyse data

↓

Report

It may be more accurate to say that these are tasks to be undertaken rather than stages to be gone through. Some researchers begin not with the problem they plan to study, but the data they can get or the people they have access to, and problems and issues emerge from that.

Some researchers begin with a set of methods, like those used in market research, and then look for opportunities to use them. In practice, then, these tasks are often intertwined and inseparable from each other.

There are many texts which begin with a set of instructions about how best to do research. Typically they recommend that researchers should state a hypothesis, specify variables or (just as bad) that they should mix qualitative and quantitative methods, as if these answers applied to any field of activity. The main justification for that sort of approach is that, in certain contexts, that is what the writers are hoping that fledgling social scientists will do. In the context of policy research, it is absolutely the wrong way to go about things. Research design begins, not with a fixed model or approach, but with the questions that have to be addressed. There are many ways of finding things out, and there are always alternative ways of doing research in practice. The issues and problems that policy researchers face are varied enough to mean that there is no general approach, method or type of activity that is right for every case.

Methodology

Research can begin with data or with theoretical analysis. All empirical research is descriptive; material has to be gathered, selected and presented. But research also has to be interpreted; the process of selection itself requires some kind of analysis, whether or not this is explicit. Research reports often label a description of research methods as their 'methodology', but that is something of a misnomer; methodology is the study of research methods, and the methodology of a particular study consists not so much of an account of the process, as a rationale for what is done and why it has been done in that way.

There are two common patterns by which research might be undertaken, usually referred to as 'inductive' and 'deductive' approaches. 'Inductive' approaches begin by collecting material and seeking to classify and organise it after it is collected. ('Induction' is a rather bad name for the process. The word refers to a common fallacy, the assumption that things which happen a lot are likely to happen again. It has been pinned on a range of research methods by people who didn't think research undertaken without preconceptions is real science.[829]

---

[829] e.g. B Russell, 1911, *The problems of philosophy*, Oxford: Oxford University Press, p 37 ff.

What induction is really about is gathering facts and looking for possible connections. A better name for this process might be 'exploratory research' – see Box 18.1 – but this is a textbook, which means that I have to use the mainstream terminology.) Induction is a common pattern of work in history and ethnography. The most basic historical method is to collect facts and information and to seek to assess the importance of different factors, or to interpret trends within it. Political analysis is similar to historical research; it relies, for the most part, on interpreting facts. Ethnographic research is derived mainly from social anthropology. An anthropologist researches into a culture by becoming immersed in that culture, living with people, collecting information, and interpreting. This is the foundation for the sociological method of 'participant observation'.

The 'deductive' approach relies on the generation of propositions which can be tested. This typically takes one of two forms:

- *Testing hypotheses* A hypothesis is a statement about reality which can be tested. The process of generalisation depends on the idea that there is some kind of connection between the factors – a causal link, or a 'generative mechanism'[830] – that explains why something is happening the way that it is.
- *Examining models* A model, like an ideal type, consists of a set of inter-related assumptions to which reality can be compared. I have used 'models' in the same sense as 'ideal types' for much of this book, because the models which I have been considering (like Titmuss's) have largely been theoretical ones. Models can also be designed to reflect a real situation rather than a theoretical construct. The facts are compared to the model; the model is gradually refined to improve its descriptive or predictive power. An example of a model in this text is Kerr's description of the thresholds that people have to pass before claiming benefits.[831] Each of these propositions can be tested independently, but together they constitute a whole series of actions.

In practice, inductive and deductive approaches are rarely completely distinct. Inductive researchers find it difficult to avoid preconceptions which direct their work, and as they gather material they are likely to form criteria by which further selections might be made. Conversely, deductive research has to start somewhere; hypotheses have to be

---

[830] R Pawson, N Tilley, 1997, *Realistic evaluation,* London: Sage, esp. ch 3.
[831] S Kerr, 1983, *Making ends meet,* London: Bedford Square Press.

generated and models constructed from some kind of factual basis. It is possible to use inductive and deductive approaches simultaneously, and there are patterns of research which operate by a constant process of interpretation and refinement of ideas.

This is the approach of 'grounded theory'. Grounded theory depends on a process of sorting material inductively, putting it into categories and stopping when there is no material left to classify.[832] The process is intended to help the development of theory; it does it by looking at material and organising it. The most basic technique is to take the data and to organise it into categories, carrying on until there is no more data, or no more categories to fill.[833] These categories become the basis on which generalisations are made, and so on which theories can be generated. Action research is another example. During action research, researchers are examining processes and, at the same time, making decisions about them.[834] The basic model is one of constant experimentation; researchers try out a range of methods, see what works and what does not, and try to select likely approaches.

Box 18.1: Known and unknown problems

'There are known knowns; there are things we know we know. We also know there are known unknowns; that is to say we know there are some things we do not know. But there are also unknown unknowns – the ones we don't know we don't know.' (Donald Rumsfeld, former US Secretary of Defense and winner of the Plain English Campaign's Foot in Mouth award for 'a baffling comment by a public figure'.[835])

Researchers in social policy don't necessarily know quite what they are going to be researching. The task of the researcher might be, for example, to go and find out what problems there are in an area; to see what a local agency, like a family centre or a community facility, is actually doing (it is not often possible to tell from the sign on the door); to find out where a process is failing; to find out the benefits of a programme; to find out what needs a

---

[832] B Glaser, A Strauss, 1967, *The discovery of grounded theory*, Harthorne NY: Aldine de Gruyter.

[833] A Bryman, R Burgess, 1994, *Analysing qualitative data*, London: Routledge, pp 4–6.

[834] R Lees, 1975, *Research strategies for social welfare*, London: RKP.

[835] Plain English Campaign, 2103, *Foot in Mouth Awards: past winners*, www.plainenglish.co.uk/awards/foot-in-mouth-award/foot-in-mouth-winners.html

group has. The answer to those questions depends on what is happening on the ground. They will almost always have several dimensions. The findings cannot usefully be classified in advance; sometimes we do not even know what we should be asking about.

Using conventional deductive research in such circumstances is problematic. Hypotheses depend on prior knowledge – on the assumption that we already know enough about the issue to disregard other factors. Blaikie explains:

> Hypotheses are tentative answers to 'why' and, sometimes, 'how' research questions. they are our best guesses at the answers. But they are not appropriate for 'what' questions. There is little point in hazarding guesses at a possible state of affairs. Research will produce an answer to a 'what' question in due course, and no amount of guessing about what will be found is of any assistance; it might even prejudice the answer.[836]

This reservation is important for policy research, where the first questions to address are usually concerned with what is happening, rather than why. Even with 'why' questions, however, there are reservations to make about hypotheses. The deductive method is liable to exclude fruitful lines of enquiry, to waste time, and to miss the point; it calls for a lot of prior knowledge to be sure that a hypothesis is worth investigating. Majchrzak argues:

> hypothesis testing ... has little place in policy research. While such an approach fosters thoroughness in scientific exploration, the potential loss and misperception engendered by taking a singular perspective on a multidimensional problem is too great a risk and luxury for policy researchers.[837]

Not knowing what might be found, or even what to investigate, has a profound impact on the design of research. When policy researchers are looking for source material and background information, they may well refer to generalised material from social science; that does not mean that they have to follow the same pattern themselves. Policy research in practice is typically exploratory; it looks for whatever might be found, rather than hunting for a specific, closed set of information. Exploratory research of this kind tends to be qualitative, intensive and flexible. The research needs to be open to unanticipated findings, and it has to be designed so as to allow definitions to be formed or reconsidered. It tends to rely on key

---

[836] N Blaikie, 2010, *Designing social research*, Brighton: Polity, p 67.
[837] A Majchrzak, 1984, *Methods for policy research*, London: Sage, p.19.

informants and insights from stakeholders. Often, that implies that policy research should be *abductive*, drawn from the perceptions and understandings of those involved in the process;[838] discussing issues with people who are affected, or who have a particular role or expertise, can be an effective way of mobilising existing knowledge. This is no panacea: abductive evidence is often partisan and committed, and key actors often control access to sources of information that might give a different perspective. Like all evidence, it needs to be corroborated and set against alternative viewpoints.

Operationalising the problem

Research problems have to be 'operationalised'. This means that concepts have to be translated into operational terms – terms which can be investigated, observed, worked with.

Definition of terms Defining terms is often important for research; if the definitions are inadequate, the whole study may be invalid. For example, a study looking at disabled people has to decide what is meant by 'disability'. An early study for the UK DHSS defined disability mainly in terms of the ability to move one's limbs or use one's organs, and found about three million adults with disabilities This excluded important areas like mental illness.[839] A 1988 OPCS study widened the 1968 definitions and found 6.2 million.[840] This was an impressive, well conducted survey; but when the surveys were repeated in 1996, the apparent number of disabled adults had increased by over two million people in less than ten years.[841]

It can be important to state terms precisely in deductive research, because the definition of the problem changes the kind of information which is collected, and small changes in definition can make large differences to figures. By the same token, however, finding out more about a topic may lead to the conclusion that the initial definition was inappropriate. In inductive research, definitions help to explain why a particular group is being focused on. It does not always matter if

---

[838] N Blaikie, 2010, *Designing social research*, Brighton: Polity, p 105.

[839] A Harris et al, 1971, *Handicapped and impaired in Great Britain*, London: HMSO.

[840] OPCS (Office of Population Censuses and Surveys), 1988, *The prevalence of disability among adults in Britain*, London: HMSO.

[841] OPCS, 1988; E Grundy, D Ahlburg, M Ali, E Breeze, A Sloggett, *Disability in Great Britain: results of the 1996/97 follow-up to the Family Resources Survey*, www.dwp.gov.uk/asd/asd5/94summ.asp

some people are included who should not be, or other people are left out; in so far as the research is collating material on factors, influences or relationships, the material which is necessary for a valid interpretation may still be there. In empowering research, discovering how people understand and use terms may be part of the exercise of the research.

Validity   The term 'validity' is often used in a specialised way in empirical research studies. It refers refer to a particular part of the process – whether or not the 'facts' collected show what they are supposed to. 'Concept validity' is the question of whether the issue which is being tested is the same as the issue which was supposed to be tested. Some issues are relatively easily identified and tested – like how many people over 75 have a bathroom. Many concepts in social science, however, are much vaguer. Issues like altruism, punishment or racism have not only to be defined, they also have to be identified within certain types of context. Many studies try to create situations in which people will act or respond in a way which can be interpreted in terms of these underlying concepts. Titmuss tested altruism by people's willingness to give blood;[842] Pinker has objected that giving blood is painless and so is not a good test of altruism.

There is a common problem in research design: the way that research is conducted has the potential to alter what the research finds. This might reflect researcher bias – which is possibly more common in social policy than in other social sciences, because many researchers have a strong commitment to a particular policy or approach, and because agencies commonly use 'research' as a means of arguing for extra funding. There is sometimes bias from the respondents – 'response bias' can occur when respondents are trying to be helpful and to give the researcher what they think the researcher wants. The researcher's presence alone can lead to differences in behaviour: people behave differently when they are being watched. [843] The description of method is important, then, because it may reveal something about the process which affects interpretation of the results.

Reliability   Reliability is also known as 'predictive validity'. Results are said to be 'reliable' if they consistently show the same thing. Reliability is important for some sorts of research, but not for all. A study can be

---

[842]   R Titmuss, 1970, *The gift relationship*, Harmondsworth: Penguin.

[843]   R Olson, J Verley, L Santos, C Salas, 2004, What we teach students about the Hawthorne studies, *The Industrial-Organizational Psychologist*, vol 41 no 3 pp.23–39

valid and the results may still be unreliable, because some methods –
particularly interpretative methods – allow for a great deal of latitude
in observation and interpretation. Equally, a study may be invalid
and produce reliable observations – because the same facts are found
repeatedly for different reasons from the ones the researcher believed.

In practice, the conditions under which social policy operates are
constantly changing, which tends to mean that the test of reliability is
less important and less useful than it is in some other fields. A study can
be valid and the results may still be unreliable, because some methods
– particularly interviews in depth – allow for a great deal of latitude
in observation and interpretation. Equally, a study may be invalid
and produce reliable observations, because the same facts are found
repeatedly for different reasons from the ones the researcher believed.
Results which are unreliable, however, may raise questions about
whether or not research is valid. There have been three waves of surveys
looking at what people in the UK think is essential to avoid poverty,
conducted in 1983, 1990 and 1999. In 1983, 64% of respondents said
that two meals a day were necessary for adults; in 1990 90% said so.
63% of people thought that people needed to give presents once a
year when the question was asked in 1983; 69% agreed in 1990; 56%
agreed in 1999.[844] This may genuinely reflect a major shift in public
perception, or a change in social conditions; but it may also indicate
that there is something about the question which led to inconsistent
responses, in which case it is difficult to tell what the true position is.
Halleröd suggests that the intrinsic problem with consensual measures
of poverty is that people's expectations and preferences are conditioned
by what they think is realistic; because the possibilities change, so do
the responses.[845]

Qualitative and quantitative research

Sayer makes the important distinction between *intensive* and *extensive*
research.[846] 'Intensive' research looks in depth at a problem or issue,
examining the relations between different elements and the processes

---

[844] J Mack, S Lansley, 1985, *Poor Britain*, London: Allen and Unwin; H
Frayman, 1990, *Breadline Britain 1990s*, London: LWT/ Domino Films; D
Gordon, L Adelman, K Ashworth, J Bradshaw, R Levitas, S Middleton,
C Pantazis, D Patisos, S Payne, P Townsend, J Williams, 2000, *Poverty and
social exclusion in Britain*, York: Joseph Rowntree Foundation.
[845] B Halleröd, 2006, Sour grapes, *Journal of Social Policy*, 35(3) pp 371–390.
[846] A Sayer, 1981, *Method in social science*, London: Hutchinson.

involved. Intensive research is concerned with questions like why and how something happens. 'Extensive' research is concerned with the context and relationships within which an issue occurs; it is concerned with the extent of problems and associations between problems and issues. The distinction between 'intensive' and 'extensive' research is helpful for policy analysis, because it tries to relate the pattern of research done to the kind of problem which is being addressed. The appropriate approach depends on what kind of problem we are dealing with. Much of my own work has been intensive – for example, I have undertaken studies of the experiences of psychiatric patients, the problems of people in minority ethnic groups in a rural area, and what kind of problems might stop elderly people in hospital being referred to services which can help them better. But other problems I have worked on have needed an extensive approach, like comparisons of poverty rates in different areas, or planning services for people with dementia in an area. The pattern of research should be the best option for the circumstances, not necessarily the one the analyst is most used to doing.

This distinction is often represented in the literature as a distinction between 'qualitative' and 'quantitative' research, though those terms are slightly misleading – quantitative work can be intensive and interpretative, and qualitative work can be wide-ranging and analytical. The main forms of qualitative research include observation, interviewing in depth and examining documents. Qualitative research is commonly aimed at producing material to help explain issues, answering questions beginning with 'why?', 'who?, 'how?', as well as some questions about process – like 'what is happening?'. Quantitative research is research which measures effects. The characteristic methods are censuses and questionnaires. Numbers are used to answer questions like 'how much?', 'to what extent?, 'what proportion?' and 'what are the differences?'. Quantitative methods can be used for tests of hypotheses, examinations of models, and predictions; numbers can also be helpful in deciding which of several factors are most important, and under what conditions certain types of things will happen.

Qualitative and quantitative methods are not, of course, exclusive. Quantitative methods do require a level of interpretation to know what the numbers mean; qualitative judgments can include some element of computation. Many studies use elements of both.[847] Because of the type of questions they address, qualitative methods are generally more appropriate for inductive approaches, quantitative methods for

---

[847] A Bryman, 1988, *Quantity and quality in social research*, London: Unwin Hyman.

deductive ones. The identification is not exact, however. Qualitative methods can be used to test some hypotheses, for example about organisational behaviour, while quantitative methods can be used to sift through information – for example, in the case of workless families, using quantitative profiles to identify the scope of the problem and potential samples in deprived areas.[848]

Whenever quantitative research is being undertaken – that is, studies which rely on the use of numbers – the design of the study is likely to be crucial. There is a general rule in computing called 'GIGO': which means, garbage in, garbage out. The first issue to address is validity. I wrote about the problems of measurement and quantification in Chapter 6; some degree of interpretation is unavoidable. If the concepts and constructs do not mean what they are taken to mean, it does not matter how sophisticated the internal mechanics of the research are. The second issue is about what it is possible to infer from the data about extents in other circumstances. That generally relies on a representative sample; where samples are produced in other ways, it may not be possible to make claims about extents and proportions. Descriptive statistics about selective samples are often fairly meaningless as they stand.

Graham and McDermott suggest that 'qualitative studies are routinely excluded from evidence review and policy development'.[849] That is less true than it used to be, but it is probably fair to say that there is some scepticism in policy-making circles about qualitative methods. The validity of qualitative studies is often challenged by people who think that numbers are more 'scientific' or credible. Evidence from qualitative responses is often dismissed as 'anecdotal' or 'unsystematic'. This is mainly based in a misunderstanding of the validity of quantitative research – rubbish is not turned into information of value by having a number stuck on it. Validity in quantitative research is based in the theoretical relationship between the data and the findings. Exactly the same is true of qualitative research.

Qualitative material is usually verified in three ways. The first is the validity of the source. Research with stakeholders and key actors is often based on the principle that these are the people who know about the issues. Second, there is external cross-confirmation. The things

---

[848] T Shildrick, R MacDonald, A Furlong, J Roden, R Crow, 2012, *Are 'cultures of worklessness' passed down the generations?*, York: Joseph Rowntree Foundation.

[849] H Graham, E McDermott, 2006, Qualitative research and the evidence base of policy, *Journal of Social Policy* 35(1) p 21.

people say may reflect experience elsewhere. Independent research reports, press reports of problems, or specialist literature may show that a problem is general, rather than specific to a particular study. Third, there is internal cross-confirmation. If several people say the same thing, that is usually evidence either of a common perception or a common experience. People sometimes confirm each other's statements because they don't like to contradict or argue; but if they say it in different places at different times, the cross-confirmation is stronger and clearer.

If the information from a qualitative study is correct, and correctly interpreted, it is as valid as any other data. There are various ways of trying to establish whether the information is correct, but most depend on 'triangulation' or cross-validation. Information which is corroborated from different independent sources – the findings of other research, the testimony of other witnesses, or the products of other methods – is more likely to be correct than information which is not. Typically, then, responses to qualitative questions are presented in twos or threes, in order to show that comments are not isolated.

The issue of correct interpretation is more difficult to determine; it depends on whether the interpretation is theoretically justified. If the research is particular – a study of a specific set of issues, in a specific setting – generalised social science can be used as a way of corroborating the interpretation. If the research is intended to deliver findings that are generalisable, it should be possible to take the findings out of that context and apply them to other settings. This can only be established either by reference to existing theory, or by looking for later cross-confirmation in subsequent studies.

Data collection

Data are gathered from many potential sources. The first, and most obvious source, is the material that other people have collated, and all research calls for some kind of review of previous work if it is to build on it and not simply to duplicate it. A literature review in policy research is mainly used

- to identify what is known about a subject. One of the purposes of reviewing literature is to avoid 'reinventing the wheel' – spending time and money on finding out information which has already been thoroughly checked out beforehand.
- to identify methods and approaches which might be useful for the analysis of the issues. The academic literature is often helpful in providing frameworks or structures for organising disparate

material relating to a field in practice. By contrast with many academic literature reviews, however, there is no place for a survey of areas of academic interest, disciplinary development, or the broader context.

- to bring evidence to bear which may reinforce or question findings from the policy analysis. If the findings are similar to findings from other places, it may be taken as confirmation of the problems.

These are limited objectives, and it follows that the literature review may also be limited. Wallace et al question whether a comprehensive, 'systematic' literature review is really necessary. They point to two main problems with comprehensive trawls. From an academic point of view, they tend to be insufficiently selective. It is important to exercise some judgment about what should be included. From a practical point of view, they are time-consuming and expensive. More is not necessarily better.[850]

When the focus is the operation of a public agency or a policy, there should be some kind of record – the process of accountability means that decisions and actions are meant to be subject to scrutiny, and that can only happen if there is a record. There should then be official notes, written statements, policy documents and files. In principle all public services should be able to track clear lines of authority in a continuous record of events. Increasingly, files are being maintained in an electronic format; the records can be searched and cross-linked much more easily than used to be the case. However, it is still not uncommon to find that they fall short. Agencies rarely collate sufficient background data while they are starting up, because when they are starting up, they don't have a pool of information to draw on, and putting it together is not usually the first thing on their minds. When they realise that they ought to have done so, because they need that information to establish what difference they have made, they often need to construct a back-story or 'baseline' in retrospect. The best information tends to be collated by long-standing agencies, like local government or the health service, where the procedures are already in place – but in those cases, the information that is collected is likely to be whatever has been formally identified, and retrieving information which does not fit the standard pattern can be difficult.

---

[850] A Wallace, K Croucher, D Quilgars, S Baldwin, 2004, Meeting the challenge: developing systematic reviewing in social policy, *Policy & Politics* 32(4) pp 455–470.

For the most part, the principal source of data in policy research comes from people – the people who establish the policies, administer the agencies, receive the services, and experience the problems that are being addressed. The most common forms of empirical research, as a result, are concerned with human activity – chiefly people's behaviour, beliefs and opinions. This tends to push social policy research towards methods which are concerned with obtaining such information, such as interviewing and observation.

Sampling The sources from which data can be drawn have to be identified. This process is usually described in terms of 'sampling', because so much research is based on selecting appropriate sources of information for quantitative studies. The earliest research was done comprehensively; the emergence of sampling methods made it possible to think to select data from only certain parts of the field being studied. Research that is supposed to describe the characteristics of a population is typically meant to be *representative*, often reproducing the features of the population in miniature. Various forms of probability sampling – random samples, quotas and structured samples – might be used to achieve this. Extensive research is often done this way; representative samples are used for citizens' panels, opinion polls and large-scale evaluations of the effects of programmes or legislation. There is a common danger here: if the sample is not representative, or biased, the results will be too. There is not much point in counting responses if the sample is not selected to support it.

Not all research is intended to reflect the characteristics of a population. The main test in most policy research is that it offers an insight into the issue being studied, and studies in social policy are often agency-based, exploratory and intensive. Many samples in policy research – arguably most – are *purposive* rather than numerically representative; they focus on a narrow group as a way of illustrating the major issues, rather than trying to reproduce distributions in miniature. Examples of purposive samples include:

- *Illustrative cases* Individuals or groups can be selected as illustrative cases. Illustrative cases do not have to be typical; there may be a value in selecting examples where issues are pronounced, so as to put the validity of the classification beyond dispute. A study of doctors can be used as a basis for discussion of professional regulation, or a sample of people who have been subject to court proceedings for debt could be the basis of a study of problems with debt.

- *Extreme cases*   The same principle can be extended further; some research is based on extreme cases, selected because they are unusually revealing. It may be appropriate to look at extraordinary circumstances, like child abuse inquiries, legal cases or historical anomalies. 'Critical incident' techniques use complaints and breakdowns in procedures to identify the key issues in service delivery.[851]

- *Self-selected samples*   People have been selected on the basis that they volunteered for an activity, or even applied for a job – which indicates they may not be like others who have not come forward.[852]   In quantitative studies, the researcher has to argue that this does not distort the issue under study.   In qualitative samples, it does not necessarily do so – the test is whether the observations point validly to issues and processes, not whether they are numerically representative. Similar arguments apply to 'snowball' samples, in which cases are drawn out of a network of contacts; they may be the only effective way to reach people who are otherwise hard to find.

- *Key groups*   Special groups like political representatives, police, social workers, claimants, are all potentially valid and interesting in their own way.   However, within an organisation, or a policy network, people in particular roles can be 'key' in a more specific way; they occupy positions which allow them both to give specific information about their activity, and to offer insights into the role of others.   It is usually possible to identify the actors, and their relationship to each other, through a process of enquiry. Bryson suggests beginning with a small group of people in a workshop, and using them to identify relationships and connections, including an evaluation of the relative contribution, power and importance.[853]   This has the advantage of speed, but it might also mislead – people's answers in a formal group are constrained, and they might reflect the formal structures rather than what actually happens. Identifying relationships and interactions is typically done over a period of time, as information from each actor is collated with others.

---

[851]   J Flanagan, 1954, The Critical Incident Technique, *Psychological Bulletin* 51, pp 327–357.

[852]   See e.g. A Rogers, D Pilgrim, R Lacey, 1993, *Experiencing psychiatry*, Basingstoke: Macmillan/MIND.

[853]   J Bryson, 2004, What to do when stakeholders matter, *Public Management Review* 6(1) pp 21–53.

- *Stakeholder research* A stakeholder can be seen either as someone who has a role relating to the issue under study, or more generally as 'any group or individual who can affect or is affected by the achievement of the organization's objectives'.[854] Stakeholder analysis has grown from a view that organisational behaviour can be understood by focusing on interactions between key actors or policy networks.[855] The people who know about an issue are often the people most closely engaged with it, and it is not possible to find out what the issues are without asking. Consulting stakeholders also has a political dimension: identifying people as having a stake in an issue is itself often a political statement. The process of discussing issues with people serves to identify their interests, and makes it possible for their views to be taken into account. Stakeholder research usually calls on researchers not just to obtain relevant information, but to engage stakeholders in the process.[856] Empowering research aims to give a voice to people within the policy process, and the methods that are adopted have to be both inclusive and enabling.

Selecting methods

One of the banes of research in social policy is the assumption that there is a single, 'right' way to do research – the randomised control trial which dominates in health services, the deductive experiment which characterises psychological approaches, or the opinion poll which is used to discover what people think. There is nothing intrinsically wrong with these methods, but whether they are appropriate depends on the circumstances where they are applied. If a policy researcher wants to find out what people think, there are alternatives to polling – for example, the range of interactive and participative methods used in the World Bank's *Voices of the Poor*. If the aim is to examine people's behaviour, it can be done through observation, examination of records or anthropological approaches, as well as through experiment. However, because research can be done in so many ways, there is often a question as to whether the way that has been chosen was appropriate. Whatever the method, it needs to be justified.

---

[854] R Freeman, cited J Bryson, 2004, What to do when stakeholders matter, *Public Management Review* 6(1) pp 21–53.

[855] R Brugha, Z Varvasovszky, 2000, Stakeholder analysis, *Health Policy and Planning* 15(3) 239–246.

[856] J Bryson, 2004, What to do when stakeholders matter, *Public Management Review* 6(1) pp 21–53.

The most common methods used in social science are probably

- enumerations (counting things)
- observation and participant observation (observing things)
- interviews (asking things), and
- experimentation (testing things).

Zelditch suggests that different types of methods are appropriate for different types of problems. He refers only to the first three sets of methods, enumerations, participant observation, and interviews; his classification is set out in Table 18.1.[857]

Table 18.1: Selection of research methods			
	Methods		
Information types	*Enumerations*	*Participant observation*	*Interviews*
Frequency distributions	Best – prototype	Usually inadequate and inefficient	Usually inadequate; efficient if adequate
Incidents, histories	Inadequate	Best – prototype	Adequate and efficient with precautions
Institutionalised norms and statuses	Adequate but inefficient	Adequate but inefficient; useful for unverbalised norms	Best – most efficient

The table is disputable: for example, institutions can also be examined by considering their records, and the quantitative examination of outcomes is not necessarily 'inefficient'. I referred earlier to the principle of 'triangulation'; it may be desirable to pick not one method, but several. But the essential point the table makes is that one has to choose the method according to the type of problem, and methods which are good for one purpose may be not very good for another.

The basic techniques for drawing information from purposive samples, like stakeholders and key actors, are qualitative research methods – individual interviews, group interviews and postal enquiries. When samples are selected for a purpose, such as finding out what relationships are, any questions that are asked should be compatible with

---

[857] M Zelditch, 1979, Some methodological issues in field studies, in J Bynner, K M Stribley (eds) *Social research: principles and procedures*, London: Longman.

that purpose. Unless samples have been selected with mathematical representativeness in mind, there is no point in questions which establish proportions or fixed answers. Questions to stakeholders and key actors generally ought to be exploratory, giving respondents the chance to identify the issues that matter. That implies that they should give the respondents the chance to identify the issues that matter from their perspective. 'Open questions' are questions which cannot be answered with a single, fixed, response, like 'yes', 'no' or 'three years ago'. 'Closed' questions are questions which can be. Closed questions are not much use in this context; questions generally should be open.

Individual interviews are probably the most used. An interview is a purposive conversation. It is a 'conversation' because there are two sides: the person being interviewed, generally with the aim of finding out information, and the person who is doing the interview, who is asking questions and trying to steer the conversation to salient points. It is possible to conduct an interview entirely with pre-set questions. This is called a 'structured interview'; its purpose is to put similar points to a range of people, so that answers can be gained in a form which can be compared directly. Structured interviewing is widely used in some specialised forms of research, such as market research and opinion polling, where set answers make it possible to quantify the results. This is occasionally helpful for policy analysis, but it is not typical of the process, and it is not a central skill. What is much more often done is interviewing in depth. These are sometimes called 'unstructured interviews', but they should not be. Interviews cannot be unstructured, because they must have a purpose; generally that means that there is an agenda, a list of topics which is to be covered, or some way of selecting and shaping the material that the interview covers. Interviews in depth are free-flowing. 'Semi-structured' interviews are a half-way process: interviewers have a set agenda, some themes, and some initial questions, but are then free to examine in issues in depth as they are raised. This is probably the most used technique for a team of analysts, because it is makes sure that different people are asking the same things, while leaving analysts the freedom to go into more details when new issues arise.

Group interviews make it possible to identify shared perspectives, and points of disagreement. They are a quick and effective way of getting material from several people at once. In practical terms, they can be difficult to record – a smart-phone may do for a one-to-one, but sound recording for a group is difficult at best, even with good professional equipment. For a researcher visiting an organisation or a community group it is hardly ever possible to choose the room or to control background noise while the interview is happening, and frankly old-fashioned note-taking works better. The disadvantage with group interviews in principle is that people will feel some pressure to make their answers consistent with each other, which happens particularly when some people in the group have higher status than others. To avoid that situation, it is possible to give participants an individual questionnaire first. For larger groups, such as the public meetings used in stakeholder and user consultations, there are a range of techniques, including breaking people up into small groups and getting someone to record on a flip chart, or using coloured sticky 'post-it' notes so that people can make comments on particular issues.

Postal and internet enquiries deserve a special mention. They are widely used in policy work, for example in getting information from stakeholders and for public consultations, and that stands in striking contrast with most social science research. The problem for social scientists has been that postal enquiries are not much use for extensive, quantitative research, where they offer poor and unrepresentative response rates – a quantitative questionnaire, sending a mailshot to randomly selected people and counting the responses to closed questions, is likely to be worthless. This comment is not necessarily relevant to qualitative work, however, and in any case there are better ways of asking questions. The issues that apply to representative samples hardly matter in work with a limited range of key actors or stakeholder groups, especially organisational representatives. If you want to find out, for example, the kinds of issue that patients' groups are taking up with local hospitals, or how housing associations go about managing empty properties, writing to them or using e-mail makes perfectly good sense. To get the broadest coverage, it helps to keep the length of the query to a practical minimum, using open questions and focusing on drawing out information which is reasonably sure to be available. The main limitation of such enquiries is that they do not give the same opportunity as an interview to explore issues which are unclear or which need further development. Where there are large numbers of potential stakeholders, however, they can be a very effective way of gathering information, giving people the opportunity to identify issues, and creating an opening for people to participate.

The analysis of data

What data show is rarely clear or obvious; 'facts' are not intrinsically meaningful, but acquire meanings through a process of interpretation which needs to be understood theoretically. Processing data is not very interesting in itself, but it is important to identify it as part of the research process in order to avoid the problems which arise when that process begins – as it must – to change the characteristics of the original data through selection, sifting and interpretation. A thorough account of method will usually refer to this process at some point.

Qualitative data are generally organised through a process of selection and thematic organisation. The method is sometimes referred to as 'open coding', 'open' because there are (or should be) no fixed categories. Data from exploratory research are sifted, sorted and classified flexibly. The basis for classification can be drawn from theoretical principles based on knowledge of social science, or, as it happens in 'grounded theory', it can be developed from a process of comparing and contrasting the material and sorting it into categories. Either approach is, at root, an interpretative process – similar to the kind of approach required of those reading and writing textual material.

There are more conventions governing the organisation and presentation of quantitative data. I have reviewed some of the traps in considering the problems of indicators in Chapter 6. Descriptive statistics consist of summaries of numbers in particular categories; usually they are presented in charts or tables. There are some common problems – for example, converting figures from small samples into percentages and passing them off as something they're not. The cardinal sin, however, is the presentation of data about samples that have been selected purposively – for example, discussions with stakeholders or selected groups of service users – as if they were numerically representative. It is important not to treat this kind of data as if it was the numbers that mattered, rather than the character of the views expressed. The validity of responses depends on the experience of the respondents and the process of corroboration, not on the quantities.

Analytical statistics (the kind taught in 'statistics' courses) are used to identify associations in the data. This approach is concerned mainly with probability, or the chance of something happening. The most obvious problem with this is the assumption that associations are likely to be evidence of a direct relationship, when they might have arisen by chance. Correlations are often misleading – many of the associations that seem to show a statistical connection disappear when they are subject to further investigation.[858] There is a danger of allowing the computer to run away with the analysis. Common problems include

---

[858] See J Ioannidis, 2005, Why most published research findings are false, *PLOS Medicine* 2(8) e124 doi:10.1371,obtained at www.plosmedicine. org/article/info:doi/10.1371/journal.pmed.0020124

- generalising results when data come from samples that cannot support a generalisation
- using parametric statistics, which assume normal distributions, on non-normal data
- treating variables from common sources as if they were all independent (such as data from a handful of countries, too often done in comparative social policy)
- violating (or simply ignoring) the assumptions required in statistical analysis – as a rule of thumb, the more sophisticated the method, the more sensitive to those assumptions it is likely to be, and
- data mining, or 'fishing', in data sets.

If we want to identify the links between different factors properly, we need to have a good, firm explanation of what is going on. Managing the mathematics is secondary to understanding the relationships.

Ethical issues in research

Many research projects have ethical dimensions, and consideration of the ethical issues is a standard part of research design. In general terms, the kinds of ethical consideration which are included in the published codes are of four kinds:

- The *impact* of the research, including:
  ° the potential implications of research for participants
  ° the potential implications of research for non-participants, and
  ° the uses to which research can be put.
- The *treatment of participants*, represented for example in:
  ° informed consent
  ° confidentiality and anonymity, and
  ° special consideration of vulnerable respondents.
- *Disciplinary considerations* Researchers are enjoined to protect the status of their discipline by trying to:
  ° maintain research of high quality
  ° display competence
  ° act responsibly towards others in their field, and
  ° advance their discipline.
- Rules concerning *research relationships*. These include:
  ° the responsibilities of the researcher to the body commissioning the research
  ° responsibilities to the host institution

    ° commitments to fellow researchers, and
    ° integrity in dealing with participants and stakeholders.

These codes offer guidelines, not rules. None of the rules that are commonly referred to (like consent or confidentiality) applies universally in every case. Social policy often implies work in both the private and public domains; people are entitled to privacy in some circumstances (such as details of their private lives) but not in others (in their operation of public services). Principles like 'consent' and 'confidentiality' are much less likely to be relevant in the public domain.

There are, however, several principles which could be argued to be particularly important for social policy research, and they are not adequately considered in conventional guidance to social scientists.[859] Some rules apply in general terms to all forms of public service. The most fundamental principle in research ethics is 'beneficence' – the question of who benefits, and who is harmed, by the research. Each person should be respected; that people should be treated as ends in themselves, rather than means; that their rights should be respected to the greatest degree possible; and that the work of the policy researcher should not lend itself to procedures which are offensive, degrading or detrimental to people's welfare. Researchers should consider the implications of their actions, including

- the implications for policy,
- conformity with other moral codes (such as equality, opposition to racism or respect for humanity), and
- a commitment to benefit the wider society.

Another important guiding principle is public accountability. Social policy research has a critical function. Public scrutiny is essential for democracy to work, and public accountability is itself an ethical principle. In a democracy, if people are functioning in a public role, they are subject to public examination and criticism in that role, whether they like it or not.

---

859 P Spicker, 2007, The ethics of policy research, *Evidence & Policy* 3(1) pp 99–118.

Box 18.2: Scandal versus research

It is well established that research in social policy hardly ever has the impact of a scandal. Research can be ignored, dismissed or qualified out of existence. Social scientists have had plenty of practice at dismissing research themselves; there is probably no research which cannot be criticised on methodological grounds. By contrast, scandal forces the hand of politicians and decision-makers; it puts them in a position when they have to respond, even if the action is ineffective or misplaced.

The distinction between research and scandal may be exaggerated. Research is nothing more than finding things out, and scandal can be a remarkably effective way of finding out the details of a process. Inquiries into child abuse are generally based on a detailed examination of every aspect of the process, reviewing the experience of all major participants.[860] Equally, the shocking details of cases in mental health have played a major part in the development of policy – most clearly, in accelerating the movement of people from institutions to the community. The principle of 'critical incident techniques' in research[861] is essentially equivalent to the process that inquiries into scandals go through; focusing on the points in a process where things go wrong is an illuminating way of identifying what the process is and where its weaknesses lie.

Conversely, research may be the way in which distasteful facts are brought to public notice. Child abuse was 'discovered' by radiologists in the 1940s and 50s – which seems a bizarre statement, because neglect and cruelty had been the subject of legislation long before. However, many professionals found it hard to credit that parents could systematically abuse their children, and problems were commonly attributed to other causes, such as bone defects. The presentation of evidence about fractures in an appropriately 'scientific' format was crucial in persuading medical professionals to take the issue seriously, as was the description of the problem as a 'syndrome' in the 1960s.[862] Problems like neglect in institutions or the misuse of drugs for control of children featured in the research literature long before they became the subject of media attention.[863] Social policy research is often intended to have an impact, and much research in the field is arranged and

---

[860] C Hallett, 1989, Child abuse inquiries and public policy, in O Stevenson (ed) *Child abuse*, Hemel Hempstead: Harvester Wheatsheaf.

[861] J Flanagan. 1954, The critical incident technique, *Psychological Bulletin* 51, pp 327–357.

[862] S Pfohl, 2003, The 'discovery' of child abuse, in P Conrad, V Leiter (eds) *Health and health care as social problems*, Lanham, Maryland: Rowman & Littlefield.

[863] M D A Freeman, 1983, *The rights and wrongs of children*, London: Pinter.

presented to get the maximum attention. Research reports typically come nowadays with a press release, a summary of main points and text on the Internet.[864]

The sociologist Gary Marx once made a spirited defence of 'muckraking' research. Muckraking is 'the searching out and public exposure of misconduct on the part of prominent individuals and the discovery of scandal and incriminating evidence.' Muckraking research, Marx suggests,

> uses the tools of social science to document unintended (or officially unacknowledged) consequences of social action, inequality, poverty, racism, exploitation, opportunism, neglect, denial of dignity, hypocrisy, inconsistency, manipulation, wasted resources and the displacement of an organization's stated goals in favor of self-perpetuation.[865]

This is research as a passionate, politically committed act.

Even if it gets attention, the most passionate research is not necessarily the best. Good academic research, in its very nature, tends to be equivocal; it looks at different sides of an argument and comes to a reasoned conclusion (often something dull like 'more research is needed'). The research that makes a splash is often the most sensationally presented – or scandalous. This, perhaps, is one reason why the social science that influences policy often comes over as simplistic and partial.

Criticising research methods

Most research studies include a methodological analysis, in which researchers try to deal with objections. Many of these are very narrowly focused on minor issues – for example, how many times researchers visited if people were out, or how long the interviews took. These are sometimes important – if they haven't been done adequately, they may cast doubt on the findings – but they are not usually central. A defective piece of research may still point to real problems, while an excellent methodology may yield results which are vulnerable to theoretical criticism, misinterpretation and political bargaining.

In order to criticise an empirical study, a number of questions have to be asked.

---

[864] Joseph Rowntree Foundation, 2007, www.jrf.org.uk/
[865] G Marx, 1972, *Muckraking sociology*, New York: Transaction Books, sourced at http://web.mit.edu/gtmarx/www/ascmuck.html.

---

1. What is the study for? The purpose of a study can affect both the perceptions of the researcher and the types of method undertaken.
2. What assumptions have been made? In other words, what are the premises of the argument? How have terms been defined?
3. Is the process which has been followed appropriate to the problem?
4. Is the study valid? Is it examining what it was supposed to be examining?
5. Do the conclusions the researcher draws follow from the results?

ISSUE FOR DISCUSSION

Is it legitimate to research social problems, like homelessness or mental illness, or personal problems, like grief or distress, without the hope of doing something about them?

CHAPTER 19

Evidence and policy

Using empirical evidence
Evaluation
Methods of evaluation
Analysing policies and services
Approaches to evaluation

Using empirical evidence

Social policy is problem-oriented, and although the term is treated by some apprehension by social scientists, the analysis of social policy is often 'positivist', at least in the methods it uses. I wrote earlier about 'real people' and 'practical problems'. This begs some important assumptions; it implies that there are conditions which can be determined empirically, which do not simply lie 'in the eye of the beholder'. Positivism is the view that scientists are dealing with an external reality, and positivistic methods are those which attempt to identify true 'facts'. One of the commonplaces of social research is that the best way to look at a topic is by 'triangulating' – that is, looking at an issue several ways at once. By doing so, it becomes less and less likely that the findings are the result of some quirk in the research method, and more likely that they reflect what is actually happening. Positivism has been the subject of withering criticism, particularly in sociology, because it disguises the kinds of value-judgment concealed in our understanding of 'reality'.[866] Arguments about 'social reality' are now more likely to be made in terms of 'critical realism', which accepts that social structures and meanings are important parts of the way that social relationships are formed, but which claims nevertheless that what we are studying is a real set of issues.[533] Social 'reality' is complex, because much of it depends on the society of which it is part; but much social policy, if not most, begins by accepting society on its own terms, and trying to identify patterns and relationships within the constraints of that society.[867]

---

[866] See A Chalmers, 1999, *What is this thing called science?*, Cambridge: Hackett.
[867] D Byrne, 2011, *Applying social science*, Bristol: Policy Press, chs 1–2.

Empirical evidence is important for social policy, but it cannot establish policy or priorities itself. Empirical material has to be interpreted; problems have to be recognised as important, evidence has to be seen as pointing to some outcome, 'facts' have to be constructed in a way which relates them to possible policy responses. What happens in social policy is that theoretical insights from different disciplines can be used to give some shape to the mass of empirical material (or 'fact') which is available, and a direction about what to look for. There are often competing, contested interpretations of the same evidence. Boaz and Pawson look critically at five systematic reviews of the evidence on the same topic in social administration (mentoring); the reviews all come to different conclusions about what the evidence says.[868] Translating evidence into policy is not straightforward; interpretation and evaluation are unavoidable.

The construction that is put on evidence is difficult to recognise when problems seem 'obvious'; if children are battered by parents, people are living on the street, or there is mass unemployment, what 'construction' is being put on the material? Some reference to the history of social policy can be helpful here, because in each of these cases there has been not simply denial of these problems but a range of political views about what the problems were, what they signified and what kind of response might be appropriate. Facts are seen through particular perspectives; the received wisdom of one generation becomes the misconception of another. In a field like social policy, theory is meaningless without some reference to empirical problems; but equally, empirical issues acquire their meaning for us only because we are able to relate them to some kind of theoretical understanding.

Box 19.1: Generalising from experience

Although policy research is typically specific to particular circumstances, there is sometimes the possibility that the findings from one study can be generalised to others. Questions like 'what works?' assume that general principles can be translated from specific examples into other contexts. There are three main approaches to generalisation. One is exploratory and empirical; a relationship which is found in one context may well hold in others. 'Grounded theory' begins by sorting the data, generating theory interactively and continuing until all the data is categorised. A second approach begins with theory – an ideal type, a hypothesis, perhaps

---

[868] A Boaz, R Pawson, 2005, The perilous road from evidence to policy, *Journal of Social Policy* 34(2) pp 175–94.

a model – and tries to examine how closely reality approximates to the theory. Examples are discussions of whether frustration leads to aggression, unemployment leads to crime, liberal values lead to lower public spending or higher benefits lead people to choose not to work. A third approach is 'realism'. Pawson and Tilley's case for 'realistic evaluation' is based in the idea that services do have an effect, that the effect can and should be explained, and that there is somewhere a 'mechanism' or causal link which can explain what is going on.[869] For example, if the theory for avoiding 'broken windows' is right, crime can generally be reduced by ensuring that small problems are remedied immediately. When everyone is made aware that a community cares, the argument runs, they will be less likely to make problems in small or large things. If this is generally true, using the same approach in other contexts should also work. However, assumptions about mechanisms can be misleading (see Box 1.2). The mechanisms are complex; it often happens that policy-makers, and policy analysts, are mistaken about the connections; and in any case, explaining issues in terms of causes does not necessarily offer any useful prescriptions for policy.

Aristotle describes alternative forms of knowledge: *episteme*, science or generalised knowledge; *techne*, or applied knowledge; and *phronesis*, or practical wisdom. Social policy depends heavily on phronesis – precepts drawn not from reason, but from experience. Examples might be the claims that

- Selective social policies characteristically fail to reach a proportion of the people they are intended to reach.[870]
- People do not claim the benefits they are entitled to because of negative attitudes to services and the costs of claiming.[871]
- There is an 'inverse care law' in health care which means that while people from lower social classes are in the greatest need, they are also least likely to receive services.[872]
- People whose priority is based on how long they have waited for service are better able to exercise choice than those priority is based in need.[873]

---

[869] R Pawson, N Tilley, 1997, *Realistic evaluation,* London: Sage, esp. ch 3.

[870] R M Titmuss, 1968, *Commitment to welfare,* London: Allen and Unwin.

[871] P Craig, 1991, Costs and benefits, *Journal of Social Policy* 20(4) pp 537–565.

[872] J Tudor Hart, 1971, The inverse care law, in G Smith, D Dorling, M Shaw (eds) 2001, P*overty, inequality and health in Britain 1800–2000,* Bristol: Policy Press.

[873] D Clapham, K Kintrea, 1986, Rationing, choice and constraint, *Journal of Social Policy* 15(1) pp 51–68.

None of these statements is self-evident, or universally true, or even genuinely 'explanatory'. Phronesis develops principles experientially, setting them against empirical evidence, and it does not need to consider underlying mechanisms to be effective.

The problem with phronesis is that it can be difficult to tell good generalisations from bad ones. Policy debates are often influenced by recurring myths – that punishment works as a deterrent, that poor people are trapped in a cycle of deprivation, that complexity in benefits is a disincentive to work – which at best are weakly supported by selective evidence, and often are maintained despite all evidence to the contrary. The voice of experience is not always the voice of wisdom.

Evaluation

Policies are evaluated mainly by scrutinising evidence in order to be able to make some judgment about them. The first thing that one needs to do in order to evaluate a policy is to establish some sort of criterion by which it can be judged. The sorts of criteria which are most often used are fairly straightforward: does this policy meet needs? does it have other benefits? is it worth what it costs? As is often the case questions like these are not as simple as they appear to be. It is not always clear just what is being evaluated, or what the standards being applied are. And the criteria which are being applied are not always explicit: economic and political constraints are often taken for granted.

Evaluation is commonly categorised in two main classes, summative and formative. *Summative* evaluation is the evaluation of a whole policy or process, focusing on the impact of policy. Most policy can be treated in terms of a series of categories – aims, methods, implementation and outcomes. A summative evaluation reviews each of the later categories to see whether or not the operation of policy is consistent with the aims. The impact of policy is most usually assessed by asking whether the policy has done what it set out to do. But summative evaluations may also take into account unintended consequences as well as the achievement of aims.

Formative evaluation is undertaken at intermediate stages in the policy cycle. Formative evaluations can take place to see whether guidelines have been followed, to see whether an agency is ready to start work, to see whether an agency is being properly managed, or to see whether contract terms have been complied with. Typically this is done for peripheral projects and voluntary organisations, to see whether funding should be approved or continued. There are times when implementation itself is the outcome that matters – in health care, which is a form of social protection, it may matter more to people that they are treated civilly, promptly and responsibly than that they are cured.[874] These issues are, legitimately, the subject of analysis in their own right. Many policy analyses, however, are not concerned with outcomes. They take place at a time when a policy or project is starting out, is beginning to engage with issues, and some initial judgment has to be made about whether the process is working. It is necessary, then, to have some criteria by which implementation processes can be judged *as processes*, rather than dealing with the more obvious question of whether they work. This is sometimes called a 'process evaluation'. The term implies a focus on the process, rather than on either policy or outcomes: that focus is inevitable if neither the policy nor the outcomes are subject to scrutiny.

The distinction between formative and summative evaluation is a technical one, concerned with the stage when evaluation takes place. Bate and Robert take the distinction a little further. People who think they are working on a 'summative' evaluation, they suggest, may be more inclined at the end of a process to believe that they are providing a final, authoritative answer, while those who think they are working 'formatively' may be more inclined to see it as part of an interactive work in progress.[875] The model of rational policy making leads back from evaluation into policy formation and development. In that sense, almost all evaluations are 'formative'.

For the most part, evaluation begins with a view about what services are supposed to do, and how they are supposed to do it. This is true of most evaluations, but it does not apply to all: sometimes the definition of aims is misleading. Policing is often assumed to be about catching criminals, but it might really about public security; social work might be assumed to be about protecting children when in reality it is much more often about supporting families; sheltered housing was initially set up to provide support in emergencies, but the evidence that emerged was that the provision of day-to-day support was much more useful. There is also, Scriven suggests, a case for 'goal free' analysis[876] to look at what policies actually do, without prior assumptions. A policy might be considered to be justified if it has had beneficial effects, even if the effects are not the effects that it was supposed to have. The distinction

---

[874] M Calnan, E Ferlie, 2003, Analysing process in healthcare, *Policy & Politics* 31(2) pp 185–93.

[875] P Bate, G Robert, 2003, Where next for policy evaluation? *Policy & Politics* 31(2) pp 249–262.

[876] M Scriven, 1991, *Evaluation thesaurus*, London: Sage.

between goal-based and goal-free evaluation is picked up in the *Magenta Book*, the UK government guide to evaluation.[877] However, their understanding of goal-free evaluation is not the same as Scriven's: to them, a goal free evaluation is one which looks at both intended and unintended consequences. This approach is not really 'goal free'; it still takes into account the aims of policy, along with other material which is additional to those aims.

Methods of evaluation

The central question behind many assessments of policy is whether a policy or an agency delivers what it is supposed to deliver. Evaluation research is research which is done to assess the value of a programme or activity. There are many specialised texts on this, but the techniques used in evaluation are not necessarily particularly specialised; the main concern is simply to find out what policy does, and what difference it makes. The simplest kind of answer is based on the outcomes of policy, but this is rarely enough to determine what works – only what does not. If outcomes are satisfactory, it is difficult to say with confidence whether the benefits are produced by the policy, or by other social conditions. For example, it is difficult to say that success in reducing crime, relieving unemployment or preserving families might be the result of what the policy has done, when these factors are heavily dependent on the external environment. By contrast, if outcomes are unsatisfactory, this is usually good enough reason to conclude that the policy has not worked. It is possible that the judgment is mistaken, but in a world where detailed examination is costly, time-consuming and difficult, evidence that things are worse, or even no better, suggests that something else should be tried.

Indicators of effectiveness and the 'black box' The simplest test of effectiveness is done by considering indicators of what the activity has done, and comparing these indicators with the aims. The available data is usually classifiable in terms of inputs, outputs and outcomes. These terms were explained in Chapter 11. Deciding whether a policy has worked should in theory be based mainly on outcomes rather than inputs or outputs. However, it can be difficult to distinguish inputs,

---

[877] Cabinet Office, 2003, *The Magenta Book: Guidance notes for policy analysis and evaluation*, www.policyhub.gov.uk/evaluating_policy/magenta_book/chapter1.asp

outputs and outcomes clearly in practice, and it is fairly common for evaluations to slide back and forward between different tests.

A focus on outcomes is sometimes referred to as a 'black box', after the work of psychologist B F Skinner.[878] Skinner argued that the best way to understand people is to look at what goes in and what goes out, and to ignore all the complicated stuff that goes on in people's heads. He suggested we treat the mechanism as a 'black box' – black because it concealed what was going on in the middle (stage magicians use black felt to make things disappear). All you do is to look at what goes in – the inputs – and what comes out – outputs or outcomes. The trick, then, is to ignore everything else you know about a process. In the same way, it may be possible to look at the behaviour of some organisations, like police or schools, without being too much concerned about procedures, culture or implementation. Studies of discrimination, for example, have sometimes been concerned simply to show that there is a problem. If the outcomes show that people are disadvantaged, that is a matter of concern. There may need to be more, detailed analysis later, explaining the process by which disadvantage has come about, but in the first instance the outcome alone is enough to establish that there is a problem, and that something ought to be done about it.

The idea of the black box is treated with disdain by some social scientists – as one reviewer of *Policy Analysis for Practice* made very clear – because they find it hard to believe that any technique can be quite so crude and still be legitimate or useful. The idea is counter-intuitive – that is, it does not make obvious sense. It asks us to ignore everything else we know about a process, when every academic instinct should be screaming that process matters, and that it cannot be possible to arrive at a considered judgment by ignoring what is happening. An example may help to explain. Let us suppose, for example, that we want to establish whether a university is putting lower-class students at a disadvantage in its admissions process. It is possible to imagine the reasons and processes by which this can happen, but we do not need to speculate or hypothesise. What we can do, instead, is to look at what actually happens. We look at the number and range of applicants, we look at their results, and we look to see who is admitted and who is not. We do not need to interview applicants, or people responsible for admissions, or to observe the process, to establish that there is a problem. We would want to do those things once we knew that there was a problem, if we want to work out why and how it is happening; but

[878] B Skinner, 1971, *Beyond freedom and dignity*, London: Peregrine Books, 1988.

the first step is to find out whether it is happening or not. That is a simple question, and a simple answer will serve.

Benchmarking and performance indicators Indicators of performance are used to test progress, and to achieve specified targets or standards. A benchmark is a standard, used to check an agency's performance against an ideal; standards relative to other agencies; or standards within the same agency over time. The topics overlap, because performance indicators are usually introduced with some standard in mind, and because benchmarks are usually expressed in terms of performance indicators, the achievement of targets or milestones. In some cases, the standard that is applied might not be practically achievable – like the aspiration that every child aged 11 should be reach certain educational standards in tests – but the benchmark can still be used to assess both the agency's performance, and the performance relative to others.

The UK government took a lively interest in benchmarking in the late 1990s, but despite the occasional flush of enthusiasm,[879] this has seemed to wane. There were ambiguities in the idea – for example, as to whether it relies on external standards or self-assessment, how far it can be used comparatively, and what kind of factors could reasonably be benchmarked. Bowerman and Ball argue that the government's expectations for the results of benchmarking were in any case based in a misunderstanding; local authorities in the UK have been using benchmarks since at least the early 1980s, and the idea that endorsing the approach after nearly twenty years' practice would lead to a radical improvement in standards was always illusory.[880]

Although benchmarks can relate to any part of the policy process – inputs, process, output or outcomes – they are more often used to test processes and outputs rather than outcomes. The problem with using them for outcomes (like a reduction in crime) is that outcomes can depend on a range of external factors; they can have more influence when the issues are within the control of the agency being benchmarked. Outcome based measures are being used, however, in attempts to pay agencies by results; the problem here, in common with performance indicators in general, is that this creates incentives

---

[879] e.g. M McAteer, A Stephens, 2013, The role of benchmarking in supporting improvement in local government, *Public Money and Management* 33(4) 381–384.

[880] M Bowerman, A Ball, 2000, Great expectations: benchmarking for best value, *Public Money and Management* 20(2) pp 21–6.

---

for 'gaming' the system, manipulating returns and tailoring activities to the requirements of the indicators rather than to best practice.[881]

Modelling One of the weaknesses of simple assessments of outcomes is that it is not always easy to tell what difference the policy might have made. Things may have got better, but can we tell it has happened because of the policy? Things may not have changed, but might it not have been worse? Evaluations are supposed to test whether something has worked. In principle, if a policy has worked, it has made a difference. There should at least be some added value – something should have happened which would not otherwise have happened. To work out whether that is true, it can help to be able to say what would have happened. Models are generally predictive, either in the sense that they duplicate a causal process, or in so far as they represent conditions which produce predictable effects. They are useful, Byrne comments,

> if they are deployed with a clear sense of their limitations. They are worse than useless, that is to say they are actually negative in their effect, if they are asserted as some proper 'scientific' account of complex social reality which should be the basis of social interventions and/or the general approach of governance to policy and practice.[882]

The standard techniques for working out what might have happened, or what might be expected to happen, were covered before in the section on forecasting. They depend on projections, the modification of parameters and modelling. It should, in principle, be possible to say what would have happened if nothing was done, what ought to happen if a plan is implemented, and perhaps even to say what might have happened with an alternative approach. (The last approach is sometimes referred to as 'counterfactual'.) It is relatively unusual, however, for evaluations to depend strongly on this kind of calculation, for three reasons. The first reason is that, in most fields, neither the causal models available, nor the core quantitative information available, are good enough to do this sort of work. The Treasury model makes it possible for governments to undertake some of this kind of analysis for UK economic policy; there is nothing equivalent for social policy.

---

881 G Bevan, C Hood, 2006, What's measured is what matters: targets and gaming in the English public health care system, *Public Administration* 84(3) 517–538.

882 D Byrne, 2011, *Applying social science*, Bristol: Policy Press, p 154.

The second reason is that most social policies, and most local policies, are too small-scale to have much relative impact. There are too many factors. As statisticians put it, there is too much 'noise', and it drowns out any sense of a possible impact. The third reason, which is probably decisive, is that detailed modelling is not actually necessary. There are ways of deciphering the impact of services without going into details about causes, and without trying to identify all the contributing factors.

Action research Action research is primarily used in policy-making. Researchers are both examining processes and, at the same time, making decisions about them. This goes beyond research taking place in a professional setting, which is a form of participant observation – the idea of action research is that the research and the practice are part of the same process. The basic model is one of constant experimentation; researchers try out a range of methods, see what works and what does not, and try to select likely approaches. Pioneering examples in Britain were the Community Development Projects[883] and Educational Priority areas.[884] There are several advantages. One is that researchers are able to try out several approaches. They are able to correct mistakes as they go. By comparison with formal evaluations like randomised control trials, if a policy is not working, researchers are not bound to carry on regardless. The main problem with action research is that the process generates commitment to policy. If a policy is not working, the practitioners and researchers have to be asked why they did not try to do something else instead. Over time, they get locked into a process where they believe that what they are doing is the best thing they can do. No-one wants to feel that they have wasted three years of their lives. Both workers and researchers become partisan, and it can be difficult for them to take a different view.

Control trials Control trials compare outcomes in different situations, so that differences between the environments can be distinguished from the effects of the policy. One option, the randomised control trial, works by assigning some subjects to a treatment group and others to a control group which is not treated. The approach is most commonly used in medicine for the trials of new pharmaceuticals.[885] Because

---

[883] R Lees, G Smith, 1975, *Action research in community development*, London: Routledge and Kegan Paul.

[884] A Halsey, 1971, *Educational priority*, London: HMSO.

[885] A L Cochrane, 1989, *Effectiveness and efficiency*, London: British Medical Journal/Nuffield.

some people get better just because they think they are being treated, people in control groups are commonly given 'placebos' – pretend drugs – and their progress is monitored relative to others. There are potential ethical problems with this, because the effect of withholding treatment can have very undesirable effects for the patient. This is commonly avoided by offering a different treatment, and examining the differences in outcomes.

In medicine, control trials are generally seen as a 'gold standard' – in this context, the best way to do things (though caution is needed, because in economics the term means something quite different). In social policy, it is often difficult to conduct experiments with people in this way, but it is not impossible; well-known pioneering examples, from a time when greater confidence was invested in the potential of social science, include experiments examining the benefits of pre-school education (Headstart in the US),[886] or the New Jersey Income Maintenance Experiment, which sought (fairly inconclusively) to identify the effects of a basic income system on people's behaviour and in particular on work incentives.[887] Much more common in social policy is the approach in which people are compared when they are subject to different policy régimes, usually as a result of a localised project.[888]

It is unusual for formal evaluations of projects to be conclusive. The problems which are being dealt with are multi-faceted, and even where the causal links are fairly widely accepted the results are subject to re-interpretation. For that reason, the construction of theory is central to the understanding of effects, and to the belief that some kinds of effect are produced by a policy while others are not. The British Medical Journal once published, as a demonstration of the dangers, the results of a randomised control trial showing that the power of prayer improved outcomes for patients in the past who had already fallen ill and recovered, even though their recovery took place several

---

[886] R Fuller, O Stevenson, 1983, *Policies programmes and disadvantage*, London: Heinemann, ch 8.

[887] J Pechman, M Timpane, 1975, *Work incentives and income guarantees*, New York: Brookings.

[888] C Weiss, J Birckmayer 2006, Social experimentation in public policy, in M Moran, M Rein, R Goodin (eds) *The Oxford handbook of public policy*, Oxford: OUP.

years before the experiment.[889] The lesson is not that retroactive prayer works; it is that randomised trials can yield random results.

Pawson and Tilley make a more fundamental, potentially devastating critique of control trials. In the first place, it is in the nature of social research that people tend to behave differently when they are being studied, and the set-up of many experiments and pilot projects makes it difficult to be confident that what is being tested is the method that is being used, rather than relationships between the people who are involved. Second, control trials are designed to neutralise the impact of the social environment. The general experience of many such trials in criminology is that initial experiments or pilots work very well, and then subsequently they fail when they are applied in other circumstances. The difference often lies in the social conditions where they are applied – and those conditions are what the methodology is meant to exclude. They argue: '... what needs to be understood is what it is about given communities that will facilitate the effectiveness of a program! And that is precisely what is written out.'[890]

User perspectives Service users in the public sector are often members of the public, receiving services on an individual basis – the public, after all, is who the public services are meant to be for. Some social services serve the public directly – social security, social work or the health service. Some, like regeneration services and community development, are aimed at groups or areas, rather than individual recipients. There are many different types of public service, and other public services may equally be serving local businesses (e.g. through economic development or city centre management), working with specialist consumers (e.g. builders, utility companies, and transport providers) or delivering services to other public sector agencies.

This covers a wide range of activity, but there are three general points to make. The first is that service users are key stakeholders. They have an interest in the policies which are followed, the terms on which services are delivered, and the way that the service performs. This overlaps with the previous consideration of user involvement – there is a growing appreciation that evaluation can be used as a means of empowering users.[891] As stakeholders, users offer an essential

---

[889] L Leibovici, 2001, Effects of remote, retroactive intercessionary prayer on outcomes with patients with bloodstream infection, *British Medical Journal*, 323 1450–1.

[890] R Pawson, N Tilley, 1997, *Realistic evaluation*, London: Sage, p 52.

[891] I Hall, D Hall, 2004, *Evaluation and social research*, Basingstoke: Palgrave Macmillan, pp 51–2.

---

counterweight to the views of administrators. The processes of policy analysis tend to have a bias to the administrators; they provide the core information, they are the ones who take policy reform forward, they are the main people with whom policy analysts establish a relationship. But services do not exist for the benefit of the administrators, and their views have to be balanced against the views of other stakeholders.

The second is that users have a particular concern with the delivery of services, and distinct perceptions of the process. I referred in Chapter 11 to Scriven's concern that focusing on the stated aims of a policy can implicitly override the concerns of users.[892] There is a potential danger here, but it does not have to be true; users want services to work, and often their concerns can be expressed in terms of the service's aims. Users' satisfaction or dissatisfaction with the service, their perspective on quality and performance, and their experience of delivery are part of the standard assessments of outcomes.

Users' ability to comment does depend on how directly they are engaged with the service. Sue Balloch and her colleagues suggest that it is difficult to get users to participate in evaluations if the policy being evaluated has not engaged users before the evaluation.[893] This is only half true – users may still appreciate the opportunity to comment, as they did in the case study which follows. Many public services take quantitative surveys of user satisfaction as basic indicators of performance. There are potential problems with these surveys in research terms. People who are asked for views by an agency do not respond neutrally: there is an implicit bias favouring the agency asking the question. In quantitative terms, feedback questionnaires are mainly useful for producing a series of indicators, so agencies know whether they have done better or worse as time goes on. In qualitative terms, they are much more valuable; they give alternative insights and a range of perspectives about what is done, and how else it might be.

The third point, which follows on from the second, is that some users may be able to offer a particular insight into the way that services operate. Complaints from users are an important source of information, and close examination of critical incidents makes it possible to identify what has gone wrong, and how to set it right. Comments, complaints and problems can be used to put together indicators, but much more

[892] M Scriven, 1991, *Evaluation thesaurus*, 4th edition, p.37

[893] S Balloch, A Penn, H Charnley, 2005, Reflections on an evaluation of partnerships to cope with winter pressures, in D Taylor, S Balloch (eds) *The politics of evaluation*, Bristol: Policy Press, p 170.

valuable is a detailed, intensive, qualitative examination, which can help to point out issues in the service delivery.

Box 19.2: User perspectives in psychiatric care

Evaluations commonly depend on collating the views of stakeholders, those who have a role and those people who are affected by services. Users have a particular insight and point of view, which can be used in conjunction with other evidence to inform the examination of service operation. The quotations which follow come from a qualitative study for a local health board, undertaken with fifty respondents.[894] Patients were given open-ended interviews in depth, on a semi-structured schedule of questions intended to give them the opportunity to identify the issues important to them. For some, those issues related to their personal experience of mental illness; for others, the main issue was the response of the health service. Often this was seen as coercive,

> 'I got told that if I didn't come here I wasn't getting home. ... I took it to mean that they would section me.'

> 'I lost my freedom being in hospital ....I was on medication.'

Two comments, though, were particularly frequent. One was that patients knew very little about their treatment.

> 'I don't know what's available in the health service. ... The only way I can find out I think is by asking the doctor who's very busy and waiting to see the next patient.'

> 'Nobody has told me how I can find out or where to go. I'm totally confused because I haven't been in this situation before so I don't know.'

The other was that no-one had the time to talk to them. Medical attention was infrequent and harassed staff did not have the time to sit and discuss issues. A common experience of being in hospital was boredom: 'I just sit around and vegetate and things get worse in the hospital.'
Psychiatric patients have often been denied a voice. In former times, this happened because mental illness was treated as a form of incapacity, which

---

[894] P Spicker, I Anderson, R Freeman, R McGilp, 1995, User perspectives on psychiatric services: a report of a qualitative survey, *Journal of the Association for Quality in Healthcare*, 3(2) pp 66–73.

invalidated anything they said. This is a misunderstanding of the nature of mental illness. Rogers et al argue:

> Our approach starts from the premise that the views of users of mental health services are valid in their own right. We do not assume that these views are a definitive version of reality or 'the truth', but they are a legitimate version of reality, or a truth, which professionals and policy-makers should no longer evade or dismiss.[895]

Currently, misinterpretations about confidentiality and the ethics of research have become a major obstacle to undertaking work relating to psychiatric care. An emphasis on privacy, ethical scrutiny and a presumption against research with vulnerable people has made it difficult to researchers to gain access to psychiatric patients. There is a risk that interviews may be intrusive or distressing, and researchers have to be sensitive to the possibility. But some people see the opportunity as a direct channel of communication to the service:

> 'Just hoping through speaking to yourself and telling you about what happened when I first got to hospital, I just hope that they can put a stop to that ...'

Giving people a voice is not a qualification to dominant ethical standards; it is an ethical imperative.

Analysing policies and services

The discussion of policy in Part 2, and the outline of the structures and approaches of different public services in Part 3, point to a series of issues which a policy analysis will probably have to consider. One of the ways of doing this was outlined in Chapter 11, which mainly focused on the operation of specific policy programmes: analysis depends on identifying aims, methods, implementation and outcomes. There are other ways of analysing social policy and administration in practice. Michael Scriven offers a 'key evaluation checklist', with fifteen main points:

- context
- descriptions and definitions

---

[895] A Rogers, D Pilgrim, R Lacey, 1993, *Experiencing psychiatry: users' views of services*, Basingstoke: Macmillan p 13.

- consumers
- resources
- values
- process
- outcomes
- costs
- comparisons
- generalisability (i.e. whether there are lessons for others)
- overall significance
- recommendations and explanations
- responsibility and justification
- report and support (i.e. follow-up work with agencies), and
- meta-evaluation (that is, evaluation of the evaluation).[896]

These are all useful terms, but the list is difficult to use. The sequence is not very clear, and with a long list of points, it is difficult to know what weight to attach to each element, or how the issues relate to each other. Some of the issues (like generalisability) are less important for analysing practical administration to managing than they are for other fields. Others which matter for practice, like considering what can go wrong, are hardly considered.

The sorts of questions that have to be asked in the analysis of policy are summarised in Table 19.1. The questions are not the only questions that can be asked, or that should be, and it may be possible, in some contexts, to leave out some which are inappropriate. This can be used as a checklist, but it does something more important than that – it is also a way of structuring information. The questions reflect a pattern of thought – the kinds of problem that social policy practitioners need, in practice, to address, and the kinds of issue that they need to consider.

Approaches to evaluation

The literature on evaluation has been characterised by two main approaches. On the one hand, there has been a methodology dominated by quantitative, scientific, non-normative analysis. On the other, there is a qualitative, naturalistic, descriptive approach.[897] The World Bank's coverage of evaluation, which is freely available on the Internet, is a

---

[896] M Scriven, 2000, *Key evaluation checklist*, at www.wmich.edu/evalctr/ checklists/kec.htm
[897] M Patton, 1997, *Utilization-focused evaluation*, pp 290–299.

Table 19.1: Policy analysis in practice		
Key stage	*Indicative questions to consider ...*	*... while reviewing the issues in the light of:*
Aims and goals	What is the policy, service or agency supposed to do? How will we be able to tell if they have achieved their aims?	The policy process Strategic objectives
Assessing the situation	What is happening? What is the evidence? What do stakeholders and key actors have to say? What is likely to happen in the future?	Aims and values
Methods	What is being done, and how? What are the options What are the constraints? What resources are there? Are the methods consistent with the aims? What happens if nothing is done? What might go wrong?	Aims and values The assessment of the situation
Effectiveness, efficiency and equity	What are the costs? What are the benefits? Are the methods cost-effective? How can costs be reduced, and benefits increased? Who gains, and who loses?	Aims and values Methods
Implementation	Is the way things are done appropriate to the task? Does the process meet the criteria and standards applicable in this field? What is going wrong? What else might go wrong?	Aims and values The assessment of the situation Methods Effectiveness, efficiency and equity
Evaluation	What impact does the policy have? What do those affected think? Has the policy met the criteria established to meet its aims?	Aims and values The assessment of the situation Methods Effectiveness, efficiency and equity The process of implementation

model of the first type.[898] It has two troubling faults. The first is that it is very difficult to understand for people who are not already schooled in the techniques. There are recurring problems in using sophisticated mathematical techniques in social science. Unless users have a very clear understanding of the assumptions behind the models, the character of the relationships being identified, and the ways in which changes in the relationships or in the parameters might affect the results being reported, both the results and any policies based on them are liable to be misconstrued.

The second fault, which is probably more important, is that these techniques rely heavily on the quality of the data that goes into them. The more sophisticated the technique, the more vulnerable it is to inadequate data. The World Bank's advice is aimed at less developed countries – countries which have fewer people involved in formal economic activity, and which tend to be poor. It is almost a tautology to say that they tend to have less developed systems for information gathering and statistical processing. The quality of information needed to make these kinds of technique work is beyond anything in my experience in the UK and Europe, and I am very sceptical about the idea that developing countries are much better equipped to provide the information than developed countries are. There are also reservations about adopting that approach more generally. Evaluation is a relative activity; its character depends on the agency where it is being done and the criteria that are being applied. In terms of specific evaluation techniques, the ones that have to be used are the ones that seem most appropriate in context. There is no single model of best practice to follow. Procedures have to be adapted to the problems they are being applied to. There are some issues which require quantitative examination, just as there are some requiring qualitative. But the discussions of consultation and user experiences point to another general issue – not about the style of the evaluation, but the basis on which the evaluation is being carried out. Participative, democratically based evaluations tend to look different from specialised, expert assessments, whether they are quantitative or qualitative.

Evaluation is also a political activity. If the evaluation is part of a participative process, or it is part of the structure of democratic accountability, the evaluator has to work within the political framework. Political constraints and issues arise even within the narrowly defined

---

[898] J Baker, 2000, *Evaluating the impact of development projects on poverty: a handbook for practitioners*, New York: World Bank, available at http://siteresources.worldbank.org/INTISPMA/Resources/handbook.pdf

position of specialist work for a particular agency. If the evaluator is someone from outside the agency – which is typical of much policy analysis – the evaluation can only have an impact if it is adopted and carried through by someone in the agency. The results are keenly anticipated and felt by staff working on the ground. Part of the task of evaluation is to engage people in consideration, to find people who are likely to take revisions forward. Evaluation calls for discussion, mediation, and responsiveness to people's circumstances. Taylor and Balloch write that evaluation 'requires the evaluator to master not just quantitative and qualitative research processes but also to develop the political acumen of a skilled negotiator and the sensitivities of an experienced counsellor'.[899]

ISSUE FOR DISCUSSION

Who should decide the criteria by which services are to be evaluated?

---

[899] D Taylor, S Balloch (eds) *The politics of evaluation*, Bristol: Policy Press, pp 251–2.

CHAPTER 20

Social policy for practice

Applying social policy
Skills for social policy
Social policy as a professional role
Social policy as public service
Social policy as an ethical activity

Applying social policy

Any adequate understanding of social policy has to be able to identify the implications of policies for practice. There are three main areas of applied policy work: policy formation, public management, and policy analysis.

- *Policy formation* The formation and development of policy depends on knowledge of the specific subject area and ideas about options and approaches. Studies in this field focus on what policies are, what they do, and how else they might be done. Because this is often done in an attempt to bring about change in policy, or to defend particular approaches, it is sometimes referred to as 'policy advocacy'.[900]
- *Public management* is mainly concerned with the process of administering policy, implementation and managing organisations. The skills include project management, resource management and working with people.
- *Policy analysis* This is about examining policy – finding out and assessing what is happening; monitoring implementation; and evaluation, or finding out whether policies do what they are supposed to do.

Social policy draws heavily on a range of academic disciplines. It cannot lay claim to a distinctive view of the world, or special methods and approaches. It is defined by what it studies, not by how it goes about it. The kind of work which I have been outlining does not mark out

---

[900] M Hill, 2005, *The public policy process*, Pearson/Longman.

social policy as a discipline, in the sense of clearly setting the analysis of social policy apart from other kinds of academic study, but it is characteristic. There are four recurring features:

1. The work is *problem-oriented*. Research and evaluation are done for a purpose, quite apart from their academic interest.
2. The general approach to analysis tends to be *pragmatic*. Given that there are problems and issues, the task of social policy analysts is to find material which can effectively serve the kinds of work they intend to do. Often, as in the use of indicators, this implies a degree of compromise; such compromises are a necessary part of the approach to the subject.
3. The work is *multi-disciplinary*. It is possible to confine oneself to one kind of approach, but this is not always consistent with the pragmatic concerns of work in the subject. The eclectic approach of social policy can be seen as a virtue, because the kinds of skill called for in practical fields require the kind of range and adaptability that social policy fosters.
4. The work is *political*. The analysis of policy is not simply a technical exercise, undertaken in order to choose the best methods for a range of agreed aims or goals; it is an intensely political activity in which arguments are being made for different kinds of philosophy, approach and outcomes. Academic work in social policy is inevitably developed in a political environment. This affects the selection of the issues: housing research has been dominated in recent years by studies of privatisation and affordability, while the implications of housing shortages – homelessness and lack of access – have been examined relatively little. It affects the understanding of the issues; educational outcomes, for example, are likely to be judged differently if they are considered in terms of academic success or social mobility. The evaluation of evidence, as Taylor argues, is heavily dependent on its social context, and politically contested.[901] The relationship between policy analysts and agencies is sensitive and sometimes difficult.[902]

---

[901] D Taylor, 2005, Governing through evidence, *Journal of Social Policy* 34(4) pp 601–618.
[902] A Wildavsky, 1993, Speaking truth to power, New Brunswick, NJ: Transaction Books; D Taylor, S Balloch (eds) *The politics of evaluation*, Bristol: Policy Press.

The applied nature of the subject means that academics working in social policy have to take into account the potential consequences of their work. Research can be a tool for changing policy – though it is important to note that the use to which work is put is not necessarily the use that researchers would wish – and those who begin with this awareness are often looking to justify a particular result. Research into poverty provides a powerful example. Most commentators want to make the same basic point – that people on benefit do not receive enough to live on. But they make the point differently, defining the issues in ways which they believe will best support their political case.[903] This is an area in which knowledge is used for particular purposes, and consideration of the implications for policy is itself a crucial part of the academic process.

This brings us back to the discussion in the introduction, about the nature of social policy as a field of study. Social policy has its own knowledge base, its own literature, and a set of common approaches. Studies in social policy have a recognisable style. But the terms in which policy is interpreted are strongly affected by perceptions of the social, economic and political context in which decisions are taken; insights from all the disciplines are important as a means of understanding that context. The remit of social policy is not confined to the academic world, and it cannot afford to emphasise its academic distinctiveness at the expense of these insights.

Box 20.1: Policy without theory

In a book which focuses on the relationship between theory and practice, it seems appropriate to pause and to ask whether theory is always the best way to go. Critiques of social policy can be scathing about responses which seem to be addressed to 'symptoms' rather than basic causes, or which 'paper over the cracks'. That position should be treated with some scepticism. There is nothing much wrong with dealing with symptoms, which at least will have some effect, and dealing with superficial issues like discomfort and misery is no bad thing. Dealing with 'fundamental' issues, by contrast, is often wrong-headed. Boxes 1.2 and 4.1 have pointed to some of the problems of relying

---

[903] e.g. P Townsend, 1979, *Poverty in the United Kingdom*, Harmondsworth; J Bradshaw, D Mitchell, J Morgan, 1987, Evaluating adequacy: the potential of budget standards, *Journal of Social Policy* 16(2) pp 165–181; S Stitt, D Grant, 1993, *Poverty: Rowntree revisited*, Aldershot: Avebury; D Gordon, L Adelman, K Ashworth, J Bradshaw, R Levitas, S Middleton, C Pantazis, D Patisos, S Payne, P Townsend, J Williams, 2000, *Poverty and social exclusion in Britain*, York: Joseph Rowntree Foundation.

on causal explanations. One of the main methods of policy development is to focus, not on what ought to work, but on what does.

There are many approaches to policy which try to find solutions to problems without necessarily understanding how a problem comes about. If, for example, governments are concerned about individual behaviour, like gambling or alcoholism, they do not need to start by analysing the causes, and they may not even need a detailed understanding of the problem. An obvious first step is to limit the opportunities to gamble or to obtain alcohol. This will not stop the problem from happening, but it will generally reduce the scale of the problem. The main limitation in practice is not the lack of knowledge, but the problem of enforceability; there is a limit to what governments can do effectively, and absolute bans, like prohibition, tend to be ineffective.

An approach which is based on taking practical steps rather than general principles is called 'pragmatism'. The test of whether a policy was beneficial, Edmund Burke argues, is not whether it fitted preconceived notions, but whether it worked. The way to develop policy, then, was incremental – trying things out, doing a little at a time, seeing what worked and what did not. It was better, in Burke's view, to end up with a patchwork of things that worked rather than a grand system which didn't. 'From hence arises, not an excellence in simplicity, but one far superior, an excellence in composition.'[904]

There are however some vexing problems with pragmatic approaches. The first is that things that work in some places do not necessarily work in others. A common experience of pilot programmes is that approaches which seem to be promising have much less effect when they are applied more generally. Pawson and Tilley argue that unless we understand the processes and relationships, it becomes almost impossible to identify which elements of a policy are having an effect.[905]

The second problem is that dealing with a problem in part is not necessarily good enough to make a difference, and it may make things worse. It may not seem unreasonable to suppose that where a problem has several dimensions, dealing with one of them will make the problem smaller and easier to solve. However, the effects of partial remedies may be no better, and may even be worse. Economists refer to this as the 'second best' problem: second-best solutions may be worse than apparently inferior choices. When, for example, inequality in education was identified as a key social issue, the response of governments in the UK was to improve equality of access, particularly in secondary schooling and higher education. Greater equality of access should in principle have led to less inequality overall. In practice, it is not clear that

---

[904] E Burke, (1790), *Reflections on the revolution in France*, New York: Holt, Rinehart and Winston , 1959, p 209.
[905] Pawson, Tilley, 1997.

---

it has done so; greater equality of access has made competition harder for those who are disadvantaged.[906] Where access is equalised and other issues are not, the outcomes in terms of examination results and opportunities for higher education seem to reinforce existing inequalities.

The third problem is that governments do not necessarily look in the right places. Welfare has been heavily influenced in recent years by policy in the United States, a notorious welfare laggard.[907] The influence of the US is partly a result of its political and economic status, partly a result of aggressive marketing (US providers have incentives to sell their products)[908] and partly a matter of convenience, because of the accessibility of English and of published information. By contrast, countries which are brimming with interesting approaches but where the language is inaccessible (like Finland) or which are less prominent politically (like New Zealand or the Netherlands) tend to be overlooked.

Fourth, regrettably, pragmatic approaches are slow. Measures have to be tried and tested, and that takes time.

In these circumstances, recourse to theory is inevitable. Evidence needs to be interpreted before it can be applied; policy-makers need to make an informed selection; often they need to do it in a hurry. The most common procedure is neither pragmatic nor theoretical, but what Etzioni calls 'mixed scanning' – switching back and forth between pragmatic and theoretical modes in order to make informed, practical decisions.[909]

Skills for social policy

Many people working in the field of social policy come to it as practitioners. The kind of work discussed in this book falls outside the common range of professional fields, like medicine, social work or policing, but there are roles within those professions where competence in social policy is a necessary complement to professional skills. Conversely, there are people working in social policy who work closely with practitioners, but they are not in practice themselves. We can dispose of one myth immediately: policy analysts, researchers and

[906] J Blanden, P Gregg, S Machin, 2005, *Intergenerational mobility in Europe and America*, London: London School of Economics, http://cep.lse.ac.uk/about/news/IntergenerationalMobility.pdf

[907] See R Goodin, B Headey, R Muffels, H-J Dirven, 2000, *The real worlds of welfare capitalism*, Cambridge: Cambridge University Press.

[908] See A Pollock, 2004, *NHS plc*, London: Verso.

[909] A Etzioni, 1977, Mixed scanning: a third approach to decision making, 87–97 of N Gilbert, H Specht, *Planning for social welfare*, Englewood Cliffs NJ: Prentice Hall.

advocates do not have to be able to do the job themselves to make relevant comments about a service. It is important for a social policy specialist to gain some working knowledge of the area which is being investigated. There is a jargon to be learned; professionals in the field will want to communicate their concerns; users ought to be able to explain about their experiences. The skills which are needed to do this, though, are not necessarily the skills of the relevant profession. It does not take a doctor to ask a patient about their treatment – in some circumstances, being associated with the medical profession may be an obstacle. It does not take a social worker to talk to the users of social work. (Despite the impression one may gain from the specialist literature, these are not just 'service users'. They are *people*.) It is important, though, to be sensitive to the situation that people are in, and to know how to ask them the questions which will produce the answers. These are the basic skills of a researcher, and there are many fields in which people learn those skills.

The academic skills that are looked for in social policy have been the main subject of this book, and at this stage it is possible to list them briefly:

- the application of theory to practice, including the process of analysis and classification;
- skills of research – identifying source material, finding it and organising it;
- the skills of selecting, processing and evaluating evidence; and
- skills of policy analysis, adopting a systematic approach which can recognise what is missing as well as what is happening.

A second set of skills relates to communication. Three kinds of communication, apart from those required in research, are particularly important:

- *work in committees*. A social policy practitioner may be a member of a committee, but just as likely is that the practitioner will be someone asked to inform a committee, as an officer, a researcher or a consultant. People working in these roles are not usually expected to argue a position, because outsiders do not make decisions; contributions in committee have to be informative and to the point. In academic seminars, students are encouraged to talk, to interact, to work out what they have to say. In a policy committee, the opposite is true. The contribution of policy analysis has to be relevant, brief and well-chosen.

- *presentations*. Policy analysts have to be able to present material directly and effectively, in a way which is tailored to a specific audience. Often the audience is non-specialised – a community group, a public meeting or elected members. The central test of a good presentation is not how the presenter performs, but how well the material is prepared and delivered for the people who are hearing it. Presentations need to be clear, accessible and engaging. Handouts, diagrams and clear layouts can help. Slide-shows and video material have to be comprehensible – there is no excuse for long sentences in tiny print, or academic references presented in a way that cannot immediately be related to the content. Most presentations need to be concise and delivered to time; it is very rare to hear someone coming out of a meeting complaining that the presentation didn't go on long enough.
- *reporting*. Reports are usually presented in writing. The tests applied to reports are simple enough: appropriateness to the audience and fitness for purpose. Sometimes several reports have to be presented at once – a short report for general readers, a fuller report for decision-makers, a technical report for specialists. Clarity is usually (but not always) preferred; references should be used sparingly, and always placed where someone can find them without having to flip through the papers (academic conventions are not helpful here, and the Harvard referencing system so beloved of universities may get in the way). Because the report will be the subject of detailed discussion, there should be a means of referring clearly and unambiguously to the main points, such as numbered paragraphs.

  Reports conventionally have an executive summary. This is not an introduction or guide to contents, nor is it a short report, though occasionally it may be the basis of a press release or website summary. The executive summary is a concise statement of the report's substantive content, and some readers will use in place of the report itself. It should be short, typically on one side of paper. Its purpose is to get decision-makers up to speed, and to focus the discussion. (One also has to say that it's a rare committee where everyone will have read all the papers before the meeting. I was instructed very early on in my career never to base a committee presentation on the expectation that people will have read more than the first page. I've found that to be good advice.)
- Many reports also include recommendations, though some decision-makers and committees may prefer statements of options, so that they are left to arrive at their own conclusions. Where

there are recommendations, they should be raised both in relation to the section which justify them, and separately in a distinct list with cross-references, enabling the points to be discussed either together or separately by decision-makers.

Third, there are skills of interaction and engagement with the policy process. They include:

- *networking and informal communications.* It helps if analysts are able to build a rapport with the people they are dealing with. It improves both the flow of information which will be used in the analysis, and it is likely to make the messages that policy specialist has to communicate more acceptable.
- *advice giving.* An adviser's task is not to tell people what to do; it is to identify options and potential outcomes so that they can make informed decisions. That calls for clarity, brevity and even-handedness.
- *negotiation and brokerage.* Some situations are adversarial, conflictual or based on competing issues. In such circumstances the task of the practitioner is often to determine what options are available that will best serve the competing interests, and so to establish what compromises are possible and appropriate.
- *advocacy.* The skills of advocacy have been referred to at several points in this book: it may refer to advocacy on behalf of a person or organisation, making and presenting a case on their behalf, but increasingly advocacy is identified with the process of voice, mingling argument with support and facilitation to enable service users to make their case to best effect.

The other part of what is required of practice in social policy is, obviously enough, academic knowledge – the kinds of issue discussed throughout this book. Much of the literature on social policy analysis is concerned with explaining what policy is, how it is developed and why it matters.[910] Understanding the process through which policy, too, is made is an important part of understanding social policy overall. But the study of social policy is not simply a study of policy, or process; it is very much concerned with outcomes. The analysis of social policy has to extend beyond description; it is important to make judgments and to consider choices for action. To do this, students and practitioners working in the subject area need to be able to collate information and

---

[910] See e.g. M Hill, 2005, *The public policy process*, Pearson/Longman.

to evaluate policy. They need to know what effects a policy is having, whether it is being implemented appropriately and, if necessary, what to do about it. The skills and approaches which are needed to do this kind of work are sometimes referred to as 'policy analysis', but it is a different kind of policy analysis from much of the material found in the academic literature. It is analysis *for* policy, rather than analysis *of* policy.

Social policy as a professional role

There is no profession of 'social policy' as such, but the applied focus of the subject, and its direct application to practice, mean that it is frequently used in a professional context. Many of the people who study social policy are practitioners in other fields, who use the insights and the approach of the subject as a complement to the work of their profession. Examples are social workers, teachers, housing officers, doctors, accountants, administrators, health workers, statisticians, community workers, planners, and research officers. Aspects of social policy are often taught in professional training as a complement to their studies. Then there are academic specialists who find themselves effectively working in social policy fields – sociologists, economists, psychologists, statisticians, management specialists and lawyers amongst them. And then there are a wide range of jobs in policy formation, public management or policy analysis or review, for which social policy offers a preparation. Social policy has many of the features of a profession – for example, the application of broad, theoretical knowledge in non-routine situations, the ethical character of the work, and the emphasis on public service. The reason why it is unlikely ever to become one is the first – the extensive contribution to social policy of people with an existing range of professional commitments, roles, education and professional organisations.

In the absence of a clearly defined professional role, the application of the methods and approaches of social policy has to be negotiated. Sometimes it will be part of a person's employment; sometimes it will be done by outsiders, as consultants, evaluators or researchers; it may be part of policy-making, possibly with elected authority, possibly with voluntary organisations; and it may be part of working in partnership with others in the public services.

Wildavsky emphasises the role of the policy analyst in 'speaking truth to power'.[911] However, the compromises that are called for

---

[911] A Wildavsky, 1993, *Speaking truth to power*, 4th ed., New Brunswick, NJ: Transaction Books.

can be problematic. There can be considerable pressure on analysts and researchers to provide analyses which are convenient, rather than truthful. At different times, I have been asked to alter the focus of the analysis being done, to change findings, to drop critical comments made by stakeholders, and to postpone disclosure of findings until after an election. I have had public statements I didn't agree with made on my behalf, and in one government-funded report had the facts I had reported in one passage replaced by other claims which said the opposite in the final publication. It all goes with the territory. Becker writes:

> officials usually have to lie. That is a gross way of putting it, but not inaccurate. Officials must lie because things are seldom as they ought to be. For a great variety of reasons, well-known to sociologists, institutions are refractory. They do not perform as society would like them to ... officials develop ways both of denying the failure of the institution to perform as it should and explaining those failures which cannot be hidden. An account of an institution's operation from the point of view of subordinates therefore casts doubt on the official line and may possibly expose it as a lie. [912]

He may be right about the pressures, but lies should be avoided. One of the characteristic elements of public service is that actions have to be accounted for; most actions are recorded, reported and open to scrutiny. Prevarication and misdirection might be excused; lies get found out.

Social policy as public service

The practitioners of social policy are public servants. That does not mean that they all work for government; it means, rather, that the work is driven by a dedication to public service, a commitment to welfare, and a sense of purpose. The huge variety of activities undertaken in the field makes it difficult to offer confident generalisations, but in general, social policy practitioners speak for others. The contemporary emphasis on governance, networks and partnerships has shifted the emphasis in social policy from technocratic expertise toward a more fluid, interactive approach to policy, heavily dependent on engagement with stakeholders and service users. Workers in the field of social policy

---

[912] G Becker, cited in A Grinyer, 1999, Anticipating the problems of contract social research, *Social Research Update* 27, http://sru.soc.surrey.ac.uk/SRU27.html

have become increasingly aware in recent years that there are different, often conflicting perspectives on issues, and it matters whose perspective is being taken. For practical purposes, stakeholders can be thought of in three main categories. The first category consists of organisations, officials or agencies who are engaged directly in policy making. These are often people with specialised knowledge. Beyond that, they are also likely to be people who may be able to take responsibility for action. Organisations, Catt and Murphy suggest, adopt three main positions in these processes. These are

- information provision: organisations pull together data from a range of sources
- 'contestation', or advocacy; organisation adopt positions in relation to policy questions
- synthesis – bringing together different types of information, position and voices.[913]

The second category of stakeholders includes people on the receiving end of policy – people who are directly affected by decisions. A decision to close a town's hospital, for example, affects the staff who work there; it affects people providing services in the vicinity, such as the local authority or voluntary organisations; it affects other services who rely on the hospital to do their own work, like general practitioners and community nurses; it affects patients, who may or may not be represented by patients' organisations; and it affects the general public, who even if they are not patients, may become so. Third, there are citizens. In a democracy, there are arguments not just for enlarging the information base, but for the general involvement of members of a political community in decision-making.[914] The concept of political 'participation' stretches from the rather limited engagement required in voting, through to active participation in deliberation and decision-making. In its most complete form, the concept of participative democracy offers an alternative approach to the policy process, but that is not the purpose of considering it here. The nub of the argument is that the public are the source of political legitimacy, and so that the public must be able to make the decisions. Every citizen is a stakeholder.

---

[913] H Catt, M Murphy, 2003, What voice for the people? categorising methods of public consultation, *Australian Journal of Political Science* 38(3) pp 407–421.

[914] A Richardson, 1983, *Participation*, London: Routledge and Kegan Paul.

David Byrne argues that social policy has to represent a commitment to welfare; but more than this, it has to think about how to achieve it.

> Speaking truth to power is not enough. Knowledge is a necessary condition of power; it is not a sufficient one. We need not just to say what is true, but to act on it. We have to think about agency and therefore about audiences with the potential for agency. [915]

The analysis of social policy in practice is, to some extent at least, a *technical* activity. It involves the application of social science techniques to practice in order to make judgments about policy. Policy analysts are commissioned or requested by policy-makers to collate essential information and to provide the basic material for judgments. The analyst is seen as an expert who uses a set of techniques – particularly economics, statistics or other forms of social science – to make an impartial, scientifically valid judgment. The technicalities mean that at times policy analysis sometimes seems devoted to blinding people with science; but, as Wildavsky comments, 'the technical base of policy analysis is weak.'[916] There are too many factors to consider, and too many normative issues, to treat policy analysis as a dispassionate, scientific activity.

Social policy is also a *political* activity. Wildavsky goes on: 'unlike social science, policy analysis must be prescriptive; arguments about correct policy ... cannot help but be wilful and therefore political.'[917] At the simplest level, social policy is political because its subject matter is political: the issues requiring analysis are often contentious and sensitive. This part of the book is less concerned with the technical issues in analysis than with interpretative skills. But policy analysis is also political in a broader sense: the work of policy analysts typically depends on networking, negotiation, and diplomacy. In a traditional hierarchy, roles and functions are determined by rules, commands and instructions. Because policy analysis is usually done by someone who is not working in the same team, policy analysts have to negotiate their relationships with policy-makers and practitioners. A good general rule, Majchrzak suggests, is that communication with policy-makers should start at the beginning of a project and should be maintained all the way

---

[915] D Byrne, P Spicker, 2009, *Ethical principles in social policy research and practice,* Social Policy Association conference, University of Edinburgh, p 10.

[916] A Wildavsky, 1993, *Speaking truth to power*, 4th ed., New Brunswick, NJ: Transaction Books, p 16.

[917] Wildavsky, 1993, p 16.

through it.[918] I expressed caution in Chapter 13 about systems that rely on good working relationships, because that implies an acceptance that services will fail if relationships break down, and formal structures should protect against routine failures. However, in a situation where there are no such structures and the activity is not routine, there may be no choice. It follows that maintaining good relationships is basic to the cooperation needed to do the job.

Social policy as an ethical activity

Social policy is partly political, and partly technical; but it is also an ethical activity. Public policy matters, in general, because it makes a difference to people; if it does not, it is using resources which ought to be making a difference somewhere else. Social policy analysis is important partly because of its effect on public policy, but also because the actions affect the staff, institutions and users of public services.

Ethical conduct in public services has been insufficiently investigated as a subject for discussion, and the literature on the subject is inadequate. Most of the strongest ethical discussions relate to professional activity, for example by doctors, teachers, nurses and social workers, whose position in relation to the public services is not fundamental to their ethical position; the ethics of the profession remain the same whether or not they are operating in the context of public service. Several aspects of professional ethics distance them from the aims of the organisations within which they work: they include individual responsibility for action, accountability to the standards of the profession through professional councils, and duties to disregard the aims of the organisation where they conflict with professional rules.

There are four main kinds of ethical rule which apply to work in the public services. They are:

- requirements for the agency to act ethically in relation to the community which it serves
- responsibilities to the agency
- individual requirements for ethical conduct, and
- ethical constraints not to abuse power or position.

Requirements for the agency to act ethically Public services have, evidently, responsibilities towards the public. I identified four main principles in the discussion of the values guiding policy in Chapter 11. These are

---

[918] A Majchrzak, 1984, *Methods for policy research*, London: Sage, pp 92–3.

beneficence, citizenship, issues of accountability and ethical procedures – that is, institutional constraints intended to ensure that agencies adhere to ethical principles.

Beyond this, many people working in public sector agencies would consider that they have further responsibilities which stem from their specific remit. Even if the task of an education department is substantially concerned with administration and finance, for example, it is rare to find an education department in which people have no sense of the value of education. The same kind of argument can be made about each of the public services. There are strong traditions: examples include the powerfully activist tradition of environmental health officers, the neo-liberal agenda associated with economic development, or the judgmental paternalism which reflects the influence of Octavia Hill in housing management.

Responsibilities to the agency The responsibilities which officials owe to the agency are often unfortunately unclear – unfortunately, because transgression of unpublished rules is not infrequently a reason for individual dismissal. There are different, and potentially conflicting, models of conduct. What, for example, should a public service worker do when offered the opportunity to combine work for the agency with an independent consultancy? Within a bureaucratic model, this would generally be unacceptable, because the role of each person has to be understood in the context of the role within the organisation. Within a management model, this is often encouraged as completing the range and diversity of actions within the agency, and the agency would expect to participate in the work. Within a professional model, the issue is a matter for the individual, and subject to the professional's judgment about meeting other responsibilities.

Saying that officials have an ethical responsibility to the agency is not equivalent to saying that they must comply with instructions; the duty of the official may be to ensure that the agency behaves ethically. 'Whistle-blowing' is sometimes called for when corrupt practice is identified within an organisation. The standard rule on whistle blowing is that people should first take such a complaint through the procedures and mechanisms provided within the organisation. This presumes that the organisation has procedures and lines of accountability which are able to deal with the problems. This is hugely problematic, especially where there are specific allegations made against individuals. The rules of natural justice mean that the person accused must have the opportunity to respond to allegations, and will remain responsible for other aspects of their work before the allegations are tested. The alternative, which is suspension pending investigation, is seen by many as punishment prior to trial – and is no less subject to abuse, because it could be used to remove people in a position to prevent problems.

Individual requirements The ethical position of each person follows a similar pattern: there are some general ethical rules, but there are also differences in codes in professional, bureaucratic and management-oriented organisations. An example of a general ethical rule is the view that no official should comply with breaches of human rights or crimes against humanity. That sounds straightforward enough, but millions of public servants have got it wrong in the course of the last century, and it is arrogant to suppose that, faced with such a policy, we would be sure to do the right thing. The defence of Maurice Papon, a senior official in the Vichy government, on trial for his role in deporting Jews, was that he thought he could help to make things better: to quit, he argued, would have been desertion.

An example of differences in codes of behaviour might be confidentiality. Confidentiality applies fairly strictly in the medical profession, but that has led to conflict with the bureaucratic structures of hospitals. (Currently the legal position is that notes made within a hospital belong to the hospital, not to the doctor.) Confidentiality does not apply within bureaucratic structures, because a report to one person is a report to the whole agency: a social worker in criminal justice, for example, is an officer of the court, and has a duty to disclose material to the court (at the risk of being held in contempt) which overrides professional discretion.

Both of these principles relate to general moral rules – rules which apply to everyone. Individual officers may also incur particular moral responsibilities in the course of their work. For example, a promise binds the person who makes it to the person who has been promised, not to every other person. The principle that people should respect the undertakings they make is usually referred to as 'integrity', though that term is also used in almost the opposite sense to indicate immunity from influence.

Constraints on the abuse of power A special category of ethical constraints refer to the abuse of power. It is legitimate to use power in circumstances where it is authorised: a teacher who disciplines a pupil, an environmental health officer who threatens to close a restaurant, or a probation officer who threatens to 'breach' a client who is considering breaking the law, are all using power, and are allowed to do so. Equally it is illegitimate to use the authority which stems from a role in public service in ways which are not directly compatible with the functions of that service. There are two obvious cases where the use of power is illegitimate: taking personal payments, and having sexual relationships with clients. What these have in common is that, even in circumstances where there are no explicit rules forbidding the action, and the action seems to be innocent, the fact that the official is in a position of power inevitably taints the relationship to the client.

The reference to seeming innocence might strike the reader oddly, but it is not always clear when action is improper. A housing association committee who are invited to dinner by an architect to discuss business, or a doctor who receives free goods from a drug company, are not being 'bribed', but there is clearly a material inducement. Sex between consenting adults is not a criminal offence. The borderlines are fuzzy, then; if they were not, it would not be so easy to fall foul of them. (I should also add a brief defence of the corruptors. When I worked as a housing officer, I was occasionally offered bribes, and there were times I had to make sure I did not see certain applicants alone. I controlled the only prospect of decent housing for people who had no resources and saw no alternatives. People do not offer bribes just because they are corrupt; sometimes they offer bribes because they are desperate. That increases the weight of moral responsibility that has to be borne by the official.)

Box 20.2: Corrupt practice

Corruption occurs when people pursue their own self-interest illegitimately. Private enterprise is based in the pursuit of self interest, and in that context it is usually approved of; the main issue is whether it is done legitimately. There may be cases where the pursuit of private interest is permitted in the system, for example through personal incentives. However, public officials are invested with the power to act for public purposes; when they subvert those purposes, or divert them to pursue their own interests instead, it becomes illegitimate.

Corruption is a major problem in the public services of developing countries.[919] The low income of public servants is an important part of the problem: it simply costs far more to bribe an official in a rich country, who stands to lose security, a good salary and fringe benefits, than it does to bribe an official in a poor one. A second element is the underdevelopment of market provision. It is common in some countries to have to pay a bribe to receive 'free' medical care, because there is no accepted system of charging; in other countries the fee would be open, predictable and legitimate. Third, systems for financial monitoring, and the cultures associated with them, are

---

[919] See Transparency International, 2005, *Corruption perception index,* at www. transparency.org/policy_research/surveys_indices/cpi/2005

often not strong enough to avoid the problems. The systems used in the west were developed in the nineteenth and early twentieth century: they include accounting practice, the division of financial authority and audit. The introduction of computerised information technology has undermined some of these systems, often removing important but poorly understood safeguards like multiple consents and personal signatures. Fourth, the ethos of the public sector may not be fully developed. In places where the public sector is underdeveloped, where business practice dominates, confidentiality can be considered more important than accountability or public awareness. Business practices are not necessarily appropriate to the needs of public services; this is visible in the influence of multinational corporations, which have often exacerbated problems through questionable financial practices.[920] That relates to the fifth factor, which is the lack of transparency. It is not coincidental that some of the world's most corrupt countries are also some of the least democratic, because transactions cannot effectively be subject to scrutiny.

Corruption is not, by any means, confined to poorer countries. Savedoff and Hussman argue that corruption is likely to occur whenever opportunities exist. The transparency of procedures, the existence of alternatives for consumers and the institutional structures all affect the scope for corrupt activity.[921] Where there is insufficient monitoring, policing or penalties, there is little reason for corrupt practice to stop.

The American Society for Public Administration code of ethics offers guidance intended generally for officials in the public sector; the central principles are to

- advance the public interest
- respect the law
- promote democratic participation
- strengthen social equity
- fully inform and advise those in authority
- demonstrate personal integrity

---

[920] S Hawley, 1999, Exporting corruption: privatization, multinationals and bribery, *Corner House Briefing 19*, www.thecornerhouse.org.uk/item. shtml?x=51975.

[921] W Savedoff, K Hussmann, 2006, Why are health systems prone to corruption?, in *Transparency International, global corruption report 2006*, www.transparency.org/content/download/4816/28503/file/Part%20 1_1_causes%20of% ; and see R Klitgaard, 1988, *Controlling corruption*, Berkeley: University of California Press.

- promote ethical organizations, and
- strive for professional excellence.[922]

The journal *Policy Evaluation* is more prescriptive: it suggests that policy analysts have a moral responsibility to take account the side effects of what they do, to be aware that their recommendations are subject to uncertainty, and to examine the risks they are exposing people to.[923] An activity which is profoundly political and ethical in its character can hardly be constructed in a dispassionate, technical, non-normative framework. There is hardly any activity in social policy that has no ethical dimensions.

It is important to recognise that social policy work is heavily constrained. Policy formation begins from a wide range of sources – ideas, networks, coalitions of interests, agencies, and so forth. Most social policy in practice, by contrast, begins with a policy that has already been decided and set, usually by someone else. Policy analysts and practitioners have only a limited scope, and limited power, to make changes in policy. The main way that changes can be brought about is by working through the formal process – pointing to undesired implications for policy, giving advice which favours better policy, and providing a focus for stakeholders who share the analyst's concerns to exercise their influence. In circumstances where a practitioner actively disagrees with a policy, the options are very limited. In serious cases, such as breaches of ethical codes, this may imply withdrawal from engagement with the policy (which generally means leaving it to someone else who does not have the same reservations), possibly including resignation. This, however, is a counsel of despair, reflecting the inability to change the policy internally, and it removes the prospect of affecting other aspects of policies in the future. Academics sometimes refer to engagement with practice as 'getting your hands dirty'. There is more than one way to read that metaphor. If you really want to avoid political and moral conflicts, you should consider taking up a different line of work.

---

[922] ASPA, 2013, Code of ethics, www.aspanet.org/public/ASPA/Resources/Code_of_Ethics/ASPA/Resources/Code%20of%20Ethics1.aspx?hkey=acd40318-a945-4ffc-ba7b-18e037b1a858

[923] Policy Evaluation, 2001, *Ethical Policy Analysis*, 7(1) pp 15–17.

ISSUE FOR DISCUSSION

Social policy practitioners are not only asked to promote welfare; they may also need to take action to coerce, direct, restrain or punish people. Often those people will be vulnerable or disadvantaged. When is it legitimate to use power in a way that is contrary to the interests of service users?

APPENDICES

Social policy: a guide to sources

Most of the material written about social policy as a subject dates from the period after the Second World War, though there are some notable exceptions. Theoretical material does not date very rapidly, but social conditions are in constant flux, and policies change like the sands of the desert. There is, in the study of social policy, something of a fetish of the new – a tendency to disregard older material, and to assume that newer material has greater contemporary relevance. The opposite may be true: older material is often useful for its theoretical relevance or method, while even the newest material is vulnerable to changes in policy or circumstances which lead to it being dated before it appears.

The Internet The World Wide Web (www)has become an invaluable source for accessible material on social policy. The place to begin is with my own website, *An introduction to social policy*, at www2.rgu. ac.uk/politics/socialpolicy/ This site gives a brief introduction to a range of topics in social policy, and links to other sites.

Because many social policy documents are ephemeral, the Web offers an excellent complement to publication – rapid and easily referenced. Government documents in particular have become widely accessible; many legal jurisdictions now place case reports on the Web. *Governments on the web*, which includes links to government sites around the world, is available at www.gksoft.com/govt/en/

New media Apart from the web, in recent years there has been a flurry of new technologies, including blogs, Twitter and RSS feeds. The immediacy of these sources also runs the risk that they will not last – it takes considerable dedication to run a Twitter feed – and I am sceptical that links in a book will stay up to date for long. There is a useful initial directory at http://docressocialpolicy.wordpress.com/2012/01/25/ hello-world/ My own blog at http://paulspicker.wordpress.com can be accessed from my website; it includes more than sixty of my published papers on open access.

Books Textbooks are used to summarise material, and to offer a range of differing opinions. Their main use is to allow people to gain an initial overview of a field; students can absorb the material and move on, occasionally referring back for different purposes. Most students using this book will also need to get a descriptive text outlining social policy and services in their own country. The facts in such books date rapidly, however, and any information should be supplemented by drawing down facts from sites on the internet.

Academic journals Academic journals are 'refereed', which means that articles are scrutinised by specialists before acceptance, The articles in journals are often difficult, and the quality is very mixed, but they are generally more up to date and much shorter than textbooks. With the advent of electronic libraries, articles in academic journals have become much easier to access in recent years. Most readers can read ten articles in the time it takes to read one book, and they will probably have covered far more ground. The leading journals in the subject are the *Journal of Social Policy*, *Social Policy and Administration* and the *Journal of European Social Policy*. There is also potentially useful information in *Critical Social Policy*, the *International Journal of Social Welfare* and *Policy & Politics*.

Collected papers Some books are collections of articles; readers can draw from them in much the same way as from a journal. Although books in the subject are also refereed, there is rather more freedom in collected books to theorise, to speculate, and to present interim conclusions. This means that the quality of collections is variable, but it has also been an important stream of ideas on social policy; much of the feminist literature in the subject, for example, has developed in this format.

Most books in social policy tend to be specialised, often putting forward a particular argument or taking a position. The contrast between views and findings from different sources becomes more striking as more ground is covered, and the wider the ground covered, the better equipped the student is to deal with the subject. Student 'readers' are, consequently, worth a special note; these are edited collections which bring together some of the major papers on a subject. They can be invaluable both as a way of extending one's range and as a fruitful source of arguments and material.

Monographs, pamphlets and working papers One of the undesirable side-effects of using academic referees is to delay publication. This, coupled with pressure to present material in an appropriate academic framework, means that books and journals are rarely able to carry basic research reports. Much of this kind of material appears instead in small and ephemeral publications, produced by academic institutions (e.g. the LSE CASE Programme), research agencies (the Institute for Fiscal Studies), charitable foundations (the Joseph Rowntree Foundation), campaigning groups (the Child Poverty Action Group) and public sector agencies. Some of the most important papers in social policy have appeared in this kind of format. It used to be difficult to track it down, but the growth of the Internet has made this kind of material much more accessible.

Newspapers and periodicals There is always a problem with books, since however accurate the book is when published, new legislation and other developments soon make parts of it out of date. Newspapers and weeklies are helpful. Most reporting on social policy is second- or third-hand, however; most journalists are not very well informed on the subject, and newspaper reports cannot be relied on. The kinds of research monograph referred to above are important sources for many journalists.

Statistical sources Official statistics have their problems, but they are a quick and easy way to check basic facts. There are many easily accessible international sources available. Columbia University Libraries have many international links at http://library.columbia.edu/subject-guides/social-sciences/stats/int.html and the United Nations has links to national statistical offices at http://unstats.un.org/unsd/methods/inter-natlinks/sd_natstat.asp

Primary sources In the discussion of research methods, I outlined a number of ways in which information might be drawn from original sources. Even for students working at a basic level, information can often be obtained directly from government, politicians, and political parties: examples are consultative documents, pamphlets, and manifestos. It is harder to get to administrative decision-makers, though not impossible by any means. Voluntary groups often bring together observations and comments from stakeholders and service users.

Further reading

Social Policy: theory and practice has been written for readers from around the world. The reading and source material which is referred to in this section, like most of the references in the book, have been selected because they are relevant to people in a wide range of circumstances. That means, however, that this book cannot hope to provide the kind of practical, up-to-date information that is the staple of textbooks in specific countries. In almost every case, this book needs to be supplemented with other material, to relate it to contemporary issues and practice in the particular context where it is being read.

The suggestions for further reading, then, are based on a special type of source material, developing the general and theoretical issues explored in this book.

The introduction The central statements of the nature of social policy were made many years ago; the most important are in R M Titmuss, *Essays on the welfare state*, (London: Allen and Unwin 1976) and D V Donnison et al, *Social policy and administration revisited* (London: Allen and Unwin 1975). There have been many restatements since, and many attempts to redefine the field; however, readers will understand that I think these works have led in the wrong direction, steering social policy away from the issues that most need attention.

Jonathan Bradshaw has posted a lecture on 'What is social policy?' at www.youtube.com/watch?v=7zUv4bHdHMc Readers should be able to identify some points of difference in our views (for example, on the importance of social administration) but he is recognisably referring to the same basic concepts as this book.

Part 1: Social policy and society There is an abundance of material outlining basic approaches to sociology, as well as collections of readings which offer an insight into a range of viewpoints. Most general texts on sociology will help to outline the social context, the relationship of the individual to society, and issues like class, gender and race. Rather less is available on the direct relevance of sociological concepts to social policy, which tends to be assumed.

The literature on social problems and needs is diffuse, likely to focus in detail on specific topics like poverty or disability, and much more likely to be specific to the circumstances of particular countries. It is important to read widely. The *Journal of Social Policy* and *Critical Social Policy* are most relevant.

Part 2: Policy The material in this part is probably the best served by the theoretical literature. Michael Hill's books *The public policy process* (Pearson Longman, 2012) and *The policy process: a reader* (Prentice Hall, 1997) offer respectively an introductory text and key readings. The literature on principles and values is extensive, but it is dogged by inaccuracies, misconceptions and political bias: misrepresentations of topics like pluralism, socialism, equality and social justice are rife. My own work in this area includes *Social policy in a changing society* (written with Maurice Mullard) (Routledge, 1997), and *Liberty, equality, fraternity,*

(Policy Press, 2006). The coverage of welfare strategies is mixed, but it is informed by some of the best-known writings in the subject, such as the work of Richard Titmuss. The most recent reader is P Alcock (ed) *Welfare and well-being* (Policy Press, 2001). David Reisman's critical synopsis, *Richard Titmuss: welfare and society* (Heinemann, 1977) is also helpful.

The coverage of welfare states and comparative social policy has become a small industry in its own right: Esping Andersen's *Three worlds of welfare capitalism* (Polity, 1990) has been the leading text, but there are many more accessible texts which offer rewarding insights. C Pierson, F Castles (eds), *The welfare state reader* (Polity, 2006) is a useful collation of readings. The leading journals are *Social Policy and Administration* and the *Journal of European Social Policy*.

Part 3: Social administration The literature on social administration is not well covered in social policy texts, and it is difficult to find academic discussions that take a synoptic view across many disciplines. Part of the field has been colonised by writers on public management : useful general guides are J Erik Lane, *The public sector* (Sage, 2000), and N Flynn, *Public sector management* (Sage, 2012). There is some coverage in books on economics: Nick Barr's textbook, *The economics of the welfare state* (Oxford University Press, 2012) has become less accessible to non-economists in recent editions, but is still worth referring to. The leading journal in this area is probably *Policy & Politics*; *Public Administration* and *Public Money and Management* are often useful.

Part 4: The methods and approaches of social policy Much of the literature on policy analysis and evaluation in practice is American: examples are M Patton, D Sawicki, J Clark, *Basic methods of policy analysis and planning* (Pearson, 2012), for policy analysis, or Michael Scriven's *Evaluation thesaurus* (Sage, 1991). Despite the centrality of this material, there is less directly related to social policy than might be anticipated; this book goes some way to fill the gap. The outstanding theoretical contribution to the field in recent years, though I disagree with much of it, has to be R Pawson, N Tilley, *Realistic evaluation* (Sage, 1997).

Texts on social research tend to be misleading; it is difficult to write a book on research without giving general advice, but in a context where methods have to be closely adapted to circumstances, general advice often turns out to be wrong. Probably the best of the recent texts (even if it does call interviews in depth 'unstructured interviews') is S Becker and A Bryman (eds) *Understanding research for social policy and practice* (Policy Press, 2012); also useful is C Seale, *Social research methods: a reader* (Routledge, 2004) and N Blaikie, *Designing social research* (Polity, 2010). *Social research update*, at http://sru.soc.surrey. ac.uk/, offers a helpful internet resource.

Glossary

Access to welfare Before people can receive welfare, either by applying or being identified as likely recipients, they have to put themselves in the position where welfare might be provided – for example learning about the service, claiming, or being able to get to an office. This is the issue of 'access'.

Accountability The process through which services can be made to answer for their actions.

Administrative law Laws which regulate the administrative processes through which services are to be delivered.

Adverse selection Commercial firms choose which demands they serve, and who they will supply: so, insurance companies may refuse 'bad risks'.

Affirmative action The policy adopted in the United States to correct the disadvantages of some groups relative to others by giving people from disadvantaged groups special treatment. The nearest term in the UK is ➜ positive discrimination.

Aims What a policy is supposed to achieve.

Ambulatory care In health care, services which people can use without requiring a stay in a hospital bed.

Ameliorism The 18th-century belief that the world is gradually improving through human effort.

Atomisation A social situation where everyone is isolated from everyone else.

Audit Initially a financial term, it has come to stand for inspection, evaluation and processes of administrative accountability.

Authority The right to make decisions affecting others.

Autonomy A person's capacity for free action, which requires lack of restraint, the power to act, and the ability to choose. In relation to organisations and professional activity, autonomy is based on delegated authority to make independent decisions.

Benchmark A standard expressed as a performance indicator, and used to gauge progress in relation to process.

Beneficence. The intention to do good rather than harm; the intention to produce good consequences.

Black box A technique based on reviewing effects without looking at internal processes.

Bloc A group of people who share common characteristics, for example. women, minority ethnic groups or older people.

Brandeis brief In the US, a legal plea which makes it possible for evidence about the social implications of an action to be taken into account.

Budget A financial plan in quantitative form.

Bureaucracy A hierarchical organisation run through a system of rules.

Bureaucrat A person working in a hierarchical organisation who performs official functions.

Capitalism In Marxism, a system of production in which the means of production is owned by a capital-owning class in order to make profits. The term is sometimes used to indicate the general character of modern economic systems.

Care The provision of services to maintain or improve people's circumstances.

Care management/care plans In community care, the selection of a package of services for a client from a range of available options.

Casework Individuated responses made to issues in the context in which they are presented.

Census A comprehensive count of every person or every issue.

Choice. Autonomous action; the selection of options.

Christian democracy A form of conservative thought, strong in European countries, which emphasises moral restraints and responsibilities.

Citizenship A collection of rights, argued by Marshall to include basic social rights and the 'right to welfare'.

Claims A call for resources, from any source; the specific process of applying for certain benefits or services.

Class action In the US, the right of people to sue as a group.

Classes Groups in society with different economic positions, variously understood in terms of the relationship to the means of economic production; groups with different economic capacity and power; or groups with different social ➔ status.

Community A group of people linked by common characteristics or culture; a group of people linked together through social relationships; people living in a defined geographical area; people who share a set of common interests.

Community action ➔ community organisation.

Community care The provision of support and practical assistance to people who have special needs, to make it possible for them to live in their own homes or as 'normal' an environment as possible. The term is, however, highly ambiguous.

Community development ➔ community organisation.

Community education Development of the social skills and collective potential of disadvantaged people.

Community organisation The attempt to develop political mobilisation and collective action in disadvantaged communities.

Community social work A form of social work which takes account both of individuals and of their social interactions in order to increase their potential in a social context.

Community work A collective approach to the problems of communities. ➔ neighbourhood work; community social work; community organisation; community education.

Comparative need ➔ Need determined by comparison with others who are not in need.

Comparative social policy Cross-national and international studies in social policy.

Conflict theory The argument that welfare is an outcome of conflict between different power blocs in society.

Conservatism A set of political beliefs emphasising social order and traditional patterns of social relationships.

Constitutional law Law which sets the framework through which policies are exercised.

Consultation. The process of asking stakeholders, service users and citizens for their views; an essential element of voice and deliberative democracy.

Contested concepts Ideas which have different, conflicting alternative meanings, so that no agreement about them is really possible.

Control group A group of people used for comparison in order to establish the effectiveness of a measure.

Convergence In comparative social policy, the argument that different countries are coming to act similarly in the face of common pressures or circumstances; in the European Union, agreement on basic principles for action.

Corporatism The exercise of power by established corporate interests: socially, a hierarchical structure of power characterised by restricted competition between a limited number of corporate groups; economically, a system of economic organisation dominated by corporate structures; politically, a system of interest group representation in which the state negotiates with and seeks to include other agencies.

Cost-effectiveness Achieving one's aims at minimum cost.

Crisis A turning point, external shock or long-standing contradiction. The term is particularly used by Marxists to emphasise the instability they argue characterises modern industrial society.

Critical incident technique A focus on non-routine events as a means of clarifying processes and problems.

Critical social policy A view of social policy which emphasises the importance of all of structured inequality and seeks to interpret problems and policy in terms of the patterned relationships of social division.

Culture Patterns of social behaviour, which may refer to language and history, common experiences, norms and values, and life-style.

Cultural diffusion The process through which cultures are shared and affect each other.

Customers People who buy services; a cant term for service users, used to imply a market relationship where there is choice, mutual consent and the right to exit.

Deadweight An aspect of inefficiency in service delivery, when help is given to those whose need would have been alleviated without that help.

Decentralisation The devolution of decisions to smaller geographical units.

Deconstruction The process of unpicking existing constructions of ideas by questioning or rejecting assumptions about their relationships.

Deductive approaches A pattern of research based on the generation of propositions which can then be tested.

Degeneracy A combination of genetic defects that were once believed to be the root of social problems.

Deliberative democracy A model of democracy based on dialogue, cooperation, negotiation and voice.

Demand The amount of service that might be used if the service was supplied at a particular price.

Democracy Government 'of the people, for the people, by the people'; the term is variously understood in terms of political ideals, approaches to governance or systems of government.

Dependency A state of reliance on the support of social services, which may be financial, physical or psychological.

Deterrence Reducing demand for services by making services deliberately awkward to reach, unpleasant or humiliating.

Dilution A means of reducing what is offered to clients by cutting the quality of what is offered, rather than refusing service altogether.

Direct discrimination Deliberate and overt ➜ discrimination.

Disability A set of problems and issues related to physical or mental capacity, understood in a social context; the functional restriction which results from impairment. ➜ impairment and handicap.

Discretion The scope for independent judgment which is left to officials when no rules apply.

Discrimination Adverse selection which places some people in an inferior position. ➜ direct discrimination; indirect discrimination; institutional racism.

Disincentives to work Factors that lead to people choosing not to work; the argument that benefits, in rewarding people for not working, influence choices about work.

Domiciliary care In health and social care, care delivered in people's own homes.

Earnings-related Benefits which vary according to previous earnings.

Economies of scale The ability that large agencies have to make savings on purchasing or production that smaller agencies do not have.

Effective demand Current existing demand, as distinct from potential demand.

Effectiveness Achieving one's aims.

Efficiency The minimisation of waste; production of units at the minimum cost per unit.

Elasticity The extent to which a change in one factor will stimulate a response in another. The 'elasticity of demand', for example, generally refers to the extent to which demand will change as a result in a change in price.

Elective surgery Surgery which people choose to have, like cosmetic surgery.

Eligibility The criteria for whether or not people should receive a service or benefit.

Empirical Factual, based on observation or experience.

Empowerment The process through which people who are relatively powerless can gain more power.

Equality The removal of disadvantage. Note that equality does not mean sameness or uniformity.

Equity A principle of fairness: like cases should be treated alike. → 'substantive' and 'procedural' fairness.

Ethnic groups A group of people distinguished from the main population by differences in history and culture.

Evaluation Judgments about policy; a stage of the policy process where effectiveness is judged; or the process of appraising policy.

Exclusion People who are not part of networks of solidarity and social responsibility, because they are left out of social networks (for example, not being entitled to social protection); because they are shut out (like migrants), or because they are pushed out through stigma.

Eugenics The belief that society can be improved through the selective breeding of people.

Executive The executive branch of government is the branch which implements policy once made.

Exit Ceasing to use a service; the term is also used for the power to withdraw from the service.

Expressed need ➔ Need which people say they have.

Externalities Economic consequences which go beyond the people involved in a transaction.

Family A special kind of social unit defined in terms of a particular network of personal and social relationships and responsibilities; most usually it refers to circumstances where people who are related by birth or marriage live together.

Family resemblance A term used in the process of classification through the identification of inter-related clusters of characteristics.

Fascism A form of collective authoritarianism in which the state, the race or the nation is more important than any individual person.

Felt need ➔ Need which people feel they have.

Feminism The general class of beliefs that women should not be viewed or treated in a way inferior to men. There are many different branches, including ➔ liberal feminism, ➔ marxist feminism and ➔ radical feminism.

Filtering A stage in rationing: a process of sifting out people who may or may not receive provision subsequently.

Financial rationing The control of expenditure.

Fiscal welfare Titmuss's term for redistribution through the tax structure.

Flat-rate Benefits paid at a single rate, by contrast with 'earnings-related' benefits which vary according to previous earnings (and so the level of contribution made).

The 'focus' of policy The kind of people or social units who the policy directly affects.

Forecasting Predicting the future on the basis of what has happened so far.

Freedom The absence of restraint and the capacity to act.

Friendly societies Mutual aid organisations developed in Britain for the protection of their members.

Functional Serving a function (in functionalism, 'useful' or serving a purpose), or pertaining to the ability to perform a function. A 'functional division of labour' is a division of labour which reflects the performance of functions, while a 'functional impairment' is an impaired ability to do something.

Functionalism A mode of analysis which argues that societies change through adaptation to changing circumstances. Adaptations are 'functional' if they support social processes and 'dysfunctional' if they do not.

Funded schemes Social security and pensions schemes which build up and pay people from a fund.

Gender roles A set of social roles, or particular expectations, which subsequently condition the activities undertaken by women and men.

Generalisation In most contexts, the process of applying particular insights more widely; in French social policy, the process of extending solidaristic networks to include as many people as possible.

Generative mechanism A cause; a set of factors and process which together produce an effect.

Genericism Generic workers work with a range of techniques with a range of different client groups.

Globalisation A process of increased communication, commerce and inter-connectivity which is seen as leading to increasingly homogenised social, cultural and economic behaviour across the world.

Goals. Loosely used to refer to aims; more specifically, operationalised objectives which are represented by specific intended outcomes or targets.

Green politics A set of political beliefs which rejects mainstream concerns, emphasising in their place conservation of the environment, the use of natural resources, and the role of humans in relation to other species and the natural world.

Gross National Product The value of a country's total production; a country's total income.

Handicap Disadvantage in a particular role or set of social roles as a result of disability.

Hawthorne effect The effect of being observed on the behaviour of the research subject.

Health Maintenance Organisations In the US, organisations which provide medical care to members for a subscription.

Health services Services for medical care and related activities.

Hegemony The maintenance of values and norms designed to further the interests of a dominant class.

Hereditability An explanation of variance between cases in terms of heredity.

Hidden curriculum In education, the idea that part of what schools teach is a concealed means of conveying rules about social behaviour. The idea is linked with ➔ hegemony.

Hierarchy A structure of power or accountability in which people are placed above and below others in some kind of rank order.

Historicism The argument that there are 'laws' of history or inexorable movements.

Homelessness Having no accommodation; having unsatisfactory or insecure accommodation.

Horizontal redistribution Redistribution between people in different social circumstances, without necessarily having regard to resources.

Household A group of people who live together, sharing resources and responsibilities.

Hypothesis A speculative proposition formed in a way which allows it subsequently to be tested.

Ideal type A theoretical model or template against which reality can be compared.

Ideology A set of inter-related beliefs and values.

Impairment A physical or mental condition implying some abnormality or loss.

Implementation The process through which policy is put into practice.

Incapacity for work The inability to continue with one's employment because of ➜ impairment or an inability to work generally because of ➜ disability.

Incentive A potential gain which motivates people to change their behaviour in order to receive it.

Incidence The rate at which new problems or issues occur.

Inclusion Bringing people into networks of social support; countering ➜ exclusion.

Income smoothing The effect intended by redistributing money from one part of a person's life-cycle to another.

Indicator targeting Targeting aimed at general characteristics, like regions, age groups, gender etc.

Indicators Figures which are used to sum up data about social issues.

Indirect discrimination Actions which, because they select some people, have an adverse effect in other ways.

Individualism A view of people which sees each person separately as being able to take action independently from other people in society. The individual is able to choose options, undertake obligations, make agreements, or to try to gain redress against injustice.

Individualistic policies Policies which focus separately on each person who has needs or problems.

Inductive approach An approach to research which begins by collecting material and subsequently looks for patterns and relationships.

Industrial-achievement/performance model of welfare Titmuss's model of welfare in which welfare is seen as a complement to industrial production and economic policy.

Inequality The position where people are advantaged or disadvantaged in social terms.

Informal sector Care not provided through formal organisations, but by communities, friends, neighbours and kin.

Inputs The resources which go into welfare provision.

Insertion The French term for ➔ integration or social inclusion; used in particular to refer to the integration of people who are 'marginal' or 'excluded' into social networks.

Institutional racism The production of racial disadvantage through the policy or practice of an agency.

Institutional welfare Model of welfare in which welfare is accepted as a normal part of social life.

Integration The incorporation of people into the available social networks.

Intellectual disability A process of slow intellectual development, leading cumulatively to slow development of physical and social functioning. The term used varies widely between countries and over time.

Intensity The depth or severity of a problem.

Inter-subjectivity The process through which understanding develops in society through a series of shared perceptions and beliefs.

Interest groups Pressure groups which are seeking to influence policy in ways which will benefit them directly. They are also referred to as 'representational' groups.

Interests Whatever increases people's ➔ well-being or ➔ utility.

Judiciary The judicial branch of government adjudicates on the operation of the law. *See* executive; legislative.

Key intervention Strategic intervention at the point in a system which will produce a range of desired effects.

Key worker A nominated worker with the main responsibility for a particular case.

Law A system of rules and procedures through which the actions of individuals and people collectively can be regulated by the state.

Leadership The role of managers in general; the aspects of their role relating to relationships with subordinates; the personal attributes of leaders; the task of motivating and influencing staff; the situation of being in charge; methods for the achievement of tasks; a pattern of behaviour; the coordination of teamwork; or the desire to invade other countries.

Left-wing Political beliefs identified with ➔ social democracy, ➔ socialism or ➔ Marxism, which are broadly in favour of collective social provision and the reduction or mitigation of disadvantage.

Legislative The legislative branch of government which makes laws, as distinct from ➔ 'executive' and ➔ 'judicial' branches.

Legitimation crisis Neo-marxists argue that the welfare state's attempt to legitimate capitalism is in conflict with attempts to foster the accumulation of capital, posing a crisis of legitimation.

Less eligibility The deterrent principle, in the English Poor Law, that the position of the person receiving support had to be less 'eligible' (less to be chosen) than that of the poorest independent labourer.

Liberal feminism The argument that women should have equal opportunities to men.

Liberalism A set of beliefs, related to individualism, which argue that individuals must be left free to make choices and that society is best able to regulate itself without state intervention.

Life cycle The series of changes in condition and circumstance which a person goes through in the course of his or her life – including, for example, childhood, adulthood and old age.

Lone parents The heads of families in which there is only one parent, through divorce, death of a partner or birth outside marriage.

Macro-economic policies Policies for the whole economy.

Manager A person who runs an organisation: the ideal type of a manager is a person who is specialised in the organisation of services, and who has general responsibility for the operation of functions taking place under his or her command.

Marginal utility The change in utility which follows from a small change in circumstances from one point to another.

Marginality People who are peripheral to social networks or mechanism of ➔ solidarity: ➔ exclusion.

Market failure Circumstances where economic markets are unable to perform as they should in economic theory because practical limitations (such as location or imperfect information) prevent mechanisms from operating effectively.

Marketisation The process of making the delivery of services more like the delivery of services in the private market, achieved either through privatisation or by turning social services into something like a market. ➔ quasi-markets.

Marxism A set of beliefs based on the idea that society is a conflict between economic classes.

Mass media The means through which people receive information. The media include the press, television, radio and indeed any other form of mass communication used for the purpose.

Means tests The process of distributing benefits or services subject to a test of income or wealth.

Mental handicap ➔ intellectual disability.

Mental illness A complex set of disturbed behaviours, perceptions and thought processes.

Methodological individualism The assumption for the purposes of analysis that society is composed of individuals, used for example as the basis of much economic theory.

Methodology The study of research methods; the rationale used for the selection of methods.

Mixed economy of welfare The description of welfare in terms of ➔ welfare pluralism.

Model A statement about the relationships between a group of factors. Some models are ideal types, and others are generalised statements about relationships, but others may be based in specific associations and described as equations.

Moral hazard The problem of insuring people who are able to control the circumstances which might produce a claim, like pregnancy or unemployment.

Multicollinearity A problem arising in statistics when variables are not truly independent of each other, so that some effects are duplicated while the influence of some important factors may be disguised.

Mutual aid The principle whereby people join with others to provide help or support for each other. Often this takes the form of mutual insurance in the event of difficulties.

Myth In social science, a belief which, true or not, affects the way that people behave.

National efficiency A term used at the turn of the century to indicate the physical capacity of people in the nation to serve their country.

Nationhood A cluster of ideas associated variously with a common history, culture or language, geographical location or membership of a political community.

Natural justice Procedural ➔ rights to be heard, and to be judged impartially.

Needs The kinds of problem which people experience; requirements for some particular kind of response; a relationship between problems and the responses available.

Neighbourhood work Developing the networks and relationships in a community in order to facilitate social action.

Non-decisions Decisions not to decide, and so to keep things as they are.

Non-takeup Failure to claim benefits and services to which one is nominally entitled.

Normal In keeping with ➔ norms.

Normalisation Enabling people to live autonomously, as others do; empowering people to act so as to participate in society.

Normative Concerned with values, expectations, standards or rules against which policies and practice can be judged.

Normative need ➔ Need identified according to a ➔ norm – probably a standard set by experts.

Norms Rules – that is, expectations coupled with sanctions (or penalties) for non-compliance; standards which are set against which actions may be judged.

Occupational welfare Welfare provided through the workplace.

Operationalisation The process through which concepts are translated into terms that can be worked with and acted on.

Parameters Assumptions about a model which can first be taken not to change, then relaxed and re-examined to discover its implications.

Participant observation A technique of social research in which the researcher seeks to become part of the process which is being studied.

Participation The process of taking part in decision-making.

Partnership An arrangement between agencies to work jointly or form policy together.

Paternalism The principle of doing things for people's benefit without their consent.

Path dependency The tendency for established institutional processes to determine what policy is possible in the future.

Pathological theories Theories which see the cause of a problem in terms of the unit which has the problem.

Patriarchy A society in which men have power over women.

Performance indicators Numerical goals or targets used to monitor how a service is performing, to test progress, and to achieve specified outcomes or standards.

Person A social actor, defined in terms of social roles and relationships to others.

Personal social services The range of services available outside health, housing, education and social security which deal with people's personal needs. This includes social work, residential care and domiciliary care.

Planned Programme Budget System (PPBS) A system of financial control in which after total expenditure has been set, areas of activity are then allocated budgets and subject to limits.

Pluralism The idea that there are many kinds of groups in society which interact in various ways; in the analysis of power, it is argued that this multiplicity of actors has the effect of diffusing power. Alternatively, a value position which argues for diversity and multiplication of the number of actors as something valuable in itself.

Policy A decision or set of decisions about a course of action; a defined sphere of political activity or governance.

Policy analysis In some literature, the analysis of policy; elsewhere, analysis for policy, including policy appraisal and evaluation.

Politics Understood narrowly, the exercise of government; more generally, any activity in which there is some form of collective social action, or in which power is exercised.

Positive discrimination ➔ affirmative action. The term in the UK goes beyond equality to an argument for preferential treatment.

Positive rights Rights which are linked to some kind of effective sanction, such as a legal norm.

Positivism The view that scientists are dealing with an external reality.

Postmodernism The argument that society has moved beyond previously established patterns, becoming increasingly diverse and unpredictable.

Potential demand Demand which might arise in certain conditions, as opposed to effective demand, which is that which currently exists.

Poverty A complex term denoting material deprivation, lack of resources, disadvantage in social relationships and severe hardship. Because the term is used morally to convey conditions which are unacceptable, the definition is much disputed.

Poverty trap The position which arises with means-tested social security benefits when benefits are withdrawn as people's needs decrease.

Power The ability to direct the conduct of others who accept that direction.

Pragmatism An approach which is opposed to changes made on ideological grounds and favours finding out what works before introducing it.

Predictions Statements about the future.

Pressure groups Groups which seek to influence the political process, either to represent their own interests or to promote causes.

Prevalence A measure of how frequently a problem or issue is found.

Primary care In health care, services provided without requiring people to come to a hospital. The distinction is slightly arbitrary and for that reason some of the literature refers instead to ➜ ambulatory care.

Principles Guides to action: in relation to welfare, the term particularly relates to normative statements about what should be done.

Priorities An order of precedence decided between competing claims.

Private sector The provision of services for profit by independent producers. Some commentators include non-profit provision by ➜ mutual aid as part of the private sector.

Probability sampling Selection of subjects for research in order to reflect the characteristics of a wider population. ➜ purposive sampling.

Procedural fairness Procedural fairness consists of rules to guarantee a fair procedure, which is a prerequisite for ➜ substantive fairness. The central rules are consistency, impartiality, and openness.

Procedural rights ➜ Rights to ensure that certain rules are followed, and to make the redress of grievances possible.

Process evaluation An ➜ evaluation or ➜ audit which focuses on implementation rather than effects.

Professions Certain classes of occupation which have a particular status and claim specialised knowledge or expertise. Professionals are allowed discretion or independent judgment in their conduct on the basis of that expertise.

Progressive redistribution Transferring resources vertically from richer to poorer people. ➜ regressive redistribution.

Projection Conditional predictions; extrapolations of existing trends into the future.

Public goods Goods of which the benefits are not directly attributable to any particular individual or group.

Public sector Agencies which are financed and managed by the state.

Public services Services for the public which carry out public policies, have a redistributive effect and are operated as a trust.

Purposive sampling The selection of specific people as subjects for research in order to examine a particular kind of problem. ➜ probability sampling.

Qualitative research Research which is interpretative and aimed at producing material which can help to explain processes and issues.

Quantitative research Research which measures effects or enumerates.

Quasi-markets Systems set up to imitate the operation of the private market in the delivery of public services.

Race A term used variously to indicate physical differences, cultural issues and historical antecedents between different groups of people.

Racism Prejudice or discrimination against other racial groups. The term is extended by some to include the production of disadvantage, whether or not prejudice or discrimination occur. ➜ institutional racism.

Radical social work A neo–Marxist critique of the role of social workers in society, coupled with a set of arguments about alternative patterns of practice.

Rational planning A model of the planning process which allows the examination of successive stages in a policy, and feeds back results into further decision making.

Rationing Balancing supply and demand outside the mechanism of the market.

Reaction In politics, extreme conservative or right wing views opposed to reform and in favour of 'turning back the clock'.

Redistribution Transferring resources from some people to others; any arrangement where one person pays and another benefits.

Redress The ability of the recipient of a service to have bad practice corrected.

Regressive redistribution Transferring resources vertically from poorer to richer people. ➔ progressive redistribution.

Regulation The process by which the state establishes the rules and settings under which welfare services operate.

Relative Socially determined, as in a 'relative' view' or poverty or morality; based in examination of differences, as in 'relative deprivation'.

Reliability In social research, the likelihood that results can be reproduced or at least that they show the same thing in the same circumstances.

Residential care Care in which help and support is provided in a residential setting – for example, an old people's home.

Residual welfare Model of welfare in which people receive welfare only when they are unable to cope otherwise.

Right to welfare Marshall's argument that the welfare state represented an extension of the rights of citizens gained in the eighteenth and nineteenth centuries into the social field.

Right wing Political beliefs identified with conservatism, liberalism and fascism, which are broadly against collective public provision for all.

Rights Rules, based sometimes on legal and sometimes on moral norms, which justify the provision of welfare in terms of the position of the recipient.

Risk Exposure to hazard; cumulative incidence; insecurity; unpredictable contingencies; or ➔ vulnerability.

Sampling Selection of subjects for research.

Secondary analysis Research done on material recorded and processed by other people. ➜ primary analysis.

Selectivity Policy which focuses resources on people in need.

Semi-professions Workers who have to perform their activities in a hierarchical organisation but who are nevertheless permitted some of the independent judgment allowed to professionals in the conduct of their work.

Service rationing Rationing which takes place at the point where services are delivered, as opposed to ➜ financial rationing.

Social administration The study of the development, structure and practices of the social services.

Social capital The value derived from collaborative and solidaristic social action, as distinct from the actions of individuals within social structures.

Social construction The development of a pattern of relationships in society which shapes social circumstances, common understandings and the perception of issues.

Social control The process through which some people are limited by others, whether for the benefit of society or for the benefit of specific groups in society. People are controlled by social services when they are being made to act in ways which they would not otherwise choose, or when their options have been restricted.

Social definition The process through which some issues are constructed in such a way as to define the terms in which those issues are subsequently understood and discussed.

Social democracy A set of political beliefs based on the acceptance of the necessity for collective social action and social protection in a mixed economy.

Social division A social structure in which people are distinguished sharply from others in terms of certain characteristics or circumstances which then become the basis for advantage or disadvantage.

Social division of welfare   Titmuss's term for the range of processes through which redistribution took place.

Social group   People who share some common social contact or network; people who have common characteristics or circumstances which lead to them being treated as a group for social purposes.

Social inclusion   The process of bringing people who are ➔ excluded into networks of social relationships.

Social justice   A distributive principle related sometimes to desirable outcomes, or more usually to outcomes that are proportionate to normative criteria, like rights, desert or needs.

Social policy   The study of the social services and the welfare state. ➔ structural policy.

Social problems   Issues defined in social terms as for which some kind of response is called.

Social security   The system of benefits for income maintenance; in some countries the term is understood more widely to include health care, while in others it is taken more narrowly to mean social insurance.

Social services   Mainly understood to include social security, housing, health, social work and education – the 'big five' – along with others which are like social services.

Social welfare   The welfare of society, or the social services provided. ➔ welfare.

Social work   Work done by social workers, including a range of techniques to maintain or change people's circumstances or patterns of behaviour.

Socialisation   The process through which people become a part of society, learning social norms, values and rules.

Socialism   Although socialism has many meanings, its principal use in Europe refers to set of political beliefs based in the values of collective action (or solidarity), freedom and equality.

Societal policy ➜ structural policy.

Society A network of networks of ➜ solidarity; a group of ➜ societal groups.

Soft law In the European Union, recommendations and generalised statements designed to encourage a response rather than to require action.

Solidarity Mutual responsibility; responsibilities to others in society, which are the basis for collective social action; policy built on a complex range of overlapping networks.

Spillovers An aspect of inefficiency in targeting which means that more than necessary is given to some people with problems.

State The formal political institutions of a society; the means through which government power is exercised.

States of dependency Titmuss's term for conditions in which people were likely to become dependent.

Statistics The popular name for ➜ indicators; quantitative data; the mathematical analysis of quantitative data.

Status A form of social identity, identifying the way that people see themselves and how others see them.

Stigma A sense of shame, which makes people reluctant to claim benefits or services; a loss of status; an attribute or characteristic which is discrediting; a pattern of social rejection.

Strategy A group of inter-related ➜ policies with a common approach or purpose.

Stratification Splitting something into a range of levels.

Street-level bureaucracy Lipsky's term for decisions made at the lowest administrative level, which effectively become policy because no other rules apply.

Structural dependency Dependency conditioned by economic position and relationship to society, rather than by people's intrinsic capacities.

Structural policy Policy which is intended to maintain or change the pattern of social relationships. This is sometimes referred to as 'societal policy'.

Substantive fairness A fair result, judged by whatever criteria are thought applicable.

Substantive rights Rights to particular outcomes.

Targeting Focusing, directing or aiming policies at a particular category or group of people.

Targets Specific goals, often represented in numerical terms as indicators.

Technological determinism In sociology, the argument that the structure of society is shaped by available technology; in social policy, this can be extended to the argument that the structure of services is shaped by the methods which are available.

Tenure In housing policy, the right by which people occupy their housing: for example, owning or renting.

Triangulation In social research, the process of looking at an issue several ways at once.

Underclass A term used variously to signify the lowest social class; people who are economically non-productive and in receipt of benefits; people who are marginal to the labour market; or people who are socially undesirable.

Unemployment Worklessness in a situation where the workless person is nevertheless considered to be part of the labour market.

Universality A method of distributing welfare based on given benefits or services to everyone, or at least everyone in a broad category (such as 'children').

Utility Perceived value to people making a choice.

Validity In social research, the question of whether the results reflect what they are supposed to reflect.

Values General moral principles or norms, used to guide or limit the scope of action.

Vertical redistribution Redistribution between people on different levels of income or wealth.

Voice Having some say in a service.

Voluntary sector Independent provision which is not for profit, usually on the basis of charity or mutual aid. Some commentators include private provision as 'voluntary'.

Vulnerability The possibility that when adverse events happen, the vulnerable person might suffer harm.

Welfare Well-being; certain categories of collective provision which attempt to protect people's well-being; in the US, social security payments to the poor.

Welfare economics A branch of economics concerned with the analysis of ➜ utility; it is not closely connected with social policy.

Welfare pluralism Like ➜ pluralism, this can be taken to indicate both the situation in which services are provided from many different sources and the argument that they should be.

Welfare rights In some literature, ➜ rights to ➜ welfare; a range of activities involving advice and support in claims for social welfare services.

Welfare society A society in which people support each other through a range of solidaristic networks.

Welfare state The delivery of social services by the state; the strategy of developing inter-related services to deal with a wide range of social problems; an ideal in which services are provided comprehensively and at the best level possible.

Index of subjects

Index of names